Contents

DVD Contents

This is a hybrid disc.

The following contents can be viewed on a DVD player:

The Movie
- *Time and Again*, the movie
- *Time and Again* commentary track

The Modules
- Intro to Writing
- Intro to Pre-Production
- Intro to Production
- Directing
- Intro to Editing

The Extras
- The Forms
- The Footage
- www.powerfilmmaking.com

The following contents can be accessed on a computer:

Footage
- 14 clips from the stickball scene

Forms
- Development
  - Script Template (Word format)
  - *Time and Again* script

Dedication

This book is lovingly dedicated to my incredibly supportive family. Mom, Dad, Aimee, and Heather, thank you for all your support over the years. I couldn't have done it without you.

Acknowledgments

I would like to thank the many businesses and individuals whose helpful advice contributed to the completion of this book.

Photo credit
  Peter Graves

Proofreading
  Derek Willis
  Kate Bernier
  Reb Groh
  Mimi Tomaric

Special thanks to
  Elinor Actipis
  Houston King
  Winnie Wong
  Andrew Huebscher
  Stephen Campanella
  John Henry Richardson
  Apple Computer
  Micheal K. Brown
  Matthews Studio Equipment
  Lowel Lighting
  Arri
  Panavision
  Kodak
  Audio-Technica
  Screen Actors Guild
  IATSE
  Writers Guild of America
  Directors Guild of America

. . . and, of course, to the cast and crew of *Time and Again,* for an unforgettable experience.

Foreword

I remember the moment as if it happened yesterday. It was a scorching summer afternoon in July 1984, and my fourth-grade friends and I stood anxiously in our spacemen costumes in the loft of my parents' barn. Surrounded by Christmas lights stuck through hastily painted cardboard boxes, we stared at the crayon-drawn view screen and yelled as the make-believe enemy ships fired their weapons at us. Throwing ourselves around the set, my Dad shook the camera as my friends threw pieces of cardboard debris on top of us. It worked perfectly. I stood up, called "cut," and we officially finished the first shot of my first movie. Looking around at the world I had created in the barn, I knew, in that moment, that I had found my calling . . . to make movies.

In the following years, I never went to film school, but learned instead by trial and error. I would shoot a movie, learn from my mistakes, and then move on and produce another one, hoping it would be better than the one before. The result was a lifelong journey of learning by doing, not by reading textbooks and listening to lectures from professors who had never stepped on a movie set. Since then, I've produced several award-winning feature films, television commercials, and music videos, making a successful living doing what I love.

I've been fortunate enough to teach at some of the country's most prestigious film schools, where they teach you how to make a $20,000,000 film. Unfortunately, I don't know of any graduate who walks out of college with an eight-figure budget to start his first movie. Film schools don't teach students the critical first steps: how first to use local resources to create high-quality movies for only a few thousand dollars and then move on to higher budget productions. As a result, this massive gap in film education has led to the failed careers of thousands of talented, aspiring filmmakers.

This book is a collection of practical experiences, tips, and tricks I've learned over the years. As I wrote this, I thought about what I wish I had known 10 years ago when I was just getting started in this industry. I needed real information from someone who had actually made a successful low-budget movie. With the right resources, information, and guidance, it is possible to make a great movie with little money. You just have to know where to start.

Be creative, persistent, and ambitious. Think big and live your dream.

Jason J. Tomaric

UNIT 1

Development

i. Begin with a strong idea, inspired by actual events, literature, personal experiences, or historical occurrences.

ii. Set-up a comfortable, quiet workspace.

iii. Determine the genre, format, and plot type of the story.

Developing the Idea

iv. Secure the rights from the author of a previous work, or from an individual whose story inspires you.

v. Contact other writers with whom you may want to partner.

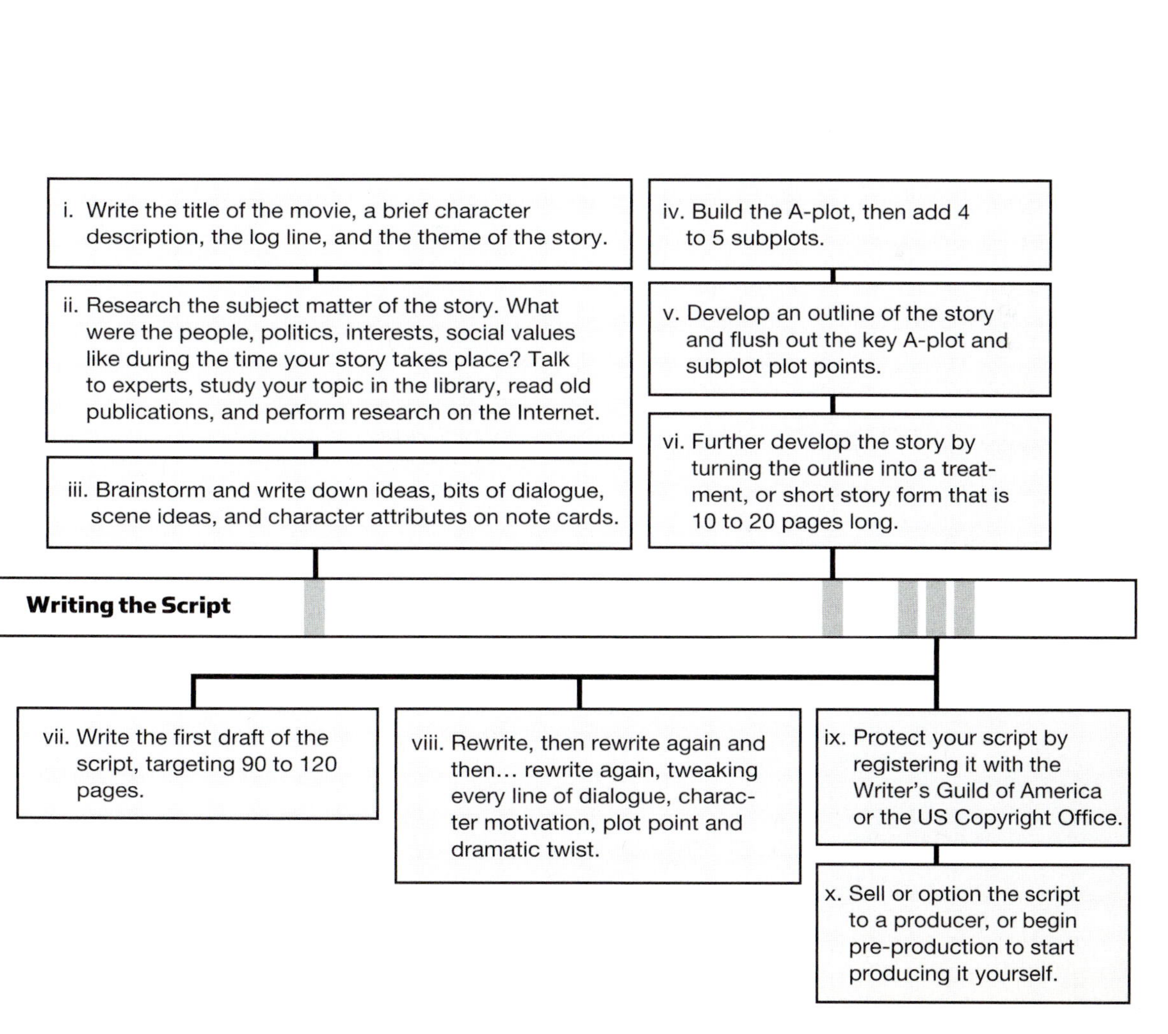
i. Write the title of the movie, a brief character description, the log line, and the theme of the story.
ii. Research the subject matter of the story. What were the people, politics, interests, social values like during the time your story takes place? Talk to experts, study your topic in the library, read old publications, and perform research on the Internet.
iii. Brainstorm and write down ideas, bits of dialogue, scene ideas, and character attributes on note cards.
iv. Build the A-plot, then add 4 to 5 subplots.
v. Develop an outline of the story and flush out the key A-plot and subplot plot points.
vi. Further develop the story by turning the outline into a treatment, or short story form that is 10 to 20 pages long.
Writing the Script
vii. Write the first draft of the script, targeting 90 to 120 pages.
viii. Rewrite, then rewrite again and then… rewrite again, tweaking every line of dialogue, character motivation, plot point and dramatic twist.
ix. Protect your script by registering it with the Writer's Guild of America or the US Copyright Office.
x. Sell or option the script to a producer, or begin pre-production to start producing it yourself.

"The Yesterdays of Tomorrow"
by
Jason J. Tomaric

CHAPTER 1

The Script

INTRODUCTION

The script is the blueprint for the story and contains dialog, character movements, and scene descriptions. Like the old adage says, "If it ain't on the page, it ain't on the stage."

Every good movie is produced around a well-written script, and it doesn't matter how big the budget is, how good the actors are, how incredible the explosions are, or how dynamic the visual effects are unless the story is moving, engaging, and believable. Films with high production values have been known to flop because the script was poorly written, and rarely has a bad script been made into a good movie. Writing a script is a craft that takes time to learn and requires a tremendous amount of discipline and understanding of story structure, psychology, human dynamics, and pacing.

Not only is writing a script is THE MOST IMPORTANT ASPECT of making a movie; it's also the cheapest. Whereas Hollywood studios spend hundreds of millions of dollars on digital effects, great actors, explosions, and car chases, the materials involved in writing a script could be nothing more than a pencil and paper—materials that cost only a few dollars.

In embarking on the journey to get the perfect script, there are three paths you can take. You can write the script yourself, you can option a script that has already been written, or you can hire a writer to write the script for you. This chapter will look at these three options and at which may be the best choice for your production.

For more information on how to write an effective screenplay, including tips from established Hollywood writers, check out the Writing modules at www.powerfilmmaking.com.

WRITING YOUR OWN SCRIPT

Developing the idea

The foundation of a good movie is a good script. The foundation of a good script is a good story. The foundation of a good story is inspiration, research, and the ability to develop an idea into a commercially viable product that audiences will want to see.

Before you decide to spend years working on a project, its important to know the purpose of the production at the very beginning. Are you going to make a movie for art's sake, so that the film is an exploration of your vision and style, or maybe even to learn the process of filmmaking? Or are you looking to produce a commercially viable movie that can be sold and (it is hoped) generate a profit?

Contrary to the popular belief of many filmmakers, these two options are almost always mutually exclusive. Most commercially produced movies tend to rely on a time-proven, revenue-generating formula designed to appeal to the widest possible audience. Because the marketing budget for most Hollywood movies is significantly higher than the production budget, the industry has to sell as many tickets as possible to cover not only the film's production and marketing costs, but also the costs of movies that fail to recoup their initial investment. Unfortunately, this commercialization tends to discriminate against artistic films that play to a smaller audience, leaving those productions to run, at best, in local art theaters and small film festivals.

Making a movie requires a lot of time and money, so be smart in the type of story you choose to tell. Carefully consider what you want the movie to do for you:

- **Do you want the movie to make money?** Then develop a concept around the industry standard formula, with marketable actors, a tight three-act structure, and high production values. This can be the most expensive option.
- **Do you want to make a movie for the educational experience?** If you want to learn filmmaking or practice your craft, produce a short film and know that you won't recoup your investment.
- **Do you want to make art?** Producing an artistic film that defies traditional Hollywood convention is risky because distributors tend to shy away from films they can't easily explain to viewers. If picked up for distribution, most art films will find homes in small art theaters and possibly on home video, although the odds of generating a profit are slim.

DIRECTOR'S NOTES

I can remember the moment when the idea for *Time and Again* struck me. I was talking with my colleague (and subsequent co-writer of *Time and Again*), Bob Noll, and he pitched me an idea about a man who escaped from prison. In the middle of the prison break, he suddenly and mysteriously found himself in the middle of an open, sunny field.

I don't even remember the rest of the pitch. All I know is that sequence haunted me so much that as I drove home, I couldn't stop thinking about this guy in this field. So, that night, I wrote out a story that roughly became the premise of *Time and Again*. Once inspiration hit, the story nearly wrote itself.

When I called Bob the next day, he was really excited about my idea and jumped at the chance to help me write the script, so within three days, we had our first 35-page draft.

I had never thought about making a 1950s movie before, but when inspiration hit, I knew that *Time and Again* was the story I wanted to tell. I don't know how I knew, I just did. I've learned that it's not really difficult to find inspiration; you just have to sit back, live life, and wait for it to hit you.

When it comes to developing a story, write what you know. The best piece of advice I ever received was to write what I've seen, what I have experienced, and what I've lived in life. How can you faithfully write a story about the joys and difficulties of marriage if you've never been married? Granted, you may have seen how married couples interact, but it's not the same as if you were to live it yourself. How can a writer write a real love story that connects with the audience if he's never been in love? Writing about love, death, betrayal, loneliness, or happiness without experiencing it seems like a formula for an empty, soulless story. Filmmaking is about truth, and writing scenes and moments that truthfully resonate with the audience can be a difficult task unless you are personally familiar with the material you're exploring.

One way of doing this is to dedicate your life to experiencing a variety of situations, cultures, and people so when it comes time to write, you have a broad range of life experiences to draw from. Many legendary filmmakers are older men and women who have put their life experiences on film, resulting in real, engaging moments that ring true to the audience.

One reason most young filmmakers' movies aren't very interesting is because they haven't had enough life experiences to draw on. If you can't experience events yourself, then draw on ideas and inspiration around you to help develop a strong idea.

- Look at real-life moments for inspiration: childhood memories; interesting happenings at work; relationships with family, friends, and love interests. Think of family conflicts, your first job or your freshman year in high school, moving out on your own for the first time, and college experiences. Drawing on personal experiences leads to strong material because you've lived and experienced it.
- Read the newspaper, listen to the radio, and watch news stories that may captivate your imagination. The old cliché says that truth is often stranger than fiction, and in many instances, it is!

- Keep a journal of interesting things that happen every day; an engaging conversation, a funny moment, an unusual or interesting person you may have encountered in public. These moments can be the seeds of not only good ideas, but also engaging characters, moments, and lines of dialog in the movie.
- Brainstorm and write down anything and everything that comes to mind. You'd be surprised what comes out. Listen to inspirational music, turn off the lights, let your mind roam free, and be ready to capture ideas as they strike.
- Study political history and the lives of dictators, emperors, famous people, and serial killers. All these peoples' lives involved extraordinary circumstances that are full of drama and conflict.
- Be original and avoid copying concepts used in other forms of media, stories from movies or television shows, or major plot lines from popular books. Audiences want to see new, unique ideas, not rehashes of old ideas. Create concepts inspired by real-life situations, people, and experiences.
- Be careful not to infringe on copyrighted work. Copyright infringement can be an expensive mistake if the original owner of the stolen property chooses to sue.
- Surf the Internet. The knowledge of the world is at your fingertips and can provide outstanding ideas and motivation for a movie.
- Try reading the yellow pages, magazines, and even advertisements for inspiration.
- Get out of your house. Traveling to a new place, whether it's going out of town or visiting a local coffee shop can help spur the imagination.
- Take breaks and don't force your imagination. A walk on the beach or through the woods can help clear your thoughts and open your mind to new ideas. I find that the less I think about my story, the more ideas pop into my mind.
- Write stories you're passionate about. Be excited and willing to explore the subject matter. Learn as much as you can about the world, people, and situations you're writing about.
- Visit classic literature; listen to operas and read books. Stories of mythology, ancient romances, and tales of adventure and heroism are the root of storytelling. If in doubt, go back to see how authors of old tackled an idea.
- Research your idea by studying the time period, characters, customs, fashions, technologies, and values of the world you're telling the story about. Learning more about the actual events or motivation behind your story will help develop ideas.
- Learn from people who resemble, or can provide insight into, your character. If you're writing a crime drama, contact a local police station and ask to shadow an officer for a week. Listen to how she talks, how she acts both casually and under pressure. Get a sense of the police environment so when it comes time to create it in a script, you can write a realistic and believable world.

Setting up your space

Bob Noll, my co-writer of *Time and Again*, works from his office at John Carroll University, a normally quiet place to work after hours.

The first step to writing a screenplay is to find a comfortable, quiet space to write. Whether it's your office, your basement, or your workspace after business hours, designate this space as your "writing room," and remove any distractions. It's important to have a designated space so that when you enter it, your brain knows it's time to start being creative.

- Find a quiet space that you use only for writing. I like to work in a particular coffee house in Burbank. For some reason, this space, the constant rhythm of the people coming and going, and the quiet ambience help me focus and allow the creativity to flow.
- Turn off the telephone and television. These needless distractions will only draw your attention away from the script. Writing is a practice in the art of focus and discipline as much as it is about storytelling.
- Be prepared with a pencil, paper, and computer. Even though I use Microsoft Word and Final Draft when I write, I find that keeping a pencil and paper nearby is handy to write down notes and thoughts I have during the writing process.
- Consider playing music from movie soundtracks or classical music that inspires you. I find that background music, especially music without lyrics that supports the theme and tone of the story I'm writing, gets the creative juices flowing.

Developing a premise

Once your space is set up, the next step is to develop the story structure for the movie. Think about whether you want the story to be fiction or nonfiction, which genre is best, and the appropriate format for the story.

STEP 1: FICTION OR NONFICTION

Fictional stories involve made-up characters in made-up situations. Based on imagination more than fact, fictional stories allow the writer to evoke emotions and thoughts outside the realm of the audience's everyday world. Fiction provides a vehicle for the writer's creativity to blossom and take form in a nearly boundless format.

Nonfiction stories are true stories based on actual people and events. Nonfiction stories include documentaries, biographies, and stories based on history, politics, travel, education, or any real-world subject matter.

Remember that if you choose to write a nonfiction story, you may need to secure the rights to the person or the events your movie is based on.

STEP 2: GENRE

A genre is a category or type of story. Genres typically have their own style and story structure, and although there are several primary categories, movies can be a mixture of two or three different genres.

Some common genres include:

- Action
- Comedy
- Crime
- Drama
- Family
- Fantasy
- Horror
- Musical
- Romance
- Romantic Comedy
- Science Fiction
- Thriller
- War
- Western

When choosing the genre for an independent film, be aware of the costs and difficulties of shooting certain genres like science fiction or westerns, for which the cost of sets, costumes, and props may be prohibitive.

Take special notice of the resources available to you in your community and through your contacts. When I wrote *Time and Again*, I knew that my hometown Chardon, Ohio, could easily pass as a town from the 1950s without much set dressing. I also knew that throughout the region, I could approach antique car owners and costume shops and scavenge the dozens of antique shops to recreate the time period easily and inexpensively. Doing this research in advance gave me a really good idea as to what resources were available as I developed my story.

STEP 3: FORMAT

Stories can be told in many different formats, each designed for a different purpose. Be mindful of your budget, the availability of resources, and time when you choose the format for your story.

The main formats include:

- **Animation.** Produced either by hand or using computer technologies, 2D or 3D movies still rely on traditional story structures, although the means of production lie strictly with the animator and rarely include live-action elements. Animated films are very time consuming and technically elaborate.
- **Commercials.** Designed to advertise a product or service, television commercials incorporate a wide range of styles, techniques, animation, narrative, and hard-sell techniques into 10-, 15-, 30-, or 60-second time lengths. Commercials are a great way for filmmakers to showcase their style and story-telling and production capabilities and are among the most lucrative, well-paying forms of production.
- **Documentaries.** Documentaries are intended to study a subject, occurrence, theme, or belief in an attempt to either explore the subject or arrive at a conclusion about the subject. Documentaries can either take on an

investigative approach, in which the filmmaker tries to answer a question or research a subject, or follow a subject and allow the story to unfold during the production. Documentaries can, in some instances, be inexpensive but time-consuming to produce.

- **Feature films.** The 90-minute narrative is the mainstay of Hollywood entertainment, and its production is the dream of millions of aspiring filmmakers. The riskiest style of production, feature films are expensive and time consuming and rarely recoup the monies invested.
- **Industrial/corporate.** These productions are typically marketing or how-to pieces for businesses. Although not very entertaining to watch or make, industrials are an outstanding way to make money in the production industry.
- **Music videos.** These highly stylized four-minute promotional videos for music artists are a great way for a filmmaker to explore unbridled creativity using any medium, any style of narrative or performance, and artistic editing. Music videos are terrific short-format pieces that easily demonstrate a filmmaker's abilities.
- **Short films.** Short films are movies that are shorter than 80 minutes. Ideally under 20 minutes, shorts are a terrific way of learning the process of making a movie, showcasing the talents of the filmmakers, and generating interest from investors in future projects. Despite the educational and career benefits, there is virtually no market for short films, making it nearly impossible to see a return on the investment. Although there are a few distributors who may release a compilation DVD of short films, filmmakers rarely see their money back or see distribution of a short film by itself.

The crew finishes a lighting setup for my short film, *The Overcoat.* Used as an opportunity to hone our skills, I knew we wouldn't make any money from the movie, but the experience we gained was invaluable.

DIRECTOR'S NOTES

If I can give one piece of advice from the years I've been working as a filmmaker, it is to produce several short films before tackling a feature. The process of learning how to make a movie is cyclical, meaning you have to go through the entire process at least once just to begin to understand the craft. For example, much of directing stems from understanding the editing process and the way shots work together to make a scene. Understanding just this one aspect will have a huge impact on your choices for camera placement and pacing when directing on set.

Don't turn your star idea into your first film . . . you'll regret it for your entire career. Start small and learn the process with a short film; then with the second and third films, hone the craft of directing, working with actors, and directing the camera. You will know when you're ready to take on a feature.

STEP 4: PLOT TYPE

At the core of every great movie is a great idea, but an idea by itself is rarely unique. Every idea you can think of has already been written, produced, told, packaged, marketed, and reconstituted a thousand times throughout history. From Shakespeare to Spielberg, the core story elements are the same. So what makes a movie new and exciting to an audience? The WAY an idea is told keeps it fresh and new.

Stories can be distilled down to a very simple premise: the main character encounters a problem and is either successful or unsuccessful in solving it. The setting, supporting characters, and details are the padding that transforms this simple skeletal structure into a multilayered, interesting, and engaging story.

As you begin crafting your script, be aware of the simple plot structure that will become the backbone of the story. Here are some of the most common:

1. **Overcoming the adversary.** The hero must find a way to overcome a threat presented by another person, society, nature, him- or herself, a supernatural force, technology, or religion. (*Terminator, Alien*)
2. **The quest.** The hero undergoes a search for something, someone, or an idea. The perils he encounters and whether the hero meets his objective are up to the writer! (*Contact*)
3. **The journey and return.** The hero undergoes a journey from home and experiences a change in character along the way. (*Lord of the Rings, The Wizard of Oz*)
4. **Comedy.** Events in the story keep the characters apart, only for a happy reunification at the end.
5. **Tragedy.** Events in the story lead to the death of a character. This usually unhappy ending is not often seen in Hollywood movies. (*Gladiator*)
6. **Resurrection.** The hero is oppressed until events in the story free her. (*The Shawshank Redemption*)
7. **Rags to riches.** The life of a character evolves from a life of nothingness to one of bounty, be it family, wealth, or fame. (*It's a Wonderful Life*)

OPTIONING MATERIAL

As a writer, you can develop a script around an existing work, such as a book, poem, short story, or even a personal account. However, to simply adapt the idea into a screenplay could violate copyright laws and expose you to legal liability.

One way of legally using this material is to option the rights to use it. An option is a short-term lease that grants a producer permission to adapt material into a screenplay and either produce it or try to sell it to a production company.

The ability to option a book or story opens up hundreds of thousands of possibilities, so one way of finding a strong story is to go to the bookstore and start reading. If you find a book that you like, call the publisher and get the author's contact information. Explain how you want to use the book and how you will adapt it and ask if the author is willing to consider an option. The author may want money up front, a percentage of the profits, credit, or any number of deal points that would need to be negotiated. If the conversation gets this far, it's best to contact an entertainment attorney to help negotiate with the author on your behalf and draw up the necessary paperwork.

WORKING WITH A WRITER

Oftentimes, writers are either skilled in writing structure or in writing dialog and character, so finding a writing partner who complements your skills can lead to a much better script. Finding a competent writing partner can be as easy as contacting local writing organizations, colleges, or university programs with writing courses or seeking writers online or through industry contacts. When looking for a good writing partner:

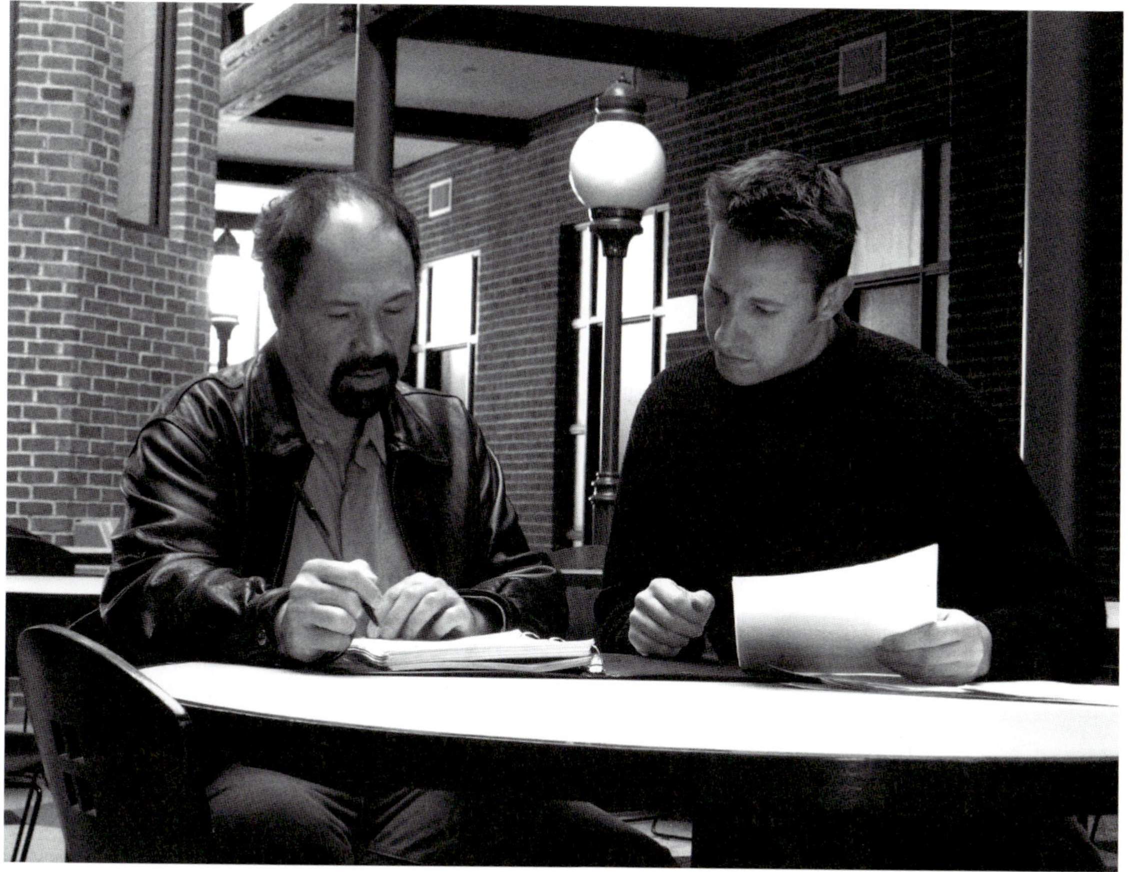

Bob Noll and I work through a scene of *Time and Again*. I found that collaborating with a writing partner is both inspirational and functional. We would often bounce ideas off each other if we were stuck, support each other if our ideas needed help, and ground each other if we felt our ideas were too good.

- Ask for a writing sample. Read through the writer's past works to see if his style, ability to write dialog, pacing, dramatic moments, structure, and plot twists are on par with the nature of the story. To get an idea of the writer's ability, read the first 20 pages of his previously written screenplays and see if the script engages you. If so, keep reading. If not, consider finding another partner.
- Find a partner whose strengths are your weaknesses. If you are good at writing structure, then find a partner who is good at dialog and characterization. A good partner will bring additional talents to the table and balance your skill set.
- Talk with your potential writing partner about the story and make sure she likes the genre, story, and characters before working with her. For example, if you are writing a romantic comedy, look for partners who specialize or have an interest in writing romantic comedies.
- Make sure your partner has the time and commitment to work on the script, especially if it's being written on spec (for free). It's difficult to complete a screenplay if your partner has to drop out in the middle of the project or has obligations that may interfere with his ability to work on the project. Write and sign a contract that outlines the details of your working relationship together. Understand that when working with a writer, you both own 50 percent of the script, so if any problems occur during the relationship, the project may go unproduced.
- Work out the credit she will receive as well as payment terms if the screenplay is sold, optioned, and/or produced.

STORY STRUCTURE

The A plot

Before you can begin writing the script, it's important to define the structure of your story. Powerful stories are made up of strong characters, sharp dialog, engaging plots, and, most importantly, a strong structure.

Stories have been told a certain way throughout history, and audiences have grown accustomed to this "formula." First, we set up the characters, setting, and circumstances of the story, then we present the problem or conflict that the main character will face. Then we sit back and enjoy the intricacies of how the character finds his way out of the problem. This is considered the basic story structure and can be broken up into three distinct parts, called acts.

Act 1

Act 1 is the beginning of the story, when the audience is introduced to the main characters and their traits, personalities, likes and dislikes, problems, and challenges. The script also establishes the setting, time period, and technology of the world in which the story takes place. In Act 1, the writers and filmmakers have the most liberty in setting the stage for the rest of the story, even though

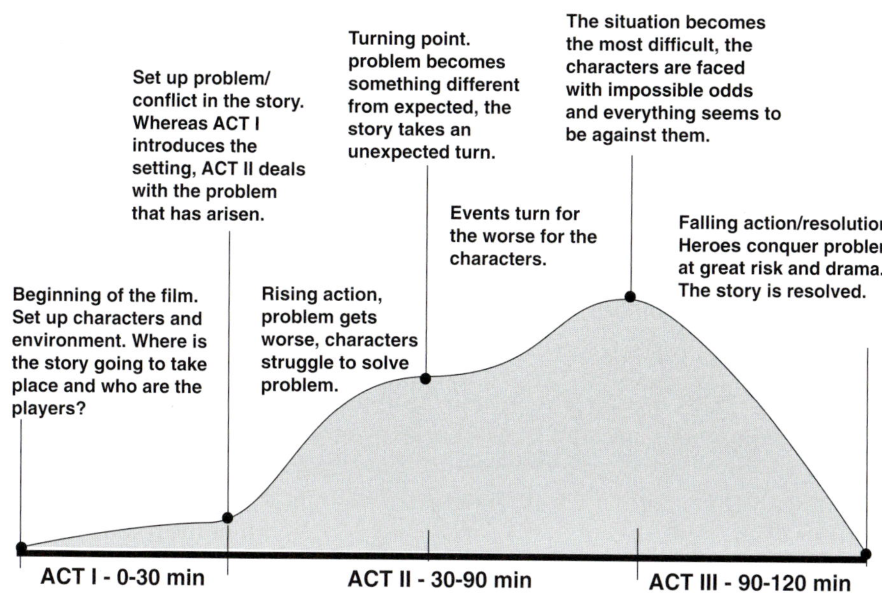

Beginning of the film. Set up characters and environment. Where is the story going to take place and who are the players?
Set up problem/ conflict in the story. Whereas ACT I introduces the setting, ACT II deals with the problem that has arisen.
Rising action, problem gets worse, characters struggle to solve problem.
Turning point. problem becomes something different from expected, the story takes an unexpected turn.
Events turn for the worse for the characters.
The situation becomes the most difficult, the characters are faced with impossible odds and everything seems to be against them.
Falling action/resolution. Heroes conquer problem at great risk and drama. The story is resolved.
ACT I - 0-30 min
ACT II - 30-90 min
ACT III - 90-120 min

The plot arc for a 120-minute movie.

it may seem a little forced. The audience will accept and understand this. Act 1 is the first 30 minutes of a 120-minute film.

Act 1 is about WHO the main characters are, WHERE the story takes place, WHEN the story takes place, WHAT is the story about, WHY the problem is occurring; and the drama begins when the characters figure out HOW to deal with the conflict.

> Timmy is a 10-year-old boy walking home from school in the residential suburb of Highland Heights, Montana. He is a quiet and shy kid who is wildly imaginative, turning the most everyday items into play toys. He is well dressed and lives in a typical middle-class neighborhood.

Act 2

Act 2 is the next movement in the story, in which the conflict is introduced. Stories are about conflict and whether that conflict is man vs. man, man vs. society, man vs. nature, or man vs. self, the conflict is the essence of the story. Without conflict, there is no story.

> Timmy, while walking home from school, is approached by a vicious, ill-tempered dog. Scared and without anywhere to run, Timmy climbs up a tree, but the dog remains, barking and snarling at Timmy.

The dog is the conflict and now our story is about how Timmy deals with the dog.

Be careful, however, because Act 2 is usually the most weakly written act in the entire script. A poor second act will bring the story to a screeching halt, so as we write, it's important to raise the stakes and increase the jeopardy against the main character. The more pain, agony, hardship, trial, and tribulation you can throw at the main character, the more the audience will root for him.

> Timmy struggles to climb higher up in the tree, but he loses his grip and begins to slide down the trunk, cutting his arms on the sharp bark. The dog, now inches from his feet, snarls and snaps at Timmy's ankles. Timmy struggles to climb onto a higher branch. He makes it and, for the moment, is safe. It starts raining and Timmy opens his backpack and pulls out his jacket. He loses his grip and the jacket falls to the ground. The dog rips it to pieces.

Turning point

The most important part of the second act is called the turning point, which occurs at the middle of the story. The turning point is the instance in which the story and plot line take a severe turn and the characters are forced to compensate for this twist.

> As Timmy watches his jacket get torn to bits, the rain continues to pour down. A car driving down the road hits a puddle, hydroplanes, and hits the tree, knocking Timmy out of the tree and onto the roof of the car.

The story has changed direction drastically from the earlier plot of Timmy and the dog to Timmy and the car. The latter half of the second act is about our characters dealing with the new change in circumstances.

> The man driving the car has been knocked unconscious in the accident. The dog moves toward Timmy, while Timmy struggles to call for help and assist the injured driver. Timmy is scared, wet, and alone as he faces this new problem.

Act 2 lasts for an hour, with the turning point occurring in the middle of the act.

Act 3

Act 3 is the last quarter of the story, when the conflict becomes the most difficult for the character and she is forced to use her skill, wit, and ability to resolve or escape from the problem with the maximum possible risk. Late in Act 3 is the point of no return, at which the character chooses a path that will lead to her ultimate success or failure.

> Timmy struggles to pull the driver out of the car while throwing pieces of his peanut butter sandwich to distract the dog. Timmy almost frees the driver when he notices a gun, a mask, and a bag full of hundred dollar bills sitting in the back seat. The man wakes up and grabs the gun and Timmy, holding him hostage, and threatens to kill him if he escapes. All the while, the dog remains outside snarling at the two.

The third act ends with the conclusion of the story when the character resolves the conflict. At this moment, the main character changes, either for the better or for the worse, through redemption, understanding the importance of love, learning to be kind and caring, or through any number ways.

> Timmy, in his most dire moment gathers up every last bit of courage and stuffs the remaining peanut butter sandwich in the robber's face. The dog jumps on the robber, giving Timmy enough time to grab the gun and hold the robber at bay. The dog then turns on Timmy, and instead of attacking, lick's Timmy's face, nuzzling him for more food. After having found the courage, Timmy waits for the police to arrive and arrest the robber. At the end of the ordeal, Timmy walks home, side by side with his new canine friend.

Act 3 is the last 30 minutes of a two-hour movie.

Subplots

We just created the primary, or A plot of the story. Movies not only contain the primary plot, but four or five smaller subplots that are interwoven throughout the movie, many of which help to develop character, pace the timing of the A plot, and give the story more depth. The subplots almost always tie into the A plot and feature four or five scenes, with each subplot wrapping itself up mid-Act 3.

In our example with Timmy, the A plot follows his plight with the dog and the robber. Some possible subplots could include:

- **The girl next door.** When he is in the tree, Timmy discovers he can see into a pretty girl's room from across the street. Reluctant to get her atten-

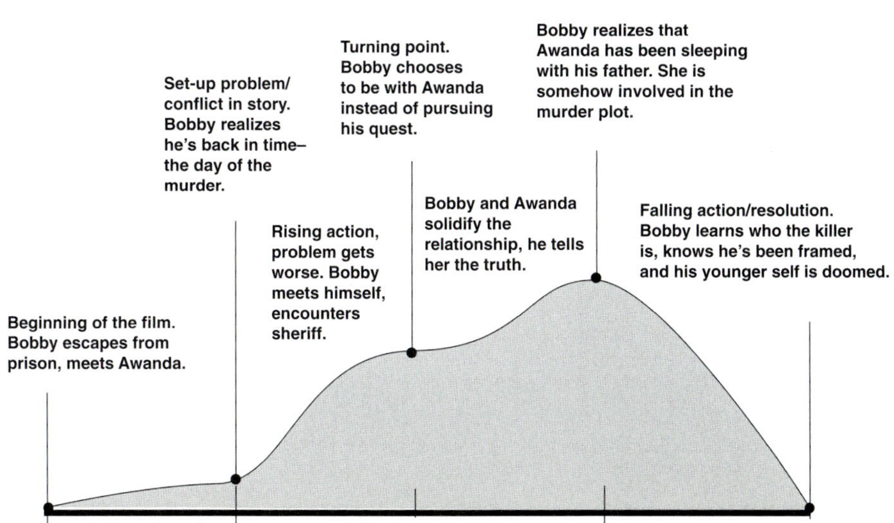

Beginning of the film. Bobby escapes from prison, meets Awanda.
Set-up problem/ conflict in story. Bobby realizes he's back in time– the day of the murder.
Rising action, problem gets worse. Bobby meets himself, encounters sheriff.
Turning point. Bobby chooses to be with Awanda instead of pursuing his quest.
Bobby and Awanda solidify the relationship, he tells her the truth.
Bobby realizes that Awanda has been sleeping with his father. She is somehow involved in the murder plot.
Falling action/resolution. Bobby learns who the killer is, knows he's been framed, and his younger self is doomed.
ACT I - 0-15 min
ACT II - 15-45 min
ACT III - 45-60 min

The plot arc of *Time and Again* is similar to that of a feature-length movie.

tion for fear that she will see him in this embarrassing position, Timmy tries hard to watch her while remaining unnoticed. At the end of the story, when the car crashes and Timmy holds the gun on the robber, the girl hears the commotion, calls the police, and finds Timmy to be a hero.

- **The report.** While Timmy was scrambling up the tree, the dog bit Timmy's book bag and his school report fell out. During the A story, Timmy attempts to use branches, even putting bubble gum at the end of a stick to try to save his report from being mauled by the dog. At the end of the story, the girl picks up the report and offers to put it in a fresh, clean binder.
- **The orphaned bird.** When Timmy climbs the tree, he finds a small bird left all alone in the tree, its nest about to crumble apart. Timmy tries to rebuild and support the nest with twigs and leaves. At the end of the story, as Timmy is walking away with the girl, he looks back into the tree only to see the mother bird return to her baby.

Every subplot ties in and supports the A plot, giving the writer several opportunities to write about during the story. If you develop a strong plot and subplots, you will have an engaging, well-paced story that will give you plenty of opportunities to develop strong characters.

The gasp moments

Every good movie has four or five gasp moments in which the audience is startled or shocked by a turn in the plot. Be sure to write these gasp moments into the story. For example:

- **The car crash.** The biggest gasp moment in the story happens when Timmy's tree is struck by a car. This unexpected moment will certainly take the audience by surprise.
- **Timmy tries to escape.** Timmy, thinking the dog has left, tries to sneak out of the tree. He barely makes it down when he turns to look and the dog is inches from his face, about ready to jump. Timmy scrambles back up into the tree.
- **The girl sees Timmy.** Timmy, while trying to build a support for the nest, pulls off his belt so he can use it to support himself on a tree branch. His pants, caught on a branch, start to slip off, and he looks over to see the girl watching him. Trying to dismiss his actions and not look foolish, Timmy tells her everything is OK and he's saving a bird.

WRITING A SCRIPT

In writing a script, it can be intimidating to craft a 90- to 120-page story, but the process can be easily broken down into a series of steps, each designed to make sure that the script is properly structured.

DIRECTOR'S NOTES

I've always hated writing. . . . It requires discipline, focus, and a willingness to go back and rewrite something again and again. I know that I'm not the only person who feels this way. Lots of my writing friends agree that writing the script is one of the most difficult parts of making a movie; it's not fun, social, or exciting. Writing is a tough process that involves you, your computer, and your life experiences.

So how do you start writing? Well, the question has the answer built in . . . you JUST START. Follow the easy steps in this chapter to help you break into the first page. After that, it's up to you to find the motivation to write.

When I wrote *Time and Again*, I was really inspired by the idea of a man escaping from jail and appearing in the middle of an open field. I started writing down ideas I had had about where he ends up, who he meets, where and when he goes. . . . All these questions helped me make a list of unconnected ideas that further spawned additional ideas. As I kept writing down ideas, the plot eventually came into being. The more ideas I had, the more I was able to work the plot.

Once I had an idea of where the story was going, I called Bob Noll, a friend of mine at John Carroll University. We had discussed the idea for this story and he agreed to help me write it. We spent numerous nights at his office, brainstorming and developing the characters, fleshing out scenes, and ultimately developing an outline that was strong enough to begin turning it into a script.

I would think of the story in terms of how the audience would see it . . . one scene at a time, from the beginning to the end. As I verbally developed these ideas, Bob would type them into the computer in an outline form. Sometimes we would write dialog, sometimes only the character's actions. But whatever we wrote, our goal was to capture the spontaneous thoughts and ideas we had during our session so we could later go back and rewrite and tighten the story.

I always looked forward to these writing sessions because they helped me as the filmmaker deeply explore the world of our characters. I found that I really enjoyed the creative, brainstorming part of writing and Bob was really good at translating my ideas to the page. Our partnership began to take form as I would pace in his office and, following the outline of the plot points the story needed to hit, develop exciting scenes that would get our character from one plot point to the next in an exciting, unpredictable manner.

We usually worked for only a few hours a night. Beyond that, our brains would turn to clay and the creativity valve would shut off. Even if we tried to push longer, the material we wrote looked really bad when we came at it again with fresh eyes the next day. The lesson I learned was to listen to my mind. When it got tired, we quit for the night.

The process of writing the script from the outline was pretty simple. The more detailed the outline, the easier the process of writing the script. Completing the first draft, no matter how good it is, is the first crucial step in making a good story. Revising and rewriting the story to make it tighter and better paced, to make the characters stronger

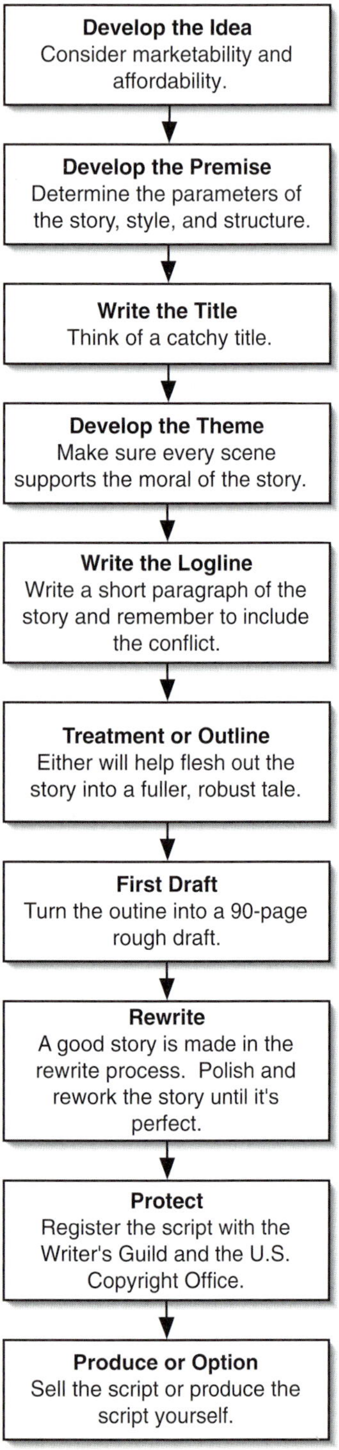

Develop the Idea
Consider marketability and affordability.

↓

Develop the Premise
Determine the parameters of the story, style, and structure.

↓

Write the Title
Think of a catchy title.

↓

Develop the Theme
Make sure every scene supports the moral of the story.

↓

Write the Logline
Write a short paragraph of the story and remember to include the conflict.

↓

Treatment or Outline
Either will help flesh out the story into a fuller, robust tale.

↓

First Draft
Turn the outine into a 90-page rough draft.

↓

Rewrite
A good story is made in the rewrite process. Polish and rework the story until it's perfect.

↓

Protect
Register the script with the Writer's Guild and the U.S. Copyright Office.

↓

Produce or Option
Sell the script or produce the script yourself.

Writing flow chart.

> and the dialog more snappy, was a lot easier once we got past the hurdle of completing the first draft.
>
> We went through several revisions of *Time and Again* before we were happy with the script and felt like it was time to go into preproduction.

Title

Title (1–5 words). Name the film. This doesn't have to be the film's final title, but a strong working title can help maintain focus of what the story is about.

> Time and Again.

Theme

Theme (5–15 words). What is the "moral of the story?" Beneath the story, plot, characters, and genre, what is the message you want to convey to the audience after they finish watching the movie? Make sure that every scene, every moment, and every character supports this theme. If you ever encounter writer's block, or don't know where a scene should go, refer to the theme and write a scenario that supports it.

> A man's quest to find the truth supersedes everything, even love and death.

Logline

Logline (15–25 words). Describe the good guy, the bad guy, the setting, and the conflict. The logline is the basic premise of what the movie is about. Think about what a movie reviewer would write up in the newspaper when trying to describe the premise of the film in a clear, concise manner. After you describe the who, what, why, when, and where, be sure to identify the conflict, or there's no story. A line like ". . . and problems arise when . . ." strongly sets up the conflict in the story.

> Time and Again is the story of Bobby Jones, a convicted murderer, who has been sentenced to 30 years in prison for a crime he doesn't remember committing. Bent on finding the real killer, he escapes from prison only to be thrown back in time to July 14, 1958, the day of the murder. Problems arise when, with six hours to work, he must reconstruct a forgotten past to save himself. When he meets the sexy diner waitress, Awanda, his true priorities are tested.

Treatment

Treatment (2–3 pages). The treatment is a short-story form of the movie that describes what happens from the beginning to the end of the film. It reads like a novel and serves as an easy way for the writer to understand the characters and events as they appear in the movie. Treatments are valuable writing tools that allow the writer to work out the story points in a short form before moving on to write the longer script.

When you write the treatment, you can begin incorporating script-formatting elements that will eventually make their way into the finished screenplay. For example, each time a new character is introduced in your treatment, type the name of the character in capital letters followed by the character's age and a brief description. For example:

> AWANDA, 31, a lonely blond bombshell who hustles men in the hopes of finding true love.

The treatment can be as long or as short as the story requires. The more detail you can write into the treatment, the easier it will be to incorporate into the script. For example:

> The fog rolls across the prison yard, streaked by moonlight. Outside, three figures, BOBBY JONES, 32, a rugged young man whose face reflects his hard prison time, and two other convicts jump the fence. Landing hard between the perimeter fences, the three men take off running inside the courtyard, as guards and their dogs rush to intercept. Spotlights flick on and sirens pierce the night as Bobby turns a corner. BAM! A shot from one of the guards takes out one of the prisoners, but Bobby keeps running. Moments later, another shot rings out, taking out the second prisoner. Now Bobby, alone, picks up his pace, despite the guards' orders to stop. As he turns another corner, a vortex opens and, before he can stop, Bobby races through, landing in a golden wheat field on a sunny day. Tripping over a branch, he crashes to the ground as he tries to get his bearings. . . .

Continue working and reworking the treatment until the entire story is fleshed out. Remember that every good story has four or five major conflicts that arise for the character, plot twists, and shocking story moments. Keep the story kinetic, with every moment leading the audience toward the next plot point. Remember the theme and ensure that every scene reflects the theme of the story. The treatment should read smoothly and include all major characters and plot points and the resolution written in short-story format.

Outline

Outline (20–30 pages). Once the treatment is written, it's time to begin fleshing out the details of each scene and every plot point. Begin outlining by writing 80 to 100 scene numbers on a piece of paper. Then break the treatment down into scenes, describing the location where each scene takes place, the characters involved, and what happens in the story. Add more details to the outline so that it becomes easier to transcribe the outline into a script. Each scene in the outline will become one scene in the script. The more detail that is written in the outline, the easier it will be to write the script.

Start out by writing the main plot points of the A story. I usually like to write this step by step in outline form, by writing simple sentences that loosely describe what happens in the movie. Writing in simple plot points makes it easy to rework, expand, and remove story points later. As you develop the A story, outline the basic plot points from the beginning of the story to the end. This process can be as simple as taking a sheet of paper, numbering each line, and writing each plot point.

For example:

1. Bobby Jones escapes from prison.
2. Bobby wakes up in a field and finds a school yard.
3. Bobby encounters a teacher from whom he learns that something is wrong.
4. Bobby treks through a field until he finds a farmhouse.
5. Bobby steals clothes from the clothesline and makes his way to the road.
6. After trying to hitch a ride, he sees a girl riding a bike down the road. It's Awanda.
7. . . . and so on.

Once the A-story points are listed out, begin adding B-story points, or subplots. There are usually four or five subplots in a movie that usually tie into the A story at some point. All subplots should resolve themselves by the end of the story.

For example:

A subplot in *Time and Again* deals with the bicycle that Bobby and Awanda crash, and Bobby needs to repair it. This subplot ties into the A story as an integral part of the plot twist.

Continue working and editing, adding and removing plot points and scenes until you are happy with the pacing and flow of the story. As you develop the outline, keep these points in mind:

- Every scene must push the story forward. If you can effectively tell the story without a particular scene, that scene should be removed.
- Every scene should support the theme of the movie.
- Know how the movie is going to end so you can write to a conclusion, instead of free-forming thoughts and ideas that may not go anywhere.

Script

Script (90–120 pages). Once the outline is finished and every plot point is described, begin fleshing out each plot point into a scene, adding dialog and detailed descriptions. Remember that one page of a properly formatted script roughly equates to one minute of screen time.

Complete the first draft of the script, regardless of how good or bad it is. Once you have a complete draft of the script in front of you, you can begin the revision process. Shorten, edit, alter, tighten, and scrutinize every line of every page until you are satisfied with the script, then register the script with the Writers Guild of America, apply for a copyright from the U.S. Copyright Office, and begin either the submission or the production process. For more information, please see page 32.

Creating characters

A movie is nothing more than a slice of a character's life, and a character's life experiences dictate how he may respond and react to the conflicts presented in the story. By developing each character's personal background, family history, personality traits, habits, and behavioral tendencies toward friends and neighbors, the writer will make them become realistic, multidimensional people.

One of the strongest techniques for creating realistic characters is to base them on someone you know. Look to friends, family, or even yourself for inspiration and draw on their personal experiences, quirks, and idiosyncrasies. The more vividly you can picture each character in your mind, the easier it will be to write his dialog and behavior in each scene. For example, if you're basing a character on your neighbor Frank, think "What would Frank do in this situation? How would he act? What would he do?"

Characters fall into three primary categories, each having a specific role in driving the story forward.

Protagonist: The protagonist is the central character or "good guy" in the story: a person who almost always undergoes a personal transformation and whose personality and motivations are explored more than any other character. The story is always about the protagonist, focusing on his journey of discovery and change. Although the protagonist is the focal point, the story may or may not be told through his eyes.

Antagonist: The antagonist is the literary opposite of the protagonist, who presents obstacles, challenges, and situations the protagonist must overcome. The antagonist has her own goals and objectives that conflict with the protagonist's desires.

It is important to note that the antagonist, although often the more fun character to write, often falls prey to being the most shallow and cliché character in the movie. This is evident in cheesy action movies in which the overzealous

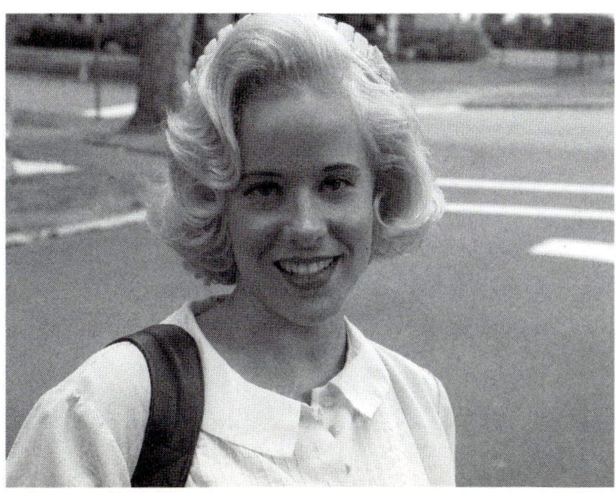

Awanda.

MAKING ORIGINAL CHARACTERS

When designing and creating characters, I find it helpful to develop a character profile that lists the traits of each character. Consider running each character through this list to flesh him out to a fuller, more real person.

Describe the character's. . . .

1. Interests and hobbies
2. Romantic successes or failures
3. Family life
4. Relationship with parents/siblings
5. Financial situation
6. Education
7. Life goals
8. Posture
9. Musical tastes
10. Culinary tastes
11. Political views
12. Travel experience
13. Favorite vacation spot
14. Worst habit
15. Biggest fear
16. Favorite occasion
17. Reaction to criticism
18. Television viewing habits
19. Behavior while drunk
20. Nickname

Another great way to create strong characters is to take a personality test as each character to identify his or her personality temperament. The results will help you when writing a character's reaction to specific problems that arise in the storyline. An outstanding book to read is *Please Understand Me* by David Keirsey and Marilyn Bates.

Russian spy plans to blow up America unless $2,000,000 is wired to his Swiss bank account. The audience never learns what drives him to commit this crime, what his life is like, how his family is reacting to the situation, or what terrible circumstances in his life led to his wanting to blow something up just for money. This lack of depth leads to a flat, boring character that simply does bad things. This character's impact on the audience is minimal and fleeting.

Supporting characters: Supporting characters are written to support either the protagonist or the antagonist, usually having similar objectives. Supporting characters work with the main characters, but never eclipse them, although supporting characters may have their own set of complexities.

In *Time and Again*, the main character is Bobby Jones, along with the supporting characters Awanda, Sheriff Karl, young Bobby Jones, Martha Jones, and Robin Jones.

Whereas these primary characters carry the story, there are quite a few secondary supporting characters helping to provide a realistic backdrop for the story. These characters include the stickball players, the high school kids outside the theater, the deputy sheriff, and the diner waitress. Although they aren't aligned with either the protagonist or the antagonist, they are vital in providing information to the main characters and pushing the story forward. If the character cannot provide this function, they must be cut from the story. For example:

- **Stickball players.** By playing stickball, they provided the opportunity for young Bobby Jones to be in the middle of the street so that older Bobby Jones could see him.
- **Diner waitress.** She helped Bobby Jones when he ran into the diner, looking for Awanda, providing him critical information that led him to his next course of action.
- **Students outside theater.** When Bobby Jones approached them, they also gave him critical information as to the whereabouts of young Bobby Jones.

Activities

ACTIVITY 1

Use a video camera to document an event . . . a birthday party, a picnic, a dinner. Then edit it into a two-minute sequence showing how the event progresses from beginning to end. Transcribe the scene into a written script, writing down word for word what people say in the scene. Study the way spoken word appears on paper and the flow of how people move and act during an event.

ACTIVITY 2

Keep a journal of interesting events you experience. Write, in detail, what you saw, how people reacted, how you felt during the event. Use this as a launching point for future scenes and ideas. Also, write down and describe interesting people you encounter. What did they wear? What were these peoples' oddities or quirks? The best characters will come from your own experiences.

ACTIVITY 3

Record a conversation between two people you know and transcribe the conversation word for word to paper. Study how the written word differs from spoken word and how the spoken phrases look on paper. This is an important skill to learn when writing realistic dialog. You'll be surprised to find just how short sentences and phrases look when transcribed.

Formatting guidelines

Hollywood has very stringent guidelines regarding how a script should be formatted. It is imperative to follow these guidelines, or your script will end up in the trash without being read. Consider purchasing a professional script writing program like Final Draft that does the formatting work for you.

The following are guidelines to formatting a feature-length screenplay.

- Use 12-point Courier font (the typewriter font), which is the standard script font. When this font is used, one page of properly formatted script is roughly equal to one minute of screen time.
- Begin each scene in capital letters and describe whether it is interior or exterior (INT or EXT), the location where the scene takes place in the

"The Day Bobby Jones Came Home" Draft 6/29/02 14.

BOBBY
Even after doing all this work?

AWANDA
That might count for something.

Bobby and Awanda get on bike.

DISSOLVE TO:

19 EXT. TRAILER -EVENING 19

Bobby and Awanda ride up to a dilapidated old trailer nestled in the middle of an overgrown field.

DISSOLVE TO:

20 INT. TRAILER - NIGHT 20

Bobby slowly, almost reverently splashes water over his face, enjoying every moment of it. He grabs a towel. He can't help but notice Awanda in the slipping out of her dress. The light plays beautifully off her bare back. Bobby watches entranced. Awanda puts on a slip and turns, catching Bobby's stare. Bobby turns away.

BOBBY
How long have you worked at that diner?

AWANDA
Six months. I used to be a substitute teacher -- kindergarten. Had a problem with the principal though -- he couldn't keep his hands off me.

BOBBY
Do you ever have any regrets about that?

AWANDA
About teaching or the principal?

BOBBY
No, teaching. If you could go back in time and change anything, anything at all... would you?

Script page.

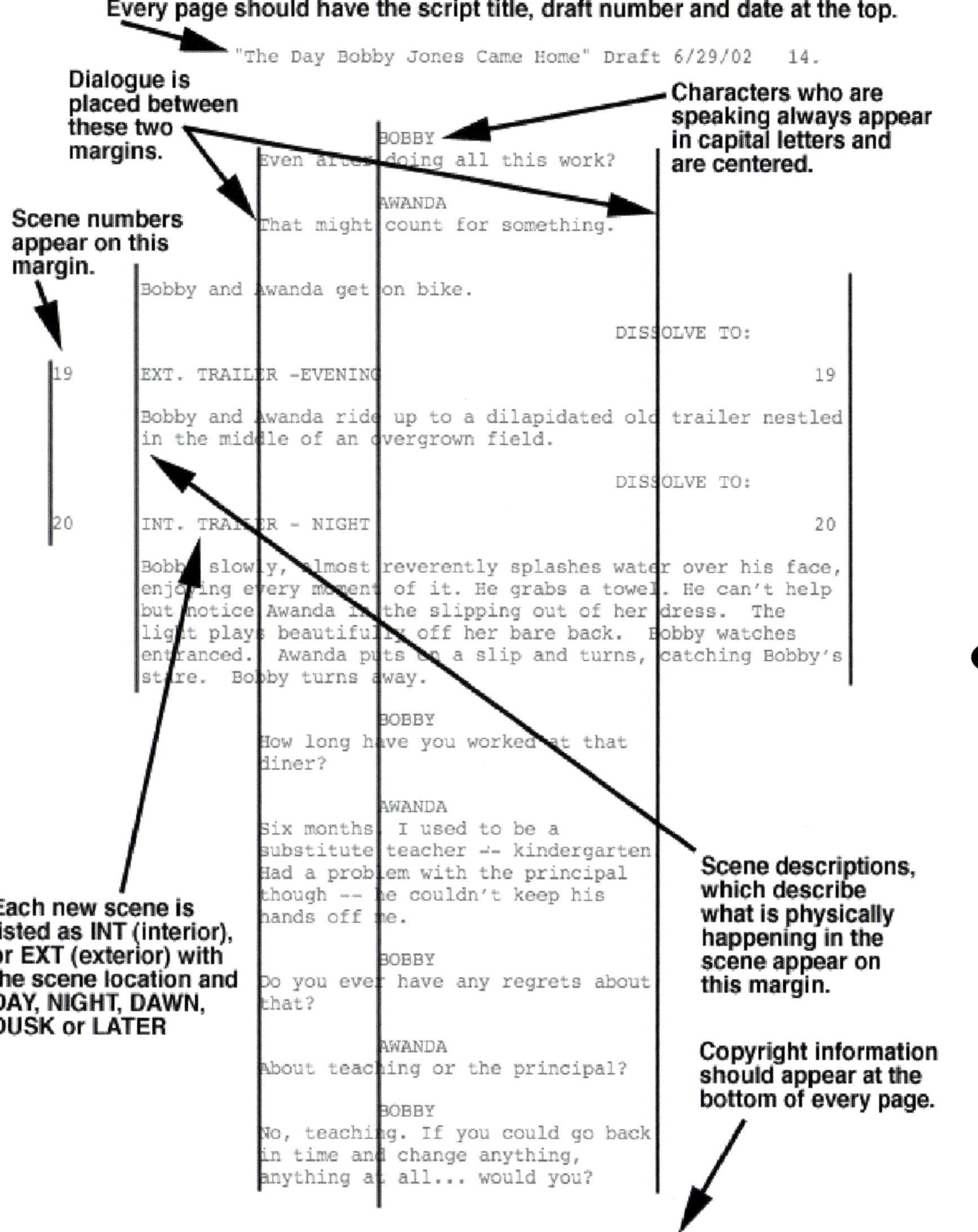
Every page should have the script title, draft number and date at the top.
Dialogue is placed between these two margins.
Characters who are speaking always appear in capital letters and are centered.
Scene numbers appear on this margin.
Scene descriptions, which describe what is physically happening in the scene appear on this margin.
Each new scene is listed as INT (interior), or EXT (exterior) with the scene location and DAY, NIGHT, DAWN, DUSK or LATER
Copyright information should appear at the bottom of every page.

"The Day Bobby Jones Came Home" Draft 6/29/02 14.

BOBBY
Even after doing all this work?

AWANDA
That might count for something.

Bobby and Awanda get on bike.

DISSOLVE TO:

19 EXT. TRAILER -EVENING 19

Bobby and Awanda ride up to a dilapidated old trailer nestled in the middle of an overgrown field.

DISSOLVE TO:

20 INT. TRAILER - NIGHT 20

Bobby slowly, almost reverently splashes water over his face, enjoying every moment of it. He grabs a towel. He can't help but notice Awanda in the slipping out of her dress. The light plays beautifully off her bare back. Bobby watches entranced. Awanda puts on a slip and turns, catching Bobby's stare. Bobby turns away.

BOBBY
How long have you worked at that diner?

AWANDA
Six months. I used to be a substitute teacher -- kindergarten. Had a problem with the principal though -- he couldn't keep his hands off me.

BOBBY
Do you ever have any regrets about that?

AWANDA
About teaching or the principal?

BOBBY
No, teaching. If you could go back in time and change anything, anything at all... would you?

© 2002 Robert T. Noll & Jason J. Tomaric

Script page marked.

story, and the time of day (DAY, NIGHT, DAWN, DUSK, LATER). For example:

```
INT. AWANDA'S TRAILER—DAY
```

Once the script is finished and each scene is numbered, add numbers to the beginning and end of the scene header line. For example:

```
46.     INT. AWANDA'S TRAILER—DAY               46
```

- Type all screen directions in the same margin as the scene header. Screen directions should explain where and how the characters move and what is happening in the scene. Use the screen directions to describe to the reader/audience what they will see on screen. For example:

```
46.     INT. AWANDA'S TRAILER—DAY               46

        Awanda walks to the refrigerator and
        pulls out a pitcher of water, all the
        while watching Bobby from the corner
        of her eye. Bobby, unaware of her
        gaze, stares out the window.
```

- When writing dialog, write the name of the character who is speaking in capital letters and center it in the page.
- Descriptions that indicate how a line must be said (for example: sarcastically, coyly, under his breath, and so on) must be placed in a margin $3\frac{1}{2}$ inches from the left side of the page.
- All character dialog appears under the name of the character who speaks the line. This is to be written $4\frac{1}{4}$ inches from the left side of the page. For example:

```
46.     INT. AWANDA'S TRAILER—DAY               46

        Awanda walks to the refrigerator and
        pulls out a pitcher of water, all the
        while watching Bobby from the corner
        of her eye. Bobby, unaware of her
        gaze, stares out the window.

                       AWANDA
                 (quietly)
        I heard you needed a place to stay.
```

- Don't use camera directions—Camera directions indicate where the camera needs to be placed within the scene. This is not the writer's job, but that of the director and the cinematographer. Write the script as a story, focusing only on the characters and what they are doing and saying in each scene.

- Don't break scenes up into shots—A change in scene reflects a change in location in the story. Shots are individual camera positions within the scene that are designed by the director and cinematographer. Break up the script only into scenes.
- Don't number your scenes—Scenes are to be numbered by the first assistant director after the screenplay is finished. If you number the scenes in advance, rewriting the script will constantly change the scene numbers and throw off the script breakdown and any department working off the breakdowns. Assign scene numbers once the script is locked.
- Check your spelling—Correct spelling and grammar are essential in presenting a professional screenplay for consideration by agents, managers, studios, and production companies.
- Covers and binding—Present the script with a white cover that states the title, the writer(s), date completed, writer(s) and/or agent contact phone numbers, WGA registration number, and copyright information. The script should be punched with three holes and "bound" with two gold clasps.
- First page—Always begin the script with "Fade in" and end with "Fade to black."
- Scene headings—At the beginning of every scene, establish INT/EXT, the location where the scene takes place, and the time of day. Always type these in capital letters.

FORMATTING GUIDELINES

Follow these guidelines to format your script to industry-standard specifications.

Margins

All measurements are from the left edge of the paper:

Scene headings: margin starts 1.5 inches from the left edge of the paper.

Stage directions: margin starts 1.5 inches from the left edge of the paper.

Character names are centered on the page.

Dialog: left margin is at 2.5 inches and right margin is at 6.5 inches.

Character directions: left margin is at 3 inches and right margin is at 5.5 inches.

Tips for writing successfully

Writing is a process that requires a lot of discipline and focus. Here are some tips to being an effective writer:

- Set daily and weekly goals. Plan to write at least five pages a day, regardless of how good or bad they are. Remember that the real writing process begins when you rewrite. The first step is to get a rough draft down on paper.
- Be organized. By starting out with an idea and flushing it out into an outline, the process of writing the script becomes easier. Also keep a clean, clutter-free work area, free of distractions so you can focus on your writing.
- Stories are about people, not explosions or car chases. When writing your story, the dimension of your characters comes out when you show the audience how they react in different situations. Describe their strengths and weaknesses, attitudes and opinions, drives and ambitions, and what they want.
- Try putting ideas on 3×5 note cards before writing the script. Write clever lines of dialog on white cards, character ideas on green, cool scene ideas on pink, and so on. Organize these cards to help when you're outlining the story.
- Develop a step outline, or a moment-by-moment description of what the audience will see in the movie. This will make it easier to write the script.
- Build your story around sequences . . . remember that shots make up a scene, scenes make up sequences, and sequences make up a film. Sequences are moments and ministories within the larger story.
- Avoid writing cliché situations, dialog, and moments that the audience has seen before. Writing fresh ideas can be as simple as taking a moment in a scene and writing down ten unique and interesting variations on how it can be played.
- What is the plot arc? How is the story set up? How do you introduce the characters? How do you introduce the conflict? Where is the turning point in the story? How does the plot build to a climax? And finally, how does it resolve itself?
- Create setups and pay-offs . . . situations, props, information, and people your characters encounter must lead to something or have some significance within the story. Remember that the audience is going to be looking for meaning in the elements you show them.
- Create interesting names for your characters by using a baby naming book or searching the Internet for random name generators.
- Remember that the characters, much like the plot, have arcs as well . . . characters should undergo changes from the beginning to the end of the story and the story should be about this journey they take.
- Choose three primary adjectives that describe your character and make sure that the character's actions, motivations, and dialog match those three adjectives in each and every scene.
- The antagonist, or bad guy, is an interesting character who simply does bad things. Give the antagonist character inner conflicts as well as those that drive him to do evil. Make him a real, multidimensional character.

RESOURCES FOR WRITERS

Web sites

www.powerfilmmaking.com

Publications

Creative Screenwriting
6404 Hollywood Boulevard
Los Angeles, CA 90028
(323) 957-1405
www.CreativeScreenwriting.com

Daily Variety
5700 Wilshire Boulevard, #120
Los Angeles, CA 90036
(323) 857-6600
www.Variety.com

Hollywood Reporter
5055 Wilshire Boulevard
Los Angeles, CA 90036
(323) 525-2000
www.Hollywoodreporter.com

Hollywood Scriptwriter
P.O. Box 10277
Burbank, CA 91510
(818) 845-5525
www.HollywoodScriptwriter.com

Script Magazine
5638 Sweet Air Road
Baldwin, MD 21013
(410) 592-3466
www.ScriptMag.com

Written By
WGA, 7000 West 3rd Street
Los Angeles, CA 90048
(323) 782-4522
www.WGA.org

Book and software stores

The Biz
1223 Olympic Boulevard
Santa Monica, CA 90404
(310) 399-6699
www.HollywoodU.com

Samuel French
7623 Sunset Boulevard
Hollywood, CA 90046
(323) 876-0570
www.SamuelFrench.com

Writers Store
2040 Westwood Boulevard
Los Angeles, CA 90025
(310) 471-5151
www.WritersStore.com

Theatre Books
Toronto, ON, Canada
(416) 922-7175

Limelight Books
San Francisco, CA
(415) 864-2265

Applause Books
New York, NY
(212) 575-9265

Drama Book Shop
New York, NY
(212) 944-0595

Software

Final Draft
11965 Venice Boulevard, #405
Los Angeles, CA 90066
(800) 231-4055
www.bcsoftware.com

Screenwriter2000
150 E Olive Avenue
Burbank, CA 91502
(818) 843-6557
www.Screenplay.com

Software suppliers

www.WritersStore.com
www.ScreenStyle.com
www.showBix.com
www.WebFilmSchool.com

- Remember that the more you write, the more you have to produce. If the budget is limited, then limit the screenplay length to 90 pages. Ninety pages of script means that 90 minutes of the movie needs to be produced.
- Always write in the present tense. Do not write, "We cut to Alan Blum who is walking down the street." Rather, write "Alan Blum casually walks down the street."

Writing on a budget

The secret to making a low-budget film is to write within your means. Be aware of the resources you have available to you before you write. I know this probably sounds hypocritical because I tackled a seemingly expensive 1950s piece on a budget of $2000, but as I wrote the script for *Time and Again*, I knew I would have easy access to locations that could sell the time period. I also knew that

Bob Noll and I knew we only had a $2,000 budget, so we wrote the script knowing our resources.

in Ohio, antique cars are plentiful, vintage costumes were easily obtained, and cast and crew members would be willing to work for free. As I wrote the script, I thought carefully about how I would realistically produce each moment of every scene, so when it came time to go into preproduction, there were no unexpected surprises.

If you are working on a low budget, think about the following factors before you begin writing:

- **Minimize the number of locations.** When you write settings into the story, make sure the locations are accessible, available, and inexpensive to secure.
- **Keep the number of characters to a minimum.** Even if your actors are willing to work for free, feeding them isn't. Casts of thousands don't come cheap. Many low-budget movies keep their character count to under ten.
- **Avoid shooting at night.** Night shooting is very expensive, as hefty HMI lighting is required to light large expanses of exterior locations and even interiors. Daytime shooting allows the cinematographer to use bounce cards to work sunlight.
- **Write a story that takes place in present day.** Avoid the need for expensive props, wardrobe, sets, or set dressing.
- **Avoid extensive special effects, stunts, makeup effects, and pyrotechnics.**
- **Keep the script to 90 pages.** As tempting as it is to write a 120-page script, remember that every page you write translates to a minute on screen. Every minute on screen will cost hundreds if not thousands of dollars to produce. Keep the script to the shortest possible length to stretch the budget as far as possible.

Your first film needs to be about people, people, and people. Let the story be about human interactions, interesting situations, and witty dialog. Save special effects, stunts, casts of thousands, and period pieces for your next project.

Rewrites

Once the first draft of the script is complete, set it aside and read it over in a week with fresh eyes. Then, begin the process of rewriting and reworking the script to improve pacing, character development, dialog, and story structure.

Often, writers will seek the advice of friends and other writers who can provide a fresh perspective on the script. Listen to the feedback, but don't be too hasty to accept a friend's opinion and make a change. Remember that not everyone will respond the same way to a script, and it's critical to filter the constructive criticism from people who simply don't like the material.

Hollywood scripts often undergo a hundred or more rewrites to ensure they are as solid as possible, before they go into production. Adopt this approach for your script to maximize the return on your investment of time and money.

Protecting your script

Once your script is complete, consider submitting it to the U.S. Copyright Office and the Writers Guild of America for copyright protection. For a nominal fee and a simple application form, both offices will retain a copy of the script, so if you ever need to prove the date the script was written and its authenticity, submission to these agencies serves as evidence in court.

United States Copyright Office
Library of Congress
Washington DC 20559
Copyright forms hotline (202) 707-9100
Screenplays: Form PA
www.copyright.gov
Cost: $35 for electronic filing, $45 for paper filing

Writers Guild of America, West
WGAW Registry
7000 West Third Street
Los Angeles, CA 90048
(323) 782-4500
www.wgaregistry.org
Cost: $20 for non-WGA members, $10 for WGA members

Optioning a script

Although you can write an original screenplay, consider taking advantage of one of the 200,000–300,000 spec scripts written each year by writers all around the world. The best way to go about producing an existing script is to option it. An option is a lease wherein a producer pays the writer a negotiated rate for a predetermined amount of time to hold, produce, or attempt to produce the script into a film. Usual Hollywood options are for around $20,000–$30,000, but in the case of independent film producers, scripts can be optioned for as little as $1.00.

The script option, which lasts for an average of two to three years, gives the producer the exclusive right to promote, shop, raise funds, produce, or even shelve the script. If the option lapses and the script has not been produced, the rights to the screenplay will return to the writer. Optioning terms are negotiable between the writer and the producer. Always put the details of your agreement in writing.

GO BEYOND THE BOOK

Check out the companion DVD and watch the "Introduction to Writing" video to see how Jason J. Tomaric and Bob Noll wrote the script of *Time and Again*.

Take the next step and listen as Hollywood writers and producers share inside information on writing a successful screenplay.

From the Emmy-winning Executive Producer of "Everybody Loves Raymond" to the President of www.inktip.com, Jerrol LeBaron, learn how to write from people who actually write for a living in Hollywood.

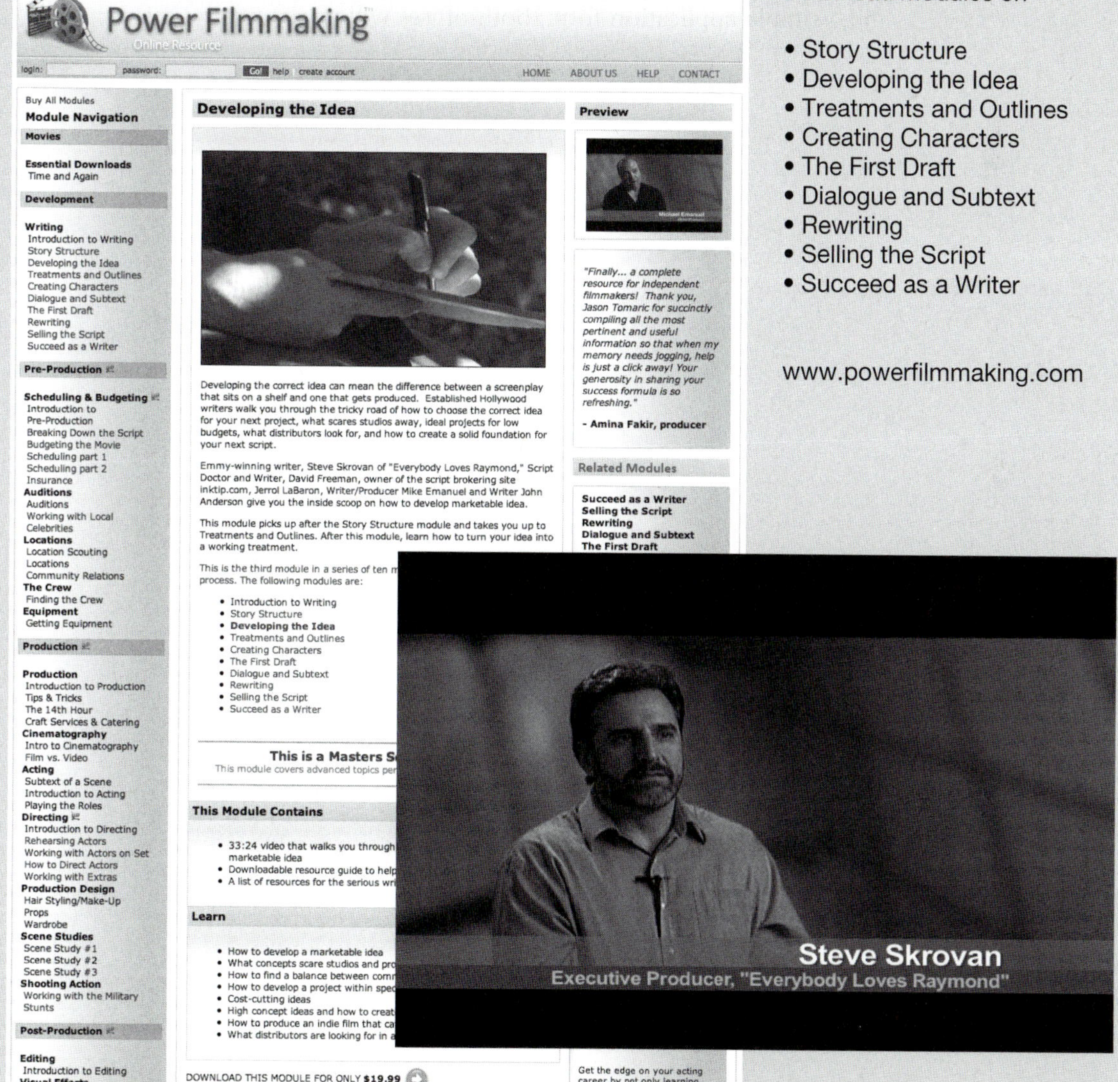

Download modules on

- Story Structure
- Developing the Idea
- Treatments and Outlines
- Creating Characters
- The First Draft
- Dialogue and Subtext
- Rewriting
- Selling the Script
- Succeed as a Writer

www.powerfilmmaking.com

UNIT 2
Preproduction

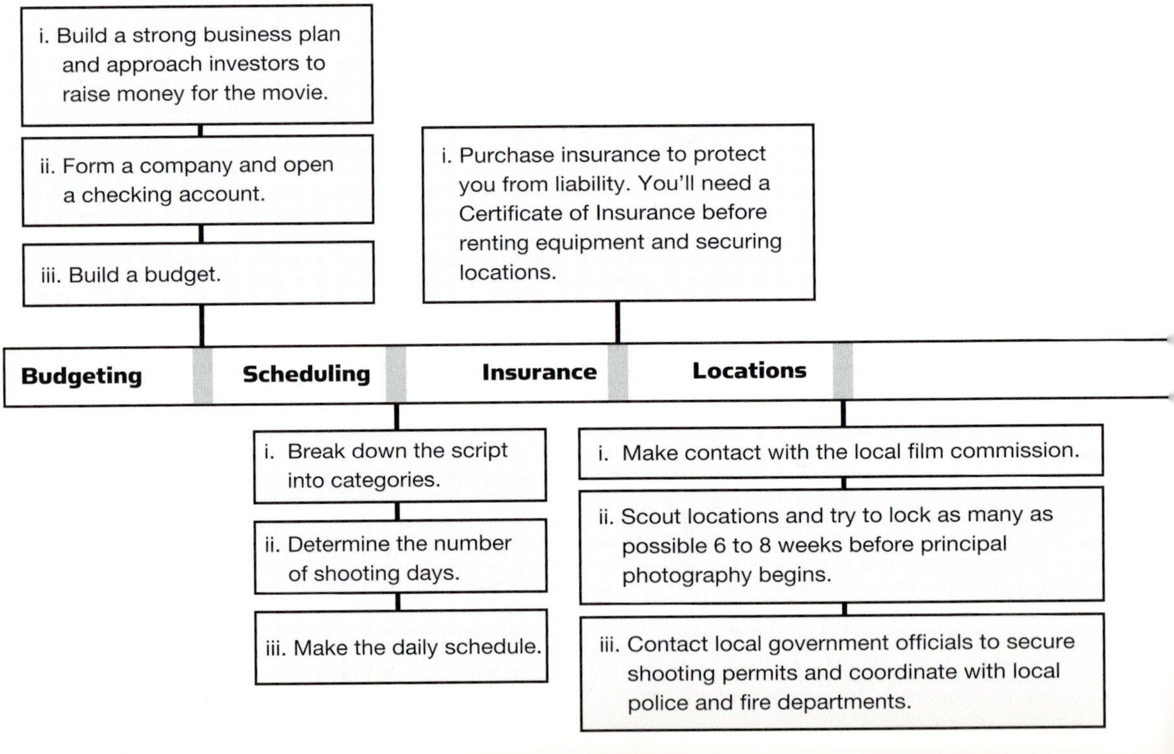

i. Build a strong business plan and approach investors to raise money for the movie.

ii. Form a company and open a checking account.

iii. Build a budget.

i. Purchase insurance to protect you from liability. You'll need a Certificate of Insurance before renting equipment and securing locations.

Budgeting **Scheduling** **Insurance** **Locations**

i. Break down the script into categories.

ii. Determine the number of shooting days.

iii. Make the daily schedule.

i. Make contact with the local film commission.

ii. Scout locations and try to lock as many as possible 6 to 8 weeks before principal photography begins.

iii. Contact local government officials to secure shooting permits and coordinate with local police and fire departments.

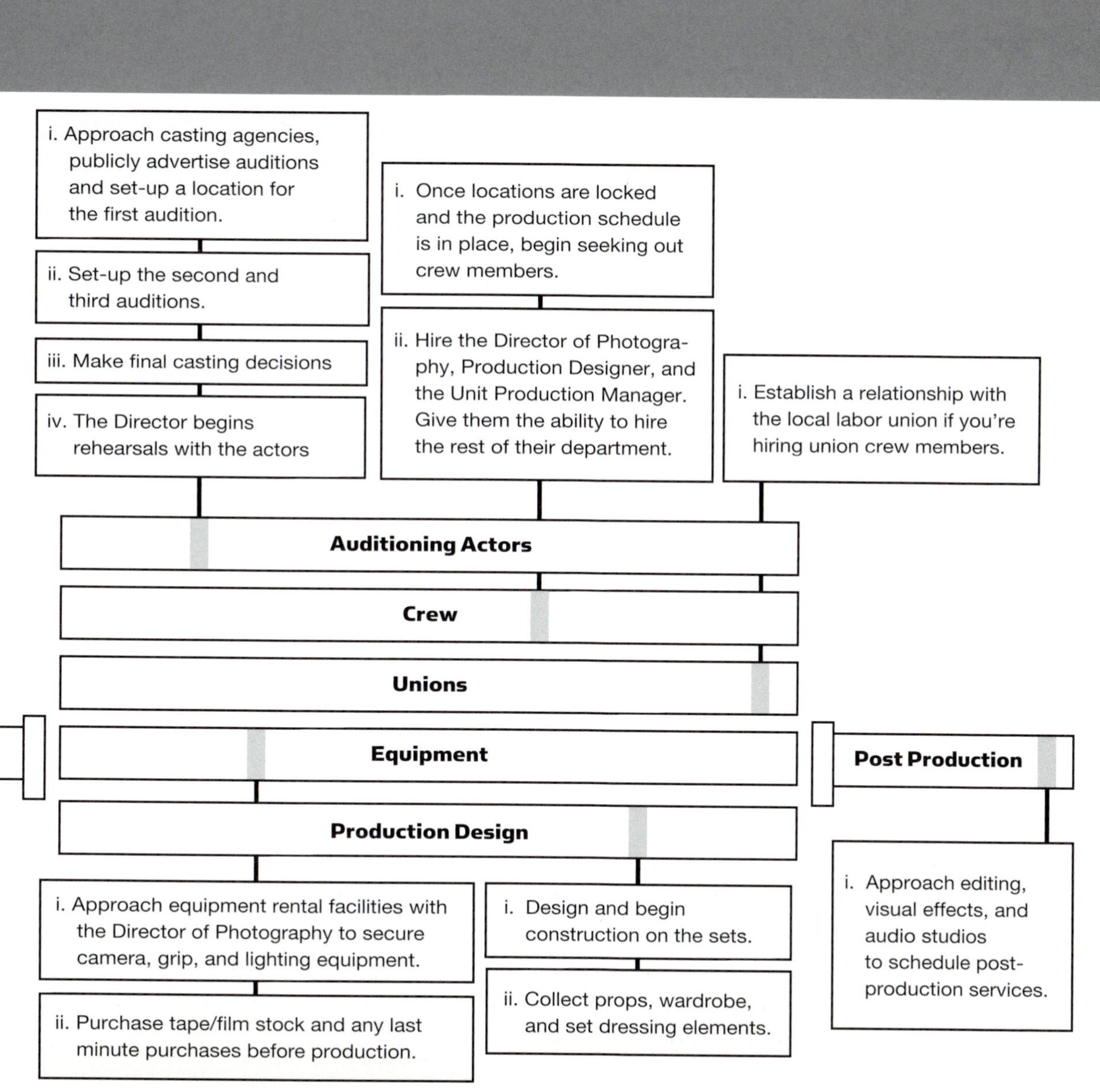
i. Approach casting agencies, publicly advertise auditions and set-up a location for the first audition.
ii. Set-up the second and third auditions.
iii. Make final casting decisions
iv. The Director begins rehearsals with the actors
i. Once locations are locked and the production schedule is in place, begin seeking out crew members.
ii. Hire the Director of Photography, Production Designer, and the Unit Production Manager. Give them the ability to hire the rest of their department.
i. Establish a relationship with the local labor union if you're hiring union crew members.
Auditioning Actors
Crew
Unions
Equipment
Production Design
Post Production
i. Approach equipment rental facilities with the Director of Photography to secure camera, grip, and lighting equipment.
ii. Purchase tape/film stock and any last minute purchases before production.
i. Design and begin construction on the sets.
ii. Collect props, wardrobe, and set dressing elements.
i. Approach editing, visual effects, and audio studios to schedule post-production services.

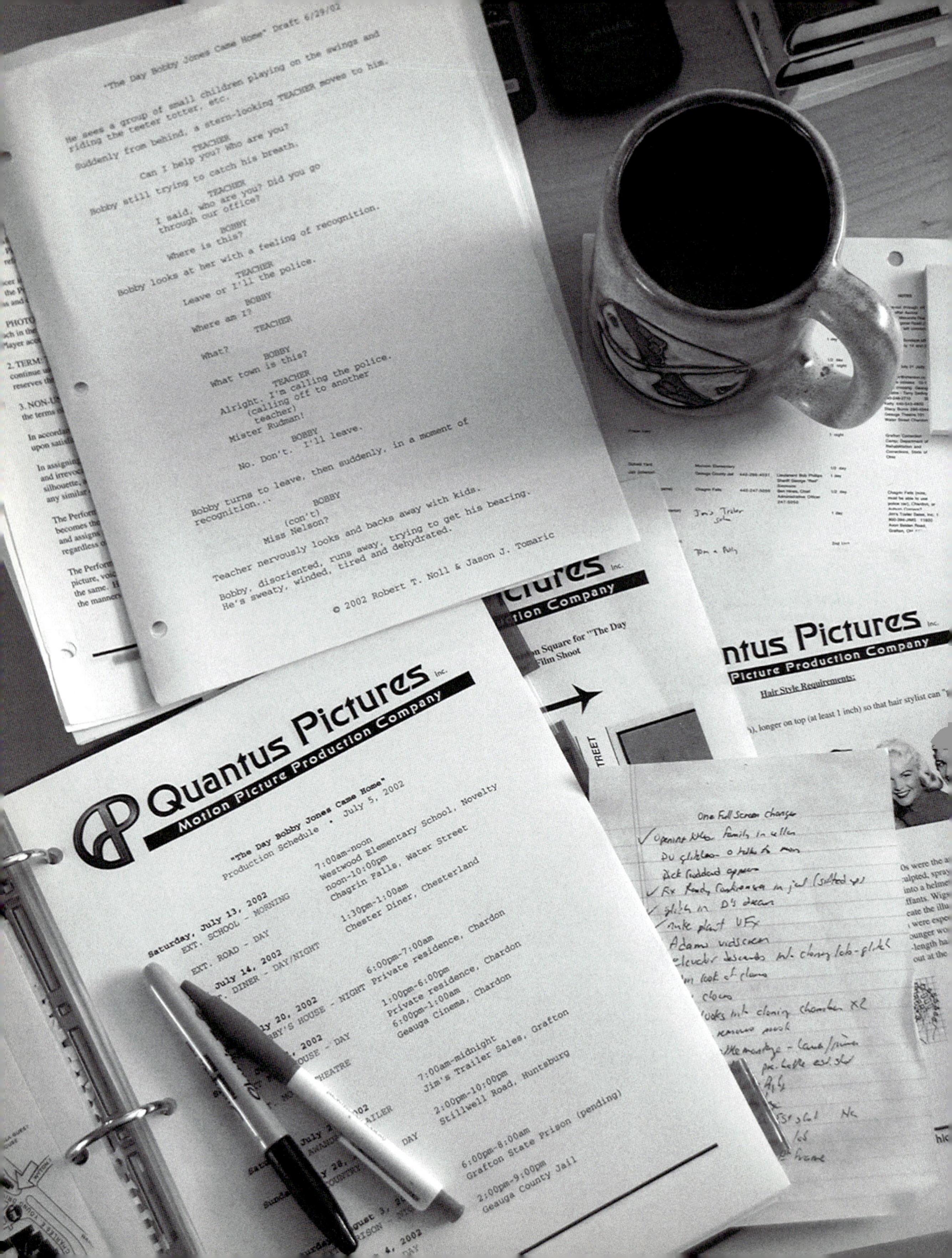

"The Day Bobby Jones Came Home" Draft 6/29/02
He sees a group of small children playing on the swings and riding the teeter totter, etc.
Suddenly from behind, a stern-looking TEACHER moves to him.
TEACHER
Can I help you? Who are you?
Bobby still trying to catch his breath.
TEACHER
I said, who are you? Did you go through our office?
BOBBY
Where is this?
Bobby looks at her with a feeling of recognition.
TEACHER
Leave or I'll the police.
BOBBY
Where am I?
TEACHER
What?
BOBBY
What town is this?
TEACHER
Alright, I'm calling the police.
(calling off to another teacher)
Mister Rudman!
BOBBY
No. Don't. I'll leave.
Bobby turns to leave, then suddenly, in a moment of recognition...
BOBBY
(con't)
Miss Nelson?
Teacher nervously looks and backs away with kids.
Bobby, disoriented, runs away, trying to get his bearing. He's sweaty, winded, tired and dehydrated.
© 2002 Robert T. Noll & Jason J. Tomaric
Quantus Pictures Inc.
Motion Picture Production Company
"The Day Bobby Jones Came Home"
Production Schedule • July 5, 2002
Saturday, July 13, 2002
EXT. SCHOOL - MORNING
7:00am-noon
Westwood Elementary School, Novelty
EXT. ROAD - DAY
noon-10:00pm
Chagrin Falls, Water Street
July 14, 2002
1:30pm-1:00am
Chester Diner, Chesterland
6:00pm-7:00am
Private residence, Chardon
1:00pm-6:00pm
Private residence, Chardon
6:00pm-1:00am
Geauga Cinema, Chardon
7:00am-midnight
Jim's Trailer Sales, Grafton
2:00pm-10:00pm
Stillwell Road, Huntsburg
6:00pm-8:00am
Grafton State Prison (pending)
2:00pm-9:00pm
Geauga County Jail
Quantus Pictures Inc.
Motion Picture Production Company
Hair Style Requirements:

CHAPTER 2

Preproduction

INTRODUCTION

Once a script is finished and "greenlit," which means it's ready to be made, the project moves into a phase called "preproduction."

Preproduction is the process of breaking down the finished script and preparing all elements of the movie for production.

The preproduction phase includes:

- Breaking down the script
- Determining the budget
- Securing the financing
- Scouting locations
- Casting
- Hiring the crew
- Securing equipment
- Scheduling the shoot dates

Preproduction is an extremely organized, methodical process similar to designing the blueprints of a house. Think about every aspect of the movie in advance and try to be as prepared as possible before arriving on the set. Remember, construction workers show up on a job site knowing exactly what must be done, because all the preparation was done ahead of time when the blueprints were being designed . . . not on the job site. The electrical contractors and plumbers are being paid to install the wiring and plumbing, not wait around while the architect decides how to build the house. The same is the case with a movie—every prop, every person, and every shot must be carefully thought out and planned so that when on set, you can make the best use of the time you have by focusing on the performances and not on logistics.

- The quality of the production is directly proportional to the amount of time taken on preproduction. The more organized the project, the smoother everything will go on set.
- Before starting preproduction, hire a good attorney and a good accountant to assist in setting up the bank accounts for the company, especially if the production is funded by outside investors.

- Preproduction is not complicated, but there are a thousand little jobs that need to be done. So although it may seem stressful, a careful and organized approach can help the process go smoothly.
- Even the best-planned shoots will encounter problems, so expect them. When they occur, don't get frustrated. Remember that if making a movie was easy, everyone would be doing it. Be prepared to deal with any problem that arises on set by thinking about possible solutions in advance.

SETTING UP AN OFFICE

Producing a movie is a time-consuming process that can turn into a full-time job. Establish a home base where production efforts can be coordinated, phone calls can be made, packages and equipment can be dropped off, and cast and crew can meet.

When setting up your workspace, be sure to have the following resources:

- Credit cards for use by office staff
- Coffee, copiers, fax machine
- Computers, printers
- Extra paper, ink, envelopes, file folders
- Crew listings from the local film commission
- Current editions of local phone books
- Locations of office supply store, USPS, FedEx, copier, rental car facility, hotels, restaurants (have delivery menus available)
- Meeting area with table and chairs for meetings and rehearsals
- Dry Erase board with markers
- Production email accounts
- Accounts with a courier service
- DVD player, VCR, and a television set
- Telephones (land lines and cell)—set up a phone number for the production office
- Small refrigerator with beverages
- Copies of deal memos, script breakdowns, location agreements, and all pertinent production forms

Even if you're shooting a low-budget independent movie and can't afford an office space, be prepared to use your home for meetings and be ready for a lot of people to come and go throughout the shoot. You will probably be storing props, wardrobe, art direction elements, and production equipment in your home.

LEGAL CONSULTATIONS

One of the first steps in beginning a production is to hire a qualified attorney to help with the legal paperwork, including contracts. If the budget is large enough, an attorney can set up a corporation or LLC (limited liability company).

There are a number of organizations that offer free or discounted rates to independent filmmakers.

Beverly Hills Bar Association
300 S. Beverly Drive #201
Beverly Hills, CA 90210
(310) 553-6644
$25 fee for ½ hour legal consultation
Contact Bill Newman for information: (310) 553-4022

Independent Feature Project/West
5550 Wilshire Boulevard, Suite 204
Los Angeles, CA 90036
(213) 937-4379

IFP/West Resource Bank
New membership benefit!
A panel of experts will provide ½ hour free consultation in three areas: legal, production, distribution.
Contact David Steiner for information: (213) 937-4379

Independent Feature Project/East
132 West 21st Street, 6th Floor
New York, NY 10011
(212) 243-7777
Other IFP benefits: seminars, screenings, discounts on services, and more!

Independent Writers of Southern California (IWOSC)
P.O. Box 34279
Los Angeles, CA 90034
(310) 558-4090
Provides members with a job referral hotline, free expert advice, and other programs and seminars.

Los Angeles County Bar Association
617 S. Olive Street
Los Angeles, CA
(213) 627-2727
Provides an attorney referral service
$25 fee for ½ hour legal advice
(213) 622-6700

During the preproduction of *Time and Again*, I called a local attorney and asked if he would donate his time to assist our low-budget production in exchange for a credit. He gladly accepted and was an excited participant in the movie, so much so that he was even an extra in one of the scenes.

RELEASE FORMS

Release forms are important contracts that protect the producer from liability on set. All cast and crew members as well as location owners must sign a form before being allowed on set to establish, in writing, the arrangement between the producer and the cast and crew members.

- All cast and crew members, as well as extras and interns, must sign a form that releases the production company of any and all liability in the event an accident were to occur on set.
- Post signs when shooting in public alerting passersby that a film is in production and that by entering the premises, they release the production company of any liability and they may appear on film in the background.
- Make sure all extras write contact information clearly on the release forms, and enter the data in a database so you can contact them when the film is finished.

BOOKS

The Complete Film Production Handbook by Eve Light Honthaner, 2001, Focal Press.

Contracts for the Film and Television Industry by Mark Litwak, 1994, Silman–James Press.

PREPRODUCTION

- Complete the final script, copy and distribute to cast and crew.
- Break down the script, create production board, and make the production schedule (it's easier to schedule the film after locations have been secured in writing).
- Set up production offices and bring on necessary interns and staff. Secure office equipment such as a copier, computer, fax machine, and telephones.
- Set up insurance, bank accounts, and company structure. Hire a good attorney and accountant to help.
- Begin location scouting.
- Begin scheduling auditions for principal actors and extras. Contact local talent agencies to assist.
- Begin talking with crew members, focusing on main crew positions. Call the film commission for the production manual that lists all local crew members.
- Prepare agreements, deal memos, and contracts with cast and crew.
- Review budget with newly hired crew members to determine feasibility.
- Research and assemble props and wardrobe.
- Contact local film commission and establish relationship for permits and city services.
- Begin set construction and set decorating.
- Negotiate with vendors for camera, film stock, lighting, and grip equipment.
- Contact postproduction services, including editors, labs, composers, and visual effects artists.

WE SEEK GOD'S ASSISTANCE
CENTRAL BANK of KUWAIT
1/2
中国人民银
BN207692XG
EKT EKP 2002

CHAPTER 3
Budgeting

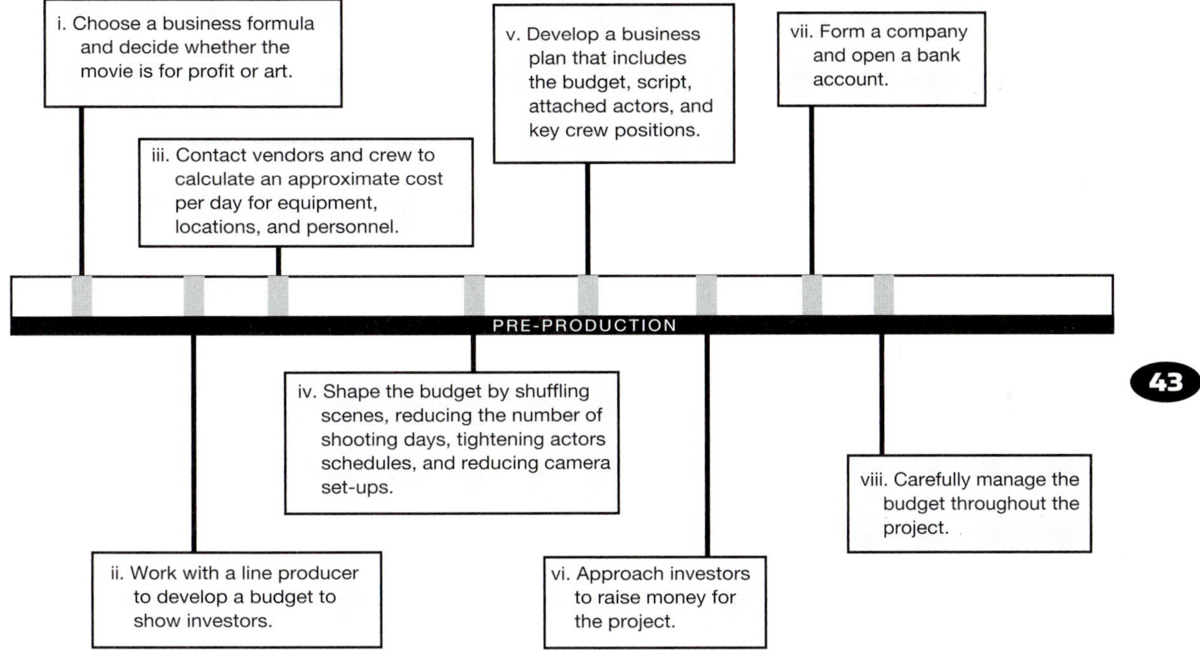

i. Choose a business formula and decide whether the movie is for profit or art.
iii. Contact vendors and crew to calculate an approximate cost per day for equipment, locations, and personnel.
v. Develop a business plan that includes the budget, script, attached actors, and key crew positions.
vii. Form a company and open a bank account.
PRE-PRODUCTION
iv. Shape the budget by shuffling scenes, reducing the number of shooting days, tightening actors schedules, and reducing camera set-ups.
viii. Carefully manage the budget throughout the project.
ii. Work with a line producer to develop a budget to show investors.
vi. Approach investors to raise money for the project.

INTRODUCTION

Of all the art forms, filmmaking is the most expensive, and securing financing can be the most difficult aspect of producing a film. It's possible to produce a high-quality, low-budget movie by managing costs, but purchases, fees, rentals, and unforeseen problems can drive even the most modest budget into the tens of thousands of dollars.

RAISING MONEY

Raising the funds needed to produce your movie can be both challenging and frustrating. Like other industries, financiers will invest money into projects whose managers have demonstrated an ability to produce a profitable product.

Unless a filmmaker has already made and sold a movie, he has no track record, so approaching an investor for a million dollars is like a recent business school graduate asking for a million dollars for a start-up company. Most investors will laugh at him and tell him to build a company out of his garage and make a profit; then, once he does, come back and ask for investment dollars. The film industry works the same way, wherein financiers flock to filmmakers with a proven track record, whose work has generated a profit in the past.

So how do new first-time filmmakers make a movie? Start in the garage, so to speak, by producing a low-budget movie with local resources. If it's a good movie, then investors may notice and consider financing the second movie.

The formula works like this:

Make a good $2000 movie and use it to raise the money to shoot a $20,000 movie.

Make a good $20,000 movie and use it to raise the money to shoot a $200,000 movie.

Make a good $200,000 movie and use it to raise the money to shoot a $2,000,000 movie.

Before you get frustrated, remember there isn't a single filmmaker in the history of cinema who had a $100,000,000 budget for his first film. Not one. Every successful director started on small projects and grew from there.

- NEVER, NEVER, NEVER spend your own money. The odds of you seeing your money back are slim to none. The first rule of independent filmmaking is to let someone else knowingly bear the financial risk of the project.
- Although increasing your credit limit or securing another home mortgage are options for securing money for your film, avoid these at all costs. The likelihood of making your money back on the film is slim, leaving massive interest-laden credit card bills or the threat of having the bank repossess your house.

BUSINESS FORMULAS

There are a number of "formulas" used in the entertainment industry to produce movies on varying budget levels. The smaller the budget, the more creative producers need to be to maximize the money they have available.

Formula 1

The primary business formula in Hollywood is to generate enough money to pay each person and vendor the proper day rate. Although this can thrust the budget into the millions, creative control remains with the producers and all employees are happily paid. This is the ideal, but not the most practical, approach for most independent filmmakers whose budgets prohibit them from paying each person on the production team.

Formula 2

One possible business plan for producing a low-budget movie is to pay everyone on the cast and crew, from the director to the production assistant, and the lead actors to the day players, $100/day. The twist is that each participant is awarded a percentage ownership in the movie. When the movie sells, 50 percent of the gross profits will go directly to the investor, and the other 50 percent is divided among the cast and crew based on their percentage of ownership. This back-end deal serves as an incentive for the cast and crew to work hard on the project and see it through to completion while minimizing out-of-pocket costs during production.

Formula 3

Offer the cast and crew deferred payment. Deferred payment means that there will be no up-front money, but the producer will pay everyone if the movie sells and makes money. Although this is extremely unlikely, many cast and crew members will appreciate the effort and will be willing to donate their time and talent to the project up front.

BUDGETING

The first step toward securing financing for your movie is to calculate how much money you need to make the movie. Remember that financiers respond better to a well-thought-out, line-item budget, rather than a request for a general dollar amount. In preparing the budget, the first step is to break down the script (see the Scheduling chapter for a step-by-step guide on how to do this) to determine the number of shooting days, cast and crew requirements, production design, camera and lighting equipment needs, postproduction expenses, and so on. Once you have an idea of the resources needed to produce the film, call vendors, cast and crew members, and locations to calculate the cost of each aspect of the movie. The result is a ballpark budget you can present an investor.

Part of the fun of making a low-budget movie is to see how many elements can be found and secured for free. The more freebies, the more money-costing line items can be removed from the budget.

- Be prepared to find actors who are willing to work for free. In *Time and Again*, none of the actors had ever acted before, but were willing to work for free for the experience. If you want to use experienced, SAG (Screen Actors Guild) actors, talk to the guild about low-budget options for filmmakers.
- When crewing up, seek recent college graduates or aspiring filmmakers in your community who are willing to work for the experience. Most crew members on *Time and Again* were independent filmmakers or recent broadcast school graduates who were excited to work on a movie. Beware, however; although inexperienced crew members may be cheap, they may

end up costing the production money in the long run because of their inefficiency on set.

- Contact local equipment rental agencies and ask them if they can donate the equipment needed, or at least offer a discount. All the equipment on *Time and Again* was secured for free through a local rental agency that was experiencing a slow month and trusted that we would take care of the equipment.
- Ask location owners if you can use their location for free. We didn't pay for a single location in *Time and Again*. I even negotiated to shut down a state prison, an entire town square, and an interstate for free, simply by presenting a professional proposal and having an open, honest conversation with the local authorities and a willingness to work with them.
- Be creative with art direction, wardrobe, and props. We talked to people in town and borrowed props, wardrobe, and set dressing, mostly for free. Many of the 1950s costumes were all rented for 75% off from a local costume shop, although some were borrowed from people involved with the production, like Sheriff Karl's police uniform.
- If you live in a large city like New York or Los Angeles, leave the city and go to areas where film production isn't as abundant. The people and local officials will be more willing to help independent filmmakers because filmmaking is more of a novelty than an everyday occurrence.

I was able to produce *Time and Again* for $2000 by approaching people, businesses, and the local authorities and asking for their help. The worst answer I would hear is "no," and my attitude was that every "no" I heard was one step closer to hearing a "yes." This attitude empowered me and made it possible to make a Hollywood-quality movie without a big budget.

Once the script is broken down and you have an idea of how much each department's needs will cost, begin typing the numbers into a budget form or enter the data into a budgeting program. You should end up with a final cost for the movie. If this cost exceeds the amount of money you have available in the budget, cut costs by reducing the number of shooting days, eliminating an effects sequence, or simplifying a scene.

Keep in mind some factors that surprise filmmakers with unexpected costs:

- Look at the costs of shooting at each individual location and plan what elements will be needed, both in front of and behind the camera. Be sure to include location fees, permit fees, and costs of hiring city officials such as police or fire marshals. Does the location have restrooms? If not, it will be necessary to rent portable toilets. If you're shooting a night interior scene, will it be necessary to block out the windows if the location is only available during the day? How much will it cost to buy or rent black fabric to cover all the windows? Does the crew need a day to prelight the set? Remember that foresight is the biggest money saver you have in your arsenal.
- Calculate the cost of crew members if they aren't willing to work for free. Most crew members will have a daily rate for short projects and a weekly

	DESCRIPTION	AMOUNT	UNIT	X	RATE	SUBTOTAL	TOTAL
	…tional…						…0.00
	Expendables/Supplies		Allow			500.00	$500.00
61							
62	STILL PHOTOGRAPHER						
63	Prep/Shoot/Wrap		Allow			125.00	$125.00
64	Rentals		N/A			100.00	
65	Film & Developing		Allow			500.00	$500.00
66	Expendables/Supplies		N/A			50.00	
67							
68	VIDEOGRAPHER (B-ROLL)						
69	Prep/Shoot/Wrap		Allow			0.00	$0.00
70	Supplies/Expendables		Allow			0.00	
71							
72							
73		Total for C-1500-00					$5,775.00
74	LIGHTING & GRIP						
75	GAFFER						
76	Prep/Shoot/Wrap	5	Days	0.00	250.00	1,250.00	
77	Overtime Charges	0	1.5 hours		0	0.00	$1,250.00
78	KEY GRIP						
79	Prep/Shoot/Wrap	5	Days	0.00	200.00	1,000.00	
80	Overtime Charges	0	1.5 hours		0	0	$1,000.00
81	DOLLY GRIP						
82	Prep/Shoot/Wrap	5	Days		150.00	750.00	
83	Overtime Charges	0	1.5 hours		22.5	0	$750.00
84	BEST BOY ELECTRIC						
85	Prep/Shoot/Wrap	5	Days		150.00	750.00	
86	Overtime Charges	0	1.5 hours		22.5	0	$750.00
87	BEST BOY GRIP						
88	Prep/Shoot/Wrap	5	Days		150.00	750.00	
89	Overtime Charges	0	1.5 hours		22.5	0	$750.00
90	RENTALS						
91	Base Package	1	Week		1,500.00	1,500.00	$1,500.00
92	Additional		Allow			0.00	
93	Additional	1	Week		500.00	500.00	
94	Expendables/Supplies		Allow			200.00	$200.00
95		Total for L-1600-00					$6,700.00
96	DESCRIPTION	AMOUNT	UNIT	X	RATE	SUBTOTAL	TOTAL
97	SOUND						
98	MIXER						
99	Prep/Shoot/Wrap	5	Days		250.00	1,250.00	
100	Overtime Charges	0	1.5 hours		0	0	$1,250.00
101	BOOM						
102	Prep/Shoot/Wrap	5	Days		125.00	625.00	
103	Overtime Charges	0	1.5 hours		18.75	0	$625.00
104	RENTALS						
105	Walkies	1	Week	10	20.00	200.00	$200.00
106	Base Package	1	Week		0.00	0.00	$0.00
107	SUPPLIES						
108	DAT Stock (50 min/10 per case)	1	Allow		50.00	50.00	$50.00
109	Batteries		Allow			200.00	$200.00
110	Expendables/Supplies		Allow			200.00	
111		Total for S-1700-00					$2,325.00
112	ART DEPARTMENT						
113	PRODUCTION DESIGNER						
114	Prep/Shoot/Wrap	2	Weeks		1,000.00	2,000.00	
115	Overtime Charges	0	1.5 hours		0	0	$2,000.00
116	Rentals		Allow			2,000.00	
117	Set Dressing		Allow			1,000.00	
118	Head Props		Allow			500.00	$500.00
119	Expendables/Supplies		Allow			200.00	
120		Total for A-1800-00					$5,700.00
121	WARDROBE/MAKEUP						
122	Staff (Prep/Shoot/Wrap)	5	Days		0.00	0.00	
123	Rentals/Purchases		Allow			1,000.00	
124	Film (Polaroid)		Allow			100.00	
125	Expendables/Supplies		Allow			100.00	$100.00
126		Total for W-1900-00					$1,200.00
127	LOCATIONS						
128	LOCATION MANAGER						
129	Prep/Shoot/Wrap	1	Week		0.00	0.00	
130	LOCATION FEE					500.00	
131	Site 1	1	Days		0.00	0.00	
132	Site 2	1	Days		0.00	0.00	
133	Site 3		Days		0.00	…00	
134	Site 4		Days		0.00		
…5	Expendables/Supp…		Allow				
		…ot…					$600…
			…N…				…OTAL

Budget form.

rate for longer projects. Several crew positions such as the director of photography, production sound mixer, and hair and makeup artists may have their own equipment they bring to the set. Negotiate with them to rent their gear as it may be cheaper than renting from a third party.

- If working with a union cast or crew, be aware of minimum payment requirements as well as overtime costs if the production goes over schedule. Remember that going nonunion is always less expensive.
- Talk with the director of photography about the camera, lighting, and grip equipment needed for production and ask her for a list of the required gear. With the list in hand, negotiate with equipment rental houses for discounts, especially for first-time, student, or independent productions.
- Consider all transportation costs including vehicle rental, airport shuttles, and vehicles to transport set pieces or large props. Some cast and crew members may ask for gas money if they travel long distances to the set.
- Speak with postproduction facilities about discounts on editing, music composition, digital effects, and final mastering. These costs can be high, but begin negotiations early. Production costs may need to be reduced to allow budget money for postproduction. ALWAYS budget postproduction costs. I know of many filmmakers who spent their entire budget on production, expecting the film to magically edit itself. The footage sat on a shelf for years because they couldn't afford to finish it.
- Consider the cost of production insurance, including adjustments for stunts, pyrotechnics, water scenes, or any other potentially hazardous activity that could raise the cost of insurance.
- Be aware that it will be necessary to compromise some of the artistic vision in a film because of budget restrictions. Be creative and think of unique ways to maintain the artistic integrity of the film while keeping the budget low.
- Always stick to the budget, no matter what happens on set. Cost overruns in production will always carry through to postproduction. Running out of money in the postproduction process means the film won't be finished.
- Include all costs of copying, postage, telephone, and other office-related items.
- Be sure to include not only money for on-set craft services and catering, but also any costs of lunches and dinners you may pay for during preproduction and second meals if the production runs into overtime.
- When budgeting the movie, allow an additional 10% on top of what you think you'll need. This "padding" will protect you if a problem occurs on set, such as a rainy day that requires you to add an additional day to the shoot.

Here are some tips on keeping the budget manageable:

- The key to keeping the budget low is to restrict the number of shooting days. Many low-budget features are shot in as little as 12 days with 12 working hours each day. If the script has 90 pages, that means that the crew needs to shoot 7.5 pages per day. This extremely tight shooting schedule and very ambitious approach won't allow for many extravagant camera moves, locations, pyrotechnics, or stunts or large amounts of extras. With this type of shooting schedule, plan for two or three locations and mostly lockdown (the camera is on a tripod) shots for most setups. Camera angles will be limited to a master shot, and in some instances, there may be time for close-ups and an insert shot or two.

- Remember that dolly, crane, steadicam, and even some handheld shots take a long time to set up and rehearse. These shots cost money and may require extra days if there are a lot of specialized shots in the movie.
- Special effects makeup, animals, children, car shots, night scenes, weather effects, and scenes in public areas, noisy areas, and hard-to-access locations always require a lot of time. Allow extra time when factoring in these elements.

For more information on how to develop an effective budget, including valuable tips from Hollywood producers, budget templates, and budgeting guides, check out the Budgeting a Movie module at www.powerfilmmaking.com.

CAST AND CREW

One important factor in determining the budget of a movie is assessing the costs of above-the-line talent versus below-the-line talent.

Above-the-line crew members include the director, producers, writers, and main actors. These positions involve negotiable salaries because of the substantial creative and marketing influence these artists have in selling the film. The more experience the above-the-line person has, the higher the negotiated salary can be.

Because most independent filmmakers wear the hats of director, writer, and producer themselves, the only substantial above-the-line cost may be the cost of the actors, if recognizable actors are cast. Non-union actors may be willing to work for free, but union actors will certainly increase the cost of making the film due to SAG requirements. In addition, casting a recognizable actor for a few days of shooting can cost up to $100,000/day, an amount that is negotiated with the actor's agent. Hiring a name actor, even if he or she appears in a few scenes, can greatly increase the chances of distributors picking up the film.

Below-the-line crew members are people whose day rates are negotiable, locked amounts. These positions are typically much easier to budget in advance and are usually lower than above-the-line costs. Independent filmmakers working with little money can finesse the below-the-line category by soliciting free or discounted services; offering flat fees to crew members for the entire project instead of paying a daily rate; offering meals, a copy of the finished film, and credit in exchange for crew members' involvement; or offering deferred pay to slim down the below-the-line costs.

This model works well with inexperienced crew members, but working professionals usually expect to be paid for their services, unless they have a personal interest in the movie. Don't be afraid to ask people to donate their time and services.

We were able to keep the budget of *Time and Again* around $2000 because of a volunteer cast and crew, donated equipment and catering, free locations, and the support of numerous businesses and individuals.

TIPS TO KEEPING THE BUDGET LOW

- Write the screenplay yourself.
- Direct the movie yourself.
- Cast actors who want to build a resume and are willing to work for free.
- Choose crew members who are willing to work for free or for a discounted rate.
- Hire crew members who own their own equipment. Even though you may need to pay for it, it will be cheaper than renting from a rental facility.
- Shoot in real locations and avoid building sets.
- Use available resources for props, costumes, and locations.
- Shoot on digital video to avoid the costs of film and processing.
- Be as organized as possible and plan as much as you can in preproduction.
- Avoid special effects, stunts, pyrotechnics, and digital effects.
- Avoid shooting with children and animals. They can be difficult to direct on set and will take up valuable time.
- Shoot during the day. Night shooting requires additional lighting and takes time to shoot.

THE BUSINESS PLAN

Now that you know how much money you need to produce the film, the next step in raising money is to create a strong business plan. The business plan describes the project, the target audience, how much money is needed, the results of similar projects, and all details of how the business will be structured. Remember that filmmaking is a business and most investors, unless they're looking to fund the arts, are looking to generate a profit from their investment. Investing in a film is risky, so presenting a professional, well-designed business plan positions you as a professional business person who can be trusted with the finances.

The business plan should include:

- **The story.** What is the film about? Include a brief one-page synopsis of the story and include information on the characters, setting, and genre.
- **How well have other films in a similar genre done?** Reference the successes of projects similar to yours and demonstrate how your project may be able to achieve similar results. Look for projects with similar budgets, casts, genres, and production value.
- **What is the experience of the cast and crew?** Investors are looking for assurance that they will see a return on their investment. Listing the accomplishments of the key players, such as the cinematographer, producer, director, and actors, improves the perception that a professional, marketable product will be produced. Packaging a movie with experienced above-the-line cast and crew helps sell the marketability and viability of the movie.
- **Who is the audience?** Know the demographic data of the age, gender, education level, income level, and geographic location of the film's intended target audience. The demographics play a key role in which actors to cast, the cinematic and editing style of the movie, and which distributors to market the movie to.
- **Try to secure distribution deals first.** Contact distributors to see how well films like yours have sold in the past and how well they are selling now. Have they made their money back? Have they taken a loss? Is the genre of your movie consistent in sales? How would a distributor approach the sales of your film?
- **The director's past credits.** What proof can be provided of the director's past successes? Film festival screenings, awards, and distribution contracts assure the investor that the director is qualified to produce a marketable film and that the odds of seeing a profit are greater.
- **How much will it cost?** Provide a detailed budget to show the investor on paper how his money will be spent.
- **What will the investor stand to profit from the film?** Discuss the investor's percentage of ownership in the project. Be aware, however, that it is illegal to guarantee a return. It is traditional for investors to recoup their investments from the first monies made from the sale of the film, before any profit sharing takes place.
- **Include any extra creative materials that may help sell the film.** Include storyboards, key art, photos of the actors, costume designs, set blueprints, and/or a mock-up poster to help the investor visualize the style and quality of the final production.

Once the business plan is complete, go to a local printer and have it professionally printed and bound using high-quality paper, or put it inside of a high-quality presentation folder with your business card. First impressions are always critical when asking for investment dollars.

With the business plan in hand, begin approaching investors by making phone calls, researching family contacts, sending letters, and setting up meetings. This is a long, time-consuming process, so don't get frustrated. Believe in your project and there's a good chance you'll find an investor.

Here are some tips to finding potential investors:

- Approach family members, friends, co-workers, local business people, and wealthy contacts. Try contacting professional business groups that are frequented by those in high-income occupations like doctors, lawyers, or business owners. Present the project with the business plan to generate interest.
- In addition to the business plan, create a web site that includes all the story information and people involved in the production. If the cinematographer for the project has a good demo reel, put his reel on the web site as an example of the potential quality of your movie. Also include actor bios and their previous acting experiences and successes. Make the business plan and script available in a secure area of the web site so investors can download and read them instantly. Consider using a password to keep the general public from accessing sensitive information.
- Instead of finding one or two investors to finance the entire film, try approaching a number of people to invest small amounts. Ten people willing to invest $10,000 will yield a $100,000 budget and may be easier to find than one investor for $100,000. The terms of the potential return on their investment are negotiable with each investor, but always consult with an attorney to make sure these arrangements are set up legally.
- Grants are free money provided to fund the arts that do not need to be paid back. Applying for a grant is a difficult and competitive process and you may want to contact a professional grant writer to assist you if your project meets the requirements for the grant.
- There are many corporations that fund the arts. Begin researching corporations that have funded concerts, art exhibits, or even movies in your area.
- Before you approach potential investors, shop the script around to distributors to see if they would be interested in buying the film when it is finished. Having a letter of intent from a distributor will help assure investors that they may see their money back.

FORMING A COMPANY

When working with investment dollars, demonstrating proper management of the money will reassure investors that your production is legitimate. Consider forming a company to manage the accounting, provide legal protection for the producers, and keep clean tax records.

Forming a company will keep the movie's financing, legalities, and liability separate from your own. Even the large studios form smaller corporate entities for each movie and television show they produce, hence the sometimes funny production company names that seem to be around for only one project. These companies serve as autonomous entities and protect the bigger company (the studio) from liability.

In the United States, there are seven major types of businesses that are recognized by law, each with its own advantages.

- A **sole proprietorship** is business conducted by an individual. None of the protections or tax benefits of a corporation carry to the individual, who is solely responsible for any liability, tax burden, and debt.
- A **general partnership** is an association of two or more people (partners) who have joint ownership in a company that is intended to generate a profit. A general partnership must be registered in the city or town it intends to operate in. The partners agree to share equally all the gains and losses that occur from the operation of the general partnership.
- A **limited partnership** is made up of two different types of partners: limited partners who provide the financial backing of the company, but have little say in the daily operation of the company, and the general partner who manages the operation of the company. The limited partners can't lose more than what they put into the company, but benefit from income, capital gains, and tax benefits. The general partner makes a percentage of the capital gains and income.
- A **corporation** is a business entity that exists completely on its own, as an individual does. Corporations protect their employees, shareholders, and partners' assets from lawsuit by making the corporation's assets liable, not the assets of the people who run the corporation. Corporations can own property, incur debt, sue, or be sued.
- A **limited liability company** (LLC) is a hybrid of a partnership and a corporation that shields its owners from personal liability, and gains and losses bypass the LLC directly to the owners without being taxed. The LLC is taxed as a partnership while offering the protection of a corporation.
- A **joint venture** is a partnership between two companies wanting to do business together. The principle of a joint venture is similar to that of a partnership, although instead of people partnering, it's other business entities partnering.
- A **nonprofit** company is an organization whose intentions are for noncommercial purposes only. Nonprofit companies require a lengthy application process and can be eligible for grants and other funding sources not normally available to for-profit entities.

Most upstart production companies choose the LLC, or limited liability company, because it offers the needed protection and tax benefits for movie production.

When forming a company, consider the following:

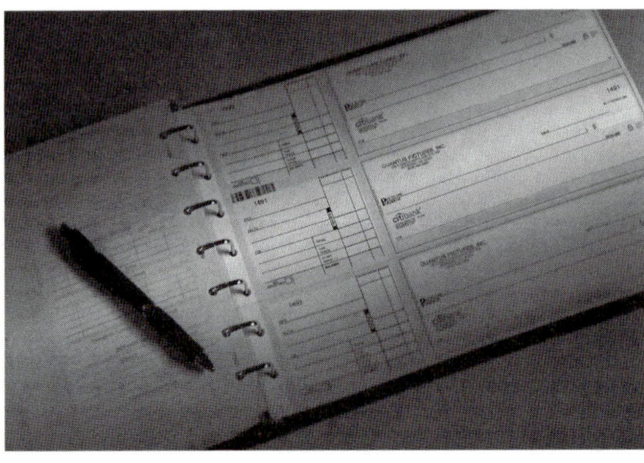

- Have a good corporate attorney draw up the paperwork. It is possible to file application papers yourself, but it can be a complicated process for the uninitiated. Generally, for a few hundred dollars, an attorney will file all applications and ensure that the business is properly set up.
- Open bank accounts in the company's name and specify who in the company is able to write checks.
- Open a checking account specifically for the film production to keep budget funds separate from your personal accounts. Keep the account strictly balanced.
- Open an escrow account, which is a neutral, monitored bank account for the investors' money, ensuring that the money is properly managed and dispersed at the correct time and place. The escrow account is managed by an escrow holder or agent who follows the agreement signed by the production company and the investors. An escrow account also protects the investors by prohibiting any inappropriate access to the account.
- If the project is large enough and the entire cast and crew is being paid, consider hiring a payroll company to handle disbursements of paychecks.

Approach an accountant or bookkeeper to assist with the handling of money for the production.

MANAGING THE BUDGET

At this point, you've broken down the script, developed a rough budget, and secured the financing for your movie. One way of keeping the movie on budget is to keep the money carefully organized, so every penny is accounted for.

- Only the line producer or unit production manager should have the ability to write checks. In the independent world, only the producer should have this ability. This shifts the burden of accountability onto the shoulders of one person.
- Keep all receipts. As is the case with all businesses, receipts are necessary to maintain a balanced budget, track the spending of the budget, and maintain detailed records for tax purposes. Remember that you need to be able to prove each and every purchase to deduct it from you or your business's income.
- Purchase an accounting program to track expenses and maintain a balanced checking account. Software solutions will make printing reports and filing taxes much easier than keeping handwritten spreadsheets.
- If you're in the United States, issue W-9 forms to every paid employee. You are legally obligated to report any payments to individuals above

$600 to the IRS. Each cast and crew member with a paycheck greater than $600 must fill out a W-9 form.

- Keep petty cash on hand, and keep careful track of who has been given money by signing out dollar amounts and putting receipts in the petty cash bag. Make sure the total amount balances out at the end of each day.

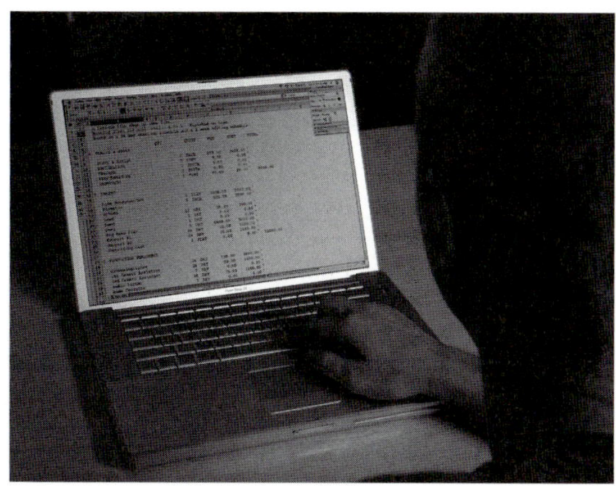

BUDGET CATEGORIES

Below are listed the most common line items for a movie budget. Use this list to help you when calculating your costs.

For help, contact a line producer to break down the script and determine the budget.

Story and other rights

- Rights and expenses

Continuity and treatment

- Writers
- Optioning screenplay
- Outline/treatment/first draft
- Rewrite
- Polish
- Xerox/photocopy script, runners to deliver
- Research
- Story editors and consultants
- Other charges
- Script timing

Direction and supervision

- Producers
- Executive producers
- Associate producers
- Directors
- Dialog directors
- Secretaries
- Receptionist
- Secretary/production coordinator
- Casting director
- Other charges

Cast—day players—stunts

- Stars
- Supporting cast
- Celebrity cameos
- Day players
- Gorgeous extras
- Stunt players
- Stunt gaffer/stuntmen/stuntwomen
- Stunt adjustments
- Overtime, looping, and other

Travel and living expenses

- Travel and living expenses
- Out-of-state flights/trips
- Room/board per diem
- Executive travel
- Executive per diem
- Food/entertainment/promotion

Production staff

- Production manager
- Unit manager
- First assistant directors
- Second assistant directors
- Script supervisors
- Location auditor
- Payroll service organization
- Technical advisors
- 3D consultant
- Production secretary
- Additional hire
- Production assistants

Extra talent

- Extras and stand-ins
- Interviews and transportation
- Atmosphere cars
- Casting fees—extras
- Other charges

Art direction

- Production designer
- Art director
- Assistant art director
- Set construction coordinator
- Set designers
- Model makers
- Sketch artists
- Storyboarders
- Set estimators
- Materials
- Expendables
- Set construction
- Set construction—materials
- Set striking

Locations

- Set operations
- Police
- Security
- Firemen
- Materials
- Purchases
- Rentals
- Repair/replace damages
- First aid
- Other charges
- Special effects foreman
- Other effects men
- Rigging—effects and explosives
- Effects—striking
- Other department labor
- Set dressing: operation and strike
- Set decorator
- Swing gang
- Manufacturing labor

Property: operations and strike

- Property master
- Assistant property master
- Animal handlers/trainers
- Animals
- Purchases
- Rentals
- Ammunition and explosives
- Picture vehicles—purchases
- Picture vehicles—rentals
- Repairs and damages
- Other charges

Wardrobe

- Costume designer
- Local labor
- Wardrobe manufacturing seamstress
- Wardrobe purchases
- Wardrobe rentals
- Wardrobe cleaning
- Wardrobe damages
- Other charges

Makeup and hairdressing

- Makeup supervisor
- Hair stylists
- Body makeup
- Purchases

- Rentals
- Hair pieces—purchases
- Hair pieces—rentals
- Other charges

Electric rigging: operations and strike

- Rigging
- Strike
- Lighting shooting company
- Gaffer
- Best boy
- Lamp and arc rentals
- Globes and expendables
- Repairs
- Generator rentals
- Fuel
- Purchases
- Rentals
- Other charges

Camera operations

- Director of photography
- Camera shooting crew
- Stillman
- Purchases
- Rentals
- Other charges

Transportation

- Drivers
- Vehicle rental
- Dressing room rentals
- Repairs and maintenance
- Fuel
- Transportation taxes and permits
- Mileage allowance
- Special equipment purchases and rentals
- Other charges

Locations

- Transportation fares
- Hotels, motels, etc.
- Meals
- Site rentals
- Office equipment rentals
- Telephone
- Shipping, stationary, postage
- Courtesy payments
- Custom fees, duties, etc.
- Export taxes
- Film shipment
- Foreign travel permits
- Flight insurance
- Location scouting
- Secretaries and typists
- Location contact
- Interpreters
- Government censors
- Policeman, watchmen, firemen
- Other charges

Production film and laboratory

- Picture negative
- Film processing
- Special laboratory work
- Stills—negative and laboratory
- Sound transfers dallies
- Other charges

Stage facilities

- Studio stage rental
- Distant location stage rental
- Test stage rental
- Additional studio facilities
- Studio personnel required
- Process—rear projection
- Other charges

Second unit: miniatures, special effects

- Production staff
- Cast
- Extra talent
- Set construction
- Set striking
- Set operations

- Set dressing
- Property
- Men's wardrobe
- Women's wardrobe
- Makeup and hairdressing
- Electrical
- Camera
- Sound
- Special effects
- Locations
- Transportation
- Purchases
- Rentals
- Other charges

Tests

- Tests
- Other charges
- Fringe benefits

Editing

- Editing
- Editor
- ADR editor
- Sound effects editor
- Music editor
- Film coding
- Projection (production and editing)
- Projection location
- Film messenger
- Cutting rooms
- Equipment rentals
- Purchases
- Video transfers
- Preview expense
- Other charges

Music

- Composer/conductor
- Musicians
- Arrangers
- Copyists
- Lyricists
- Coaches, vocal instructors
- Singers, chorus
- Labor, moving instruments
- Synchronization license (from publisher)
- Recording rights
- Music reuse fees
- Special instrument rental
- Other charges

Postproduction sound

- Transfer
- ADR facilities
- Foley facilities
- Scoring
- Narration
- Temporary dub
- Predub
- Magnetic stock
- Optical track negative—stock and transfer
- Music and effects track (foreign)
- Other purchases
- Rentals
- Other charges

Postproduction film and lab

- Reprints—one light color
- Black and white reversal work prints
- Negative cutting
- Answer print
- Protective master positives
- Internegative
- Optical effects
- Develop sound track negative
- Process plates
- Stock footage
- Video cassette
- 16 mm release print
- Shipping charges
- Sales tax
- Other charges

Main and end titles

- Main and end titles
- Foreign textless version

- Publicity
- Publicity firm fee
- Unit publicist
- Negatives, prints, supplies
- Production publicity costs
- Other charges

Insurance

- Cast insurance
- Negative insurance
- Errors and omissions
- Faulty raw stock and camera
- Liability
- Worker's compensation
- Local insurance requirements
- Miscellaneous equipment
- Comprehensive liability
- Property damage liability
- Other charges

Miscellaneous

- Telephone
- Printing and copying
- Local meals
- MPAA rating fee
- Dialog continuities
- Entertainment
- Office supplies
- Production servicing organizations
- Other charges

Fees and charges

- Accounting fee
- Legal fee
- Other charges

Deferments

- Deferment breakdown

GO BEYOND THE BOOK

Want more tips on how to develop an accurate budget? Check out the budgeting module at **www.powerfilm-making.com.** Listen as Hollywood 1st Assistant Directors Julia Lennon and Matthew Feitshans guide you through every step. Then, download budget templates you can use for your own projects!

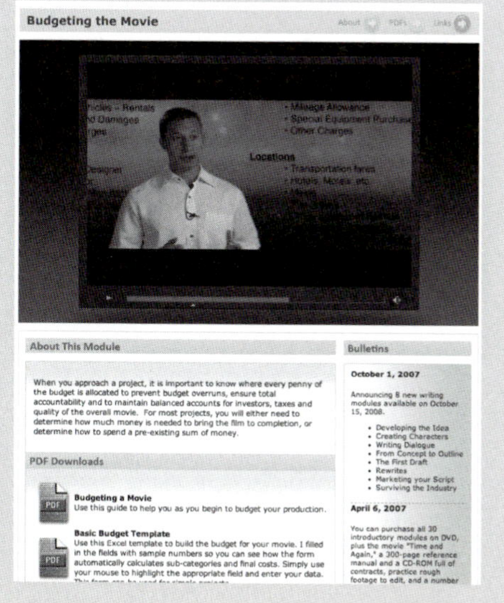

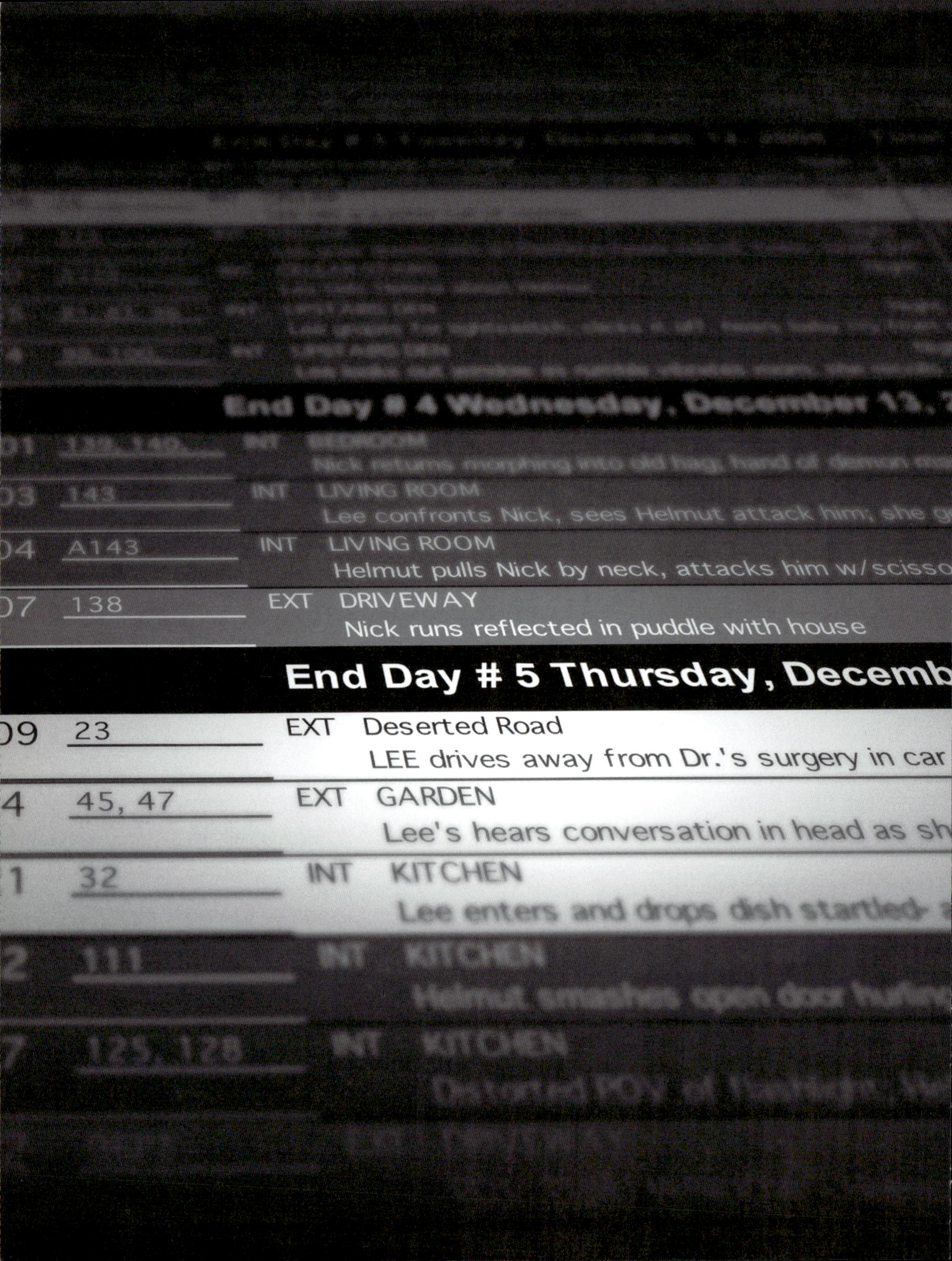

End Day # 4 Wednesday, December 13,

01	139, 140	INT	BEDROOM	Nick returns morphing into old hag, hand of demon
03	143	INT	LIVING ROOM	Lee confronts Nick, sees Helmut attack him; she g
04	A143	INT	LIVING ROOM	Helmut pulls Nick by neck, attacks him w/scisso
07	138	EXT	DRIVEWAY	Nick runs reflected in puddle with house

End Day # 5 Thursday, Decemb

09	23	EXT	Deserted Road	LEE drives away from Dr.'s surgery in car
4	45, 47	EXT	GARDEN	Lee's hears conversation in head as sh
1	32	INT	KITCHEN	Lee enters and drops dish startled-
2	111	INT	KITCHEN	Helmut smashes open door
7	125, 128	INT	KITCHEN	Distorted POV

CHAPTER 4
Scheduling

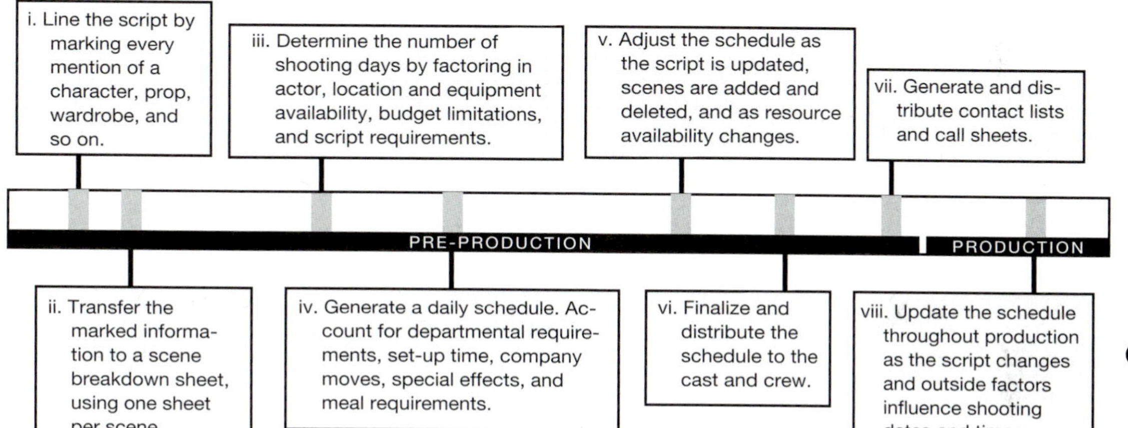

i. Line the script by marking every mention of a character, prop, wardrobe, and so on.
ii. Transfer the marked information to a scene breakdown sheet, using one sheet per scene.
iii. Determine the number of shooting days by factoring in actor, location and equipment availability, budget limitations, and script requirements.
iv. Generate a daily schedule. Account for departmental requirements, set-up time, company moves, special effects, and meal requirements.
v. Adjust the schedule as the script is updated, scenes are added and deleted, and as resource availability changes.
vi. Finalize and distribute the schedule to the cast and crew.
vii. Generate and distribute contact lists and call sheets.
viii. Update the schedule throughout production as the script changes and outside factors influence shooting dates and times.
PRE-PRODUCTION
PRODUCTION

INTRODUCTION

Believe it or not, this is the phase of the process in which most independent movies start to fall apart. Projects usually fail because they are not properly organized in preproduction, a problem that doesn't become apparent until production begins.

Even though the following steps may seem extraneous, you'll be really happy that you went through the effort when the production runs smoothly. DO NOT SKIP THIS PROCESS.

The first step in preproduction is to analyze the script and begin making lists of every single element you need to start gathering. This process, called "breaking down the script," involves combing through the script and identifying every prop, location, character; every instance of extras; and every vehicle, stunt, animal, or any other person, place, or thing that needs to be acquired. Making these lists is the first step toward developing the production schedule.

STEP 1: LINING THE SCRIPT

Let's start at the beginning. Print out a copy of the script, get 10–12 different-colored markers, and comb through each page of the script and mark each instance of the following categories:

- **Actors**—mark in red
- **Props**—mark in violet
- **Stunts**—mark in orange
- **Vehicles/animals**—mark in pink
- **Special equipment**—draw a box around every instance
- **Extras**—mark in green
- **Wardrobe**—circle every instance
- **Special effects**—mark in blue
- **Makeup/hair**—mark an asterisk
- **Sound effects/with music**—mark in brown

On big-budget Hollywood movies, the first assistant director usually performs this task. On independent movies, the producer usually lines the script if there is no first assistant director.

STEP 2: SCENE BREAKDOWN SHEETS

The next step is to print out a stack of blank scene breakdown sheets. The scene breakdown sheet is broken down into a grid with one square designated for each category. Start at the beginning of the script and copy each marked item on the script to its corresponding category on the breakdown sheet, using one breakdown sheet per scene. If the script has 32 scenes, you will end up with 32 scene breakdown sheets.

As a way of helping keep the breakdown sheets and scenes organized, use multicolored paper to help differentiate between interior and exterior scenes and day and night scenes.

Day interior—white paper
Day exterior—yellow paper
Night interior—blue paper
Night exterior—green paper

Note that every scene breakdown page has a space for the scene number, whether the scene is an interior (INT) or exterior (EXT) scene, a brief description of the scene, whether the scene takes place during the day or night, and the length of the scene in the script (always measured in increments of 1/8 of a page . . . for example, a scene that is a page and a half would be marked as 1 4/8 pages).

"The Day Bobby Jones Came Home" Draft 6/29/02 24.

The Figure drops a flashlight which hits the ground aiming back up into her face REVEALING BOBBY'S MOTHER, MARTHA JONES.

BOBBY
(under his breath)
Mom ... Oh my God, you killed her!

The door to the house opens REVEALING Young Bobby in his pajamas, holding a bandage to his head. He steps outside, listening.

YOUNG BOBBY
(calling out)
Anybody out here? Hello?

Young Bobby takes a few more steps. Stepping back inside, he turns on the porch light and MARTHA JONES bolts.

YOUNG BOBBY
Hey! Wait! What are you doing out here? Hey, come back here.

Bobby runs to follow, but trips over Awanda's body and comes face to face with the bloody body*

Police cars pull up to driveway and Karl jumps out. Young Bobby rises as the officers focus their spotlights on him.

KARL
We've got a report of suspicious activity here.

YOUNG BOBBY
(stammering)
I didn't do it, I didn't do it.

Karl tilts down the spotlight to reveal Awanda's dead body.*

KARL
Good lord!

Karl pulls his gun and aims it at Young Bobby as the DEPUTY sneaks to a position behind Young Bobby.

KARL
(continuing)
Alright, son, keep your hands where I can see them. Back away from her.

YOUNG BOBBY
I didn't do it. I just found her.

Young Bobby starts to cry.

Lined script.

Add additional prop, wardrobe, and extra information to the breakdown sheets even though the script may not directly mention them. For example, in a scene that takes place in a car repair shop, even though the script may mention only the mechanic and the wrench he is holding, describe any additional wardrobe requirements like mechanics uniforms or set-dressing elements like tools, an air compressor, and work lights. The purpose of a breakdown sheet is to have as complete a list as possible of all the elements needed to film each scene in the movie, so the crew can look at the breakdown sheet and gather everything needed.

Once complete, the finished scene breakdown forms form the "bible," which should be copied and distributed to the head of each department. If the script changes, be sure to update immediately and issue a new scene update form.

STEP 3: DETERMINE THE NUMBER OF SHOOTING DAYS

The third step toward building the shooting schedule is to determine how many days it is going to take to shoot the movie. The number of shooting days and the time frame for the production are dependent on a number of factors.

- **Budget.** The biggest determining factor in calculating the number of shooting days is how many days you can afford to shoot. Knowing how many crew members are needed, their day rates, the cost of equipment rental, the cost of hiring actors, the cost of craft services and catering, the location costs, and a number of other factors may limit the number of days in production. It's not uncommon for low-budget features to be shot in 10 or 12 days with a slimmed-down crew.
- **Actor availability.** If you have a name actor, your production schedule may have to accommodate the actor's schedule. Be sure to work closely with the actor's agent or manager before locking in a schedule. It's not uncommon for productions to be placed on hold until even a few days before shooting is scheduled to begin because the actor hasn't committed.
- **Location availability.** Do the locations have restricted hours of shooting, limited hours for production, or other schedule conflicts you may need to schedule around?
- **Equipment availability.** If other productions are shooting in your area, will equipment availability be an issue? Consider scheduling your shoot so it doesn't coincide with other projects that may be shooting at the same time.
- **Weather.** Will the production need to be scheduled during a certain season? Would adverse weather affect the shooting schedule? How likely is the shooting area to be affected by changing weather?

Determining the number of shooting days can be tricky and is largely based on the experiences a first assistant director has had on set in the past. Be careful

Scene Breakdown Sheet

Production: "The Day Bobby Jones Came Home" Page #: 9

Production Company: Quantus Pictures, Inc. Date: July 14, 2002

Director: Jason J. Tomaric Producers: Jason J. Tomaric & Adam Kadar

Location: Chester Diner (main restaurant and bathroom)

Scene Number	INT/EXT	Description	Day/ Night	# Pages
11	INT	BJ discovers newspaper	DAY	6/8
12	INT	INT BATHROOM - BJ discovers the date	DAY	5/8
15	INT	BJ talks to man at counter	DAY	6/8
23	INT	BJ barges in, looking for Awanda	NIGHT	1 2/8

Cast Members	Extras	Stunts	Wardrobe	Props
Bobby Jones Awanda Sheriff Karl Waitress Man at counter Policeman	(2) sets of 20 1 set for morning scene, 1 set for night scene Families/Couples	none	BJ standard A standard K standard Extras, day attire Extras, night attire Man at counter	Daily Newspaper Newspaper cutout Burning food Dishware Photo of A/RJ Guitar Coffee Pot Food for Extras Set Dressing
Special Effects	**Vehicles**	**Special Equipment**	**Livestock**	**Hair/Make-Up**
Fire plate for VFX as A burns food	none	none	none	BJ standard (no scar in scenes 11-15, scar in scene 23) standard for BJ/A/K standard for extras

NOTES: Check diner for 1950's props and remove any current appliances, posters, etc. Address removal of stored food from refrigeration units. EXT of diner will be at Annabelle's in Mentor, OH. Make sure daily paper has appropriate sports scores

Scene breakdown.

BREAKDOWN SHEET

DATE: ______________

PRODUCTION COMPANY	PRODUCTION TITLE	BREAKDOWN PAGE NO.
SCENE NO.	SCENE NAME	INT. OR EXT.
DESCRIPTION		DAY OR NIGHT
		PAGE COUNT

CAST Red	**STUNTS** Orange **EXTRAS/SILENT** Yellow	**EXTRAS/ATMOSPHERE** Green
SPECIAL EFFECTS Blue	**PROPS** Violet	**VEHICLES/ANIMALS** Pink
WARDROBE Circle	**MAKE-UP/HAIR** Asterisk	**SOUND EFFECTS/MUSIC** Brown
SPECIAL EQUIPMENT Box	**PRODUCTION NOTES**	

Day Ext. - YELLOW Night Ext. - GREEN Day Int. - WHITE Night Int. - BLUE

not to make the schedule overly ambitious, because if you begin falling behind, it's extremely difficult to catch up, scenes will need to be cut, and the quality of the movie will be compromised. Some tips to keep in mind when scheduling:

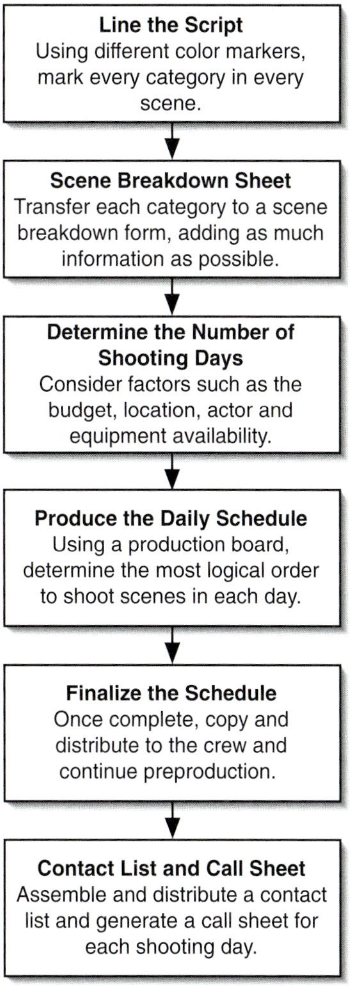

- Hollywood movies shoot one to three pages of the script per shooting day. Most independent movies must shoot upward of five or six pages per day because of budget restrictions. Avoid scheduling more than six pages per day or the production value will begin to suffer. Three to five pages per day is a comfortable amount, allowing the director and actors time to work and giving the director of photography and other department heads time to do their jobs properly. The greater the number of pages, the faster the crew has to work, and the sloppier the work becomes.
- When calculating the number of pages per day, look at the level of complexity in shooting each scene. A three-page dialog scene between two characters in a restaurant can be shot much faster than three pages of an FBI agent combing through a building in search of a bomb. The various location changes, camera setups, and lighting setups will take much more time. Consider the number of setups and look at the director's storyboards to determine how much coverage is needed for each scene. Remember that simple 90-page scripts with limited cast and locations are easier and cheaper to shoot.
- Allow six to eight weeks for the rest of preproduction before the first day of shooting. This will allow enough time to hire the cast and crew, rehearse with actors, assemble equipment, dress locations, gather props and wardrobe, and attend to all the other details prior to shooting.
- Schedule as many consecutive days as possible. It's easier for cast and crew members to commit to "every weekend in July" or "the next eight days" than to scattered production dates over a long period of time. Keeping the schedule tight maintains the pace of the production and increases camaraderie among the cast and crew.

Line the Script
Using different color markers, mark every category in every scene.

↓

Scene Breakdown Sheet
Transfer each category to a scene breakdown form, adding as much information as possible.

↓

Determine the Number of Shooting Days
Consider factors such as the budget, location, actor and equipment availability.

↓

Produce the Daily Schedule
Using a production board, determine the most logical order to shoot scenes in each day.

↓

Finalize the Schedule
Once complete, copy and distribute to the crew and continue preproduction.

↓

Contact List and Call Sheet
Assemble and distribute a contact list and generate a call sheet for each shooting day.

Scheduling flow chart.

One of the biggest problems independent producers encounter is writing a script that requires more resources to produce than are available. It is possible to shoot a high-quality feature film in 12 days if you obey the following guidelines:

- **Minimize the number of locations.** Choose a script that can be shot in one or two locations. A horror film that takes place in one house. A romantic comedy that takes place in an apartment and a coffee shop. If you have multiple locations, there needs to be time allotted for the crew to relocate from one to another, time to load and unload equipment each day, time to dress and restore each set, and time to light each location.

- **Minimize camera setups.** Shoot each scene with a master shot, close-ups of each actor, and an insert shot. Eliminate any complicated camera moves and put the camera on a tripod or handheld. Dolly, crane, jib, and steadicam moves require a lot of time to set up, rehearse, and break down.
- **Work with a professional crew.** Although they may work for free, film students, actors who haven't memorized their lines, and first-time directors usually take more time to shoot the same scene and may require added shooting days.
- **Minimal number of characters.** Choose a script with a small number of actors and no extras, no public scenes, and minimal wardrobe changes.
- **Shoot inside.** Interior locations guarantee a degree of control and protect the production schedule from weather issues.
- **Avoid special effects.** Avoid stunts, special effects, pyrotechnics, firearms, and makeup prosthetics.
- **Avoid elaborate elements.** Scenes that incorporate elements beyond the control of the production team, weather, crowd scenes, shooting in public spaces, working with animals or children, stunts, pyrotechnics, limited location access, makeup prosthetics, and incorporating special effects can increase time requirements in the schedule.

For more information on how to schedule a movie properly, tips and tricks from Hollywood first assistant directors, and sample movie schedules and scheduling templates, check out the Scheduling modules at www.powerfilmmaking.com.

STEP 4: MAKING THE DAILY SCHEDULE

After you've determined the number of shooting days, it's now time to figure out what scenes to shoot during those days. With so many variables to consider like location availability, actor availability, and multiple scenes within the script that take place in the same location, production boards are used to help simplify the process.

A production board is made up of a series of ½-inch multicolored strips of paper that each contain the information written on the scene breakdown sheets. Each strip represents one scene and the colors represent:

Yellow strips—day exterior
White strips—day interior
Green strips—night exterior
Blue strips—night interior
Black and white strips—day dividers
Solid black strips—week dividers

Referring to the scene breakdown sheets, create a traditional production board (or use a scheduling software program like www.filmmakersoftware.com to make one electronically) by writing the scene number, a brief scene description, the characters involved in each scene, the number of pages, the time of day, the location, and a description of the scene on each strip of paper. Scenes with the same actor, time of day, and location can be placed on the same strip.

Arrange and rearrange the strips to figure out the most logical way to shoot the scenes within each production day. Try to schedule scenes shot in the same location on the same day, and place scenes with the same actors together. Remember that because movies are not shot from the beginning of the story to the end, you can group locations together, or the days an actor is shooting together, to maximize the efficiency of the shoot. Use a black strip to identify the end of each day of production.

- It's easier to schedule a day if you know how many camera setups the director wants in each scene. The director should provide this information to the first assistant director prior to scheduling each day.
- Schedule at least 12 hours between consecutive shooting days. If you're working with a union crew, cutting into 12 hours will result in overtime

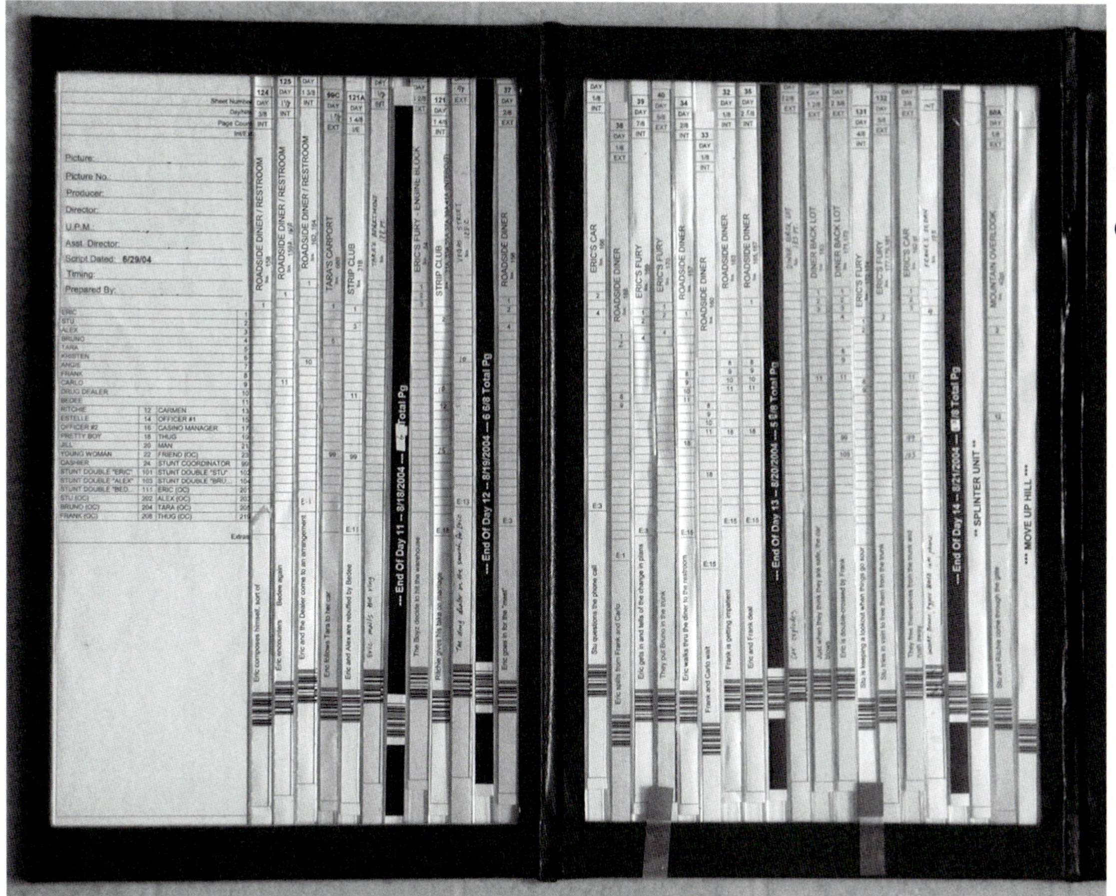

Production board.

Breakdown Page #'s		1	2nd DAY - 6/8 Pages	9	10
Day or Night		N		D	N
Scene(s)		1,36		11,12,15	23
# of pages		6/8		2 1/8	1 2/8
		EXT. PRISON		INT. DINER	INT. DINER
Title: The Day Bobby Jones Came Home					
Director: Jason J. Tomaric					
Producers: Jason J. Tomaric & Adam Kadar					
Assistant Director: Kailyne Waters					
CHARACTER / **ACTOR**					
Bobby Jones / Brian Ireland	1	1		1	1
Awanda / Jennie Allen	2			2	
Sheriff Karl / Bob Darby	3				3
Martha Jones / Paula Williams	4				
Robin Jones / Rick Montgomery	5				
Teacher / Jeannie LaLande	6				
Young Bobby Jones / Andrew Zehnder	7				
Prisoners	8	8			
Stickball Players	9				
Extras	X			X	X
		1. Bobby and prisoners escape from jail 36. Bobby Jones is dead		Bobby discovers newspaper, looks at it in bathroom and talks to man at counter	Bobby rishes in, looking for Awanda

Sample strips from the *Time and Again* production schedule.

and penalty fees. If you have SAG actors, they are limited to 8 hours on set per day. Be sure to check union requirements when scheduling.

- ALWAYS allow time for the cast and crew to eat. Schedule a major meal every six hours. If call time is 6 AM, then lunch needs to be served at noon. Assuming an hour is scheduled for lunch, the next six-hour time block begins at 1 PM. Dinner should be served at 7 PM.
- If the crew has to perform a "company move" or change location during the day, be sure to allow ample time for striking the set, moving personnel and equipment to the new location, and setting the equipment up again. Allow more time if the crew is inexperienced.
- Never underestimate the amount of time it will take to shoot a scene. Always plan for more time on set, and if there is a company move from one location to another in the same day, make sure enough time is allotted for the move.
- When filming exterior scenes, always have a backup interior scene to shoot if it rains or the weather prohibits filming. With the entire cast and crew present, don't waste a day just because of bad weather—shoot another scene.
- Allow more time to shoot scenes early in the day. Production is always slower early on and picks up pace.
- If possible, shoot any establishing shots, nondescript insert shots, and special effects shots after you complete principal photography (shooting any shots that involve the main actors).

DIRECTOR'S NOTES

The preproduction process can be pretty frustrating because of the number of different tasks you have to juggle as a producer. After I wrote *Time and Again*, I had about six weeks of preproduction, so I had very little time to get everything ready. The trick I found to work is that I started looking for locations immediately, because the entire schedule hinges on their availability. During the same time, I would stop and visit thrift shops and antique stores to collect props and wardrobe after work each day, storing them in boxes at home until the shoot. I was also calling prospective crew members and organizing the auditions, while preparing my application for production insurance and contacting the city for shooting permits.

The secret to success is to multitask and understand that EVERYTHING WILL TAKE LONGER THAN YOU INITIALLY THINK. Remember that preproduction isn't difficult, it's keeping the hundreds of small tasks organized that is the challenge.

I always keep a Dry Erase board by my desk where I can keep track of all the small details I need to accomplish, checking off the ones that are finished, and always adding new ones.

Although the chapters in the Preproduction unit are in a certain order, in reality, you will have to be working on each of these tasks at the same time. It can be a daunting task, but by being prepared and organized now, you should have a shoot that runs smoothly and without too many problems.

Quantus Pictures Inc.
Motion Picture Production Company

"The Day Bobby Jones Came Home"
Production Schedule • July 5, 2002

Saturday, July 13, 2002	7:00am-noon
EXT. SCHOOL - MORNING	Elementary School, Novelty
	noon-10:00pm
EXT. ROAD - DAY	Chagrin Falls, Water Street
Sunday, July 14, 2002	1:30pm-1:00am
INT. DINER - DAY/NIGHT	Chester Diner, Chesterland
Saturday, July 20, 2002	6:00pm-7:00am
EXT. BOBBY'S HOUSE - NIGHT	Private residence, Chardon
Sunday, July 21, 2002	1:00pm-6:00pm
EXT FARM HOUSE - DAY	Private residence, Chardon
	6:00pm-1:00am
EXT. MOVIE THEATRE	Geauga Cinema, Chardon
Saturday, July 27, 2002	7:00am-midnight
INT. AWANDA's TRAILER	Jim's Trailer Sales, Grafton
Sunday, July 28, 2002	2:00pm-10:00pm
EXT. COUNTRY ROAD - DAY	Stillwell Road, Huntsburg
Friday, August 2, 2002	6:00pm-6:00am
EXT. BOBBY'S HOUSE	Private residence, Chardon
Saturday, August 3, 2002	6:00pm-8:00am
EXT. PRISON - NIGHT	Grafton State Prison (pending)
Sunday, August 4, 2002	2:00pm-9:00pm
INT. JAIL - DAY	Geauga County Jail
Sunday, August 28, 2002	9:00am-9:00pm
EXT. COUNTRY ROAD	Stillwell Road, Huntsburg
Saturday, October 5, 2002	8:00am-8:00pm
EXT/INT BOBBY'S HOUSE - DAY	Private residencce, Chardon

The rough shooting schedule for *Time and Again.*

- Be aware of any city or location events that could affect your production days, including holidays, fund-raisers, parades, or even road maintenance. Always check your production dates to make sure they don't conflict with any other function.

STEP 5: FINALIZING THE SCHEDULE

Once you organize the production strips into the most logical order and have a shooting schedule, it's time to move to the next step of preproduction.

- Begin scouting locations.
- Begin auditioning actors.
- Begin assembling props and wardrobe.
- Begin seeking qualified crew members.
- Approach equipment rental houses for camera, lighting, and grip equipment.

Try to secure locations before you schedule the cast and crew. With locked production dates, you can confirm the number of days each cast and crew member needs to dedicate to the production, making it easier for them to commit to the project. If locations are NOT secured and you try to lock cast and crew members for dates that keep changing, you will appear unprofessional and stand to lose the commitment from those volunteering their time.

STEP 6: DURING PRODUCTION

Even though the schedule has been created in preproduction, it will always change and need to be updated throughout production. Two major documents that need to created, updated, and circulated are the contact list and call sheets.

Contact list

Assemble a contact list of each vendor, actor, and crew member and distribute to everyone on the project. Include phone numbers, email addresses, and physical addresses and keep the information updated frequently.

- If working with a well-known actor, do not distribute his or her personal contact information on the contact sheet; rather use his or her agent's contact information.
- Circulate cast and crew phone lists as soon as possible. Make sure everyone on the production knows how to reach everyone else.
- Keep the contact list updated and distribute the list not only on paper, but also by email to everyone in the cast and crew.

Call sheets

Each actor and crew member needs to know where the location is for the next shooting day, the address, and the time he or she needs to be on set, as well as

(NAME OF MOVIE)		CALL SHEET	Date:	Tuesday, May 1st, 2007
			Day:	1 of 13
			1st Shot:	9:30 AM
Producer:	(insert name) (insert phone number)	Crew Call Time 8:00 AM	Weather:	Partly Cloudy
Director:	(insert name) (insert phone number)		SUNRISE:	6:08AM
			SUNSET:	7:32PM
UPM:	(insert name) (insert phone number)	Craft Services At: 7:30 AM	High:	69F
			Low:	55F
1st AD:	(insert name) (insert phone number)	Lunch Served 2:00 PM	Hospital	(hospital name) (hospital address 1) (hospital address 2) (hospital phone number)
		DAY 1		

I/E	SET DESCRIPTION	SCENE	CAST	D/N	PAGES	LOCATION
I	Jim's Office	13	1, 12	D2	3	(Location name) (Location address 1) (Location address 2) (City, State, Zip)
	Jim receives "call to adventure"					
I	Alan's Office	17	2	D2	1 4/8	
	Alan writes letter					
	SERIES: A-I					(Parking, loading info)
I	Hallway	8	2,3,4	D2	3 5/8	
	Alan and Jim meet	9				
		11				
						CREW PARKING
						free street parking always read all signs normal traffic laws in effect
				Total Pages:	8 1/8	

#	SWF	CAST/DAY PLAYERS	PART OF	RPT MU/WARD	ON SET	OUT
1	SW	(actor's name)	Jim	8:30 AM	9:30A	
2	SW	(actor's name)	Alan	12:00 PM	1:00 PM	
3	SW	(actor's name)	Sam	2:45 PM	3:30 PM	
4	SW	(actor's name)	Billy-Bob	2:30 PM	3:30 PM	
12	SWF	(actor's name)	Diva Mary	7:45 AM	9:15A	

ADVANCE SCHEDULE

DATE	DESCRIPTION	SCENE	CAST	D/N	PAGES	LOCATION
Thursday	Hallway	28	2		1/8	Location #4
May 3rd	Alan's house	29	2		1/8	1234 Main Street
	Alan's house	30	1		1/8	Suite N
	Restaurant	6	1,2		2 3/8	LA, CA 90046
	Green Screen	26	1,2		1/8	
	Green Screen	14	1		2/8	
	Alan leaves	2	1		6/8	

DIRECTIONS TO LOCATION:

FROM Westside Take 43 E to 101N to 112N
FROM Eastside get to 112N
FROM the Valley take 18 East to 5-South to 112N

US-112 NORTH
Take the AVE 40 exit- EXIT 20.
Turn LEFT onto S AVENUE 40.
Turn RIGHT onto Bloom RD.

Front page of a call sheet.

any information pertinent to the day. This information is relayed on a form called a call sheet.

The second assistant director (AD) compiles call sheets for the next day, with input from department heads. Once approved by the line producer, the second AD distributes the call sheets to each cast and crew member before he or she leaves the set. Call sheets are updated to reflect overtime, extended turn-around time, and any last-minute changes. The second AD also emails the call sheets to everyone on the production.

Call sheets include:

- The name of the movie
- The date of production
- Day *x* of *y* days (day 12 of 16 days)
- Location of the shoot, including address and phone number
- Parking information: where to park and where not to park, including restrictions and time limits
- Contact information for key crew positions
- Suggested dress code (rain gear, cold weather, and so on)
- Scenes scheduled to be shot for the day as well as a brief five- to ten-word description of each scene
- Call times denoting what times cast and crew members need to arrive on set. The call times can be different for various departments depending on how much work they need to do before the day begins. For example:
    - Hair/makeup—is there any special-effects makeup that needs to be applied? Or does the hair stylist need to arrive early to create 1950s hairstyles?
    - Grip/lighting
    - Special effects department
    - Stunts
- Rough schedule for the day
    - Call times for main crew
    - Makeup and wardrobe times
    - Scenes to be shot
    - Travel time if there is a company move from one location to another
    - Breaks, including meals
    - Estimated wrap time
- Weather forecast for the day of production
- Directions and contact information for the nearest hospital
- Directions and contact information for the nearest police station
- Information on equipment to be used
- Contact information for the production company
- Vendors (companies from which equipment/services are being rented)

When determining what time each department needs to arrive the next day, consider the following:

- When making the call sheet, determine whether actors need to arrive early for makeup, hair, or wardrobe and schedule the makeup, hair, and wardrobe departments accordingly.
- One of the biggest problems on independent film sets is that cast and crew members are scheduled to be on set all day, even if not needed. This only tires and frustrates the cast and crew, reducing the morale on set. Figure out which scenes are being filmed at what point during the day and schedule the necessary people to arrive half an hour before they are needed, unless special requirements require them to arrive earlier.
- Be sure to create a detailed map with directions to the location from the north, south, east, and west. Drive the directions before you pass them out to the cast and crew to eliminate the possibility of errors.
- Always include the name of a contact person and phone number on the call sheet in the event that cast or crew members get lost en route to the set.
- If traveling from a hotel or if cast and crew members live close to each other, consider carpooling to minimize the number of cars parked at the location.
- Include any parking permits that need to be posted on production vehicles along with the call sheet, if available. All parking details must be handled before the day of production.
- Always bring extra copies of the script, call sheets, deal memos, and all production paperwork on set. Cast and crew members, and even the director, will invariably forget theirs.

GO BEYOND THE BOOK

Knowing how to properly schedule a production can mean the difference between an on-time, on-budget movie and a disaster. Learn from working Hollywood pros as they walk you through the scheduling process.

www.powerfilmmaking.com

CHAPTER 5
Insurance

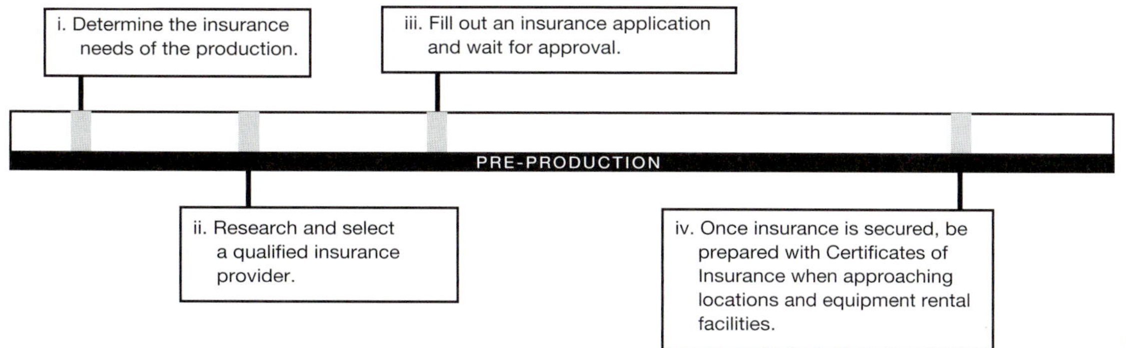

i. Determine the insurance needs of the production.
iii. Fill out an insurance application and wait for approval.
PRE-PRODUCTION
ii. Research and select a qualified insurance provider.
iv. Once insurance is secured, be prepared with Certificates of Insurance when approaching locations and equipment rental facilities.

INTRODUCTION

Anything can happen on a movie set: equipment can be stolen, cast or crew members can be hurt, or locations can be damaged. What happens if a light falls and burns the carpet or a grip trips and sprains an ankle? In each of these instances, you, the filmmaker, are personally liable. With the high costs of equipment replacement or repair, medical costs, and lawsuits, it is essential to have production insurance. In most instances, the production will be required to provide proof of insurance when you rent equipment or use a location.

INSURANCE TYPES

There are several types of production insurance to choose from and it is best to discuss your needs with a qualified insurance company.

General liability insurance

The most common type of insurance policy, general liability insurance protects you and your production in the event of property damage and claims for personal injury on set. The minimum accepted liability policy would cover you up to $1,000,000, although several factors will determine how much coverage the policy needs. For example:

- Will you be staging any stunts or other potentially hazardous activities that increase the risk of injury to cast or crew?
- Will you be shooting on or around water?
- Will you be using pyrotechnics, squibs, or explosives?
- Does your location add additional danger, such as shooting near a cliff or in an airplane?

Cast insurance

Cast insurance reimburses the production company for certain expenses incurred due to the death of, illness or accident to an insured artist or director.

Film and video tape insurance

Especially important when shooting film, this policy covers you if the film is ruined at the lab, there is a problem with the film stock, the film is lost in transit, and so on. The insurance will provide necessary funds to reshoot the footage.

Equipment insurance

This protects your equipment from theft and damage. Most production companies will require that you provide proof of coverage before they will rent you equipment. Some rental houses require that you obtain your own insurance, but others will add insurance for an additional fee. Be sure to check with the rental company before you arrive to pick up gear.

Worker's compensation

Worker's compensation covers both employees and volunteers who work for you should they be injured on the job. This insurance is calculated as a base percentage of the payroll and is required by state law.

Errors and omissions insurance

This insurance is generally needed only when a film is picked up for distribution. Distributors do not want to be liable for any legal issues you neglected to resolve. Errors and omissions insurance (or E&O for short) protects both you and the distributor from copyright infringement lawsuits, extras who may not have signed a release form and later sue, or placement of products in the film that you did not get permission to use. Typically, the E&O company will review all your documentation and, by awarding this insurance, confirms that your production has all legal documents in order and assumes responsibility should a law suit arise.

- Purchase insurance policies only for the time period you need them. If you require a short-term policy, it may be cheaper to buy coverage for a week rather than for one day. If you plan on shooting often during the year, it may be even cheaper to purchase a year-long policy instead of on an as-needed basis.

- Some locations and rental facilities require that they be listed as "additionally insured" on the policy, which ensures that they are recognized and covered by the insurance agency should a problem occur.
- Be prepared to present a certificate of insurance when approaching a location or rental house. Most will require that you have insurance and the certificate is the proof. To obtain the certificate, simply call the insurance agency and request a copy.
- Be honest with the insurance agency about what you're planning on doing on set. If you're using pyrotechnics, tell them. While this will raise your premium, the insurance policy WILL cover you should an accident occur. If, for example, you tell them that the entire film will be shot on land and you then do a scene in a boat on the ocean and someone is injured, then insurance company will decline to cover the accident.
- When choosing an insurance company, make sure they provide production insurance. Homeowner's insurance is not enough and will not cover all incidents that occur on set. In addition, homeowner's insurance covers ONLY the owner's home and will not protect the production outside of the home.

For more information on production insurance, including forms, applications, and a video on what you really need to know, check out the Insurance module at www.powerfilmmaking.com.

WHAT DO YOU REALLY NEED?

Insurance is an expensive and sometimes confusing aspect of moviemaking. When confronted with the list of potential insurance packages understand that there are four types of insurance every production needs to purchase:

- **General liability insurance.** Purchase a $1,000,000 general liability policy. Most locations will require at least this amount of coverage, although use of stunts, pyrotechnics, or any other factors outside of what the general policy covers will require an increase in coverage. A one-year, $1,000,000 general liability policy in Los Angeles costs around $2150. This premium may change depending on the city in which you live. Although there are short-term policies available, the year-long is the most affordable.
- **Equipment insurance.** Purchase the amount needed to cover the cost of replacement of all the equipment on set. If you're shooting with $100,000 worth of equipment, then purchase a $100,000 equipment insurance policy. All camera and equipment rental facilities will require you to provide proof of equipment insurance before giving you the gear.
- **Worker's compensation.** Any employer must, by law, have worker's comp insurance to cover any injuries to cast and crew on set.
- **Errors and omissions insurance.** Usually purchased when a film is about to be picked up by a domestic distributor, E&O insurance may be paid for by the distributor.

ACORD **CERTIFICATE OF LIABILITY INSURANCE** OP ID JE URACL-1

DATE (MM/DD/YY) 07/09/02

PRODUCER

THIS CERTIFICATE IS ISSUED AS A MATTER OF INFORMATION ONLY AND CONFERS NO RIGHTS UPON THE CERTIFICATE HOLDER. THIS CERTIFICATE DOES NOT AMEND, EXTEND OR ALTER THE COVERAGE AFFORDED BY THE POLICIES BELOW.

INSURED

INSURERS AFFORDING COVERAGE

INSURER A: Insurance
INSURER B:
INSURER C:
INSURER D:
INSURER E:

COVERAGES

THE POLICIES OF INSURANCE LISTED BELOW HAVE BEEN ISSUED TO THE INSURED NAMED ABOVE FOR THE POLICY PERIOD INDICATED. NOTWITHSTANDING ANY REQUIREMENT, TERM OR CONDITION OF ANY CONTRACT OR OTHER DOCUMENT WITH RESPECT TO WHICH THIS CERTIFICATE MAY BE ISSUED OR MAY PERTAIN, THE INSURANCE AFFORDED BY THE POLICIES DESCRIBED HEREIN IS SUBJECT TO ALL THE TERMS, EXCLUSIONS AND CONDITIONS OF SUCH POLICIES. AGGREGATE LIMITS SHOWN MAY HAVE BEEN REDUCED BY PAID CLAIMS.

INSR LTR	TYPE OF INSURANCE	POLICY NUMBER	POLICY EFFECTIVE DATE (MM/DD/YY)	POLICY EXPIRATION DATE (MM/DD/YY)	LIMITS	
A	GENERAL LIABILITY X COMMERCIAL GENERAL LIABILITY CLAIMS MADE X OCCUR GEN'L AGGREGATE LIMIT APPLIES PER: POLICY PRO-JECT LOC		04/22/02	04/22/03	EACH OCCURRENCE	$ 1000000
					FIRE DAMAGE (Any one fire)	$ 50000
					MED EXP (Any one person)	$ 5000
					PERSONAL & ADV INJURY	$ 1000000
					GENERAL AGGREGATE	$ 2000000
					PRODUCTS - COMP/OP AGG	$ 2000000
	AUTOMOBILE LIABILITY ANY AUTO ALL OWNED AUTOS SCHEDULED AUTOS HIRED AUTOS NON-OWNED AUTOS				COMBINED SINGLE LIMIT (Ea accident)	$
					BODILY INJURY (Per person)	$
					BODILY INJURY (Per accident)	$
					PROPERTY DAMAGE (Per accident)	$
	GARAGE LIABILITY ANY AUTO				AUTO ONLY - EA ACCIDENT	$
					OTHER THAN AUTO ONLY: EA ACC	$
					AGG	$
	EXCESS LIABILITY OCCUR CLAIMS MADE DEDUCTIBLE RETENTION $				EACH OCCURRENCE	$
					AGGREGATE	$
						$
						$
						$
	WORKERS COMPENSATION AND EMPLOYERS' LIABILITY				WC STATU-TORY LIMITS / OTH-ER	
					E.L. EACH ACCIDENT	$
					E.L. DISEASE - EA EMPLOYEE	$
					E.L. DISEASE - POLICY LIMIT	$
	OTHER					

DESCRIPTION OF OPERATIONS/LOCATIONS/VEHICLES/EXCLUSIONS ADDED BY ENDORSEMENT/SPECIAL PROVISIONS

CERTIFICATE HOLDER | N | ADDITIONAL INSURED; INSURER LETTER: ___

CANCELLATION

SHOULD ANY OF THE ABOVE DESCRIBED POLICIES BE CANCELLED BEFORE THE EXPIRATI[ON] DATE THEREOF, THE ISSUING INSURER WILL ENDEAVOR TO MAIL 10 DAYS WRITTEN NOTICE TO THE CERTIFICATE HOLDER NAMED TO THE LEFT, BUT FAILURE TO DO SO SHAL[L] IMPOSE NO OBLIGATION OR LIABILITY OF ANY KIND UPON THE INSURER, ITS AGENTS OR REPRESENTATIVES.

AUTHORIZED REPRESENTATIVE

ACORD 25-S (7/97) ©ACORD CORPORATION 1988

Certificate of insurance.

CERTIFICATE OF INSURANCE

When securing a location or renting equipment, you may need to provide proof that the production is insured. The official form that is used is called a "certificate of insurance". You can obtain one for free simply by calling your insurance company and requesting a certificate of insurance. They will ask you the name, address, and phone number of the company or individual you are providing the certificate to and whether you want that company or person to be listed as additionally insured. This will place their name on the policy, so in the event of a claim, they can call it in and collect for themselves.

GO BEYOND THE BOOK

While insurance is not the most glamourous part of making a movie, it is one of the most important. Production insurance specialist Winnie Wong simplifies the world of production insurance and helps you understand what you really need.

Download insurance applications, simple guides to insurance, and see what types of policies are available.

Simply visit www.powerfilmmaking.com and click on the insurance module.

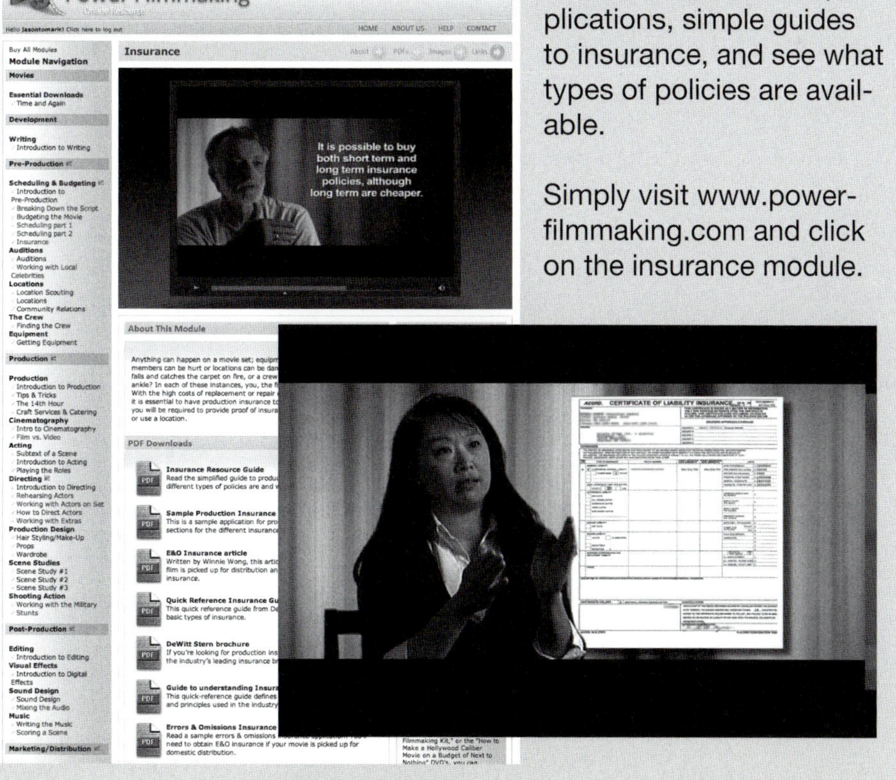

CHAPTER 6

Locations

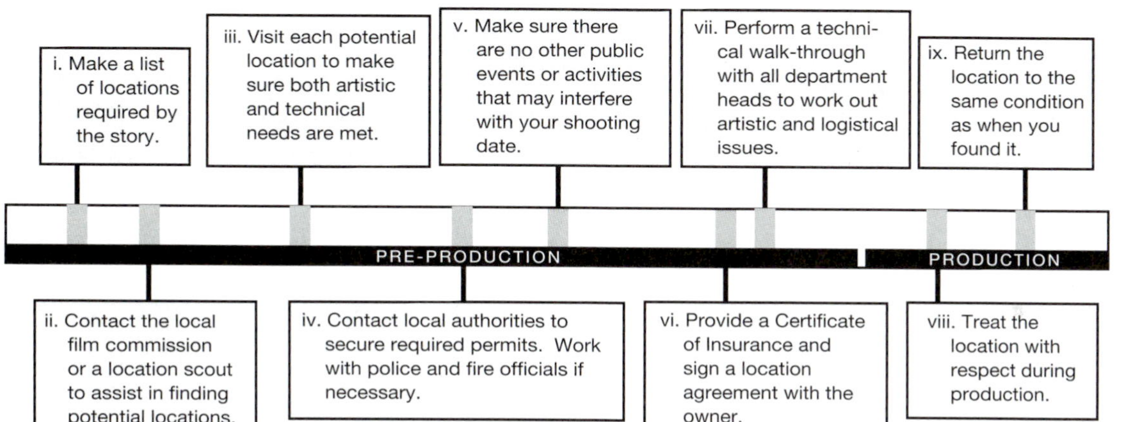

i. Make a list of locations required by the story.
ii. Contact the local film commission or a location scout to assist in finding potential locations.
iii. Visit each potential location to make sure both artistic and technical needs are met.
iv. Contact local authorities to secure required permits. Work with police and fire officials if necessary.
v. Make sure there are no other public events or activities that may interfere with your shooting date.
vi. Provide a Certificate of Insurance and sign a location agreement with the owner.
vii. Perform a technical walk-through with all department heads to work out artistic and logistical issues.
viii. Treat the location with respect during production.
ix. Return the location to the same condition as when you found it.
PRE-PRODUCTION
PRODUCTION

INTRODUCTION

Movies can be filmed either on a soundstage, where sets are constructed and the environment is completely controlled, or at an existing location that meets or can be altered to meet, the requirements of the story. Shooting on location can add to the realism of the scene, but can also increase costs and complicate logistics.

Shooting on location presents innumerable challenges that, if unaddressed, can significantly hinder the production process. Remember that locations were built to be functional, not to serve as movie sets, so they often need to be altered to fit the needs of the production. Find locations that require minimal alterations to save money on set construction or dressing.

FINDING LOCATIONS

Scouting locations is the process of researching and looking for places that fit the look of your movie. Convincing a location owner to allow you to shoot on

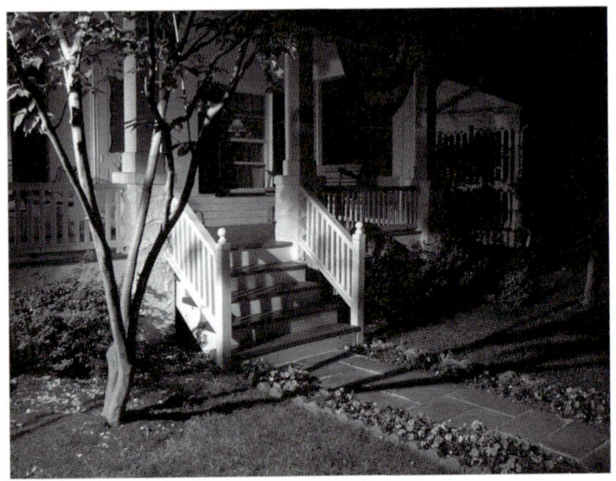

We chose to shoot the majority of the movie in the small towns of Chardon and Chagrin Falls, Ohio. When we went looking for the porch location for when Bobby fixes the bike, we stumbled across a quaint street and simply asked a number of homeowners if we could shoot on their porch. The first person we asked said yes, and their porch is now immortalized!

his property is a lot like selling a product or service in that you have to persuade the owner to accept the inconvenience of having a movie crew present for little or no money. The trick is to sell the story and vision behind the project. Make the owner feel like he is a valuable part of the production process and that his contributions will help make the project successful.

In high-production cities like Los Angeles and New York, the frequency of big-budget movie and television show productions has raised location owners' awareness of location fees, and it's not uncommon for studios to pay thousands, if not tens of thousands, of dollars a day for the use of a location. This is problematic when an independent, low-budget movie producer asks to use the same location. If you can't write a check, then the owner will probably decline your request.

Once secret to finding cheap locations is to get out of the major cities into the suburbs where movie production isn't as common. The novelty of having a movie made is still an enticing factor that may sway an owner to allow you to shoot.

When I produced *Time and Again*, I deliberately chose to shoot in the towns of Chardon and Chagrin Falls in Ohio, neither of which had been often used for film productions. We received a warm reception not only from the residents and businesses, but also from the mayors and city councils of each city. I was able to secure locations such as street corners, the Town Square, restaurants, parks, and even prisons for free, which added extraordinary production value to the movie.

Some states even offer tax incentives and rebates for productions that shoot in their state. Contact the film commission in each state for more information.

Before you begin searching for prospective locations, list all the locations mentioned the script, whether they are interior or exterior, and whether the scene needs to be shot during the day or at night. Once the list is complete, you can begin the search.

As you begin your search for locations to use in the movie, consider the following tips:

- Contact the local film commission and send them the list of locations you're looking for. Many film commissions have a file full of production-friendly locations they can direct you to, complete with contact information.
- Patronize businesses you're considering shooting at. Use this as an opportunity to get to know the owner so that when you approach her with the request to shoot, you're not walking in cold off the street.

Working with the local theater guild not only allowed us access to the theater as a location, but also attracted hundreds of local actors to be extras in the movie.

DIRECTOR'S NOTES

Locations are vital to providing a realistic backdrop for the characters, especially in producing a period movie like *Time and Again*.

We used numerous locations, from diners and trailers to prisons and town streets, locations that we never paid a penny for, but were allowed to use legally.

The secret to securing locations is to establish a relationship with the owner of the location and show that you are serious and your production is organized and professional.

When we needed a 1950s street for the stickball scene, I looked at several towns before we found Chagrin Falls, Ohio . . . a quaint country town with the charm and appeal the story needed.

I spent several hours looking at streets and houses trying to find not only the look I wanted, but also an area that would work logistically. The area we selected was within an eighth of a mile of a municipal parking lot, which the local residents could use to park their cars, allowing us to populate their driveways with our 1950s period cars. Also, there was a clean shot at either end of the street, so I couldn't see modern buildings or freeways from the set.

After I drew up a map of the area, I called city hall and asked to speak with the mayor. She was very polite, listened to my request, and asked me to submit a proposal. Because I had already done the location scout, I had all the information I needed, not only where I wanted to shoot, but how the logistics could be worked out.

The proposal went well and we were approved for the shoot, but I was asked to pay a $1000 location fee to shoot. Knowing that that was half the budget, I called the mayor and explained to her that we weren't a Hollywood production, but independent filmmakers making a no-budget movie. All of our locations, props, and wardrobe were donated and the cast and crew were all local volunteers. Once she understood this, she reconsidered and waived the location fee.

We then approached the police chief with our request and began the process of working with the local officials to coordinate the closure of four city blocks for the shoot.

When the day of the shoot arrived, everything worked like clockwork and the shoot went without incident.

We couldn't have done it without the help of the Chagrin Falls officials who were exceptionally helpful and accommodating. The moral of the story is that we were able to shut down four residential blocks with the assistance of local officials for free, just by asking!

I'm directing Brian in a cell of the county jail, which we procured for free, simply by asking.

- Always scout and secure the locations in writing BEFORE scheduling cast and crew members. Determining the shooting schedule is largely dependent on location availability and it's difficult to reschedule people if a location falls though. Location availability will often affect the production schedule.

Location scouting tips

- When scouting locations, bring a digital camera, flashlight, tape measure, electrical outlet tester (available from a hardware store for $5), business cards, a notebook, and a pencil.
- Take pictures or videotape the location during the scout so you can reference it later in preproduction meetings.
- Check for parking availability: are you permitted to use parking lots? Are there restrictions on parking on the street? What days are designated for street cleaning? Will your parking affect the neighboring residents or businesses? Are certain streets permit-only parking past a certain time? Do you need the police to reserved metered spaces? When issuing call sheets, be sure to include parking restrictions.

- Note where and when the sun rises and sets and where on the location it shines throughout the day. Factor in the sun's position when scheduling the shooting schedule.
- Check to see where you can load equipment into the location. Is there a loading dock or cargo elevators you can use? If you're using the regular elevators, do you need protective padding for the walls or floor?
- Determine where you can stage the equipment during the shoot so that it is close to the set yet secure.

INFORMATION AND ADVICE FOR SHOOTING IN LONDON

Film London
Telephone: +44 207 613 7676
www.filmlondon.org.uk

- Where can you park the production vehicles? Cast and crew vehicles? Equipment trucks? Is the area secure or do you need to hire a security guard or assign a production assistant to watch the vehicles?
- Check the breaker box to determine the number of circuits and the electrical load that can be drawn from each. If you cannot identify all the outlets or circuits, consult the building manager or maintenance department for assistance in finding other breaker boxes. Map out the circuits to determine power load.
- Check for anything that may make noise and figure out how to disable it, especially refrigerators and air conditioning units. When turning off a refrigerator, put your keys inside to remind you to turn it back on at the end of the day.
- Locate the restrooms. If you are shooting in a park or an area without restroom facilities, identify a location to place a portable toilet.
- Determine where you can set up craft services and catering and determine refrigeration, heating, and power requirements.
- Measure the room, including ceiling height and door width (can the dolly track fit in the door?). Note the number of windows and doors and what the switches on the wall control.
- Listen for outside sounds such as nearby airports; trains; freeways; sirens from hospitals, police or fire stations, and schools that may disrupt the audio. List the times throughout the day that are the busiest, for example, when school lets out, or when air traffic stops for the night. Understanding these schedules will help plan the shooting schedule to compensate for these uncontrollable audio sources.
- If shooting in a public area, make sure that precautions are taken to secure the set. Place warning signs around the perimeter notifying the public of the shoot. Use production assistants to control pedestrian traffic flow, and use caution tape to close off restricted areas. Work closely with the authori-

We shot at a private residence and took special care of the property by cleaning up after ourselves, being mindful of where we parked our vehicles, and involving the location owners in our intentions.

ties or location owner when coordinating shoots that could potentially affect the public.

- Make sure when shooting in a location such as a restaurant or store that the owner is able to close the business during the shoot. On-set production is difficult enough. Dealing with customers and the associated liability could seriously affect the production.
- Be aware of any art, photographs, posters, logos, or any other copyrighted images on the walls or surfaces that may need to be replaced with approved artwork. Using copyrighted work without permission in the movie increases your liability and exposure to a lawsuit.
- Check to see if you need any special permits from the city or if you are required to have a police officer or fire marshal present during the shoot. Many cities, especially high-production towns, require a fire marshal on set, regardless of whether the shoot occurs on private or public property.
- Be honest and open with the location owner in terms of what you want to do at the location, the number of people involved, parking needs, power consumption, food usage, if any stunts or pyrotechnics will be required, and if you need to change or move anything. It's better to work out the details in advance than for the location owner to arrive the day of the shoot and be surprised by elements he didn't expect. He would be within his rights to kick the crew off the property.
- Most locations will require that you show proof of insurance. Insurance will protect both you and the location in the event that an accident occurs that results in damage to the location or injury. Be prepared to discuss the type and amount of coverage of your insurance policy.
- Be sure to scout the location BEFORE you go into production. During the scout, plan the actors' blocking, camera positions, and lighting ideas as well as production design, props, wardrobe, and set-dressing needs.
- Bring key department heads to the location scout, such as the director of photography, production designer, set dresser, and production sound mixer. Listen to their input and seek to address any technical concerns with them during the location scout.
- If you approve of a location, check to see if you need further approvals from neighbors, nearby businesses, or other entities. Some cities require an approval form from neighboring residents and businesses.
- Locate local hospitals and prepare directions and emergency information for the cast and crew in the event of a medical emergency on set.
- Locate local hotels if the location is distant. Negotiate reduced rates for extended stays.
- Confirm directions to the set and double check to make sure call sheets and maps are correct. Do not trust online mapping web sites without driving the directions given before the shoot.

Locations to avoid

- Avoid white-walled locations like apartments, classrooms, or offices, unless the white walls are the desired look. These locations are extremely difficult to light and shoot in because preventing the walls from overexposing takes valuable production time. If you have total control of a location, consider repainting the walls a light gray. The walls can be lit to appear brighter, but under normal lighting conditions will read much better on camera than white.
- Be wary of locations with low ceilings that restrict the placement of a microphone boom over the actors or the height at which lights can be rigged.
- When the script calls for a small room, consider shooting in a larger set. It's easy to make a large room appear small by shooting in a corner and creatively dressing the set. It also makes it much easer for the production team to work by allowing room for placement of lights, camera, and production personnel.
- Avoid any locations that you cannot reasonably control during the shoot. Important factors include shooting in public where people can trespass on set, locations that restrict alterations or moving furniture, noisy locations, and locations that are subject to the weather.

SECURING A LOCATION

If a location serves both the artistic and the technical needs of the production and you and the owner agree to terms of access, payment, and time and date of usage, then you can submit a contractual package to the owner. The package usually includes:

- **Location agreement.** This contract confirms the use of the location, the dates and time of use, what parts of the location the crew is allowed to use, parking, restroom access, craft service/catering setup location, load-in/load-out location, permission to move furniture or rearrange the location, and definition of use of pyrotechnics or stunts. The location agreement also includes the waiver of liability, which protects the owner in the event of an accident on set, acknowledgment of insurance, and any special permission to use the location. Always have a signed location agreement before scheduling and locking that location.
- **Certificate of insurance.** This document, obtained from your insurance company, serves as proof to the location owner that you have production insurance. The certificate also identifies the amount of coverage and can list the owner as additionally insured, essentially placing the owner on the policy.
- **Production schedule.** Give the location owner a schedule for the shooting day so he understands what will be happening at his location. This allows the owner to prepare and know what to expect the day of the shoot.

Once a location is secured, call the local city hall or the film commission to file for any necessary permits.

Quantus Pictures Inc.

Motion Picture Production Company

Location Agreement

Agreement entered into this ____th day of ______________, 2002 by and between Quantus Pictures, Inc.("Production Company") and ____ ("Grantor").

1. **Identity of Filming Location:** Grantor hereby agrees to permit Production Company to use the property (____) located at ____ ("Property") in connection with the motion picture tentatively titled, "______________________________" ("Picture") for rehearsing, photographing, videotaping, filming, and recording scenes and sounds for the Picture. Production Company and its licensees, sponsors, assigns and successors may exhibit, advertise and promote the Picture or any portion thereof, whether or not such uses contain audio and/or visual reproductions of the Property and whether or not the Property is identified, in any and all media in which currently exist or which may exist in the future in all countries of the world and in perpetuity.

2. **Right of Access:** Production Company shall have the right to bring personnel and equipment (including props and temporary sets) onto the Property and to remove same after completion of its use of the Property hereunder. Production Company agrees not to photograph, film, videotape and use in the Picture the actual name, if any, connected with the Property or to use any other name directly associated with the Property. If Production Company depicts the interior(s) of any structures located on the Property, Grantor agrees that Production Company shall not be required to depict such interior(s) in any particular manner in the picture.

3. **Time of Access:** The permission granted hereunder shall be for the period commencing on or about ______________AM/PM on ______________________ and continuing until __________AM/PM. If the weather or other conditions are not favorable for such purpose on such date(s), the date(s) shall be postponed to a date to be determined by mutual agreement between Grantor and Production Company. This within permission shall also apply to future retakes and/or added scenes.

4. **Payment:** For each day the Production Company uses the location, it shall pay Grantor the sum of $_____________________ in consideration for the foregoing which represents costs of personnel only. Grantor agrees to waive any and all location fees associated with granting the right to film, videotape and record on or about the Property.

5. **Alterations to Location:** Production Company agrees that if it becomes necessary to change, alter or rearrange any equipment on the Property that belongs to Grantor, Production Company shall return and restore said equipment to its original place and condition, or repair it, if necessary. Production Company agrees to indemnify and hold harmless Grantor from and against any and all liabilities, damages and claims of third parties arising from Production Company's use hereunder of the Property (unless such liabilities, damages or claims arise from breach of Grantor's warranty as set forth in the immediately following sentence) and from any physical damage to the Property proximately caused by Production Company, or any of its representatives, employees, or agents. Grantor warrants that it has the right and authority to enter into this agreement and to grant the rights granted by it herein. Grantor agrees

(continued)

Quantus Pictures Inc.

Motion Picture Production Company

(continued from page 1)

to indemnify and hold harmless Production Company from and against any and all claims relating to breach of its aforesaid warranty. Production Company will return and or/restore Property to the same condition as it was found prior to Production Company's entrance onto Property. Production Company is fully responsible for any damage caused to the Property during the period of access by the Production Company, its employees, representatives or agents and will repair or renumerate the cost of repair (at Production Company's discression) within a period of thirty (30) days of the time of access.

6. **No kickbacks for use:** Grantor affirms that neither it nor anyone acting for it gave or agreed to give anything of value to any member of the production staff, anyone associated with Picture, or any representative of Production Company, or any television station or network for mentioning or displaying the name of Grantor as a shooting location on the Property (except the use of the Property) which was furnished for use solely on or in connection with the Picture.

7. **Release:** Grantor releases and discharges Production Company, its employees, agents, licensees, successors and assigns from any and all claims, demands or causes of action that Grantor may now have or may from now on have for libel, defamation, invasion of privacy or right of publicity, infringement of copyright or violation of any other right arising out of or relating to any utilization of the rights granted herein.

The undersigned represents that he/she is empowered to execute this Agreement for Grantor.

Accepted and Agreed to:

Signed ______________________________ Date ________________

Producer ______________________________ Date ________________

ENTERTAINMENT INDUSTRY DEVELOPMENT CORPORATION (EIDC)
PERMIT EMAIL/FAX REQUEST

7083 Hollywood BL, 5th Floor, Los Angeles, CA 90028

Fax this request to (323) 962-4966 or
email to permitapps@eidc.com by clicking on the link on the last page

PAGE 1

Applicant (Company Name): ____

Production Title: ____

Type of Production: Please Select a Production Type

If other please describe ______________________________

Production Company Representative: ____

Location Assistant: ____________________________

Producer: ____________________________ Director: ____________________________

1st A.D: ____________________________ Production Manager: ____________________________

Production Numbers:

Office: Production Company Fax:

Pager: Cell: (

Production representative email address (required for online submission): ____________________________

Assistant's cell:

Vehicle Breakdown: (Number of each)

Large trucks: ______ Other trucks: ______ Motor Homes/Trailers: ______ Vans: _____ Generator: _____

Picture Vehicles: ______ Cast/Crew cars: ______ Camera Cars:______

Cast:________ Crew: __________ Extras: ___________

Where is extras holding? ____

PERMIT SERVICE, IF APPLICABLE ____________________ PERMIT SERVICE REPRESENTATIVE: ____________________

PERMIT SERVICE FAX: __________________________

PERMIT EMAIL/FAX REQUEST (Cont.) **PAGE 2**

Location # 1 Type of location (house, apt. bldg., etc): ____
Open to the public: [ ] or Closed to the public: [ ] PLEASE CHECK ONE

THOMAS GUIDE PAGE # & GRID ________

Address and/or street name: ____ Type (ST, AV, DR etc.): __________

Date(s): _________to __________Time: ________to __________ ***PLEASE NOTE ARRIVAL/DEPARTURE IN MILITARY TIME**

Prep date(s): __________________ Strike date(s): ___________________________

Summary of scenes (include all activities such as traffic & pedestrian control, wet down, animals, etc.):

Other Activities:

Gunfire: [Choose One] Type of gunfire: Automatic: [ ] Semi-automatic [ ] Single Shot [ ]
Load: Full [ ] Half [ ] Quarter [ ]

Special Effects: [Choose One] F/X # _______________
Type of F/X: Squibs/Bullet hits: [ ] Explosion: [ ] Fire effects: [ ] Sparks: [ ] Other: _________________

Description of F/X scene:

Parking:

Posting "No Parking" signs

(Please indicate which side of the street: W/S-west side E/S-east side, N/S-north side, S/S-south side or B/S-both sides)

Lane/full closure:

Base camp: ________________________________ Crew parking: ____

COMMUNITY RELATIONS

Permits

Many cities require filmmakers to secure a permit. Sometimes free, these permits help the local authorities coordinate with filmmakers to ensure public safety, coordinate traffic and parking, provide necessary police and fire personnel, and schedule public events around the shoot.

- Contact city hall or the chamber of commerce of the city you are shooting in to see what the permitting and insurance requirements are. Be sure to begin the process at least a month before the proposed shoot date.
- Although there may be a fee for the permit or a cost of hiring city officials such as police or firemen, avoid shooting guerilla-style. Permits alert the city of your presence and will prevent any other city services from interfering with your shoot. Besides, it is difficult to manage a production when you're always hiding from the police.
- In many instances, shooting in public parks is free, although you still need a permit. Be sure to contact the parks and recreation department for details.
- Some cities may require that you hire a police officer or a fire marshal for the duration of the shoot, especially if it involves pyrotechnics, fire, and/or the operation of a generator. Some cities may allow you to negotiate these rates with the individual officers.
- Always carry a copy of the shooting permit with you on set at all times. If the police visit the set, they will ask to see the permit. Have it handy to minimize any delays to shooting. If you choose to shoot without a permit, the police can shut down the production, issue a fine, or even arrest the location manager or producer.
- The local or state film commission may be able to assist in getting city permits through faster or may be able to help get a discount for independent film productions. Most city governments work with filmmakers through the film commission.

Working in a community

Many people have a rosy view of the film production industry until a production comes to their town. Trucks clogging the road, bright lights and noise at all hours of the night, pushy production personnel, and the general inconvenience of having to work around the film crew often taint this view.

You can take steps to ensure the production experience is pleasant for both the community and the film crew.

- When approaching city council, be sure to present a professional, organized proposal of what you want to do. Include a letter of introduction, maps and diagrams of the areas you want to shoot in, a list of the number of people involved, insurance information, and any other materials that would make it easier for the city to approve your request.

Quantus Pictures Inc.

Motion Picture Production Company

July 9, 2002

Dear Chagrin Falls, Water Street Resident,

On Saturday, July 13, 2002 from 1:00pm-6:00pm we will be closing Water Street between West Washington and Center Street for a film shoot. The scene is from a short subject we are producing for international film festival release, tentatively titled, "The Day Bobby Jones Came Home."

"The Day Bobby Jones Came Home" is the story of convicted murderer Bobby Jones who has the chance to exonerate his name by jumping back ten years earlier to the day before he allegedly committed the murder that sentenced him to a lifetime in prison. Falling in love with the sexy diner waitress Awanda in his old home town, Bobby uncovers the true murderer, only to learn that Awanda is the victim. Framed by the very evidence he left during his relationship with Awanda, the police arrest and convict the innocent 15-year-old Bobby Jones, creating a paradox that will haunt Bobby Jones to his death.

The scene we are shooting on Water Street involves several high school kids playing stickball when, for the first time, Bobby Jones sees his younger self.

Because this story takes place in the summer of 1958, we will be bringing in several period cars to park both on the street as well as in various driveways up and down Water Street. We are kindly requesting that, from 1:00pm-6:00pm, you park your cars in the Municipal Lot. Although we will allow local access for residents of Water Street, the street will be closed to public traffic. We would also ask for your support in allowing us to park a period car in your driveway. All shooting and equipment setups will be on the street, so cast and crew will not be on your property for the shoot.

Thank you again for your kind assistance and we're looking forward to making Water Street look terrific! If you have any questions, feel free to call our offices at 216-299-1690.

Warmest regards-

Jason J. Tomaric
Director

Letter to residents.

Quantus Pictures Inc.

Motion Picture Production Company

Dear Chardon Square Tenant,

Awanda and Bobby Jones

On Sunday, July 21, 2002, the southwest corner of Chardon Square will be closed for a film shoot from 6:00pm to 1:00am. South-bound Main Street traffic will be routed down Court Street, north-bound traffic on South Street will not be able to turn left onto Water Street but can turn right, and east-bound traffic on water street will be diverted down Ferris Avenue.

The film, tentatively titled "The Day Bobby Jones Came Home" is the story of convicted murderer Bobby Jones who has the chance to exonerate his name by jumping back ten years earlier to the day before he allegedly committed the murder that sentenced him to a lifetime in prison. Falling in love with the sexy diner waitress Awanda in his old home town, Bobby uncovers the true murderer, only to learn that Awanda is the victim. Framed by the very evidence he left during his relationship with Awanda, the police arrest and convict the innocent 15-year-old Bobby Jones, creating a paradox that will haunt Bobby Jones to his death.

Sunday's shoot will take place in front of the western shops and the Geauga theatre on the square. Since the film takes place in 1958, we will have nearly 100 extras, all in period costumes, make-up and hairstyles, and dozens of vintage 1950's vehicles. Anyone interested in watching the shoot is welcome on the Chardon square lawn, allowing a terrific view without interfering with the production. We are requesting that all the stores on ground level from Cameo Jewelers due west to the theatre dress the windows with a patriotic theme and with any elements representative of the 1950's. The main character will be running down the strip, in front of each store, allowing us to showcase Chardon's classic look.

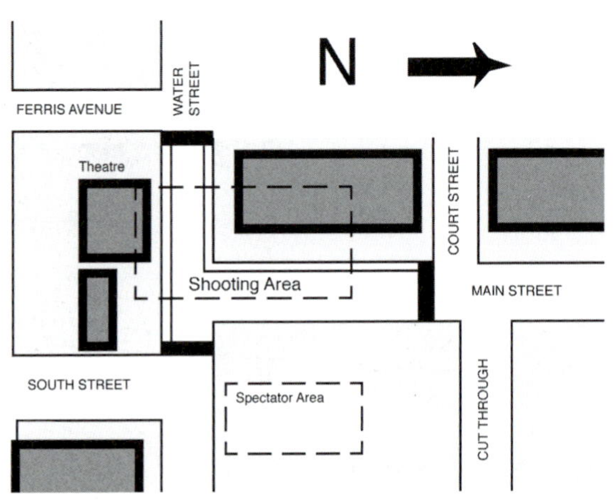

To the left is a diagram illustrating the closing. If you have any questions, please call our production offices at 216-299-1690. Thank you so much for your cooperation in making this shoot successful!

This document is intended for reference only and is not intended as a legal binding contract.

Letter to tenants.

- If shooting exteriors, alert nearby businesses and residents in writing as to the nature of your shoot and how it will affect them.
- If you require public parking, work with the police to see if they can reserve parking spots for your production vehicles. You may need to pay for the revenue the parking meters could have generated for the city during the time they were reserved for you.

Activity

Contact the local city government and find out what the process is for shooting a movie.

- Are the permits dependent on shooting on private or public property?
- Do you have to pay for a city official, such as a police officer, firefighter, or ranger, to be present?
- How long does it take for the permit to be approved?
- Do you have to present your case to the city council?
- How much does the permit cost?
- Is the permit cost dependent on activity, that is, is it more expensive to shoot near water, use firearms, or use pyrotechnics? How about large numbers of extras?
- Are there reduced fees for student or independent projects?
- What are the insurance requirements to film?
- How long does it take to receive the permit once the application is submitted?

Filmmakers' code of conduct

The Los Angeles film production office has compiled the following guidelines for all movie crews shooting on location. Abiding by these unofficial guidelines makes it easier for productions in our industry to shoot in communities, homes, and businesses. Consider distributing these guidelines to all crew members at the beginning of production.

- Production companies arriving on location in or near a residential neighborhood should enter the area no earlier than the time stipulated on the permit and park one by one, turning engines off as soon as possible. Cast and crew must observe designated parking areas.
- When production passes that identify employees are issued, every crew member must wear the pass while at the location.
- Moving or towing vehicles is prohibited without the express permission of the municipal jurisdiction or the vehicle owner.

Shooting the windmill for the opening title shot.

- Production vehicles may not block driveways without the express permission of the municipal jurisdiction or the driveway owner.
- Meals must be confined to the area designated in the location agreement or permit. Individuals must eat within the designated meal area. All trash must be disposed of properly upon completion of the meal.
- Removing, trimming, and or cutting of vegetation or trees is prohibited unless approved by the owner or, in the case of parkway trees, the local municipality and the property owner.
- Always clean up garbage, water bottles, construction materials, food, and paperwork at the end of the shooting day. Try to leave the location in better condition than when you found it, and always haul your own trash away from the location. Do not use public trash containers.
- All signs erected or removed for filming purposes will be removed or replaced upon completion of the use of the location, unless stipulated otherwise by the location agreement or the permit.
- When departing the location, all signs posted to direct the company to the location must be removed.
- Noise levels should be kept as low as possible. Generators should be placed as far as practical from residential buildings. Do not let engines run unnecessarily.
- All members of the production company should wear clothing that conforms to good taste and common sense. Shoes and shirts must be worn at all times.

- Crew members must not display signs, posters, or pictures that do not reflect common sense and good taste.
- Cast and crew are to remain on or near the area that has been permitted. Do not trespass onto a neighboring resident's or merchant's property.
- Cast and crew must not bring guests or pets to the location, unless expressly authorized in advance by the production company.
- Designated smoking areas must be observed, and cigarettes must always be extinguished in butt cans.
- Cast and crew must refrain from using lewd or offensive language within earshot of the general public.
- Cast and crew vehicles parked on public streets must adhere to all legal requirements unless authorized by the film permit.
- Parking is prohibited on both sides of public streets unless specifically authorized by the film permit.
- The company must comply with the provisions of the permit at all times.

For more information on locations, location scouting, and working with a community and to see how Jason worked with NASA and nuclear power plants and even secured a free ballroom for his first feature film, *Clone*, check out the Location modules at www.powerfilmmaking.com.

FILM COMMISSIONS

When a production company is looking for a city to shoot in, there are several factors the company must consider. Permits, local laws regarding film produc-

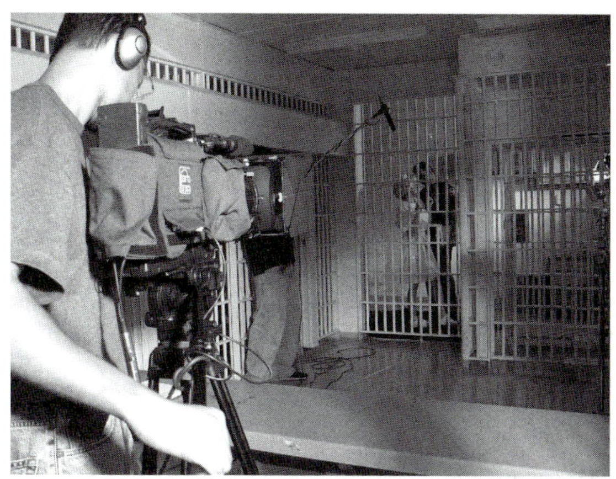

Although we didn't work through a film commission for *Time and Again*, we were able to secure the support of the local government. The police department of Chagrin Falls even gave us permission to use their 1950s police car in the film!

tion, tax incentives, and coordination between police, fire, and other city departments will affect the budget and shooting schedule. Because the production company may not be aware of the local regulations and procedures, each state has set up a film commission to work with the production company.

In addition to state film commissions, large cities may have their own. Film commissions serve to provide the following services to filmmakers:

- **Production manual.** Film commissions usually produce a yearly directory of all the film production personnel, equipment rental houses, casting agencies, hotels, travel accommodations, and postproduction services in the area. This directory is usually free to filmmakers and is a tremendous resource. Get one.
- **Locations.** Film commissions often maintain a database of thousands of photographs of locations available in the region and can assist filmmakers in finding and securing locations. Locations in high-production cities may be broken up into those that are available for free or for a slight fee and those with larger rental costs for bigger budget productions. When shooting in another state, that state's film commission may mail location photos to the producer to assist with finding locations.
- **Coordination with city services.** Film commissions work with the city to help secure permits, coordinate police and fire officials, shut down streets, or perform any other service needed to ensure a smooth production. Without the film commission, filmmakers would need to apply for each of these services separately and could encounter needless delays.
- **Coordination with local residents and businesses.** Film commissions help the filmmaker work with local businesses and residents, especially if production activity interferes with traffic or access to stores and businesses.

Finding production-friendly locations can be a challenge, so use your resources. Contact the film commission!

Film commissions can also help deal with local complaints and concerns over the production.

Film commissions are responsible for increasing film business in their state by promoting and marketing their state's resources to film producers. Tax breaks, free permits, and other incentives help cities attract productions that could bring in millions of dollars of revenue to businesses, restaurants, and hotel, not to mention the fame a city receives from being the setting for a big Hollywood film.

Film commissions are also sensitive to independent filmmakers whose projects may not carry the financial backing of a Hollywood blockbuster. Independent filmmakers who are successful may just want to come back when they are Hollywood moguls, so film commissions see a low- to no-budget independent film as a possible investment in future business.

Contact your local film commission to arrange details for your next production. Remember, they are a resource . . . use them.

ALABAMA
(334) 242-4195
www.alabamafilm.org

ALASKA
(907) 269-8190
(907) 269-8125
www.alaskafilm.org

ARIZONA
(800) 523-6695
(602) 771-1193
www.azcommerce.com/film

ARKANSAS
Film Hotline (501) 682-7676
http://www.1800arkansas.com/film/

CALIFORNIA
(800) 858-4749
(323) 860-2960
www.film.ca.gov

COLORADO
(303) 620-4500
www.coloradofilm.org

CONNECTICUT
(800) 392-2122
(860) 571-7130
www.ctfilm.com

DELAWARE
(800) 441-8846
(302) 739-4271
http://www.state.de.us/dedo/new_web_site/frames/film.html

DISTRICT OF COLUMBIA
(202) 727-6608
http://film.dc.gov

FLORIDA
(877) 352-3456
(850) 410-4765
www.filminflorida.com

GEORGIA
(404) 962-4052
www.filmgeorgia.org

HAWAII
(808) 586-2570
www.hawaiifilmoffice.com

IDAHO
(800) 942-8338
(208) 334-2470
www.filmidaho.com

ILLINOIS
(312) 814-3600
http://www.illinoisbiz.biz/film/index.html

INDIANA
(317) 232-8829
www.filmindiana.com

IOWA
(515) 242-4726
www.filmiowa.com

KANSAS
(785) 296-2178
www.filmkansas.com

KENTUCKY
(800) 345-6591
(502) 564-3456
www.kyfilmoffice.com

LOUISIANA
(504) 736-7280
www.lafilm.org

MAINE
Hotline (207) 624-7851
www.filminmaine.com

MARYLAND
Hotline (410) 767-0067
www.marylandfilm.org

MASSACHUSETTS
(617) 523-8388
www.massfilmbureau.com

MICHIGAN
(800) 477-3456
(517) 373-0638
http://www.michigan.gov

MINNESOTA
(612) 332-6493
www.mnfilmandtv.org

MISSISSIPPI
Hotline (601) 359-2112
www.visitmississippi.org/film

MISSOURI
(573) 751-9050
www.mofilm.org

MONTANA
Hotline (406) 444-3960
www.montanafilm.com

NEBRASKA
(800) 228-4307
(402) 471-3746
www.filmnebraska.org

NEVADA
(877) 638-3456
(702) 486-2711
www.nevadafilm.com

NEW HAMPSHIRE
(603) 271-2220
www.filmnh.org

NEW JERSEY
(973) 648-6279

NEW MEXICO
(505) 827-9810
www.nmfilm.com

NEW YORK
(212) 803-2330
www.nylovesfilm.com

NORTH CAROLINA
Hotline (800) 232-9227
www.ncfilm.com

NORTH DAKOTA
(800) 435-5663
(701) 328-2525
www.ndtourism.com

OHIO
(614) 466-8844
www.ohiofilm.com

OKLAHOMA
(918) 584-5111
www.oklahomaproductionguide.com

OREGON
(503) 229-5832
www.oregonfilm.org

PENNSYLVANIA
(717) 783-3456
www.filminpa.com

PUERTO RICO
(787) 758-4747 x2251
www.puertoricofilm.com

RHODE ISLAND
Hotline (401) 222-6666
www.rifilm.com

SOUTH CAROLINA
Hotline (803) 737-3022
www.scfilmoffice.com

SOUTH DAKOTA
(800) 952-3625
(605) 773-3301
www.filmsd.com

TENNESSEE
Hotline (615) 532-2770
www.filmtennessee.com

TEXAS
Hotline (512) 463-7799
www.governor.state.tx.us/film/

UTAH
(800) 453-8824
(801) 538-8740
www.film.utah.gov

VERMONT
(802) 828-3618
www.vermontfilm.com

VIRGINIA
(800) 854-6233
(804) 371-8204
www.film.virginia.org

WASHINGTON
(206) 256-6151
www.filmwashington.com

WASHINGTON DC
(202) 727-6608
http://film.dc.gov

WEST VIRGINIA
(304) 558-2200
www.wvfilm.com

WISCONSIN
(608) 261-8195
www.filmwisconsin.org

WYOMING
(800) 458-6657
(307) 777-3400
www.wyomingfilm.org

DURING PRODUCTION

Once a location has been secured, it's important to respect the location, owners, neighbors, and general public while shooting. Be mindful of the behavior of the cast and crew, keep the location clean and neat, and always make sure you put everything back the way you found it.

- Make sure set dressers take detailed photographs around the set to ensure that if something is moved that it will be put back in it's proper place at the end of the shoot.

- Post signs, especially in public areas, notifying passersby of your activities and alert them that they are potentially in the shot. Consider having a production assistant present at sidewalks to stop pedestrians temporarily while the crew is rolling during a take and manage foot traffic safely around the set.
- If shooting in the owner's home, place cardboard or furniture pads on the floor to avoid dirtying or scratching the floor, especially if setting up dolly track and heavy light stands.

GO BEYOND THE BOOK

Check out the Movie Contracts file on the companion disc for a printable location agreement you can use on your own productions.

Now that you've read about scouting locations and choosing the proper location for your story, follow along as Jason takes you on a location scout of the diner from *Time and Again*.

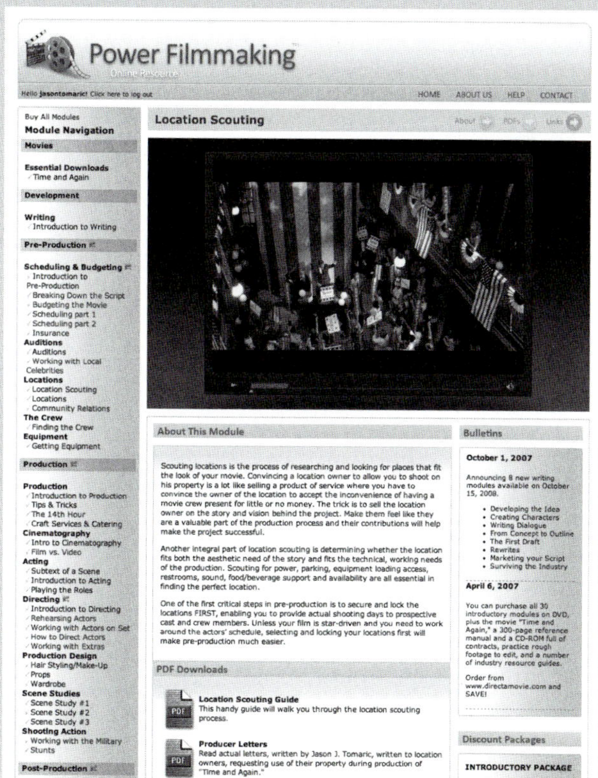

Also, download letters Jason wrote to owners of locations he successfully secured, location agreements, crew codes of conduct, public notification flyers and much more.

In the Locations module, watch how crew members accessed a nuclear power plant and even shot at NASA for free for Jason's first feature film, *Clone*.

Michael K. Brown
Actor - SAG
HM(818) 558-4043
C(818) 416-1699
Actormkb@yahoo
DVD DEMO
2 Minutes
Tara Radcliffe

CHAPTER 7

Auditioning Actors

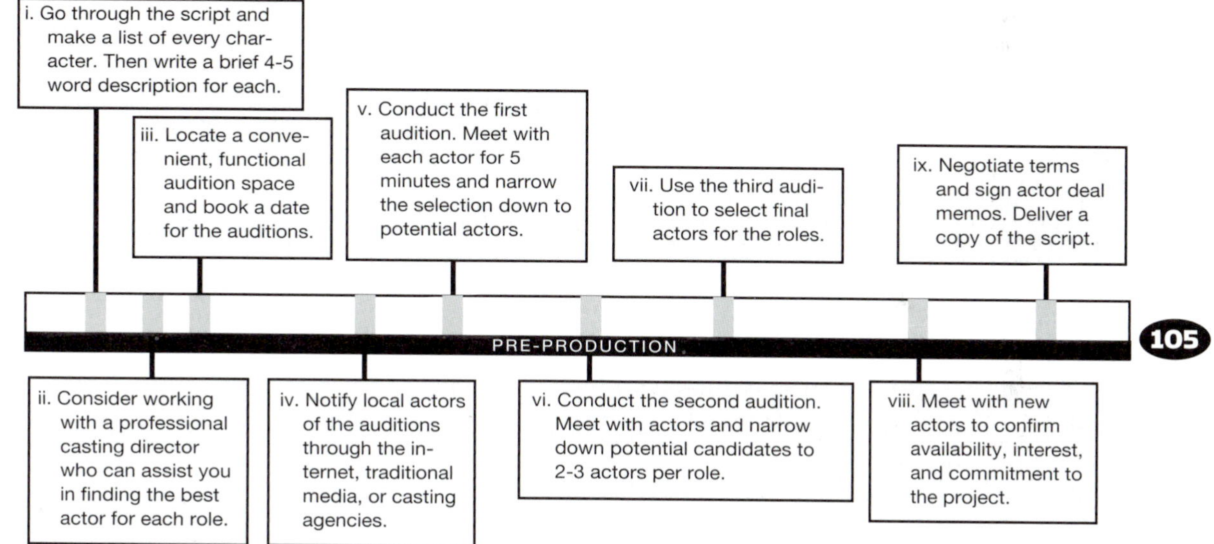

i. Go through the script and make a list of every character. Then write a brief 4-5 word description for each.
ii. Consider working with a professional casting director who can assist you in finding the best actor for each role.
iii. Locate a convenient, functional audition space and book a date for the auditions.
iv. Notify local actors of the auditions through the internet, traditional media, or casting agencies.
v. Conduct the first audition. Meet with each actor for 5 minutes and narrow the selection down to potential actors.
vi. Conduct the second audition. Meet with actors and narrow down potential candidates to 2-3 actors per role.
vii. Use the third audition to select final actors for the roles.
viii. Meet with new actors to confirm availability, interest, and commitment to the project.
ix. Negotiate terms and sign actor deal memos. Deliver a copy of the script.
PRE-PRODUCTION

INTRODUCTION

Auditions are the process of finding the best actor to play each role in the film. It can sometimes be complicated, because as a director, you're forced to select strangers with whom you will be working for possibly months on a project.

When a movie is finished, the believability of the story hinges on the quality of the acting, so it's important to find actors who can convincingly play the role while working professionally on the set.

As you begin the search for actors, avoid casting friends and family AT ALL COSTS. It may seem like a fun idea, but you will never see true, realistic performances from your friends. Working with friends will make it difficult to focus while you're on set, and joking around is a great way to ruin your production. If you want to make a Hollywood-quality movie, then look for Hollywood-quality actors. Remember that like any profession, acting is a serious craft that

Actor Brian Ireland, playing the role of Bobby Jones, was a professional wrestler who had never acted before. After seeing him in auditions, I knew he had not only the right look for the part, but also an outstanding attitude that made it easy to work with him.

requires years of training and practice, so seek out professionals who will make your characters real and believable.

FINDING AN AUDITION SPACE

The goal of auditioning is to systematically meet and cast your actors from a vast pool of acting talent. Finding an audition space that is easily accessible, is well laid out, and allows for the organized processing of actors will not only help the auditions run smoothly, but also let prospective actors know that the movie is being produced by professionals.

- Don't hold auditions in your house or apartment. It will scare people away and you will appear to be an amateur. Auditioning members of the opposite sex alone in your apartment or house is also dangerous, because it can lead to liability issues and possibly to lawsuits.
- Find a large, central, easy-to-get-to location like a library, office building, coffee shop, school gym, or classroom to hold the auditions. It will make publicizing the audition easier and will help establish you as a professional. Most public buildings with meeting rooms will allow you to use them for free if your project is not-for-profit.
- When setting up the audition space, designate a large waiting room for the actors to wait in and a second room for conducting the individual auditions. Station a production assistant in the waiting area to distribute the audition forms, collect headshots and resumes, lead the next actor into the audition area, and manage the incoming actors.
- Consider setting up a television in the waiting area to show clips from previous films you've worked on to excite the actors as they wait.

DIRECTOR'S NOTES

For *Time and Again*, I contacted a local independent casting agency, North Coast Central Casting, which used the top floor of a martial arts dojo for meetings and auditions. Because most actors in Cleveland knew where it was, it made sense to hold the auditions there. I spoke with the owner, Ray Szuch, and he let us use the space for free for six hours on a Saturday afternoon. We had over 300 people show up to audition and everything worked out without a problem.

ATTRACTING ACTORS TO THE AUDITION

There are two different ways to attract actors to auditions. The first is to put out general audition notices in newspapers, acting magazines like *Backstage West*, classified ads in the newspaper, postings on web sites like www.craigslist.org, and announcements on the local news. The benefit is that hundreds of people will show up . . . the downfall is that the general notice will also attract a lot of unqualified actors who will take a lot of time to sift through. Casting a wide net will collect a lot of fish . . . both talented and untalented.

- When posting audition notices on flyers or in the newspaper, listing a brief five- or six-word description of the roles you are casting will help narrow the actors down before the auditions. As an example, Awanda was listed as a spunky 20- to 30-year-old 1950s diner waitress. Bobby Jones was listed as a rugged late-20s prison convict.
- Consider posting an audition notice on www.craigslist.org. This free listing web site is extremely popular in large cities and is frequented by hundreds of thousands of people each day.
- Contact local community theaters, theater guilds, and university acting programs to spread the word of the upcoming auditions.

CASTING RESOURCES

UNITED STATES

www.Lacasting.com
www.nowcasting.com
www.actorsaccess.com
www.craigslist.com
www.mandy.com

GREAT BRITAIN

PCR—Production and Casting Report
P.O. Box 11
Broadstairs
London N1 7JZ, UK
Telephone: +44 2075668282
Fax: +44 2075668284
http://www.pcrnewsletter.com/

Spotlight
7 Leicester Place
London WC2H 7RJ, UK
Telephone: +44 2074377631
www.spotlight.com
UK Screen
www.ukscreen.com
Shooting People
www.shootingpeople.org

"Time and Again" Character and Casting Information

MAIN CHARACTERS:

Bobby Jones - Built white male mid-late 20's, escaped prisoner convicted for murder who maintains his innocence.
Awanda - Late 20's early 30's buxom 1950's diner waitress. She knows what she wants and can play men like cards. Has strong sexual presence.
Karl the policeman - 40's white stocky male, small town Sheriff, knows everybody and his very presence keeps the peace.

SUPPORTING CHARACTERS:

Prison Escapees (2) - 30's-40's stocky males (race unimportant), prison convict type
Prison Guards (4) - Men 30's-40's
Teacher - Early 30's pretty white female school teacher
Man in Diner-60's-70's an old timer who probably started eating in the diner when it first opened
Diner Waitress - White female, mid-late 20's high school student?
Policemen (2)- 30's-40's white male
Adam and teenage friends(5) - High School students mixed races and sexes
Young Bobby - 15 year old built white boy, is younger version of Bobby Jones
Bobby's Mother - early 50's white housewife.
Bobby's Father - early 50's white blue collar man

About the Story:

"Time and Again" is the story of convicted murderer Bobby Jones who has the chance to exonerate his name by jumping back ten years earlier to the day before he allegedly committed the murder that sentenced him to a lifetime in prison. Falling in love with the sexy diner waitress Awanda in his old home town, Bobby uncovers the true murderer, only to learn that Awanda is the victim. Framed by the very evidence he left during his relationship with Awanda, the police arrest and convict the innocent 15-year-old Bobby Jones, creating a paradox that will haunt Bobby Jones to his death.

About the Director:

Jason J. Tomaric has directed several productions including television commercials and music videos for clients such as McDonald's and RCA Records. Having recently won five national Telly Awards, Tomaric's most well-known work is the feature-film, "Clone" that premiered in Cleveland's lavish Palace Theatre.

About the Writers:

Written by Jason J. Tomaric and internationally-renowned writer Bob Noll, Bob Noll now teaches script writing at several venues including John Carroll University and the Cleveland Film Society. After working in Los Angeles for several major studios, Bob Noll is the recipient of dozens of international awards and enjoys worldwide publishing success of hundreds of scripts.

The Purpose of this Project:

"Time and Again" is being produced for two purposes: to produce an educational DVD for independent filmmakers to teach the filmmaking process, and to provide content for the international film festival market as a way of increasing the filmmakers' exposure in the industry.

Casting information.

- Get a copy of the local film commission production manual and look up the casting agencies in your area. Oftentimes, these agencies sign on talented actors with little experience, so the agency may be willing to direct those actors to your audition.

The second option is a more precise way of attracting actors, wherein you can search a number of acting web sites that post actor's headshots, resumes, and contact information. Much like a dating web site, filmmakers enter the desired physical traits and a search engine will produce a list of actors who meet the requirements. Contact the actors who fit the characters you're looking to cast and invite them to the audition. Although this is more time consuming, it provides more control over the time you spend auditioning actors.

WORKING WITH CASTING AGENCIES

Casting agencies represent actors and assist filmmakers in finding the right actor for the part, provided the actors will be paid. For a percentage of the actor's wages, the casting agency negotiates terms on the actor's behalf, finds work by soliciting production companies looking to cast, sets up auditions, and negotiates pay wages. Although casting agencies look for paying productions, independent films are a terrific opportunity for new, inexperienced actors to build a demo reel and add credits to the resume, so don't be afraid to contact casting agencies and propose your project to them. The more professional the presentation, the greater the likelihood the agency will assist you with your casting needs.

In addition to contacting casting agencies, contact individual agents who represent actors the same way as an agency. Larger agents will be unwilling to help for free, although there are plenty of smaller agents, especially in major production cities, who may welcome the exposure for their actors.

HOW TO CONDUCT AN AUDITION

The first audition

Auditioning is a nerve-wracking experience for the actor, and it's your job to make them feel as comfortable as possible. The more comfortable the actor, the better the performance, and the better the performance, the more of their skill you will see.

Paula Williams played Martha Jones and, although it was a small role, her few moments of screen time needed to effectively portray a woman capable of murder.

- **Organizing the space.** Set up the audition space in a room with at least an eight-foot table off to one side that you, the producer, the casting director, and any other crew members who want to attend sit behind. Then, in the center of the room, place a chair or a stool for the actor. In the waiting area, station two production assistants who welcome arriving actors and give them audition forms, collect headshots, and schedule audition times if there is a large turnout.

- **Beginning the audition.** When you're ready for the first audition, have one of the production assistants from the waiting area bring the first actor to the audition room. When the actor enters, greet him, take his audition form and headshot, and thank him for coming. Always be polite and courteous; these actors are taking time out of their schedules to come to your audition with the hopes of helping you make your movie. Be appreciative of that.
- **The monolog.** After the introductions, if you require a monolog of the actors, ask the actor to begin and watch for body language and believability. In major cities like Los Angeles and New York, experienced actors rarely, if ever, use monologs for auditions and are accustomed to performing a dry read of the script.
- **The first read.** After about 30 seconds, stop the actor, even if he's not finished with the monolog, and give him a two-page scene from a script other than from the movie you're casting for. Don't use the script from the movie, as this may give the actor you're auditioning a premature idea of the character. Character development should happen between the director and the actor in a rehearsal setting, not the audition. Instead, use a script from another movie with a tone, characters, and dialog similar to those of the film you're casting. Briefly introduce the scene and explain what is happening: "You are playing the role of Joe, who just left his job of 30 years after having found out he's been laid off. This scene takes place in the diner across the street from the factory between Joe and his old friend, Jean, the waitress." After the actor briefly reads over the script, have him perform the scene opposite a reader you brought to the audition who will read for the opposite part. Watch for realism and spontaneity in the performance.

Learn how to approach, cast, and work with local celebrities in the Working with Local Celebrities module at www.powerfilmmaking.com.

- **Give direction.** After the scene is finished, ask the actor to perform the scene again, this time changing the approach to how he plays the scene: "Try it again, but this time, instead of being laid off, you just received a $5000 bonus." Watch carefully to see how well the actor takes last-minute direction, how he changes his approach, and if he successfully incorporates your new direction into the scene. This is an important ability for the actor to have because there are often directorial changes on set and the actor needs to be quick to adjust his performance.
- **Wrap up.** After the second read, thank the actor and, if you feel he may be right for the part, give him a flyer for the callback, or second audition, the following week. Be sure to have the second auditions already scheduled so you can invite actors to it during the first audition. If you don't

like their performance, thank the actor for coming in and politely let him know that you will be notifying him of the audition results. Have a production assistant draft a friendly email and send it to the actors you did not choose. Be sure to thank them for their time, as you may work with them in the future and don't want to burn any bridges.

- **The next actor.** Once the actor leaves, the production assistant from the waiting area should bring in the next person. Each audition should last about five minutes and is designed to sift quickly through the actors into people who could fit a role and the people who couldn't.

Auditions are mentally and physically draining for the director and the casting director. Being prepared will help you make the best choice for each role after the auditions conclude.

- Bring a digital camera to photograph each auditioning actor as a reference in case he or she doesn't have a headshot. This will help you remember what each person looks like after the audition. Attach the photo, headshot, and resume to the audition form. Also consider videotaping each audition if you want to compare one actor against another at a later time.
- If videotaping the auditions, have each actor face the camera and state his or her name before beginning the audition. This will help you keep track of who each actor is.
- Bring several people to help you at the audition. Not only is it helpful to have someone with you in the audition itself, but you will also need people to sign the actors in, coordinate time sheets, answer any questions the actors may have, and escort the actors to the audition room. Remember that the more organized the audition is, the more professional you will appear.
- If you have a large turnout for your audition, consider setting up an appointment schedule so actors don't have to wait for hours before their audition. Scheduling on the hour will not only simplify the process, but will let the actors know that you are running a professional production.
- When auditioning actors and before casting them for a role, look for the following attributes during the audition.
  - **Physical traits**—Do they look the part?
  - **Vocal traits**—Do they sound real and convincing?
  - **Personality**—Are they easy to work with and friendly?
  - **Directability**—Do they respond well to your direction or is there resistance or no change in performance?

Bob Darby had never acted before, but his realistic performance in the auditions helped him land the role of the Sheriff.

Quantus Pictures Audition Form

You are auditioning for a role in a short film tentatively titled "Time and Again." This piece is intended as an educational project and will run the international film festival circuit. Understand that this is a NON-PAYING, NON-UNION production. Please fill out all the questions listed below.

Name ________________________ Age _____ Sex ______ Ht. _____ Wt ______

Address ________________________ Eye Color ________ Hair Color __________

________________________ Phone __________ Pager/Cell/Fax __________

E-Mail Address ________________________

Film/Television Experience ________________________

____

1. We are estimating 7-8 shooting days in July, mostly weekends. Each day would involve roughly 12-16 hours of shooting at various locations in Cleveland. What is your availability?:

Saturdays in July _____
Sundays in July _____
Weekdays in July _____

2. Are you affiliated with an agency or union? ________________________

3. Understanding that, due to budget restrictions, you will not be paid, why are you interested in participating in this production? ________________________

____

FOR OFFICE USE ONLY

About the Film: "Time and Again" is the story of convicted murderer Bobby Jones who has the chance to exonerate his name by jumping back ten years earlier to the day before he allegedly committed the murder that sentenced him to a lifetime in prison. Falling in love with the sexy diner waitress Awanda in his old home town, Bobby uncovers the true murderer, only to learn that Awanda is the victim. Framed by the very evidence he left during his relationship with Awanda, the police arrest and convict the innocent 15-year-old Bobby Jones, creating a paradox that will haunt Bobby Jones to his death.

About the Director: Jason J. Tomaric has directed and produced several productions including television commercials and music videos for clients such as McDonald's and RCA Records. Having recently won five national Telly Awards, Tomaric's most well-known work is the feature-film, "Clone" that premiered in Cleveland's lavish Palace Theatre.

About the Writers: Written by Jason J. Tomaric and internationally-renowned writer Bob Noll, Bob Noll now teaches script writing at several venues including John Carroll University and the Cleveland Film Society. After working in Los Angeles for several major studios, Bob Noll is the recipient of dozens of international awards and enjoys worldwide publishing success of hundreds of scripts.

"Time and Again" audition form 6-6-02

Audition form.

- **Awareness**—Are they aware of and able to adjust their performance based on on-set requirements and changes?
- **Professionalism**—Will they be on time and remain dedicated to the production? Are they reliable?
- **Acting ability**—Can they deliver a convincing performance?
- **Experience**—What have they done before? How can this experience help them play the role in your film?

Monologs

Monologs are an outstanding tool in the audition room for many reasons. First, they separate the wanna-be actors from the more serious actors, as monologs are difficult to prepare and deliver. Often, inexperienced actors will not respond to audition notices that require monologs.

Second, they give the director an opportunity to see the actor perform a piece that she is comfortable with. Watch not only the vocal delivery of the monolog, but also the actor's physical performance. The performance will indicate if the actor is more theatrical and "over-the-top" in her performance or if she understands the nuances of subtle performances, which work better on camera.

Understand that professional, working actors in high-production cities will probably not have monologs prepared. They are used to reading from a script in the audition because their credits and past experience are usually sufficient in proving their acting abilities.

The second audition

The second audition is similar to the first; however, this time you know that the attending actors meet your initial physical requirements of the characters in your film. The setup of the audition space is the same, with actors waiting in the waiting area until it is their time to audition. They are taken, one by one, to the audition room. This time, be sure to set up a video camera to tape the second audition so you can review each actor's performance later before making your final casting decisions.

When the actors arrive, have several scripts ready in the waiting room for them to look over while they wait for their turn. Whereas the first audition is a cold read, this time allow the actors more time to go over the audition scripts to build a character, understand the scene, and even memorize the lines. Avoid using scenes

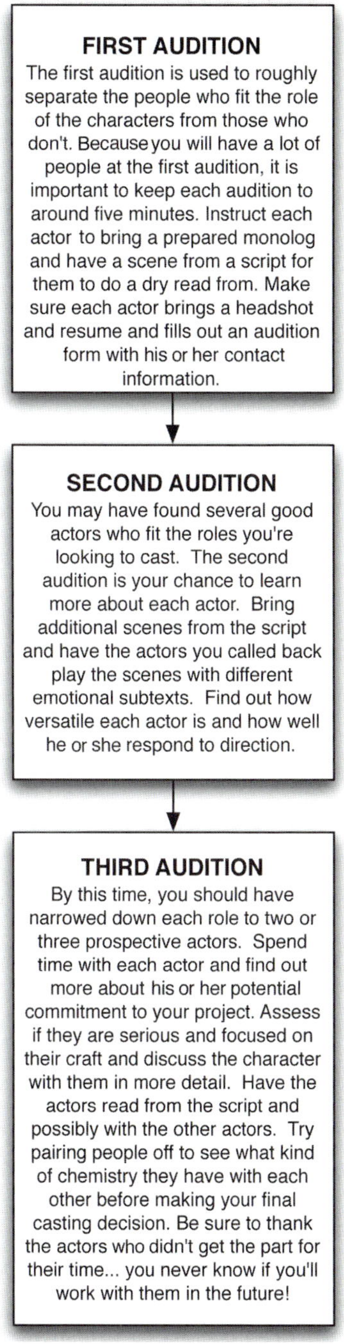

FIRST AUDITION
The first audition is used to roughly separate the people who fit the role of the characters from those who don't. Because you will have a lot of people at the first audition, it is important to keep each audition to around five minutes. Instruct each actor to bring a prepared monolog and have a scene from a script for them to do a dry read from. Make sure each actor brings a headshot and resume and fills out an audition form with his or her contact information.

↓

SECOND AUDITION
You may have found several good actors who fit the roles you're looking to cast. The second audition is your chance to learn more about each actor. Bring additional scenes from the script and have the actors you called back play the scenes with different emotional subtexts. Find out how versatile each actor is and how well he or she respond to direction.

↓

THIRD AUDITION
By this time, you should have narrowed down each role to two or three prospective actors. Spend time with each actor and find out more about his or her potential commitment to your project. Assess if they are serious and focused on their craft and discuss the character with them in more detail. Have the actors read from the script and possibly with the other actors. Try pairing people off to see what kind of chemistry they have with each other before making your final casting decision. Be sure to thank the actors who didn't get the part for their time... you never know if you'll work with them in the future!

Audition flow chart.

We always had fun on the set of *Time and Again.* Casting actors with a positive, fun attitude can help balance the stress of working on set.

from your movie, but choose similar scripts for the actors to read from.

Begin the audition by having the actor perform each scene three different times, prompting him with different emotional subtexts for each performance. Watch for the range of his performance, believability and realism, and, most importantly, how he responds to your direction. Be aware of how the chemistry is shaping between you and the actor. If he is invested in the part and is agreeable to your direction, the relationship should feel very easygoing and kinetic.

If you like the actor and can envision him playing one of the roles, chat with him about why he wants to do the movie, his availability, and what his interests are. Learn more about his personality and what it would be like to work with him for months on set.

Each of the second auditions lasts 10 to 15 minutes and should result in two or three finalists for each main role.

Within a couple of days, call the actors you'd like to see a third time and invite them to the third and final audition.

The third audition

The third audition is the last round, in which you choose the actors for the roles. At this point, you should know the individual capabilities of each actor but not yet the chemistry between actors.

I have a pretty unorthodox approach to the third audition, in which I put all the actors in the same room, pair them up, and have them act out scenes together to see how they relate, who works well with whom, and what the chemistry is like between them.

What's interesting about this approach is that all the actors become much more comfortable with one another and the material so they feel more confident, their personalities come out, and I get a sense of who they are as individuals.

I can immediately tell who will get along with whom, which actors are the scene hogs, the introverts, the sensitive types, the pranksters, and the intellects, and I like to take advantage of this by pairing up different people to see how the dynamics of the scene changes with each actor. This is a great way of casting the lead roles.

By the end of the audition, you should have a pretty good idea of which actors you want to cast. Be sure to thank all the actors and tell them that you will notify them of your final casting decision in a week.

AUDITION WARNING SIGNS

The audition process is a short period of time relative to the length of a film shoot, so selecting the right actor for a role is critical, from both a creative and a professional standpoint.

Use the casting process to find an actor who fits the role, has a good work ethic, is excited about the project, understands the financial limitations, and acknowledges the intense schedule and the need to sacrifice outside activities for the sake of shooting the film. If an actor has even the slightest reservation about any of these points in the audition, no matter how small, then chances are good that these problems will reoccur later in production when it's too late to recast.

Warning signs to look out for during the audition:

- Actors who questions the lack of pay and expresses concern about their financial ability to get involved.
- Experienced actors who patronizes the director, especially if the director is new to filmmaking. This is an immediate warning sign that can develop into a major problem on set. It is difficult for the director to do his job when an actor constantly questions his experience and skill set.
- Actors who question the project's time commitment or mention a job schedule that may be difficult to work around may not show up on set if their boss schedules them to work.
- Actors with no prior experience may seem excited at first, but the time demands and intensity on set may turn them away from the project later.
- Actors who want rewrites of the script before learning and understanding their characters are not interested in the director's vision but their own.
- Actors showing up late to the auditions may be indicative of future behavior.
- Actors who show up to auditions without memorized monologs, headshots, or resumes. Be especially wary of people who arrive "off the street" with only a Polaroid or family picture. They are not professionals.

If you notice any of these warning signs, no matter how subtle, seriously consider casting a different actor. It's better to recast in the audition phase than halfway into production.

When auditioning actors, look for these positive traits:

- Actors with prior acting experience or training who understand the demands of producing a film.
- Actors who are excited about the material and are inquisitive about their character and the storyline.
- Actors who are willing to take time off of work or at least be flexible for the production schedule.
- Actors who are prepared during the audition with memorized monologs, headshots, and resumes. Being prepared for an audition demonstrates that they care about their craft and want to move ahead with their career.

ACTIVITY

Look in local newspaper listings for auditions in your area and go to them to audition. Watch to see how the process works and what the director asks of you. Take what you learned and use these tips on your own audition.

Questions

- How did you feel during the audition and did you receive the information you needed to perform the role?
- What could the director have said to you to make the audition easier for you?
- What importance did each of the audition segments serve and what would you do differently the next time?
- What local resources can you use to cast both actors and extras for your movie?

AFTER THE AUDITIONS

After the third audition is complete and the final contenders have been narrowed down to one actor per role, meet with each actor and discuss the project in greater detail. Explain the production requirements, on-set demands, possibility of shooting pick-up shots even after the film is edited, ADR (Automated Dialogue Replacement), voice-over requirements, and all other expectations before signing the actor deal memo. This is especially important with inexperienced actors and will reduce the likelihood of them dropping out of the project in the middle of production.

Do not call to notify finalists that they did not receive the role until you are 100% positive that the primary choice for each role will work out. Once you are confident, be sure to call each finalist and thank them for their time.

After you congratulate each actor on winning the role, supply a packet that includes a letter of introduction and welcome, a production schedule, an actor deal memo, a rehearsal schedule, a character description, and a list of contact numbers for key crew people.

Schedule the first rehearsal and script readthrough within the first week following the final audition.

Quantus Pictures Inc.

Motion Picture Production Company

June 10, 2002

To the cast of "Time and Again"

Dear Sirs and Madams,

Congratulations on winning your role in the short film tentatively titled, "Time and Again." I thank you most sincerely for your interest and willingness to work on this project and hope that this will be a mutually-beneficial venture for everyone involved. The purpose of this project is twofold: practice our art form so as to improve our story-telling abilities as director, actors and crew members and to create a piece to run the worldwide film festival circuit in an effort to circulate our work in the mainstream.

My team and I pride ourselves on crafting top-quality productions in a time-conscious and budget-sensitive manner. We respect your time as much as your talent and will maximize our efforts in the allotted time. Therefore, by the end of June when I return from my trip, we will have a final call sheet and shot breakdown for you. Our goal is always to minimize the on-set surprises by properly preparing every detail beforehand.

Enclosed, please find a copy of the shooting script as well as an Actor Deal Memo. This legal document is a standard form that acknowledges our working relationship on this project. If you should have any questions about this form, do not hesitate to contact me. If you agree to all the terms, please sign it and return it to the address on the letterhead. Be sure to make a copy for yourself.

Please plan on a cast meeting on Saturday, June 29, 2002 in the evening. I will contact you about a location when I return. The purpose of this meeting is to read through the script, discuss the characters, plan on the look and feel of the project, discuss schedules, shooting dates and times, and how our sets operate. This is a critical meeting that everyone is strongly requested to be in attendance.

Although there is written dialogue, the success of "Time and Again" will come from your characterizations through the dialogue. MEMORIZE your lines and know them well. Then we can play with delivery and create some memorable moments.

Thank you again for your participation and I am honored and very excited about working with you. Happy reading and feel free to call me at any time if you have any questions.

Most sincerely,

Jason J. Tomaric
director

Once I cast each character, I sent this letter to the actors along with a copy of the script, a rough shooting schedule and an actor deal memo.

Quantus Pictures Inc.

Motion Picture Production Company

ACTOR DEAL MEMO

THIS AGREEMENT is made and entered into as of the _______th day of ________, 2003, by and between Quantus Pictures, Inc. (herein referred to as the Producer), and ____________________________________ (herein referred to as the Player).

Producer intends to produce the project tentatively titled, "______________________________________" (herein referred to as the Production) and wishes to utilize the services of the Player in connection with the Production upon the terms and conditions herein contained.

1. PHOTOPLAY, ROLE, SALARY AND GUARANTEE: Producer hereby engages Player to render services as such in the role of ______________________________ in the screenplay, at a salary of $0.00 dollars per day. Player accepts such engagement upon the terms herein specified.

2. TERM: The term of employment hereunder shall begin on or about _________________________ (the "Start Date") and continue until _____________________________, or until the completion of the photography and recording of said role. Producer reserves the right to discharge the Performer at any time.

3. NON-UNION: The Performer acknowledges that he/she is not affiliated with any union that could conflict with the terms of this contract. Performer understands that Production is a strictly non-union project.

In accordance with the Immigration Reform and Control Act of 1986, any offer of employment is conditioned upon satisfactory proof of applicant's identity and legal ability to work in the United States.

In assigning these rights, the Performer grants to the Producer and its successors, assigns, and licensees the full and irrevocable right to produce, copy, distribute, exhibit, and transmit the Performer's voice, image, shadow, silhouette, and likeness in connection with the Production by means of broadcast or cablecast, videotape, film, or any similar electronic or mechanical method of present or future use and innovation.

The Performer acknowledges that any picture or recording taken of the Performer under the terms of the license becomes the sole and exclusive property of the Producer in perpetuity. The Performer and the Performer's heirs and assigns shall have no right to bring legal action against the Producer for any use of the pictures or recordings, regardless of whether such use is claimed to be defamatory or censorable in nature.

The Performer further acknowledges that the Producer shall have the right to use the Performer's name, portrait, picture, voice, and biographical information to promote or publicize the Production and to authorize others to do the same. However, nothing shall require the Producer to use the Performer's name, voice, or likeness in any of the manners described in this license or to exercise any of the rights set forth herein.

(continued)

Actor deal memo page 1.

Quantus Pictures Inc.

Motion Picture Production Company

(page 2 of 2)

The Performer warrants and represents that he or she is free to enter into this license and this agreement does not conflict with any existing contracts or agreements to which the Performer is a party. The Performer agrees to hold the Producer and any third parties harmless from and against any and all claims, liabilities, losses or damages that may arise from the use of the Performer's voice or image in the Production.

The Performer relieves and indemnifies Producer, its owners, employees, officers, agents, licensees, heirs, and assigns from any and all liability for any injuries or damage caused the Performer or to other persons or property during the period of association with the Production. In the event that the Performer is responsible for damage to person, property, or equipment, the Performer will remunerate costs of repair or replacement (at the discretion of Producer) within a period of thirty days following the incident.

It is agreed that the foregoing grant of rights is made for promotional consideration only, and the Producer's exercise of the grant of rights shall be deemed full consideration for such grant.

AGREED AND ACCEPTED:

Performer ______________________________ Date ______________

Address ____

____

Social Security Number ____________________________

Phone Number ______________________________________

Producer ______________________________ Date ______________

Actor deal memo page 2.

CHAPTER 8

The Crew

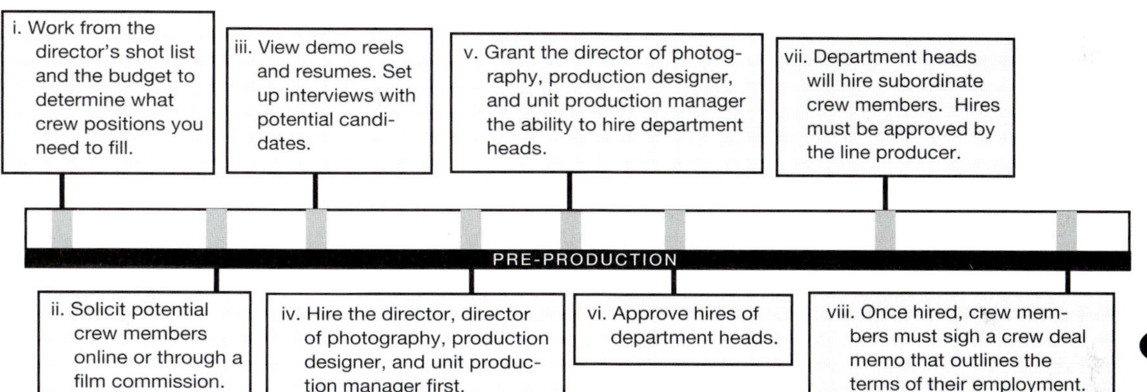

i. Work from the director's shot list and the budget to determine what crew positions you need to fill.
ii. Solicit potential crew members online or through a film commission.
iii. View demo reels and resumes. Set up interviews with potential candidates.
iv. Hire the director, director of photography, production designer, and unit production manager first.
v. Grant the director of photography, production designer, and unit production manager the ability to hire department heads.
vi. Approve hires of department heads.
vii. Department heads will hire subordinate crew members. Hires must be approved by the line producer.
viii. Once hired, crew members must sigh a crew deal memo that outlines the terms of their employment.
PRE-PRODUCTION

INTRODUCTION

From cinematographers, boom operators, costume designers, and production designers to property masters, hairstylists, grips, and assistant directors, there are many creative people involved in providing the technical and creative support a director needs to realize his vision.

Although the number of people listed in the credits of a Hollywood movie may seem extreme, each crew position is essential in the moviemaking process.

CREW POSITIONS

A movie crew comprises numerous departments, with each department having its own staff. The number of people within each department is dependent upon the complexity of the production and the size of the budget. For example, a period film is going to require a bigger art department than a present-day romantic comedy.

Listed here are the main crew positions in a Hollywood movie shoot. Although it might not seem like it, even small independent productions can benefit from

The cast and crew of *Time and Again* was made up of both experienced and inexperienced people, all of whom volunteered their time and talents.

having a similar crew setup. Take a look at the crew graphs later in this chapter for a better idea of what crew positions you really need on your set.

The producers

- The **executive producer** oversees the entire production, sometimes multiple productions, but is not involved in the daily operations of the film, deferring those duties instead to the producer. The executive producer is typically the financier of the production, providing most, if not all, of the funding. Often, the executive producer has distribution ties or can actually be the distributor. Executive producers are usually the general partner of a limited partnership whose role is to raise financing for the project. The ideal executive producer is a businessperson who recognizes good commercial material and has an understanding of how to package and sell it.
- The **producer** is responsible for finding a script, attaching a director and actors, securing financing, coordinating the hiring of cast and crew, supervising the production and postproduction processes, and assisting with the sales and distribution of the film. The producer is in charge of all business components of the production. In the independent film arena, the director may actually hire the producer to manage the business duties of the production.
- The **associate producer** is an associate to the producer who is able to bring some resource, be it financial or technical asset, to the film. In recent years, however, this title has been diminished, as the "associate producer" credit is handed to people who may not actually fulfill the duties of a producer, being used as a bargaining tool at the negotiating table.
- The **line producer** is responsible for the daily operations of the film production and approves any and all expenditures for locations, cast, and crew. Whereas the producer handles the overall production, the line producer is in charge of daily tasks, working closely with the unit production manager, first assistant director, director, art director, editor, and composer to prepare the production budget and shooting schedule. The line producer is aware of local resources and knows the below-the-line personnel in a region and can manage these resources to ensure a cost-effective, timely production. The line producer is the ultimate liaison between the production team and the producers.

The production department

- The **director**—In independent movies, the producer/writer is, more often than not, the director. If this is not the case, finding the right director for a project is of key importance. The director is responsible for translating the script to the screen by working with actors to achieve the ideal performance. The director collaborates with creative departments to build a convincing world in which the action takes place. The producer often brings on the director early and, while the production manager hires the majority of the below-the-line crew members, the director usually selects the key creative personnel. The director is also involved in every aspect of the filmmaking process, from casting actors and choosing locations to working with editors, composers, and digital effects houses. Directors can also be writers and producers on the same production.

- The **production manager**, also known as the unit production manager (UPM), is in charge of the daily details of planning and managing the business side of the production. The production manager prepares the budget, may work out the preliminary shooting schedule with the first assistant director, negotiates with and hires the below-the-line crew, and works with locations by organizing the scouting of, traveling to, and securing permissions from the location before giving these responsibilities over to the location manager. The production manager is responsible for ensuring that the production runs as smoothly and efficiently as possible, staying on schedule and on budget. The production manager also helps manage the daily budget by managing salaries, equipment rental, and other production costs. Even though the department heads can choose the crew positions below them, all hires and rates must be approved by the UPM.
- The **production coordinator** is in charge of booking all personnel and equipment. From cast to crew, equipment, and transportation, the production coordinator ensures that equipment and materials are at the right place at the right time, that crew members are in place and have all the necessary materials to perform their jobs, and that the actors have their contracts and are on set.
- The **assistant director** (or 1st AD) is not so much the assistant to the director as he or she is in charge of running the set, much like a stage manager's duty in theatre. The 1st AD's primary duties include creating the shooting schedule, coordinating the crew departments on set, ensuring the production remains on schedule, scheduling locations and actors, scheduling the day's shooting, serving as a buffer for the director, and solving on-set logistical problems so the director can work with the actors. The 1st AD is also in charge of directing extras, freeing the director to focus on the principal actors. The director and director of photography are the only positions that supersede the 1st AD's authority on set.
- The **second assistant director** assists the 1st AD with preproduction and production tasks, signing actors in and out as they arrive and depart each day, completing on-set paperwork, and managing production assistants.
- The **script supervisor** is in charge of the continuity of each scene and logs dialog spoken, number and duration of takes, lenses and filters used, actor's movements, camera coverage, and positions of props and set pieces so that scenes and shots can be perfectly reproduced.

- The **casting director** is responsible for finding, auditioning, and ultimately, with the producer's and director's approval, casting the actors and extras for a film.
- The **production assistants** are the runners and general assistants, both in the production office and on set. They are responsible for assisting in whatever matters are asked of them, including making copies, running errands, getting coffee, keeping the public away from the film set, standing in for an actor, and transporting actors to and from set.
- The **location manager** is responsible for coordinating the use of a location with its owners; coordinating logistics between all departments to ensure the location meets all production needs; working with local officials to secure permits and approvals; securing parking, changing rooms, restroom facilities, and other support services; and making sure the location is in clean, working condition before the film crew leaves.
- The **location scout** is responsible for finding locations that meet the director's vision and production requirements. The director and his creative team assemble lists of possible locations, and the scout will travel to these locations and photograph and videotape each one, bringing the photos back to the director for consideration.
- **Craft services** provides noncatered food and beverage services on set. Craft services usually maintains a table with snacks and beverages during each day of production.
- A **stand-in** is a person who bears a resemblance to the actor in height, skin, and hair color and who replaces the actor while the director and director of photography light and set up the shot, so as not to fatigue the actual actor. Once the technical setup has been completed, the real actor is brought on set for final lighting tweaks.
- The **still photographer** takes behind-the-scenes photos of the production, cast, and crew for use in press kits, marketing materials, and DVD features.
- The **storyboard artist** works closely with the director and production designer to map their ideas into rough drawings called storyboards that help the creative team previsualize the film, either on paper or using storyboarding software.
- **Talent agents** represent actors, voice artists, and models in an effort to generate work for them on film, television, radio, or print projects.

The director of photography (DP) and the camera crew

The DP is responsible for the photographic look of the movie image through use of light and the lens. In charge of the camera and lighting departments, the director of photography works closely with the director to achieve a cinematic feel that supports the director's vision. The director of photography is also known as a cinematographer. The director of photography gives the gaffer lighting instructions and the key grip rigging instructions and tells the camera crew where to set up the camera equipment.

In choosing a DP for a project, avoid hiring a film school graduate, but rather an experienced DP who has worked his way up through the ranks. In the Hollywood system, many film school graduates begin their careers by working in a camera rental facility sweeping floors, driving trucks, and trying to make connections with cinematographers as they come in to rent cameras for real productions. If they are successful in making a good contact, they may get a job as a second assistant camera (2nd AC) on a feature. The 2nd AC is in charge of loading the film, maintaining camera logs, and marking each shot with the clapboard. After working on a few dozen features as a 2nd AC, he will be able to move his way up to a 1st AC. Responsible for pulling focus and setting up, maintaining, and moving the camera, the 1st AC will work in this capacity for several dozen films until she graduates to the camera operator position. The camera operator operates the camera and will work in this capacity for several movies until he is asked to DP a film. This is the standard path most people take toward working as a director of photography.

The crew of *Time and Again* waits for the next take outside Awanda's trailer.

Film school graduates lack this practical experience, especially when shooting 35mm film. With film being the largest expense on a shoot, few producers are willing to risk bringing an inexperienced DP on set, especially with a first-time director.

The DP is the single most important asset to the director, especially an inexperienced director. By assisting the director with choices of camera placement and even blocking, an experienced DP will help shoot footage that will edit together well and shoot enough coverage for the editor to have choices in the editing room.

If shooting a three-week feature film, the DP should be paid between $2000 and $3000 a week, with several days allotted for preproduction to allow for location scouting and prep work.

The director of photography's salary can be based upon a weekly rate that she charges the production, or the production may pay her a set rate that may be lower. Another factor that influences the DP's rate is whether she brings her own equipment to the set. Camera and lighting gear may be part of the DP's package, which will increase her rate. It is common for the DP to be part of the creative team, at which point he may receive deferred payment or a reduced pay scale. However, the DP is often the highest-paid crew member on the set.

If you are shooting an independent film, ask the DP to hire the rest of the camera crew and give him a budget to do so. Usually a DP will have crew members he enjoys working with and trusts and will appreciate the opportunity to bring his colleagues onboard. The DP should hire:

Camera operator
First assistant camera
Second assistant camera
Gaffer (the gaffer can suggest electricians and the generator operator)
Key grip (the key grip can suggest grips and the dolly grip)

Even though the DP can select the camera crew, the unit production manager must approve all hires.

The director of photography coordinates the photographic operations of the movie with three department heads, the camera operator, who heads the camera department; the gaffer, who heads the lighting/electric department; and the key grip, who heads the grip department. Each of these department heads manages the crew in their department and relays orders from the DP to these crew members.

The members of the camera department include the following:

- The **camera operator** runs the camera during shooting. In many instances, especially on low-budget films, the director of photography operates the camera. The camera operator is the highest position in the camera department and is responsible for relaying orders from the DP to the rest of the camera crew. Always present with the DP when the director is blocking a scene and giving direction, the camera operator will coordinate the camera placement with the 1st AC.
- The **assistant camera** is responsible for setting up, maintaining, cleaning, and repackaging the camera and camera accessories, including lenses, magazines, eyepieces, filters, and other camera parts. In addition, the 1st AC will set and pull focus for each shot.
- The **2nd AC** is responsible for loading the unexposed film stock in the magazines, threading film through the camera, marking each shot with the clapboard, and maintaining camera logs. The director of photography will typically hire the 1st and 2nd ACs.
- The **video assist** sets up and operates a video feed from the camera that is recorded and can be played back per the director's request.

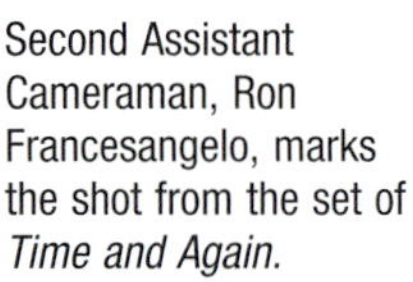
Second Assistant Cameraman, Ron Francesangelo, marks the shot from the set of *Time and Again*.

The grip department

- The **key grip** is the department head and is in charge of all grips. The key grip supervises the setup, moving, adjustment, and teardown of chromakey screens, lighting and camera support equipment (C-stands, flags, nets, silks, reflectors, and so on), creature comforts (dressing rooms, craft services tables, tents, and so on), operating dollies and cranes, and pulling cables on set. The key grip answers to the director of photography and issues orders to the best boy grip.

- The **best boy grip** is the main assistant to the key grip and usually remains on the grip truck to prepare and issue equipment to the other grips.
- The **dolly grip** is responsible for setting up the camera dolly and dolly track as well as operating the dolly during a take. In larger productions, the dolly grip answers to the camera crew, although she may play double duty between the camera and the grip departments.
- **Grips** are responsible for moving, setting up, and tearing down camera support and light equipment. They are the movers on the set and do much of the carrying, lifting, and rigging.

Visit the Crew module at www.powerfilmmaking.com and learn specific duties of each position from Hollywood crew members.

The electric department

- The **gaffer** is the chief electrician on the set and is responsible for rigging the lighting per the director of photography's request. The gaffer supervises the electrical

The dolly grip tests the track on the set of *Time and Again.*

crew and answers to the director of photography. The gaffer is an expert at lighting and sometimes plays a more creative role, if permitted by the director of photography.

- The **best boy electric** is the primary assistant to the gaffer and works on the grip truck, preparing, maintaining, and repairing equipment.
- The **electrician** is responsible for rigging, wiring, and plugging in electrical cables and answers to the best boy and the gaffer.
- The **generator operator** is responsible for the transportation, maintenance, and operation of the generator on set.

The art department

The **production designer** is responsible for designing the overall look of the world in which the story takes place, including the look of the sets, props, and costumes. The production designer works closely with the director and is involved early on in the preproduction process, developing drawings, plans, and models around the director's storyboards. Often working with a large budget, production designers have many responsibilities to the producer and work closely with the director of photography and costume designer to ensure that all departments create a compatible look for the film.

When shooting an independent movie, look for a production designer with experience on a number of features. Experienced production designers also have numerous contacts in the industry and will be able to help identify and locate art elements at a discount or for free.

Ask the production designer to hire the following crew positions:

- **Art director**—The art director works under the production designer and supervises the art department crew, coordinating the implementation of the production design.
- **Set designer**—This is the lead architect who drafts tangible blueprints and designs of the sets based on the direction and guidance of the production designer.
- **Assistant art director**—There can be several assistants to the art director based on the complexity and work involved. Assistant art directors are responsible for daily duties, including measuring set spaces, assisting in set design, and serving any of the art director's needs.
- The **set decorator** works under the production designer or art director and is responsible for coordinating the furnishings on set that are not touched by the actors. The set decorator researches, acquires, places, and then strikes any artistic element that helps improve the look and design of the sets.
- The **buyer**—Working directly under the set decorator, the buyer is responsible for finding, buying, and renting set-dressing elements.
- The **lead man** is the foreman of the set decorating crew.
- The **set dresser** works on set and physically dresses, alters, updates, maintains, and removes the set dressing. Set dressers are responsible for any creative elements on a set, from doorknobs and windowpanes to furniture

and drapery. Although most of the set dressing work is done prior to shooting, an on-set dresser remains on set should any changes be required.

- **Key scenic**—This person is responsible for all set surfaces, from wood and marble to stone. The key scenic works closely with the production designer and oversees a team of painters to create the exact look of each set.
- The **construction coordinator** oversees the construction of set pieces, orders materials, schedules tradesmen, and manages the construction crew.
- The **head carpenter** is the foreman in charge of the carpenters.
- The **greensman** is responsible for setting and dressing any plants, trees, and foliage, both real and fake. The greensman usually works for the set decorator except in productions in which greens are an integral aspect of the set, in which case he reports directly to the production designer.

Hairstylist Deb Lilly begins transforming Jennie Allen into Awanda.

The prop department

- The **property master** is in charge of identifying, acquiring, and maintaining all props used in the film. Props are handled by the actors and fall under the control of the property master. Elements not handled by the actors are considered set dressing and fall under the responsibility of the set decorator.
- The **props builder** designs and builds original props for the movie.
- The **armorer** works exclusively with firearms and weaponry and has the necessary licenses to do so.

The hair and makeup department

- The **hairstylist** creates and maintains the actors' hairstyle on set. From working with the actors' natural hair to employing wigs, the hairstylist will style the actors' hair at the beginning of the day and be on set to touch it up between takes. There may be several hairstylists on set depending upon the number of actors and the complexity of the hairstyles in the film.
- The **makeup artist** is responsible for maintaining the cosmetic look of the actors. With duties ranging from applying the initial makeup at the beginning of the day to touching up the makeup between takes, makeup artists can create everything from realistic, natural looks to special effects makeup such as blood or wounds or prosthetics using foam latex, rubber, or bald caps.

The wardrobe department

- The **costume designer** designs and oversees the creation of the costumes, working closely with the director to create a look that matches his vision of the story.

- The **wardrobe supervisor** is responsible for maintaining the costumes and accessories for the actors and extras. Working closely with the costume designer, the wardrobe supervisor ensures that wardrobe is ready, prepped, and cleaned for the actors each day and that continuity is maintained from scene to scene by taking Polaroid photos of the actors.
- The **costume standby**—Always present on set, the costume standby is responsible for helping dress the actors if necessary and maintaining the continuous look of the actors' costumes from take to take by tweaking and adjusting as necessary.
- The **art finisher**—When wardrobe needs to be worn, torn, or altered, the art finisher comes in to distress new garments.
- The **buyer** locates and purchases fabric and material for costumes.

The audio department

- The **production sound mixer** is responsible for setting, monitoring, and recording the audio on set. She is responsible for choosing and placing the proper microphones, monitoring the sound levels during a take, and coordinating with the camera and lighting crews to ensure the microphone is out of the frame and not casting shadows. She will notify the director of any problems with the audio during a take, such as background noise or poor audio levels.
- The **boom operator** places the microphone in the optimal position over the actors without breaching the camera frame or casting a shadow on the actors or set.

The stunts/special effects department

- **Special effects** is responsible for all mechanical and/or physical effects that occur on set, such as glass breaking, furniture breaking, weather effects, and gags.
- **Stunt coordinators** create, rig, and execute the stunts for a scene, ensuring maximum safety while creating spectacular stunts.
- The **stunt people** replace actors for any shots that require potentially dangerous physical actions. Stunts include everything from freefalls, fights, running, and trips to car stunts, including any activity that could potentially cause injury.
- The **pyrotechnician**—Licensed and experienced in explosives, Pyrotechnicians are responsible for building, rigging, detonating, and securing explosions, gunshots, sparks, and any chemical-based reaction that causes an explosive effect. Pyrotechnicians need to be state and federally licensed.

The transportation department

- The **transportation captain** is responsible for getting the cast and crew to the location as well as vehicle movement and parking. All drivers report to the transportation captain.
- **Drivers** transport talent and key crew members to and from the set.

Postproduction

Sound Designer Mike Farona mixes the audio at the Neon Cactus Studio.

- The **composer** will write the score for the film, using a live orchestra or a MIDI computer setup. Working closely with the director, the composer is usually the last person to work on the film and has a strong understanding of music styles, instrumentation, and composition.
- The **editor** is responsible for taking the rough footage shot on set and assembling it into a linear, sensible story. Editors, while not on set, can provide an objective viewpoint for the director, ensuring that the film is well paced and makes sense.
- The **sound designer** is responsible for editing the soundtrack for a movie. In the independent world the sound designer can also record ADR and Foley and mix the final soundtrack of the movie.
- The **Foley artist** is a sound effects artist who is responsible for recreating and recording the normal, everyday sounds in a scene, such as footsteps, clothing movement, doors opening and closing, items being picked up or handled, and any sounds an actor would make when interacting with the environment.
- The **animator/compositor** is a digital effects artist who can either create or supplement existing footage with 2D or 3D animation or composites to accentuate the look of the movie. Often working on shots immediately after they are shot, animators are involved in the creative process from the beginning, helping to ensure that footage to be altered is properly shot.

HOW TO HIRE THE CREW

It's easy to get overwhelmed by the long list of crew members that need to be hired for a production. Instead of worrying about each position, hire the department heads, give them a budget and the freedom to hire the rest of their crew.

As the producer, the four positions that are necessary to hire are:

Director
Director of photography
Production designer
Unit production manager

Crew structures

If you've ever watched the closing credits of a Hollywood movie, the seemingly endless list of people who worked on the film may seem like overkill, but in reality, the logistics and demands of a large production require each one of the artists, technicians, and coordinators.

To get an idea of the complexity of a Hollywood production, here's a simplified structure of an average-sized Hollywood crew.

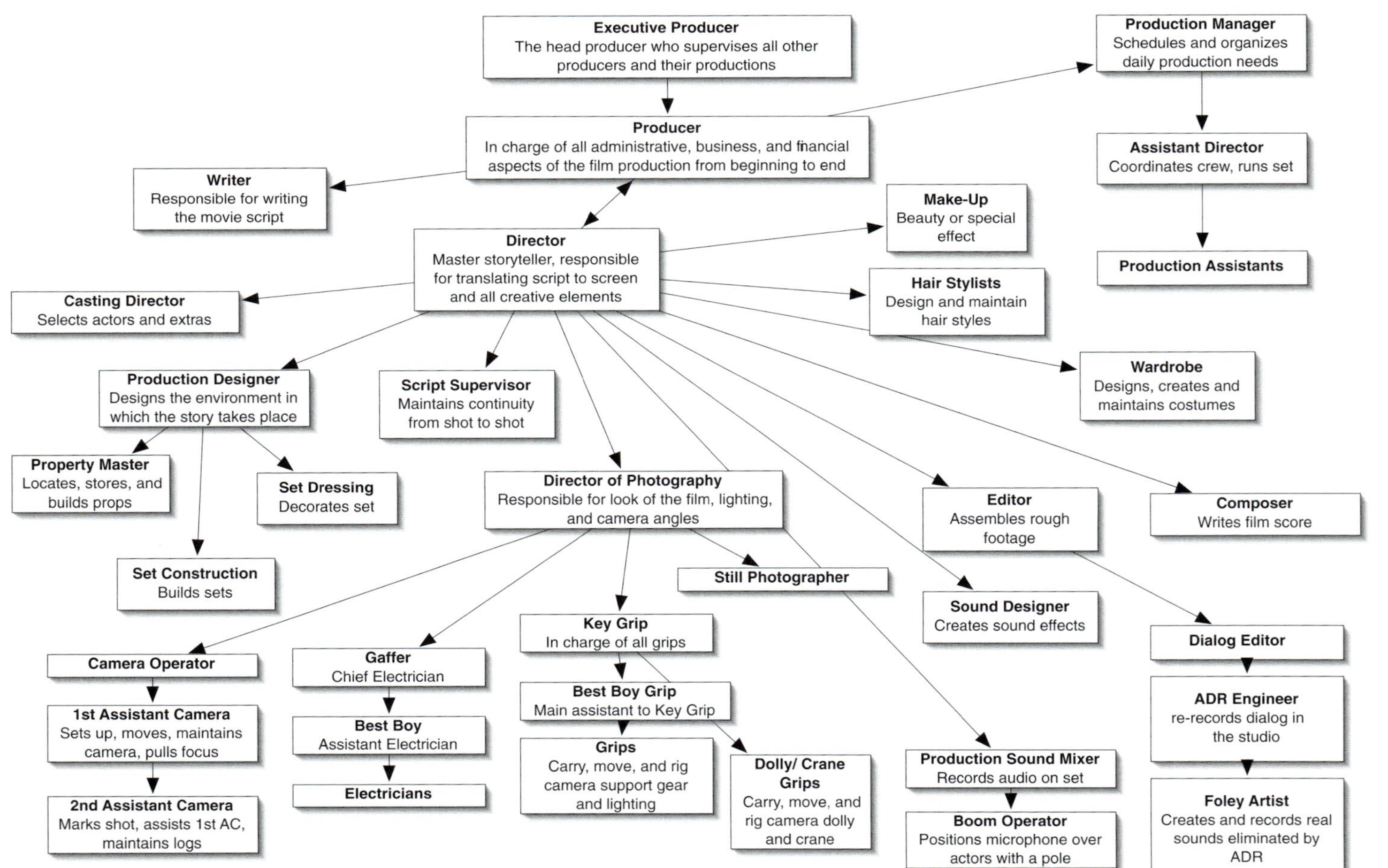

Traditional Hollywood crew structure.

In an independent film, elaborate Hollywood crews are not only unnecessary, but unaffordable. As an indie filmmaker, who do you really need to have on set? If you could compile a wish list for your productions as they grow in size and complexity, what positions do you need and which ones can you do without?

The ultrasmall crew structure

This crew structure is the most basic and is ideal for small scenes involving one or two actors in a location that doesn't require significant lighting and needs virtually no major props, wardrobe, hairstyling, or makeup. This ultrasmall crew can be very fast and mobile, but when taking on larger scenes, can become quickly overwhelmed.

The cost of hiring an ultrasmall crew is around $675/day, provided you're hiring crew members new to film, out-of-work professionals, or crew members looking to work in another position. These rates are based on a low-budget, nonunion production. The cost of hiring professionals may be significantly higher, so remember that productions this small may be better served with aspiring filmmakers and film students to keep costs low.

Producer, writer, director—$0. This person is probably you.
Director of photography—$300/day.
Grips (two)—$125 × 2 = $250/day.
Boom operator—$125/day.

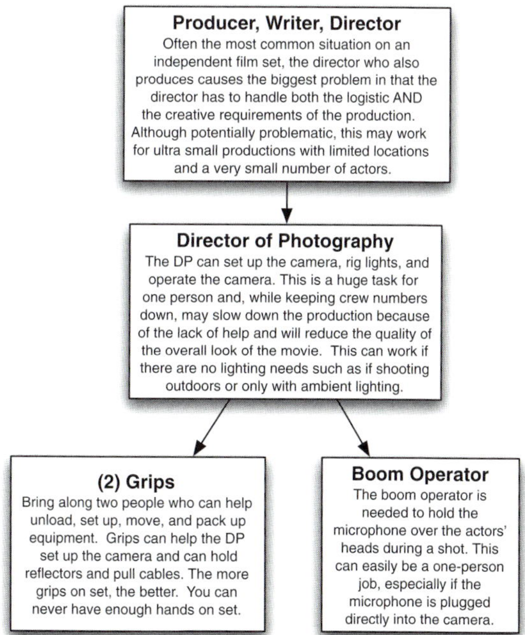

Producer, Writer, Director
Often the most common situation on an independent film set, the director who also produces causes the biggest problem in that the director has to handle both the logistic AND the creative requirements of the production. Although potentially problematic, this may work for ultra small productions with limited locations and a very small number of actors.
Director of Photography
The DP can set up the camera, rig lights, and operate the camera. This is a huge task for one person and, while keeping crew numbers down, may slow down the production because of the lack of help and will reduce the quality of the overall look of the movie. This can work if there are no lighting needs such as if shooting outdoors or only with ambient lighting.
(2) Grips
Bring along two people who can help unload, set up, move, and pack up equipment. Grips can help the DP set up the camera and can hold reflectors and pull cables. The more grips on set, the better. You can never have enough hands on set.
Boom Operator
The boom operator is needed to hold the microphone over the actors' heads during a shot. This can easily be a one-person job, especially if the microphone is plugged directly into the camera.

The Ultra Small Crew Structure.

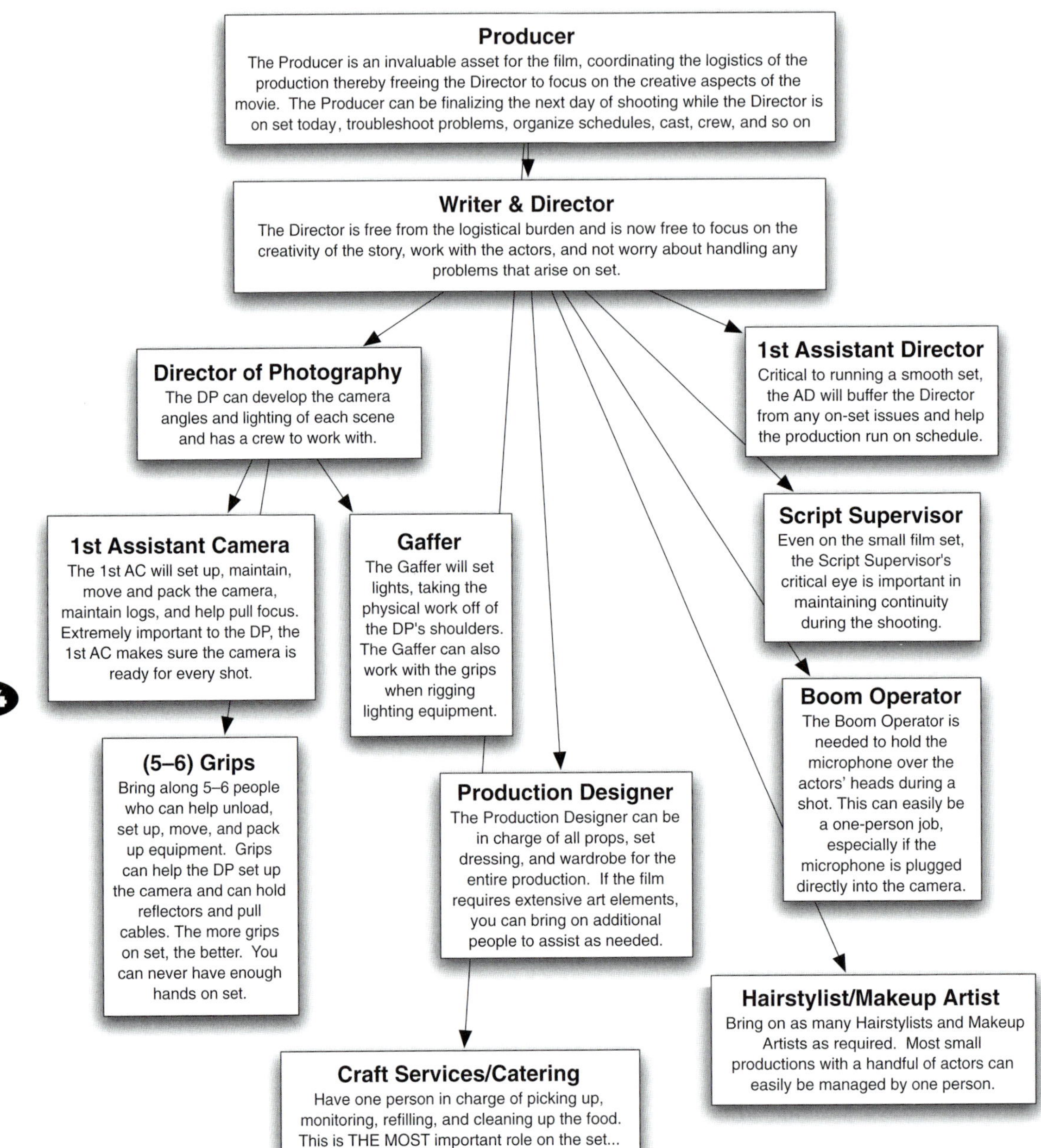

Producer
The Producer is an invaluable asset for the film, coordinating the logistics of the production thereby freeing the Director to focus on the creative aspects of the movie. The Producer can be finalizing the next day of shooting while the Director is on set today, troubleshoot problems, organize schedules, cast, crew, and so on
Writer & Director
The Director is free from the logistical burden and is now free to focus on the creativity of the story, work with the actors, and not worry about handling any problems that arise on set.
Director of Photography
The DP can develop the camera angles and lighting of each scene and has a crew to work with.
1st Assistant Director
Critical to running a smooth set, the AD will buffer the Director from any on-set issues and help the production run on schedule.
1st Assistant Camera
The 1st AC will set up, maintain, move and pack the camera, maintain logs, and help pull focus. Extremely important to the DP, the 1st AC makes sure the camera is ready for every shot.
Gaffer
The Gaffer will set lights, taking the physical work off of the DP's shoulders. The Gaffer can also work with the grips when rigging lighting equipment.
Script Supervisor
Even on the small film set, the Script Supervisor's critical eye is important in maintaining continuity during the shooting.
Boom Operator
The Boom Operator is needed to hold the microphone over the actors' heads during a shot. This can easily be a one-person job, especially if the microphone is plugged directly into the camera.
(5–6) Grips
Bring along 5–6 people who can help unload, set up, move, and pack up equipment. Grips can help the DP set up the camera and can hold reflectors and pull cables. The more grips on set, the better. You can never have enough hands on set.
Production Designer
The Production Designer can be in charge of all props, set dressing, and wardrobe for the entire production. If the film requires extensive art elements, you can bring on additional people to assist as needed.
Hairstylist/Makeup Artist
Bring on as many Hairstylists and Makeup Artists as required. Most small productions with a handful of actors can easily be managed by one person.
Craft Services/Catering
Have one person in charge of picking up, monitoring, refilling, and cleaning up the food. This is THE MOST important role on the set... don't believe me? Ask any crew member.

The Basic Crew Structure.

The basic crew structure

The basic crew has the basic crew departments, often run by only one person, but is structured so that each major component of the production is addressed. Although it seems like a lot of people, this 15-person crew is an ideal size for small- to medium-sized productions. The number of bodies on set is low, but no one department is overwhelmed. Most independent films with a modest budget should try to build this type of crew.

The average cost of the basic crew is approximately $2100 per day.

Producer—variable, negotiate this price.
Director—$0. This person is probably you.
First assistant director—$200/day.
Director of photography—$300/day.
First assistant camera—$150/day.
Script supervisor—$175/day.
Gaffer—$200/day.
Grips (four)—$125 × 4 = $500/day.
Production designer—$175/day.
Boom operator—$125/day.
Hairstylist/makeup artist—$150/day.
Craft services—$125/day.

FINDING QUALIFIED CREW MEMBERS

When beginning a new movie, having a strong crew is critical to a smooth-running production. Avoid the temptation of doing everything yourself. You'll get burned out and won't turn out quality work. Instead, surround yourself with people who know their individual responsibilities, are professional, have experience, and have a strong work ethic. Finding crew members is as easy as looking at your local resources:

- **Film school graduates.** Use the phone book to find local film schools or colleges that have a communications program. They may be willing to let you speak with a class, contact local graduates, or otherwise solicit students to work on your crew. The benefit to using film school students or graduates is their hunger to learn and willingness to work for free and shoot for long hours. The drawback is their lack of experience. Film students are a terrific asset as production assistants or grips (only if they know how to use professional production equipment), but should never be employed in key positions. Also beware the "Film School Attitude," which is the tendency to think that they know better than anyone else on set.
- **Internet.** Posting crew calls on web sites like www.craigslist.org, www.mandy.com, and www.productionhub.com is a great way of reaching potential crew members, especially in large cities. Craft a professional posting that describes the production, the dates, and approximate rates. A good online post will read:

A feature film being shot in Chicago in July is hiring the following crew positions:

- Gaffer
- Grip
- Etc.

Production will span 14 days and 3 nights, will be fully catered, and will be paying. If interested, please email your resume, link to an online demo reel, and your contact information. Our production office will be in contact with you within the week. Thank you for your interest.

- **Film commission.** Contact the local film commission and ask for a copy of their production directory. This directory includes the names, credits, and contact information for most below-the-line crew members, equipment vendors, stages, postproduction facilities, and rental facilities in the state. The people in the directory range from recent film school graduates to experienced production personnel. Don't be afraid to call them and ask if they are interested in working on the movie. Even if they aren't available, they may be able to refer you to someone else in the area.
- **Film festivals.** Attending local film festivals is a great way of networking with other independent filmmakers. Be sure to bring plenty of business cards. After screening a movie seek out any crew members in attendance. Many of these people are willing to work for low or deferred payment just for the experience.

When hiring creative positions, ask to see a demo reel of past projects the person worked on, as well as a resume that lists all past projects, awards, film festival credits, and educational experience.

Demo reel: When looking at this collective sample of a candidate's work, look only at what his or her contributions were, not at elements out of his or her control. For example, if you're looking to hire a cinematographer, look at the quality of the camera work and the lighting, but don't let bad sound or bad acting affect your decision. When looking at the quality of work on the reel, think about whether you'd be happy with that quality on your movie.

References: Ask for references from past producers and directors with whom this person has worked. Ask about his or her work ethic, attitude, and involvement in the film.

Interview: Finally, meet with the candidate and talk about the film and what you're willing to offer in exchange for his or her services, and generally get a feeling about his or her personality. Remember that, much like auditioning actors, you have only a few short meetings to determine if you want to spend hours working in a stressed environment with this person.

Above all, remember that the candidate is also interviewing you, trying to determine the type of working relationship he or she will experience, how organized you are, how passionate you are about the project, and your attitude. Good teamwork and successful productions are a result of solid relationships with a strong team of people. Build a good one.

- It's a good idea to have the production schedule in place BEFORE you start contacting crew members. It will be easier for them to commit to the project if they know specifically when you need them. You will also appear professional and organized, which may help attract more experienced people to your production.
- Be aware that working with inexperienced crew members like volunteers or film students may require more time on set for them to learn how to use the equipment. It's a good idea to have an orientation before the shoot to show the crew how to use the equipment and your set policies and procedures. The equipment rental company may be willing to host this orientation.
- When scheduling students or crew members new to production, it's a good idea to schedule more people than you need because not everyone will show up. Consider a crew member reliable if he has proven, through action, his reliability. Don't go on someone's verbal commitment alone. It's better to have too much help than not enough.
- When selecting crew members, be aware of people who appear even the least bit hesitant about the time requirements or who aren't enthusiastic about the project. They not only will be difficult to work with on set, but may not be reliable, often coming up with excuses to leave early or miss shoots entirely.
- Crew members, especially those who are working for free, are giving two very important elements: their talents and, more importantly, their time. Be appreciative and supportive of their efforts, and always be sure to thank them profusely for their dedication to the production.
- Schedule a meeting with the crew before the first day of shooting to go over the script, storyline, schedule, and what is expected of them. You want the crew to be as prepared as possible when they arrive on the set the first day.
- If necessary, schedule an equipment review with the crew, possibly at the equipment rental facility, to make sure that everyone knows how to set up, use, and pack up the gear.
- Avoid scheduling the crew too far in advance. Experienced crew personnel may be hesitant to book a job too far in the future. A good rule of thumb is to begin booking crew members within about three weeks of production.

PAYING CREW MEMBERS

Compensating crew members can be an expensive process, but consider that many new, aspiring filmmakers would be willing to work for other types of compensation.

Money

Paying crew members is the best form of compensation, although in most cases your budget may prohibit you from paying the crew. Typical crew wages are based on a daily basis for short projects and discounted weekly rates for long-term projects. Crew wages are dependent on the length of the project, if travel is required, how experienced the crew member is, and how many potentially qualified people are available for the job. Talk with each potential crew member and work out a deal for his day rate and offer to rent his equipment or kits as an incentive for him to accept a lower daily rate.

If you are paying the crew, it is customary to issue a check either at the end of the production, if it is a short project, or every two weeks if the production is a feature.

Discuss the rate in advance and include the rate in a crew deal memo. The crew deal memo is a contract between the production company and the crew member that states the terms of employment. Other factors to include are:

- **Overtime:** When crew members work on a full-paying or union job, their daily rate usually covers a 12-hour day. It is customary to pay two times the hourly rate for any time over 12 hours. However, this can get costly, especially on a low-budget independent film, so negotiate a standard day rate regardless of the number of hours worked.
- **Per diem:** If the production spans distant locations, cast and crew members are given a per diem, or additional daily money to cover food purchases. Per diems are always negotiated before the production begins and range from $30 to $75 a day. Each crew member is given the per diem amount in cash at the beginning of the day.
- **Expenses:** If the budget allows, offering to pay for travel expenses such as gas may attract higher-caliber crew members. Even on low-budget movies on which crew members may be working for free, offering gas money is a powerful and inexpensive incentive that will help bring and keep people onboard.
- **Time of payment:** Most cast and crew members expect to be paid by the last day of production. Write checks for the full amount and have them ready for the crew on their last day of work. Paying crew members late will tarnish your reputation in a community and make it difficult to crew up your next production.
- **Payroll:** Most independent movies will pay the cast and crew as subcontractors, meaning the production is not responsible for taking out taxes. In projects that involve a large number of cast and crew members, or ones that span a long period of time, consider hiring a payroll service to cut

checks and take out taxes, making the cast and crew members employees of the production. Be sure to consult your accountant.

There are several factors that determine the rate of pay for crew members:

- How experienced is the crew member? In most instances, the more experienced crew member will request a higher daily rate, unless she is excited about the project. Try to sell each person and get them excited and you may be able to negotiate a lower rate.
- How many qualified crew members are there in the production area? In major cities where the crew pool is large, it's easier to negotiate lower rates because of increased competition.
- Are there any other productions that are hiring crew members at the same time? In cities where there isn't a large crew pool, competent crew members will go to the production with the higher rate, making it difficult to staff your movie. Consult with the local film commission before making the shoot schedule so as not to conflict with another production.
- Is there a nearby film school that can provide students or recent graduates willing to work for free? If so, then professionals may be willing to lower their rates to compete with the free labor.
- Are the crew members union or nonunion? Nonunion crews are often willing to work for more reasonable rates, longer hours, and fewer creature comforts than experienced union crews.

Deferred payment

Another method of paying crew members is to pay them from the money a film makes after it is sold. Deferred payment is risky for the crew because they will get paid only if the movie makes money, which is not a guarantee. Most seasoned crew members consider this arrangement "working for free" and will accept the job because they like the project, not because of the promise of back-end money.

Some productions will pay crew members a percentage of their usual rate upfront and defer the balance.

Credit

If you can't afford to pay crew members upfront, or do not foresee your film making a profit, offer what you can . . . credit. Credit is the listing of the crew member's name and job title in either the opening credits or the film's closing credits. Oftentimes, first-time film crews are excited at the prospect of gaining the experience of working on a film and seeing their names in the credits, which may lead to future jobs.

Andrew Zehnder, who plays young Bobby Jones, waits as the crew finishes the lighting.

Quantus Pictures Inc.

Motion Picture Production Company

CREW DEAL MEMO

Production ______________________ Production Company ______________
Name ______________________
Crew Position ______________________ Start Date ______________
Address ______________________ Weekly Rate ______________
____
Phone ______________________

In accordance with the Immigration Reform and Control Act of 1986, any offer of employment is conditioned upon satisfactory proof of applicant's identity and legal ability to work in the United States.

Quantus Pictures, Inc. (herein referred to as Producer) reserves the right to discharge the undersigned (herein referred to as Contractor) at any time. Start date is subject to change and the final duration of this contract is at the discretion of the Producer. By signing this agreement, Contractor acknowledges that the following terms and conditions represent the entire agreement between the parties:

In assigning these rights, Contractor acknowledges that the motion picture tentatively titled "The Day bobby Jones Came Home" (herein referred to as the Production) is the sole and exclusive right of the Producer.

Contractor warrants and represents that he or she is free to enter into this license and this agreement does not conflict with any existing contracts or agreements to which Contractor is a party. Contractor agrees to hold Producer and any third parties harmless from and against any and all claims, liabilities, losses or damages that may arise from the Production.

Producer shall be the owner of all the results and proceeds of Contractor's services and shall have the right to use Contractor's name, image, voice, picture and likeness in connection with the Production, the advertising and publicity thereof, and in any promotional film or clips without additional compensation.

Contractor understands that services rendered for Producer will be compensated with a rate of $0.00/ day. Said compensation shall become due and payable within a period of 90 days following the final date of work with the Production.

No additional compensation shall be made payable to Contractor for the rendering of services at night, on weekends or during holidays.

Use of drugs or alcohol during hours of employment shall result in the immediate termination of Contractor.

(continued)

Crew deal memo page 1.

Quantus Pictures Inc.

Motion Picture Production Company

(continued from page 1)

Contractor relieves and indemnifies Producer, its owners, contractors, officers, agents, licensees, heirs, and assigns from any and all liability for any injuries or damage caused Contractor or to other persons or property during the period of association with the Production. In the event that Contractor is responsible for damage to person, property, or equipment, Contractor will remunerate costs of repair or replacement (at the discretion of Producer) within a period of thirty days following the incident.

AGREED AND ACCEPTED:

Contractor ______________________________ Date ______________

Producer ______________________________ Date ______________

Crew deal memo page 2.

CONTRACTS AND DEAL MEMOS

Deal memos are contracts between the production company and the crew members, which identify the crew member's job, working dates, daily/weekly rate, overtime pay, per diem, credit, travel allotment, and any additional factors that you negotiate with the crew member.

The crew deal memo is signed before production begins. A copy is given to the crew member, whereas the master is kept on file in the production office. Once signed, the arrangements of the contract are sealed, alleviating any possible future conflicts over the terms of the agreement.

If paying the crew in the United States, have each crew member fill out a W-9 form for tax and accounting purposes before the production begins.

CREW WAGES

It is often difficult to determine appropriate crew wages for a film production because rates are dependent upon where in the country the film is being shot, the number of qualified crew members available, the number of shooting days, and the format on which the movie is being filmed. The following is a list of average crew rates for a $1 million, nonunion film production shot in a major metropolitan area in 20 days. Understand that there is no standard rate chart for nonunion productions, so the following scale is a starting point for negotiating crew wages on your production. These rates have been calculated for a six-day week, 12 hours/day, with 12-hour turnaround shooting schedule.

Position	Rate
Production manager	$300–400 per day
First assistant director	$300–400 per day
Second assistant director	$200–300 per day
Production assistant	$0–150 per day

Most production assistants are interns willing to work for free for the experience.

Production designer	$1500–1700 per week
Art director	$1200–1500 per week
Assistant art director	$1000–1200 per week

Art department positions are usually hired on a per-week basis.

Script supervisor	$200–250 per day or $800–900 per week
Director of photography	$500–800 per day or $2000–3000 per week
First assistant camera	$200–250 per day

Second assistant camera	$175–225 per day or $1000–1100 per week
Camera operator	$175–225 per day
Film loader	$150–175 per day or $850–950 per week

Film loader rates are dependent on film vs video. If shooting film, this position requires a much more experienced person, which can increase the rate.

Key grip	$200–250 per day or $1000–1200 per week
Best boy—grip	$175–225 per day
Grip	$125–175 per day or $800–900 per week
Dolly grip	$175–225 per day

The dolly grip rate is usually the same as that for the best boy position.

Gaffer	$250–300 per day or $1000–1200 per week
Best boy—electric	$175–225 per day or $900–1000 per week
Electrician	$150–200 per day

Usually, the first assistant cameraman, key grip, and gaffer make the same scale. The second assistants/best boys in those categories make the same, and the third tier/film loader make the same scale. Grips and electricians make slightly less.

Production sound mixer	$275–350 per day or $1200–1400 per week

The production sound mixer usually has his own equipment, which can raise the rate.

Boom operator	$125–175 per day or $500–600 per week
Makeup	$225–275 per day or $1000–1100 per week
Assistant makeup	$200–250 per day or $900–1000 per week
Prop master	$200–250 per day or $900–1100 per week
Assistant prop master	$175–215 per day or $800–900 per week
Body makeup	$150–200 per day or $750–850 per week

Makeup artists may also charge a kit fee, which includes all the makeup materials necessary for the film shoot. When negotiating rates, some makeup artists will be willing to work for free but may charge the kit fee to cover the costs of materials.

Key hairstylist	$200–250 per day or $900–950 per week
Hairstylist	$175–215 per day or $800–850 per week

Hairstylists may also charge a kit fee to cover materials and equipment.

Wardrobe	$200–250 per day or $900–950 per week

Costume designer	$400–500 per day or $1900–2200 per week
Key costume	$175–225 per day or $800–850 per week
Stunt coordinator	$900–1100 per day or $3800–4100 per week
Stunt person	$600–700 per day or $2400–2600 per week

Hollywood stunt people are also paid for each time they perform a stunt, making complicated stunts with multiple takes very expensive. This is in addition to the base daily or weekly pay.

Construction foreman	$190–220 per day or $800–900 per week
Craft services	$175–225 per day
Editor	$50–55 per hour
Assistant editor	$28–32 per hour
Music editor	$40–45 per hour
Sound editor	$40–45 per hour

In many instances, postproduction positions may charge for the project or on an hourly basis. Some studios will sell "blocks" of time at a discounted rate. The rates charged are dependent on the size and experience of the studio, the studio's current workload, or how involved your project is.

CHAPTER 9

Unions and Guilds

INTRODUCTION

Unions and guilds are long-standing organizations that protect the rights of, monitor the working conditions of, provide benefits for, and guarantee minimum levels of payment for their members. The primary unions and guilds in the American motion picture industry are the Screen Actors Guild, Directors Guild of America (DGA), Writers Guild of America, and International Alliance of Theatrical Stage Employees (IATSE).

None of the cast or crew members working on *Time and Again* were members of a union or guild. This allowed me to keep my costs at a minimum, although we still adhered to proper set guidelines, mealtimes, turnaround, and scheduling.

- Producing a film with union cast and/or crew members can add to the cost of production, as minimum wages must be paid, payment to pension and health care plans must be made, and on-set work practices and restrictions must be enforced.
- Actors and crew members must demonstrate proficiency and experience in their crafts in order to be eligible for union membership. Although membership to a union or guild means the member met admission requirements, it by no means ensures their talents, work ethics, or abilities.
- There are dozens of unions and guilds for various crafts within the entertainment industry, such as the Motion Picture Editors Guild and the Writers Guild of America. Contact these guilds for lists of qualified artists for your production.
- Some locations may have contracts with a union or guild specifying that union members must be hired if a film crew is shooting on that location, regardless of whether it's a union film or not. Always be sure to ask before locking a location.
- Artists who join a union or guild are entitled to health benefits, guaranteed wages, controlled work hours, union representation in the event of a dispute with an employer, and many other benefits in

exchange for dues, which are paid as a first-year entry fee and as annual fees. As a producer hiring union crew members, you may need to pay into their health and pension funds in addition to paying their daily rate. There may also be residual payment requirements depending on the nature of the project. Contact your local union representative for more details.

- Using union actors in a nonunion film production violates the regulations of the union, but the U.S. Supreme Court established a principal called "Financial core" that protects union members from being punished by their union for taking nonunion jobs. Financial core applies not only to actors, but also to unions for all industries in the United States.
- Actors and crew members have daily rates; however, working on a long-term production can be expensive, so the union offers weekly rates. Essentially, in guaranteeing the union member work for a certain length of time, the filmmaker can benefit from a slightly reduced rate.

As an independent filmmaker, the only union you may need to consider involvement with is the Screen Actors Guild, especially if you're working with SAG actors. The other unions are not as influential in the production of your movie and although they can boycott your production, they may not have the power or ability to shut it down. If you choose to go nonunion, union members working on your movie may feel compelled to leave because of pressure and obligations to the union.

Don't be afraid to work with your local union or guild, but be sure to take the time to understand your obligations and requirements as a producer. Be aware that you do not need to enter into a long-term agreement as a signatory, but you can negotiate terms on a project-by-project basis. As is the case with any legal document, always read and understand any contracts you may be asked to sign. Most unions are happy to answer your questions.

DIRECTOR'S NOTES

When I produced *Time and Again*, I worked exclusively with a nonunion cast and crew for a number of reasons. First off, my budget didn't allow me access to professional union workers, and second, I wanted to make a film using local resources, in much the same way you would. I've worked on dozens of films as a director and cinematographer, and even on projects with budgets up to a million dollars, the only union members that we employed were the actors.

Hiring a union crew member is a very important decision because you will be required to pay union minimum wages and pay into each crew member's health care and pension plan. These costs are significantly more expensive than working with a nonunion crew.

Be advised that even if working nonunion, it's still a good idea to honor the basic on-set work practices set forth by the unions.

- Keep shooting days under 12 hours unless you're able to pay overtime.
- Always schedule a turnaround time of 12 hours from the time the crew wraps to the call time the next day.
- Always feed the crew a meal every 6 hours.
- Always provide a safe working environment.

These practices will not only keep morale and dedication to your project up, but will also promote a safe, healthy, and productive work environment.

The Stickball Players from *Time and Again* were all non-SAG actors.

SCREEN ACTORS GUILD

The Screen Actors Guild is designed to protect the rights of actors and ensure that filming conditions, payment rates, and overall production conditions are professional. The Guild also ensures that actors meet strict eligibility requirements upon entering, both professionally and artistically.

As an independent filmmaker, the union you are most likely work with is the Screen Actors Guild. SAG provides a number of options for low-budget productions, allowing union actors to work on smaller independent and student films.

SAG actors have all met the guild's requirements for work experience and have paid the necessary dues to enter the union. Although there are many talented actors in SAG, SAG membership is not an endorsement of an actor's capabilities and talents.

Part of the SAG regulations specify minimum (or scale) payment requirements for SAG actors depending on the budget of the film. Unfortunately, these requirements made it nearly impossible for independent filmmakers to use the high-quality, experienced actors in SAG until the guild created a multitiered low-budget structure specifically designed for student and low-budget filmmakers. The following are the various options available to independent filmmakers:

Student film agreement

For students enrolled in film school. Performers may defer 100 percent of their salaries.

Short-film agreement

- Total budget of less than $50,000.
- 35 minutes or less.
- Salaries are deferred.
- No consecutive employment (except on overnight location).
- No premiums.
- Allows the use of both professional and nonprofessional performers.
- Background performers not covered.

Ultra-low-budget agreement

- Total budget of less than $200,000.
- Day rate of $100.
- No step-up fees.
- No consecutive employment (except on overnight location).
- No premiums.
- Allows the use of both professional and nonprofessional performers.
- Background performers not covered.

Modified low-budget agreement

- Total budget of less than $625,000.
- Day rate of $268.
- Weekly rate of $933.
- No consecutive employment (except on overnight location).

- Six-day work week with no premium.
- Reduced overtime rate.

Low-budget agreement

- Total budget of less than $2,500,000.
- Day rate of $504.
- Weekly rate of $1752.
- No consecutive employment (except on overnight location).
- Six-day work week with no premium.
- Reduced overtime rate.
- Reduced number of background performers covered.

Diversity casting incentives

The Diversity in Casting Incentive applies to the Modified Low-Budget Agreement and the Low-Budget Agreement only. If the producer has demonstrated diversity in casting, the total production cost maximum may be increased to the following amounts:

Modified Low-Budget Agreement: from $625,000 to $937,500

and

Low-Budget Agreement: from $2,500,000 to $3,750,000.

The producer demonstrates diversity in casting by meeting the following criteria:

- A minimum of 50 percent of the total speaking roles and 50 percent of the total days of employment are cast with performers who are members of the following four protected groups: (1) women, (2) senior performers (60 years or older), (3) performers with disabilities, or (4) people of color (Asian/Pacific Islander, Black, Latino/Hispanic, and Native American Indian) AND
- A minimum of 20 percent of the total days of employment are cast with performers who are people of color.

Background actor incentive

The Background Actor Incentive applies to the Modified Low-Budget Agreement only.

The total production cost maximum may be increased by an additional $100,000 if the producer employs a minimum average of three SAG-covered background actors for each day of principal photography, provided that the producer notifies SAG in writing of intent to utilize this incentive prior to the start of production.

Be sure to read the restrictions and requirements for working with SAG actors, including working within the eight-hour limit per day of production. These factors are important when you schedule and budget your movie, so contact SAG so that you understand your obligations.

For additional information about SAG and the SAG independent filmmaker agreements, check out www.sagindie.com. Special thanks to the Screen Actors Guild for providing this information.

WRITERS GUILD OF AMERICA

The Writers Guild of America (WGA) is a labor union composed of the thousands of writers who write the television shows, movies, news programs, documentaries, animation, CD-ROMs, and content for new-media technologies that keep audiences constantly entertained and informed.

Their duty is to represent WGA members in negotiations with film and television producers to ensure the rights of screen, television, and new-media writers. Once a contract is in place, the WGA will enforce it. Because of the WGA's long-term efforts, writers receive pension and health coverage, and their financial and creative rights are protected.

In addition, the WGA is responsible for determining writing credits for feature films and television programs—a responsibility with far-reaching impact, financial and artistic. Writers' livelihoods often depend on the careful and objective determination of credits.

The WGA monitors, collects, and distributes millions of dollars in residuals (payments for the reuse of movies and television programs) for writers each year.

The Writers Guild also sponsors seminars, panel discussions, and special events for its members as well as the public at large.

For more information, check out www.wga.org. Special thanks to the Writers Guild for providing this information.

Writers guild low-budget contract

The Writers Guild of America has set up several guidelines for independent filmmakers to deal with option agreements with writers.

- The Low-Budget Agreement is offered to WGA members and nonmembers for purchases of existing screenplays and one rewrite. It is not for development.
- The agreement applies to films budgeted at $1,200,000 and below.
- The agreement must be requested by the writer. With the writer's consent, the agreement allows a company to defer payment of all or part of the compensation for the screenplay purchase and/or all or part of the compensation for the first rewrite in an amount negotiated between the writer and the company, provided the total amount does not fall below applicable Guild minimums. However, upon commencement of principal pho-

tography (if the budget of the film is between $500,000 and $1,200,000), the company must pay $10,000 to the writer and apply this against any deferred monies owing on the screenplay purchase price. The company may defer the remaining portion of money due until receipt of first revenue after (1) recoupment or (2) commercial distribution, whichever is earlier.

- The company must pay a script publication fee of $5000, which is due 30 days after final determination of the writing credits on the picture. For films budgeted at $500,000 and below, however, upon the writer's request, the fee may be deferred along with the screenplay purchase and/or first rewrite compensation. The fee gives the company the right to publish the screenplay on videodiscs/videocassettes.
- Original screenplays may not be rewritten without the permission of the writer. Writers of an adapted screenplay shall be offered the opportunity to perform the first rewrite.
- Writers may also negotiate for increased back-end minimums or back-end residuals, a percentage of gross profit participation, and/or additional creative rights.
- The company must be or become a signatory to the WGA Theatrical and Television Basic Agreement and sign all required documents. If applicable, the Low-Budget Agreement will also be signed and apply to the particular film project.
- Except as modified by the Low-Budget Agreement, all other provisions in the Guild contract apply, including but not limited to residuals, credits, pension, health benefits, and separated rights.
- If the budget of the film exceeds $1,200,000, WGA Theatrical and Television Basic Agreement low-budget (between $1,200,000 and $5,000,000) or high-budget (above $5,000,000) minimums are immediately due and payable.
- If the film is not made within 18 months, the writer is entitled to reacquire the literary material.

Most independent moviemakers who choose to work with a union writer are able to do so without the express permission of, or signing a contract with, the WGA. The WGA does not police the activities of its members and cannot force minimum payments if you are not a signatory company.

For more information about the WGA Low-Budget Agreement, call the Writers Guild of America, West, at (323) 782-4731 or Writers Guild of America, East, at (212) 767-7800. Information is available online at www.wga.org.

IATSE (INTERNATIONAL ALLIANCE OF THEATRICAL STAGE EMPLOYEES)

IATSE is a union that services many of the behind-the-scenes crafts, including:

- Animation/computer-generated imagery
- Front of house
- Laboratory

- Makeup and hair
- Motion picture and television production
- Postproduction
- Projection and audiovisual
- Scenic artists
- Stagehands
- Television broadcast
- Trade shows/exhibitions
- Treasurers and ticket sellers
- Wardrobe

IATSE has local chapters around the world, so go to their web site at www.iatse-intl.org for more information.

Working with IATSE crews can be very expensive and is generally an option only for productions with budgets over a million dollars. Once a production "goes union," a significantly higher portion of the budget must be apportioned to the union crews to cover higher rates and overtime and penalty pay.

Most low-budget filmmakers cannot afford to go union, but many IATSE chapters are interested in working with you to provide at least a few quality crew members, provided you can pay union wages.

DIRECTORS GUILD OF AMERICA

In much the same way that SAG represents actors, the DGA represents directors. The DGA guarantees various creative and legal rights to its members as well as pension and health plans. Membership to the guild is possible when a director is hired to direct a film by a signatory company.

THEATRICAL MOTION PICTURE MINIMUMS 7/1/06 to 6/30/08

Rates effective July 1, 2006 to June 30, 2007	HIGH BUDGET	SHORTS & DOCUMENTARIES
Weekly Salary	$14,172	$10,122
Guaranteed Preparation Period	2 Weeks	2 Weeks
Guaranteed Employment Period	10 Weeks	1 Week + 1 Day
Guaranteed Cutting Allowance	1 Week	0
Compensation for Days Worked Beyond Guarantee	$2,834 Day	$2,024 Day
Daily Employment Where Permitted	$3,543 Day	$2,531 Day

Rates effective July 1, 2007 to June 30, 2008	HIGH BUDGET	SHORTS & DOCUMENTARIES
Weekly Salary	$14,597	$10,426
Guaranteed Preparation Period	2 Weeks	2 Weeks
Guaranteed Employment Period	10 Weeks	1 Week + 1 Day
Guaranteed Cutting Allowance	1 Week	0
Compensation for Days Worked Beyond Guarantee	$2,919 day	$2,085 day
Daily Employment Where Permitted	$3,649 day	$2,607 day

Please see Low Budget Work section for films with budgets of less than $7 million.

DGA rates.

Membership to the DGA requires an initiation fee as well as yearly dues that are based on yearly earnings. For more information, visit www.dga.org.

If you're dreaming about directing the big projects, check out the payment rates for DGA directors for motion picture production. There are several pay scales for other types of productions such as television and made-for-television movies. Visit the DGA web site for more information.

GUILD AND UNION CONTACT INFORMATION

U.S. guilds and unions (above the line)

Directors Guild of America (DGA)
7920 Sunset Boulevard
Los Angeles, CA 90046
(310) 289–2000
www.dga.com
110 West 57th Street, 2nd Floor
New York, NY 10019
(212) 581–0370

Screen Actors Guild (SAG)
5757 Wilshire Boulevard
Los Angeles, CA 90036
(323) 954–1600
www.SAG.com
1515 Broadway, 44th Floor
New York, NY 10036
(212) 944–1030

Writers Guild America/West
7000 W. Third Street
Los Angeles, CA 90048
(323) 951–4000
www.wga.org
555 West 57th Street
New York, NY 10019
(212) 767–7800

U.S. guilds and unions (below the line)

International Alliance of Theatrical Stage Employees (IATSE)
10045 Riverside Drive, 2nd Floor
Toluca Lake, CA 91602
(818) 980–3499
www.IATSE.im.com
1430 Broadway
New York, NY 10018
(212) 730–1770

American Federation of Musicians (AFM)
7080 Hollywood Boulevard
Hollywood, CA 90028
(323) 461–3441

American Society of Cinematographers (ASC)
1782 N. Orange Drive
Hollywood, CA 90028
(323) 969–4333
www.cinematographer.com

Art Directors Guild
11969 Ventura Boulevard
Studio City, CA 91604
(818) 762–9995
www.artdirectors.org

Costume Designer's Guild
4730 Woodman Avenue, #430
Sherman Oaks, CA 91423
(818) 905–1557
www.costumedesignersguild.org

U.S. guilds and unions (below the line)—continued

Makeup Artists & Hair Stylists Guild
828 N. Hollywood Way
Burbank, CA 91505
(818) 295–3933
www.Local706.org

Motion Picture Editors Guild
7715 Sunset Boulevard, Suite 200
Los Angeles, CA 90046
(323) 876–4770
www.editorsguild.com

U.S. Associations

Academy Motion Pictures Arts & Science (AMPAS)
8949 Wilshire Boulevard
Beverly Hills, CA 90211
(310) 247–3000
www.Oscars.org

Academy Television Arts & Sciences (ATAS)
5220 Lankershim Boulevard
North Hollywood, CA 91601
(818) 754–2800
www.emmys.org

Casting Society of America (CSA)
606 N. Larchmont Boulevard, #4B
Los Angeles, CA 90004
(323) 463–1925

Producers Guild of America (PGA)
8530 Wilshire Boulevard, #450
Beverly Hills, CA 90211
(310) 358–9020
www.ProducersGuild.org

GREAT BRITAIN GUILDS AND UNIONS

Director's Guild of Great Britain
4 Windmill Street
London W1T 2HZ, UK
Telephone: +44 2075809131
Fax: +44 2075809132
www.dggb.org

DPRS—Directors' & Producers Rights Society
20–22 Bedford Row
London WC1R 4EB, UK
Telephone: +44 20 7269 0677
Fax: +44 20 7269 0676
www.dprs.org

UK Film Council
10 Little Portland Street
London W1W 7JG, UK
Telephone: + 44 20 7861 7861
Fax: +44 20 7861 7862
www.ukfilmcouncil.org.uk

The Production Guild
N&P Complex
Pinewood Studios
Iver Heath
Buckinghamshire SL0 0NH, UK
Telephone: +44 1753651767
Fax: +44 1753652803
www.productionguild.com

Equity (actors union)
Guild House
Upper St Martins Lane
London WC2H 9EG, UK
Telephone: +44 2073796000
Fax: +44 2073797001
www.equity.org.uk

CHAPTER 10

Equipment

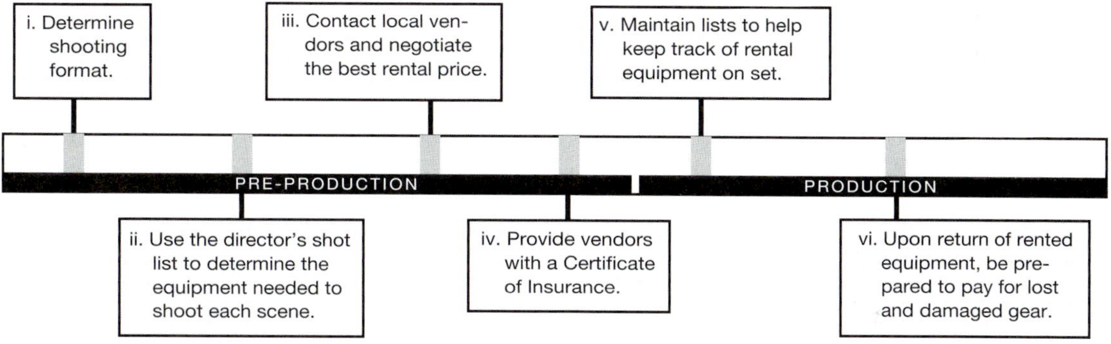

i. Determine shooting format.
iii. Contact local vendors and negotiate the best rental price.
v. Maintain lists to help keep track of rental equipment on set.
PRE-PRODUCTION
PRODUCTION
ii. Use the director's shot list to determine the equipment needed to shoot each scene.
iv. Provide vendors with a Certificate of Insurance.
vi. Upon return of rented equipment, be prepared to pay for lost and damaged gear.

INTRODUCTION

Getting the right equipment is essential to producing a high-quality movie. Because purchasing the camera, lights, and other production equipment is an expensive proposition, there are a number of rental facilities that may be willing to rent gear to filmmakers for a discount or even for free.

One common misperception filmmakers have is that they can use existing light, handheld cameras, and onboard microphones to achieve a "natural" look. This disastrous approach results in an unwatchable film; the audience can't hear the actors; the image is dark, grainy, and shaky; and the focus shifts constantly during a shot.

I'm shooting Bobby Jones as he approaches his parents' home using a JVC-GY-DV500 DV camcorder and a Doorway dolly with 32 feet of track.

Both film and digital media react to light in a way much different from that of the human eye, so often, large quantities of light are required to light a scene, even if you're striving for a natural look. In addition, camera support equipment gives filmmakers the flexibility to move the camera in artistic and creative ways, without distracting the audience with shaky camera moves.

Investing in the proper equipment is the first step in crafting controlled, creative shots that will not only increase the production value of the movie, but also help engage the audience deeper into the story.

The first part of tackling the equipment issue involves determining what kind of gear is needed for the shoot. The most important piece of equipment is the camera.

CAMERAS

Choosing a camera and a format to shoot on is one of the most important decisions you'll make when selecting gear for your production. There are many different options among video and film formats. If you choose to shoot film, you could use the inexpensive Super8 format, but the image quality will be poor; or you could choose high-quality 35 mm film and pay tens of thousands of dollars on the camera rental, film, and processing. Video offers the same array of choices, from inexpensive miniDV to professional-quality high-definition video, each with an equal array of benefits and drawbacks. Consider all the factors of cost, quality, and even distribution requirements when choosing a format.

VIDEO VS FILM

Filmmaking has always been an elitist medium that costs a massive amount of money, and unless you have a rich uncle or a spare quarter-million dollars, it is next to impossible to produce a professional-looking 35 mm or even 16 mm feature film at the independent level. This financial requirement has kept many people from realizing their dreams . . . until the digital revolution. In the late 1990s, a digital format called DV (digital video) was developed, which revolutionized moviemaking. By producing broadcast-quality imagery, the average person can easily afford technology that in past years would have cost ten times the amount. Digital video opened the doors and empowered the masses to explore, produce, and tell stories through the visual medium.

Listen to Hollywood experts discuss the pros and cons of shooting video and film in the Video vs Film module at www.powerfilmmaking.com.

But the debate as to whether film or video is superior still rages. Both media have their pros and cons. Film is much more expensive to shoot when one considers the cost of film stock, processing, and equipment rental. However, the look of film, to many, is vastly superior to the look of video by providing greater contrast range, depth of field, and image resolution. A movie shot on film is also easier to sell to foreign distributors than a movie shot on video, as video has a reputation of looking cheap and amateurish. Film can be easily adapted and transferred to one of many broadcast and exhibition formats around the world.

When you begin your filmmaking career, consider shooting your first few projects on digital video so that you can focus on the process of making a movie (directing, working with actors, and working with the crew) instead of the technical challenges of shooting film. Once you feel comfortable with the process and have a few short films under your belt, then consider shooting a project on film. Too many people invest thousands of dollars into film stock and processing on their first movie and because they are inexperienced in the process, the movie ends up being shelved due to bad acting, poor script, loose directing, sloppy editing, and so on—and the money spent on film is wasted. Focus on the process, then shoot on film.

SHOOTING FILM

Film is a strip of plastic that has several chemical layers, the most important being a layer of light-sensitive silver–halide crystals, made up of silver nitrate and halide salts. These crystals come in a variety of sizes, shapes, and composition and can be modified in the manufacturing process to produce different speeds of film. Once film is exposed to light, it then needs to be processed for the image to be visible.

During the developing process, the image appears as a negative of the original image, with blacks and whites inverted, and in the case of color film, the colors inverted. The lab then produces a positive from the negative, which displays the scene as it is supposed to appear.

Film formats

Film comes in a variety of sizes. Each film stock is measured diagonally, corner to corner, in millimeters. The larger the frame, the more "resolution" and detail the film is able to capture.

Film formats.

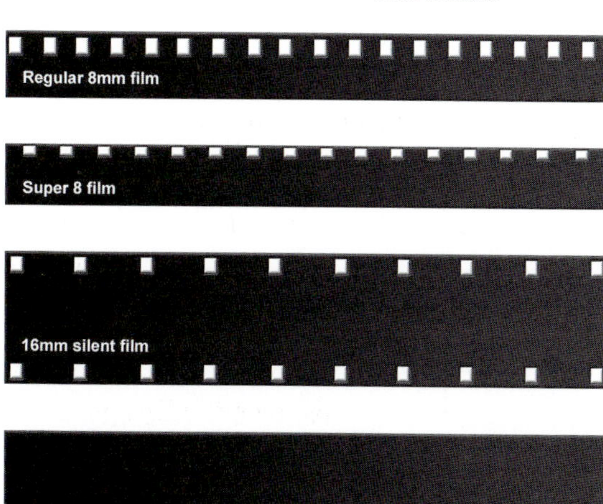

- **8 mm:** Primarily used for home moviemaking, 8 mm and Super8 formats were the predominant formats before video cameras became standard in the home. You can purchase the film and process it for around $10.00 per minute. Although this is the cheapest film stock, it is also the poorest quality.
  - The film is eight millimeters wide and has perforations on only one side.
  - The aspect ratio is 1.33 : 1, the same as NTSC television.
  - Super8 includes an oxide stripe, which allows sound to be recorded onto the film.

Table 10.1 Film vs Video

Film	Video
Costs $55 to buy and process 1 min of 35 mm film	Costs $4.50 for 1 hour of DV tape stock; DV doesn't need to be developed
Minimal number of takes, dependent on budget allotted for film stock	Unlimited number of takes, tape stock is cheap
Cameras are heavier and bulkier	Cameras can be smaller and easier to handle
Requires more time to light and set up each shot	Can set up shots quickly
Cannot see footage until the film is processed	Can see the image immediately and on playback
Very high resolution, images are crisp and defined	Lower-quality formats have limited resolution and won't hold up well on the big screen, but higher-quality formats rival 35 mm film quality
Requires a separate sound recording device, because you cannot record audio onto film	Can record audio directly to the tape; audio remains in sync with the video image
Film needs to be processed and transferred to tape before editing	Footage can go immediately into an editing suite
Distributors are much more likely to pick up a movie shot on film, especially in the foreign market	Distributors are much less likely to pick up a movie shot on video, especially in the foreign market
Has significantly shallower depth of field	Has significantly deeper depth of field
Has a greater contrast ratio (6–10 *f*-stops, depending on the film stock) and handles overexposure much better	Has a narrower contrast range in lower-quality formats and does not handle overexposure as well; high-quality formats have contrast ranges that equal that of film
Is much more complicated in postproduction, especially if the final result is to go back to film	A much simpler postproduction process, although costs of printing video to film are high
Film generally has a more aesthetically pleasing look	Video generally has a harsher look
Film is able to capture an infinite range of colors, making images vivid and deeply saturated	Video must compress color information, so saturation and the chroma range are limited
If film is underexposed and pushed in processing, film is subject to granularity and graininess	If underexposed and gain is used, the video image is subject to noise
Film is very expensive to duplicate and loses quality with each generation	Video is inexpensive to duplicate at a high quality

- All 8 mm and Super8 cameras run at 18 frames per second, and many cameras can run at 24 frames per second.
- Super8 is sold in 50-foot lengths and is rolled in a plastic cartridge that is inserted into the camera. The camera automatically loads the film. This amounts to 3:20 of shooting time if you roll at 18 frames per second, or 2:47 if rolling at 24 frames per second.
- Due to environmental legislation regarding manufacturing, Kodak no longer makes film stock with sound recording capabilities.
- Super8 film costs around $25 per roll to purchase and about $15 per roll to develop.

- **16 mm:** This film stock is ideal for student and experimental filmmakers. Able to provide excellent quality, especially when viewed on television, 16 mm film is used for low-budget applications and documentaries. Beware, 16 mm film may look good on the small screen, but not necessarily on the silver screen. A common film format is Super16, which eliminates the perforations on one side of the film, allowing a greater area to be exposed. Super16 film features a wider aspect ratio and is a format of choice for filmmakers who are looking for a lower-cost option to 35 mm film.
  - Measuring 16 millimeters from corner to corner, 16 mm film is perforated either on one side (single perf) or on both sides (double perf), although single perf, one sprocket hole per frame, is becoming the standard.
  - The aspect ratio of 16 mm film is 1.33:1.
  - Super16 film has an aspect ratio of 1.66:1 and is always single perf.
- **35 mm:** The primary format of choice in professional filmmaking, 35 mm film is able to capture enough detail in the image to hold up well on the silver screen. The only drawback is its $55.00 per minute cost for film stock and processing.
  - The film measures 35 millimeters across.
  - The 35 mm aspect ratio is 1.78:1.
  - There are a number of variations of the 35 mm format, including Super35 and 35 anamorphic, so talk with your film supplier about which format is the best choice for your project.
  - This film can hold SDDS, Dolby Digital, analog optical, and DTS timecode tracks.
  - This film runs at 16 frames per foot, 24 frames per second, 90 feet per minute.

- **70 mm:** This is the primary format for IMAX presentations for which the frame must contain enough visual information to hold up on the big screen. This film format is generally not used for traditional moviemaking. The aspect ratio for 70 mm film is 2.20 : 1.

Table 10.2 Running Time of Film Rolling at 24 Frames Per Second

Length of film	16 mm (36 ft/min)	35 mm (90 ft/min)
100 ft	2.77 min	1.11 min
200 ft	5.55 min	2.22 min
400 ft	11.11 min	4.44 min
800 ft	22.22 min	N/A
1000 ft	27.70 min	11.11 min
1200 ft	33.30 min	N/A

Buying film

Approach the purchase of film as you would buying a car—be prepared to NEGOTIATE. First, when preparing a budget for a movie, you need to know how much film you will need to shoot the movie.

- Assume you are shooting a 90-minute movie. If 35 mm film at 24 frames per second at 90 feet per minute is pulled through the camera, you can calculate that a 90-minute movie has about 8100 feet of film.
- Next, calculate the ratio between footage shot and the amount of footage used in the final movie. This is called the shooting ratio and shouldn't be more than 6 : 1. This means that for every setup, the director will shoot six takes with the intention of using one take. So 8100 feet × 6 = 48,600 feet. For the sake of discussion, round the number up to 50,000 feet. You will need to buy 50,000 feet of film to produce a 90-minute feature with a 6 : 1 shooting ratio.
- 35 mm film comes in two lengths: 400-foot rolls that are used for handheld and steadicam shots and 1000-foot rolls for everything else. Go through the script and determine how many pages are to be shot handheld or steadicam. The number of pages you count equals the number of minutes of the movie that will be shot handheld. Multiply by 6 for your shooting ratio, and you have the number of minutes you need to buy in 400-foot rolls. For example, if your script has eight pages of handheld setups, one page in the script equals one minute in the movie. Eight minutes of movie time times 6 (the shooting ratio) equals 48 minutes of footage. Forty-eight minutes of footage equals 4320 feet, which, if purchased in 400-foot rolls, comes to 11 400-foot rolls of film. The remaining 45,680 feet will be purchased in 46 1000-foot rolls. Next, calculate which scenes will be lit with

daylight or tungsten lighting and calculate how many feet of daylight film and how many feet of tungsten-balanced film you'll need.

- The retail cost of 35 mm film is around $0.65 per foot. Negotiate the cost down to around $0.40–$0.50 per foot by talking with both Kodak and Fuji.
- Instead of buying new film from the manufacturer, you can save money by purchasing:
  - **Buybacks**—If a production purchases film but doesn't use it, they sell the unused, factory-sealed film to resellers like Dr. RawStock, Short Ends, The Tape Store, and The Film Center. Purchase buybacks for approximately $0.35–$0.40 per foot.
  - **Recans**—When a production company purchases film, loads it into magazines, and doesn't use it, they repackage it, tape it up, and sell it to film resellers. Recans sell for around $0.25 per foot.
  - **Ends**—When a 400- or 1000-foot roll is loaded in a magazine and the filmmakers expose only part of the roll, the remaining film is cut, unloaded, and recanned. Purchase ends of more than 700 feet (long ends) for $0.18–$0.20 per foot and short ends of less than 400 feet for $0.10–$0.12 per foot.
- In addition to the film size, you can also purchase film with varying sensitivity to light. Film's sensitivity is measured by how fast or slow the film is. Faster film has a higher ASA number and is more sensitive to light. While this may seem like a good thing, faster film stocks are often grainier because the silver-halide crystals in the film are much larger. Larger crystals are more light sensitive, but because they are larger, there are also fewer of them in one film frame, lessening the image resolution. Talk with the director of photography to determine the amount of lighting of each scene and the optimal required film speed before purchasing film stock.

Panavision 35mm film camera.

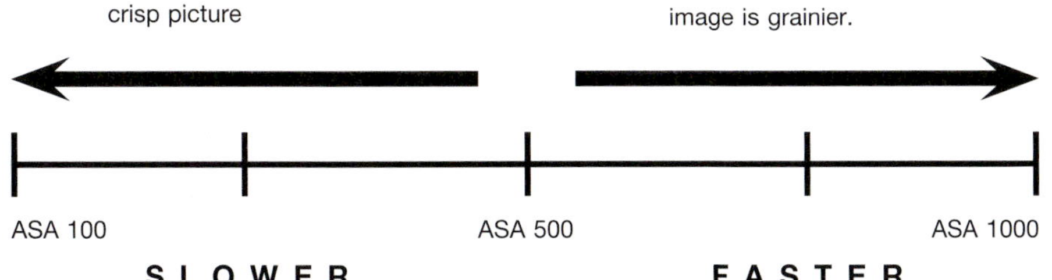

Better suited to outdoors or brightly-lit sets. Produces sharp detail and a crisp picture
Better suited to low light situations, film stock is more sensitive, but image is grainier.
ASA 100
ASA 500
ASA 1000
SLOWER
FASTER

Another factor in shooting film is the cost of camera and support equipment, purchasing the film stock, processing, and postproduction. The options and choices of format, amount of footage, and camera gear are dependent on many factors including:

- **What the final exhibition format of the movie will be.** Do you want to print the movie back to 35 mm film for a theatrical screening or is the final movie going to be exhibited on video or DVD? The cost of creating a 35 mm film print is extremely expensive and can cost thousands of dollars depending on film format and length of the movie.
- **How bright the locations will be.** Cleaner images require a slower film, which requires more lighting and production equipment for proper exposure. Will the budget support the additional lighting equipment and the crew to rig it?
- **Increased crew requirements.** Will you have qualified crew members who know how to load and operate a film camera?
- **Whether there will be any digital effects.** If you're shooting on film and there are a lot of digital effects, the cost of printing these effects will add to the postproduction costs.
- **Availability of labs and rental facilities.** Not all labs can handle all types of film, nor are all rental facilities able to support all formats. Renting or processing in another city or out of state can be costly.

Film is ultimately a higher quality format than video and increases the prospects for distribution, especially if 35 mm film is used. However, film is much more expensive and difficult to work with and may not be the best choice for your early projects.

Film workflow

Traditional postproduction

1. Once the film is shot on location, the exposed film stock is taken to a film processing lab to be developed, making a workprint. Also called dailies or a rush print, the workprint is the footage the filmmaker uses to edit and assemble the movie.
2. Once the edit is complete on a lower budget film, the editor will then physically cut the original film negative so that the edits match the edit performed on the workprint. On higher budget films, a copy of the negative is edited to preserve the integrity of the original negative and create different cuts of the film. This process is called conforming or negative matching.
3. This newly cut negative is the actual film that was exposed in the camera and the only master of your movie, so if something happens to it, the film could be irreparably damaged. That's why filmmakers make a copy of the negative to make an interpositive, also called a master positive. It's at this stage that titles, transitions, and special effects are spliced into the movie.

4. Once the master positive is complete, the movie can be transferred to video using a telecine process. Or the lab can duplicate the interpositive to make an internegative (or "dupe negative"). Prints for theatrical screenings are made from the internegative.

Digital postproduction 1

1. Film is exposed on set and then delivered to a lab for processing (developing). The cost of processing varies depending on the format you're shooting on.
2. If you want to edit the footage digitally using a nonlinear editor like Avid or Final Cut Pro, you need to telecine your film footage, which is the process of cleaning the film and running it through a high-resolution scanner to convert it into a digital format. Once scanned in, the lab will sync your production audio to the digitized film.
3. The scanned footage is then recorded to one of the following formats: HD, Digital Betacam, Betacam, DVCPRO, DVCAM, DV, or miniDV.
4. Once you have the footage digitized into your editing system, begin to edit the footage.
5. Color correct; add digital effects, titles, and music; mix your sound; and build the final movie in your editing system.
6. Render and output to a format of your choice. You can hire a film lab to transfer your movie from its current digital format back to film using high-resolution printers that essentially print each frame, one at a time. Although the price has dropped significantly, you can still expect to pay upward of $30,000 for a 90-minute feature.

Digital postproduction 2

1. Film is exposed on set and then delivered to a lab for processing.
2. The film is run through a telecine process and delivered on a video format of your choice.
3. The video version will be digitized into a nonlinear editor and an editor will edit an offline version of the movie.
4. Once the edit is complete, the editor will provide an EDL, or edit decision list, to a negative cutter who will physically cut the negative so it conforms to the offline edit. Digital effects, titles, and transitions can be performed optically, or digitally generated, and then printed back to film.

Film processing labs can brighten or darken the exposed film if the film wasn't properly exposed, there was too much or too little light used on set, or a special look is desired. When the lab brightens the film by lengthening the time of development, this is called pushing, or forcing, the film. Pushing by a stop won't adversely affect the image quality, but pushing more than a stop will begin to degrade the image by increasing grain and washing out shadows. Conversely, pulling is the process of darkening overexposed film.

16 mm color production lab costs

Developing	Per foot
Camera negative	$0.1620
Interpositive/internegative	$0.1620
Force develop one stop (min $25.00)	$0.069
Sound track	$0.090
Telecine prep	$0.023
Dolly prints	
One-Lite	$0.2390
Timed	$0.5100
Answer print	
From A&B roll negative	$1.4100
For each additional roll, add	$0.1390
Simple corrections	$0.5530
One-Lite from balanced dupe negative	$0.3290
Timed reversal check print A&B roll	$0.6630
Intermediates/after answer print	
Interpositive(contact) from A&B roll negative	$0.9070
Internegative (contact) from interpositive	$0.7000
Internegative (contact)	
From reversal or color print	$1.5880
Release prints	
Single print	$0.2440
2–9	$0.2070
10–49	$0.1660
50+	By quote
Low contrast (from telecine transfer)	$0.3020
A 3% threading charge (10-foot minimum) will be added to all pinning rolls.	
Minimum	$49.00 per item

Prices subject to change without notice.

35 mm color production lab costs

Developing	Per foot
Camera negative	$0.1620
Interpositive/internegative	$0.1620
Force develop one stop (min $25.00)	$0.069
Sound track	$0.090
Telecine prep	$0.023
Dolly prints	
One-Lite	$0.2810
Timed	$0.7000
Answer print	
From A roll negative	$1.3110
From A&B roll negative	$1.4350
Simple corrections	$0.8370
One-Lite from balanced dupe negative	$0.5250
Intermediate/after answer print	
From A roll negative Interpositive	$1.3770
Internegative (for interpositive)	$1.3770
From A&B roll negative Interpositive	$1.5160
Release prints	
Single print	$0.2940
2–9	$0.2380
10+	By quote
Low contrast (from telecine transfer)	$0.3490
A 3% threading charge (10-foot minimum) will be added to all pinning rolls.	
Minimum	$49.00 per item

Prices subject to change without notice.

Benefits of shooting film

- Film's rich, organic look is due, in part, to the random mosaic of silver halide particles that makes each frame unique. Unlike video, which captures light and converts it using a grid of light-sensitive sensors, film's chemical process mimics the way the human eye operates. Its high resolution is similar to an eight-megapixel still image, compared to HD's two-megapixel image quality. Be aware that after film has been processed and undergone copying, generation losses degrade the film you see in theaters to the same resolution quality as HD.
- Film offers a greater contrast range, color saturation, and resolution than digital video. Film is more sensitive to light and is able to capture low-light scenes and high-contrast scenes much better than most video sources. Film is also more forgiving in over- and underexposed areas of the image.
- Film cameras are able to offer a wide range of shooting speeds of 400+ frames per second.
- Film is the most universally accepted distribution format. Any country will accept a film-based movie, in part because of the ease of transferring it to other mediums.
- Film offers a shallower depth of field than digital acquisition systems.
- Film lasts longer than video formats.

Drawbacks of shooting film

- The cameras are heavy and may require additional camera personnel to operate them.
- Film is expensive to purchase and process.
- You cannot see what you've shot until the footage is processed at the lab.
- Audio needs to be recorded separately and then synced in postproduction, which is an expensive, time-consuming process.
- Film is susceptible to dust, scratches, and debris that may damage the coating.

SHOOTING VIDEO

Video has been an evolving format over the years, coming close to, and in some times equaling, the quality of film. Recently, high-definition and uncompressed formats have begun leveling the playing field between video and film. Today, the high quality and low cost of shooting digitally allows filmmakers to tell their stories like never before.

There is a significant difference in the image quality, resolution, contrast range, and color space between the old analog formats such as VHS, Hi8, 8 mm, and VHS-C and the new digital video formats of miniDV, DV, DVCPRO, and DVCAM. If you are serious about producing a commercially viable movie, consider investing in or renting a high-quality HD camcorder. Consider a system that allows you to capture uncompressed video footage.

DIRECTOR'S NOTES

When making the decision whether to shoot standard definition or high-definition video, high-definition formats should warrant careful and serious consideration. The recent proliferation of HD content has made consumers more willing to invest in HD television sets, prompting media providers to create more HD content.

Any filmmaker willing to invest money in a movie should be using a format that meets current and near-future broadcast and distribution specifications. Most distributors will no longer accept standard definition product because of the limited resolution, the poor aesthetic quality, and the inability to sell it to HD-savvy audiences.

Fortunately, HD has been a working format long enough that rental and purchase prices of HD cameras and postproduction solutions have dropped significantly, making them more affordable than ever.

Standard definition

The NTSC (National Standards Television Committee) color television signal hasn't changed since its inception in the late 1940s. Termed "standard definition," today's televisions, DVD players, tape players, and broadcasters all utilize the same signal specifications:

720 × 480

This refers to the number of horizontal pixels to the number of vertical pixels in the television image. Sometimes referred to as the lines of resolution, the NTSC signal contains 525 lines of resolution with several lines reserved for closed captioning, timecode, and other data hidden in the signal. Nonlinear editing systems digitize NTSC video at resolution of 720 × 480. Not all televisions display all lines of data, so although televisions have improved in picture quality over the past half-century, the signal itself hasn't changed.

4:3 aspect ratio

The aspect ratio refers to the ratio of the width of the frame to the height. All NTSC television signals are 4:3, which equates to four blocks wide by three blocks high. The NTSC aspect ratio is sometimes described as 1.33:1.

I've shot several movies on HD that have been distributed. Provided each shot is carefully lit, framed, and exposed, you can take full advantage of the benefits of the digital medium.

29.97 interlaced frames

The NTSC signal operates at 29.97 frames every second. Color televisions use cathode-ray tubes (three to be exact, one for each primary color), or CRT, which operate like a gun that shoots a stream of electrons at a photosensitive screen, causing it to glow. Electromagnets surrounding the CRT pull the electron stream across the screen systematically scanning each and every of the 525 lines of the frame. The engineers who created this system discovered that they could fit more lines of resolution into the frame if the electron beam were to scan every EVEN line first and then jump back to the top of the frame and scan every ODD line. Each of these passes is called a field, so we have the even field and the odd field. These two fields together make one frame. This is why NTSC television is called interlaced. So the NTSC television standard consists of 29.97 frames per second and 60 fields per second. Elsewhere in the world, the European television standard, phase alternating line (PAL), has 25 interlaced frames per second consisting of 50 fields.

Let's say that you're watching an action movie on VHS and pause the tape to get popcorn out of the microwave. When you come back, you notice that in the frame you paused at, the action hero, who is running in front of a bus, is jumping back and forth. Even though you paused the *frame*, you're seeing the interplay between the odd and even *fields*.

Benefits of shooting video

- Video is much cheaper than film, doesn't need to be processed, and can be viewed instantly for playback on set or in the editing room.
- The postproduction workflow is much easier when shooting video. It's even possible to transfer the footage to a laptop on set and assemble a rough cut before finishing a day of shooting.
- What you see is what you get. There is no need to wait for the developed film to come back from the lab to determine if there were any mistakes made in exposure, framing, or coloring. The image you see on the monitor is the image that has been recorded.
- The cameras tend to be smaller and lighter, making it easier to set up the camera for a new setup.
- It's possible to schedule more setups in a day, shortening the number of days needed to shoot a film and keeping the budget lower because it's easier to set up the camera.
- The audio can be recorded directly to tape, eliminating the need to sync the sound in postproduction.

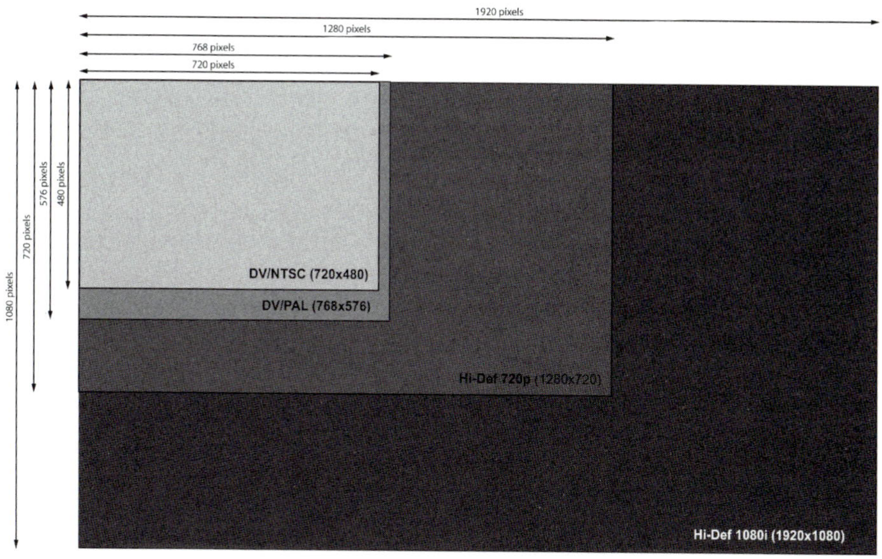

Compare the size and aspect ratios of common standard definition and high definition formats.

Drawbacks of shooting video

- Video is an electronic process that forces the image into a grid of pixels that can result in aliasing.
- Shooting a movie on video may hurt its chances for distribution, as most distributors still prefer movies shot on 35mm film.
- Shooting video has a limited contrast range and much less sensitivity to light than film.
- Filmmakers tend to get lazy when working with video, spending less time crafting each frame, the lighting, and the camera settings.
- Video cameras are limited in their ability to overcrank and undercrank. Certain HD cameras can shoot only up to 60 frames per second.
- Compression, especially in consumer formats like DV and HDV, eliminates a lot of color detail, causing artifacts, blockiness, and flat colors in favor of smaller file size.

HIGH DEFINITION

High-definition video is the long-awaited replacement to standard definition and offers huge improvements in resolution, variable frame rates, detail, and color. Designed as the new worldwide standard, there are two primary high-definition formats that are used.

720p

The smaller of the two HD formats has a resolution of 1280 × 720. Used for television broadcast where the larger HD format is too big for current broadcast carrier waves, the 720 format boasts an impressive array of features.

The 720 format has a 16 × 9 aspect ratio. Like its 1080 HD brother, it has a frame shape similar to 35 mm film. Much wider than standard definition, HD offers a much more aesthetically pleasing shape and image.

The 720 format supports a variety of frame rates as well as progressive and interlaced frames.

Television standards

Television standards are like languages. Each is unique and incompatible, but can be translated to another format. Below are listed the major television formats of the world:

NTSC

- Used in most of North and South America
- Screen aspect ratio is 4 × 3
- 525 lines of horizontal resolution
- 29.97 frames per second
- Each frame is made of two fields
- Roughly 30 MB per second uncompressed

PAL

- Used in western Europe and Australia
- Screen aspect ratio is 4 × 3
- 625 lines of horizontal resolution
- 25 frames per second
- Each frame is made of two fields

SECAM (SEQUENTIAL COULEUR AMEMORIE)

- Used in France and various parts of the Middle East and Africa
- Screen aspect ratio is 4 × 3
- 819 lines of horizontal resolution
- 25 frames per second
- Each frame is made of two fields

HIGH DEFINITION

- Screen aspect ratio is 16 × 9
- Resolution is either 1280 × 720 or 1920 × 1080
- The frame rate is 23.98, 24, 25, 29.97, 30, 50, 59.94, and 60 frames per second
- HD can be recorded in either interlaced or progressive modes
- Roughly 300 MB per second uncompressed

1080i/p

The larger of the two high-definition formats, 1080 boasts a resolution of 1920 × 1080 pixels in either interlaced or progressive mode. With a 16 × 9 aspect ratio, the 1080 format provides the highest resolution and image quality of the two formats.

Camcorder purchasing tips

The first step to shooting on video is buying a high-quality camera that will give you the control you need over the image. Buying a camcorder can be an intimidating and frustrating experience, but here are some guidelines for buying a camera that will serve your motion picture shooting needs:

- **Optics.** Buying a consumer camcorder will be cheaper, but it does not offer the same quality in optics, image quality, or control that a prosumer or professional camcorder offers.
- **Make sure the camcorder has three CCDs.** A CCD is the imaging chip that converts light into an electrical signal that is later processed by the camera and recorded to tape. Bigger CCDs have more sensors that make for a sharper image. Higher-end camcorders split the light that enters the lens with a prism and use three separate CCDs to capture the red, green, and blue colors. The results are sharper and ultraclean images with vibrant colors that don't bleed. In addition, the larger the CCD, the shallower the depth of field, resulting in a more film-like look.
- **Ensure the camcorder has manual controls.** YOU want to control the image, NOT your camcorder. Therefore, manual focus, exposure, shutter speed, white balance, and audio level controls are extremely important.
- **Look at the quality of the lens.** The better the lens, the sharper the image. Most consumer camcorders have plastic lenses, whereas professional camcorders have glass lenses. Although glass is vastly superior in quality to plastic, it is also very expensive, so manufacturers have begun using lenses made of fluorite—a composite plastic material that is still inexpensive, but offers a high picture quality and low-light sensitivity. Also consider purchasing a camcorder that has removable lenses, like the Canon XL-2 or the JVC GY-DV5000. Removable lenses give you the option of

Cameras like the Panasonic HVX-200 can achieve professional results for a very reasonable price. This camera is outfitted with a matte box, follow focus unit, and HD monitor.

upgrading or even renting a lens appropriate to the project. And finally, always purchase a camcorder with a better optical zoom, which actually zooms in on the subject, as opposed to a digital zoom, which simply blows up the pixels, resulting in a pixilated, low-resolution image.

- **Select miniDV or HDV formats.** The days of analog video such as Hi8, 8 mm, SVSHS, or VHSC are over. The high-quality digital formats today rival professional broadcast quality formats and work in conjunction with nonlinear editing systems like Apple's iMovie or Final Cut Pro. MiniDV is a standard definition format and HDV is the prosumer version of high-definition format. Consider buying the DVCPROHD format, which is superior to HDV in many ways at a similar price point.
- **Capture 24 fps.** If your movie is intended for the small screen, consider a camcorder capable of filming in 24p mode, which emulates the look of film. Although not perfect, 24p technology is the closest to achieving the film look without postproduction processing.

Shooting video is a cost-effective way to make a movie, especially for independent moviemakers on a budget. It can be challenging to make video look good, but with strong lighting techniques and solid preplanning, it's entirely possible for video to resemble the look of film closely. As an example, we shot *Time and Again* on the miniDV format using a JVC GY-DV500 camcorder. As a result, the movie bears a remarkably professional look given the $2000 we had to spend.

In addition, cheap tape stock will give you the flexibility to shoot as many takes as you want and really focus on the process of making the movie. All in all, digital video is the smartest choice for low-budget movies.

CAMERA SUPPORT

Camera support equipment helps stabilize the shot by moving the camera in a smooth, controlled manner. There are a variety of different types of support tools, including tripods, dollies, and cranes, that you can use to improve the production value of your movie.

Tripod: The biggest problem with independent movies is that the camera is handheld too often, drawing the audience's attention to the shaky camera and away from the story. Although the handheld technique has its place in action sequences and point-of-view shots, nothing can beat a steady camera, carefully panning and tilting on a tripod through each shot. A tripod is made of two different parts: the legs, which are the three supports, and the head, which is the pan/tilt mechanism the camera sits atop. There are several types of tripod heads:

- **Friction head** ($50–$100): These tripods are the least expensive and are designed for still cameras and lightweight camcorders. The tension controls on the head increase and decrease pressure on two metal plates. Although ideal for lock-down shots in which the camera doesn't need to move, panning and tilting actions are not smooth because of the two plates grinding against one another. These tripods are also very lightweight, so even the steadiest camera operator will have a difficult time getting a stable shot, especially if the camera is zoomed in on the subject.
- **Fluid head** ($250–$1,500): Fluid-head tripods rely on a thick oil to increase and decrease tension in the head, resulting in a smooth panning and tilting movement. The cost of fluid-head tripods is dependent on their size. Bigger cameras need bigger heads. Because fluid-head tripods are used mostly in professional applications, they can be configured in many different ways to suit the needs of the production. Legs and heads can be purchased separately so you can build your own tripod.
- **Gear head** ($10,000–$20,000): Used to support large 35 mm cameras, the gear head is used to precisely control the camera, whose weight may make it difficult to handle on a conventional fluid head. The gear head has two wheels, one on the side that controls tilt and one on the back that controls the panning movement. These wheels have gear settings that control the responsiveness of the wheels so the operator can, by moving the wheels the same speed, pan and tilt quickly or very slowly, depending on the requirements of the shot. Rarely used in video, gear heads are usually seen on shoots utilizing larger film cameras.

Doorway dolly.

Dolly (free–$500/day to rent): A dolly is a platform with wheels that moves the camera in a smooth, controlled manner. Always pushed by an operator, the dolly can be used with oversized tires if the ground is smooth, or it can operate on a track, which gives the dolly grip precise control over the camera's movements. Dollies can be cheaply constructed by mounting skateboard wheels parallel to each other on an angled piece of steel and then attaching them to the

bottom of a piece of plywood. Track can be made out of PVC pipe, cut to whatever length you need. Professional dollies, like the Matthews Doorway Dolly, can be rented for $50–$70 a day with eight-foot pieces of track renting at around $15–$25 a day. Using professional equipment will be much easier in setting up controlled shots. Large, pneumatically controlled dollies like the Super PeeWee or the Chapman are heavy, sophisticated dollies that can raise and lower the camera and are designed for heavy motion picture cameras. They can be rented for $300–$500 a day.

Crane ($400–$1000/day to rent): Cranes are camera support devices with long arms that can raise and lower the camera or arm the camera over a crowd or set. Some cranes are able to support only the camera, whereas others can support the camera and two people. Always counterbalanced with weights, a crane grip will raise, lower, and arc the crane around for the shot. Cranes usually come with an operator who will set up, operate, and tear down because of the unit's complexity and risk.

Steadicam ($400–$1000/day to rent): Steadicams are counterbalanced devices, either handheld for small cameras or worn on a vest for heavier cameras, that absorb the shock of the operator's movements, allowing the operator to walk and run. The result is a smooth shot much like that from a dolly, but it frees the operator to walk up and down stairs, run on rocky terrain, or secure a smooth shot impossible to get with a dolly or crane. Smaller steadicams can be purchased for around $1000 for small cameras, whereas the bigger rigs cost around $15,000–20,000.

IF YOU'RE SHOOTING IN ENGLAND, CHECK OUT THESE RESOURCES

Lighting equipment hire

Direct Lighting

200–203 Hercules Road

Waterloo

London SE1 7LD, UK
Telephone: +44 870 204 6000
Fax: +44 870 204 6001
www.directlighting.co.uk

HD camera equipment hire

On Sight
14/15 Berners Street,
London W1T 3LJ, UK
Telephone: +44 20 7637 0888
Fax: +44 20 7637 0444

LIGHTING

In order to meet the exposure requirements of the medium you're shooting and the artistic requirements of the story, be sure to have access to a wide range of lighting instruments. From inexpensive lights available from the hardware store, to practical lights seen in the shot, to professional high-wattage fixtures, professional tools are the key to creating a Hollywood-quality movie.

There are a variety of light fixtures, including halogen metal iodide (HMI), fluorescent, and tungsten lighting, that can be configured into harsh, soft, direct, and diffused sources of different color temperatures to provide filmmakers with varying degrees of control.

Two basic categories of lights are open face and fresnels.

- **Open-face lights** feature an exposed lamp placed in front of a focusing reflector. Using nothing more than a wire scrim in front of the lamp and a lever to focus or spot the light, the basic functionality of the fixture makes them inexpensive and versatile.
- **Fresnels** are lights with a built-in lens that focuses the light. Generally sturdier and more easily controlled, fresnels provide greater, more focused light output and more flexibility for the user than open-face fixtures.

Tungsten light.

Although inexpensive solutions may provide the light output needed to light a scene, the lack of control over the light will ultimately create a problem. Some features to look for in a light fixture include:

- **Barn doors:** These four metal flaps help shape the light roughly. Completely configurable, barn doors are the first line of flagging, shaping, and reducing the spill of the light. Gels and diffusion can be clipped to barn doors.

Light kit.

- **Flood and spot:** A dial or lever on the side of the light will move the lamp closer to and farther from the reflector, focusing the light beam into a narrow beam or spreading the light across a greater area.
- **Lamps:** Professional lights accept industry standard bulbs. Although expensive, these bulbs are designed to generate light at a specific color temperature and wattage.
- **Lenses:** Some fresnels, such as HMI Pars, come with interchangeable lenses that give the user greater flexibility in shaping the pattern of light emanating from the fixture.

Remember that the secret to good lighting is about controlling the attributes of the light, a capability delivered only by professional-grade motion picture lights.

Tungsten

Using the same element found in most household light bulbs, tungsten light fixtures produce a warm orange light (3200K). These fixtures are among the least expensive and provide a wide range of flexibility and control.

At the cheap end, you can purchase construction work lights from a hardware store or use the clamp on pie-tin utility lights that use standard light bulbs. Whereas these lights are inexpensive, they lack the control that you have with professional fixtures.

Professional lights produced by companies like Lowel (www.lowel.com) or Arri (www.arri.com) are much more expensive, costing anywhere between $100 and $2000 per light fixture, depending on the wattage and output of the light. These fixtures offer a much greater degree of control over the light by allowing the user to flood or spot the light, use barn doors to shape the light, and add scrims to reduce the light. Professional lighting equipment can also be rented from a local rental company.

Fluorescent

Tungsten light fixtures require a lot of electricity and generate a lot of heat, making them ineffective in small, tight quarters, so filmmakers often use fluorescent lights instead. Ideal for creating a soft wraparound, these fixtures are cool and energy efficient, although a single fluorescent lamp does not produce as much light as a tungsten lamp. Light kits of two or three fixtures cost around

$3000 and can be purchased from Kino-Flo (www.kinoflo.com) or Videssence (www.videssence.com).

Kino-Flo four foot, four bank fixture.

The lamps can be easily switched in fluorescent fixtures between daylight (5600K) or tungsten (3200K) lamps so the color temperature matches the ambient light.

Professional fluorescent lights differ from consumer fluorescents in a number of ways:

- **Flicker:** Professional fixtures utilize a special, flicker-free ballast. Unlike consumer fluorescents, which flicker when recorded on a 24 frame per second camera, professional lights will not flicker on screen.
- **Dimmability:** Professional fluorescents can be dimmed from the ballast to reduce the light output.
- **Color temperature:** Professional fluorescent fixtures can be outfitted with special bulbs that match the color of either tungsten or daylight, allowing them to be used in either lighting condition.
- **Durability:** Professional fluorescents are designed and built to withstand the rigors of film production and provide a number of controls, from barn doors to egg crates, to craft and focus the light.

HMI

Halogen metal iodide lights are fixtures that use a gas globe instead of a tungsten bulb and produce roughly five times the amount of light as a tungsten lamp at the same wattage. HMIs produce a blue light that matches the color temperature of sunlight and cost around $8000 for one light. A 1200-watt HMI, which is the largest HMI that can run off a household circuit, can be rented for around $120/day from most rental companies.

- **High light output:** HMIs generate five times the light of a similarly watted tungsten light and run much cooler in temperature.
- **Cost:** HMIs are expensive to purchase and maintain. A 1200-watt globe costs about $450 to replace. HMIs can also be very finicky and fail to strike if power conditions aren't perfect. Repairs and maintenance of HMIs can also be costly.
- **Work outdoors:** The primary light fixture of choice when shooting during daylight, the color temperature of an HMI matches the color of sunlight, eliminating the need to add gels.
- **Dimmable and timed:** HMIs have both dimming controls and the ability to work in flicker-free mode, making them ideal when working with film.

Soft boxes

Softboxes are tungsten or HMI lights with a black fabric housing mounted on the light fixture with a soft white diffusing material that softens the light.

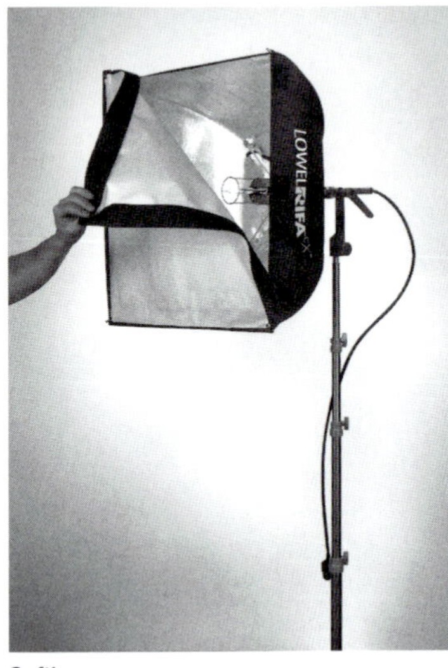

Softbox.

Ideal for filming people, the softbox smoothes the light, making much softer shadows. Softbox lights can be purchased or rented as an all-in-one unit that also includes the light fixture, or you can obtain a Chimera (www.chimeralighting.com), which is a separate softbox that can be added to virtually any light fixture.

One outstanding softbox is the Lowel Rifa-Lite. This all-in-one-unit contains a hardwired lamp mounted inside a collapsible umbrella, leaving a very small storage footprint.

Light kits

Lights can be purchased or rented individually or in a kit. Kits generally include two to four light fixtures, light stands, barn doors, and accessories in one case. This is, in most instances, the best option for filmmakers. A light kit with a 1000-watt light, a 500-watt light, and a 250-watt light should be sufficient for most small-sized indoor scenes.

LIGHTING SUPPORT

Anyone can set up a light and turn it on, but the real craft of lighting a scene is in controlling the light. Lighting control tools, called grip equipment, include flags, nets, silks, and C-stands, which are used to shape, craft, reduce, and diffuse light.

Nets are netted fabric material stretched across a metal frame that, when placed in front of a light source, reduce the amount of light. A single net will cut the light by one-third of an *f*-stop. A double net will reduce the light by two-thirds of an *f*-stop and a triple by a full *f*-stop. Nets come in a variety of sizes and are often held in front of the light source with a C-stand.

Silks are similar to nets, but instead of a netted material that reduces the light, a silk has a solid white material that softens the light. Silks are used to reduce the harshness of a light source and, like nets, come in a variety of sizes.

Nets, flags, and silks.

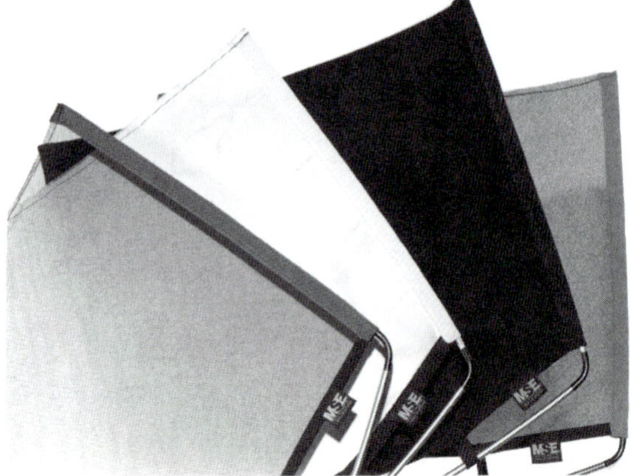

Flags are frames with a solid black material that completely blocks the light. Used to cast shadows, flags are a good tool to help shape the light so that it falls only where you want it.

C-stands are multipurpose stands with a grip head and an extendable gobo arm that can hold flags, nets, silks, and even lights.

There are hundreds of different stands, clamps, and rigs that you can use to mount lights and lighting control instruments.

Gels

In addition to controlling the quality of light, it is also important to control the color of light using thin films called gels, by placing them in front of the lights. Gels are multicolored pieces of film that will tint your light a certain color, sometimes for aesthetic reasons and other times to balance the color of the light to match the color of other lights within the scene.

The two most common types of gels are CTO (color temperature orange), which is designed to convert the color of sunlight to match the color of tungsten light, and CTB (color temperature blue), which converts tungsten light to match sunlight. To learn more about color temperature, refer to the Cinematography chapter.

You can get a free sample book that includes a variety of gels by contacting Lee Filters or Rosco Filters. Gels can be purchased from a local rental company for around \$6.00 per 2 × 2-foot sheet.

Diffusion

Whereas gels will tint the color of the light, diffusion will soften the light. There are several types of diffusion, each with varying intensities. A gel sample book will also include samples of diffusion.

C-stands.

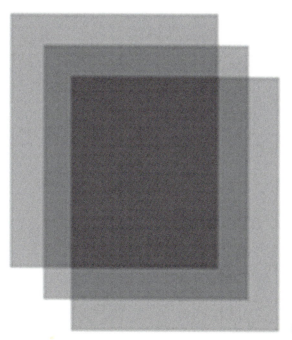

Gels.

Both gels and diffusion can be cut with scissors and attached to a light's barn doors using C-47s (the fancy technical term for clothespins).

MICROPHONES

Good audio is critical to a movie, so it is important to have a high-quality shotgun microphone, a boom pole to suspend the mike over the actors, a shock mount to suspend the mike at the end of the boom pole to minimize extraneous sounds, several XLR audio cables, and a good pair of headphones.

Do not use the built-in camera microphone because the distance from the microphone to the subject will vary from shot to shot, introducing too much ambient sound. Instead, by placing a microphone at a constant distance over the actors, regardless of the camera position, the dialog will be strong and noise-free.

Audio-Technica makes high-quality on-set microphones. See the Audio Recording chapter for more information on microphones and on how to make an inexpensive boom pole.

WHAT DO YOU REALLY NEED?

The list of equipment necessary to shoot a scene can be really complicated and intimidating, so here are some guidelines for the basic must-haves on every film shoot:

- The camera
- A tripod
- A portable television monitor
- Shotgun microphone with a boom pole, XLR cable, and headphones
- Reflector
- Basic lighting kit (one 1000-watt light, one 500-watt light, one 250-watt light)
- White foam core reflector
- Extension cords

In addition, every filmmaker should have a production bag with the following items:

- Screwdrivers, both flat head and Phillips
- A small crescent wrench
- Pliers and needle-nose pliers
- Tape measure
- Small level (used to level pictures and posters hung on set)
- Walkie-talkies
- Light meter
- Volt meter
- Pens, pencils, Dry Erase, and permanent markers
- First-aid kit

- Lens cleaners, camel hair brush
- Can of compressed air
- Small and large flashlights
- Clapboard
- Gaffer's tape, two-inch black and one-inch white
- Video cables and adapters
- C-47s (springed clothespins)
- Book of sample gels
- Swiss Army Knife
- Utility knife
- Camera filters
- Spare fuses
- Leather work gloves
- Bug spray
- Dulling spray (reduces glares on reflective surfaces)

LOW-BUDGET ALTERNATIVES

For cash-strapped filmmakers, here are some low-budget options for building an inexpensive equipment package. Understand that by using cheaper tools, you're reducing the amount of control you would normally have by using professional fixtures.

- **Work lights:** When I started shooting my movies, I purchased several construction work lights from the hardware store. Costing $25 each, these lights are switchable between 500 and 1000 watts and included a light stand and power cable. Although they put out a lot of light, the color of the lights is really warm, much more so than tungsten. Consider buying some one-half CTB, or color temperature blue, gels to correct the light to a standard tungsten light. Also be careful about putting gels or diffusion too close to the lamp. The heat will burn the gels and cause a fire hazard. One major drawback of construction work lights is that the light they generate is very broad and extremely difficult to control.
- **Clamp light:** Available for around $8 each from your local hardware store, these clamp-on lights accept standard tungsten light bulbs and feature a screw-on pie-tin shape reflector. These lights are extremely versatile and the lip of the reflector is perfect for attaching diffusion or gels using C-47s.
- **China lanterns:** China lanterns feature a standard light socket with an expandable two-foot paper globe that dramatically softens the light. Used on major movie sets, China lanterns are a great way of creating a soft ambient source. You can purchase these for under $10 at discount home furnishing stores.
- **Microphone boom pole:** Boom poles are used to suspend a microphone over the actors on set. Real boom poles cost nearly a thousand dollars. For a hundred dollars, you can make an effective boom pole yourself. Purchase a paint roller extension handle and a nice paint roller from the

Be prepared for every potential problem by having any tools, equipment, and materials on hand the day of the shoot.

local hardware store. Make sure the paint roller handle will screw onto the end of the extension pole. Next, buy a $50 microphone shock mount from a music or instrument store. Remove the wire and roller from the paint roller handle and screw the shock mount in its place. The result is a retractable boom pole with a removable shock mount that even has a handle.

- **Diffusion:** A frosted shower curtain or a bed sheet, placed a safe distance from a light source, can create a really great diffused light. Also try using tracing paper as diffusion on low-wattage, 100 watts and below, clamp lights to soften the light. Always maintain a safe distance between the diffusion and the light source to avoid a fire.
- **Reflectors:** Professional shiny boards used to reflect sunlight can cost hundreds of dollars to purchase. For an inexpensive alternative, visit the hardware store and purchase a sheet of Tyvek insulated foam. This inch-thick foam has shiny paper on either side and serves as a rugged reflector. Also try white foam core for a softer reflector and foam core wrapped in aluminum foil for a harsher reflector.

APPROACHING A RENTAL FACILITY

Go to the phone book and look up "video production," "stage and lighting rental," or "equipment rental," or contact the state film commission for a list of rental houses in the area. Most major cities will have some type of rental company that rents lights and grip gear, although much of their equipment may be for theatrical productions. There's a big difference between movie production equipment and theater equipment, so be sure to ask which they stock. Renting cameras may require contacting a rental facility in a larger city, especially if it's specialized equipment like a 35 mm or high-definition camera.

Once you find an equipment rental house near you, call them up and ask them about their services and get to know the rental agent. Talk about your project and be excited, but don't talk about prices or discounts yet. Use this as an opportunity to build a relationship.

CONTACT INFORMATION

Cameras

Sony
(877) 865-SONY
www.sony.com

Panasonic
(800) 405–0652
www.panasonic.com

JVC
(800) 252–5722
www.jvc.com

Lighting

Lowel
(800) 334–3426
www.lowel.com

Arri
(323) 650–3967
www.arri.com

Gels

Rosco Filters
(800) 767–2669
www.rosco.com

Lee Filters
(800) 576–5055
www.leefilters.com

Grip equipment

Matthews Studio Equipment
(800) CE-STAND
www.msegrip.com

Audio

Audio Technica
(330) 686–2600
www.audio-technica.com

Equipment distributors

B&H Photo/Video
(800) 606–6969
www.bhphotovideo.com

Film stock/video tape

Kodak
(800) 621–3456

Fuji
(888) 424–3854

Dr. RawStock
(800) 323–4647

ShortEnz
(888) 729–7865

Tape Company
(800) 851–3113

Supplies

Enterprise Stationers
Contracts and forms
(323) 876–3530
www.enterpriseprinters.com

Earl Hays Press
Production boards
(818) 765–0700

Studio Depot
Expendables
(323) 851–0111
www.studiodepot.com/store

Schedule a time to visit and bring the script, storyboards, and production schedule. This will show that you are serious about your project. Remember that rental companies have dozens of filmmakers walking in off the streets asking for free stuff. They say no, because the filmmakers are never organized and don't have a plan. Show them you're organized and know what you're doing. Talk to them about the dates of production and ask them for advice on what equipment you may need.

Once you assemble an equipment list, talk to them about your budget and ask if they would be willing to cut you a deal on the rental costs of the gear. Always show your excitement and conviction for the project. This is your best sales tool.

Many rental houses will have a daily rental rate or a three- or four-day rental week. This means that if you rent the gear for a week, you will only pay for three or four days. This is an incentive for companies to rent gear for a week at a time. Negotiate this rate down to two-day weeks or even one day a week.

A lot of rental houses will let you use the equipment for free, but if a paying client comes in and wants the same gear, you will have to give it up. This can cause major problems, especially if you have an entire shoot scheduled, cast and crew arriving, and locations secured. You don't want to find out the day before that your gear is suddenly unavailable. Paying a little money may be a solution to avoid this problem.

- Look in the phone book or local film production manual (available from the local film commission) for equipment rental facilities and schedule a tour and demonstration of the types and variety of lighting and grip equipment they carry.
- A rental facility can help you select the proper equipment for your production and can even show you how to use the gear if you're not familiar with it. Many of the people who work at rental facilities crew on movies, so they know the ins and outs of how the gear works. In addition, rental companies are very uncomfortable renting their equipment to people who don't know how to use it. Such rentals could result in costly repair or replacement bills. Having educated renters is in the equipment rental house's best interest.

- When shooting a film, approach a rental company with a plan. Show them how serious you are about your production and prove to them why they should let you have their equipment at a discounted rate or for free.
- Most rental facilities give student discounts if you can prove your project is school-related. Get a letter from the school on school letterhead as proof. Don't be afraid to ask for a discount or for free equipment.
- Always check the equipment at the rental facility to make sure it works properly. If you don't check the gear until you're on set, problems with equipment can cause costly delays.
- Make sure you have the proper insurance to cover the rental of the equipment. Many rental agencies will require a certificate of insurance before letting you leave with the gear.
- Make sure you have a list of every piece of equipment you're renting so you can check off each item when returning it to the rental facility.
- If you're not sure how to use a piece of equipment, ask. The rental agents will be happy to help you.
- Think about how you're going to transport the equipment from the rental house to the set. Will you need to rent a van or truck?
- Bring along a friend to help load and unload gear. The more hands, the easier the work.
- NEVER leave equipment in an unattended parked car, especially cameras and lenses. If any items are stolen, you are personally liable and will be responsible for the cost of replacement.

It's possible to rent a complete grip and lighting truck, such as the Mobile Movie Studio. Outfit with complete grip and lighting gear, a production office, editing suites, tables, chairs, walkie-talkies and generators, trucks like these often cost less than renting from dozens of different vendors.

CHAPTER 11
Production Design

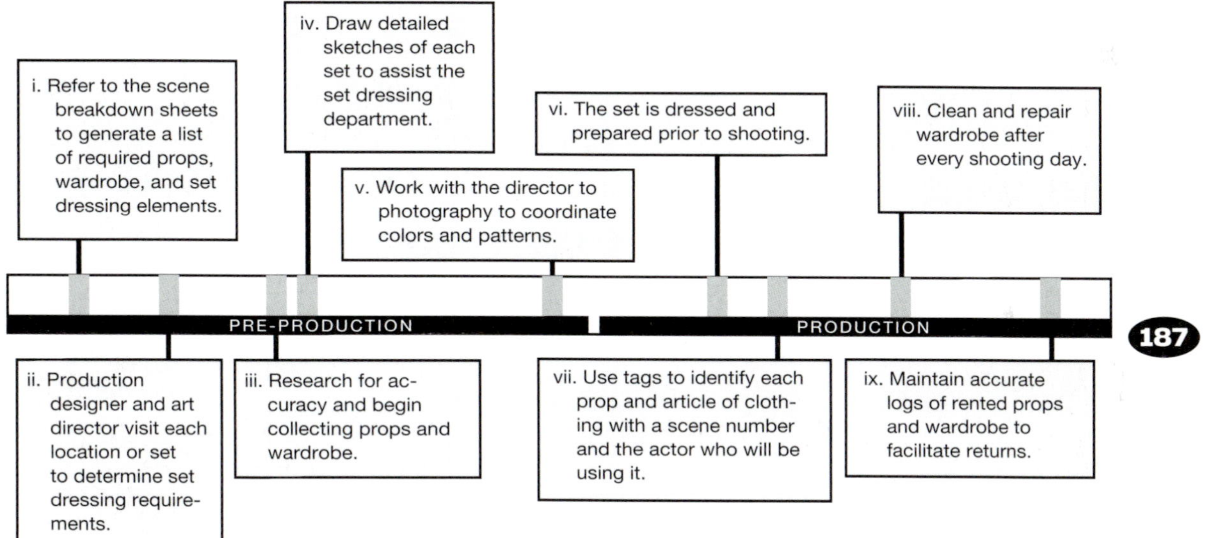

i. Refer to the scene breakdown sheets to generate a list of required props, wardrobe, and set dressing elements.
iv. Draw detailed sketches of each set to assist the set dressing department.
v. Work with the director to photography to coordinate colors and patterns.
vi. The set is dressed and prepared prior to shooting.
viii. Clean and repair wardrobe after every shooting day.
PRE-PRODUCTION
PRODUCTION
ii. Production designer and art director visit each location or set to determine set dressing requirements.
iii. Research for accuracy and begin collecting props and wardrobe.
vii. Use tags to identify each prop and article of clothing with a scene number and the actor who will be using it.
ix. Maintain accurate logs of rented props and wardrobe to facilitate returns.

INTRODUCTION

Production design involves designing and constructing sets, props, and costumes. The production design team includes the production designer, art director, assistant art director, set designer, and set decorator, as well as prop and costume departments. Production design departments are responsible for the look of the visual elements of the production short of the lighting and shooting of the scene. Production design includes set design, construction, dressing, props, and wardrobe.

When figuring out what production design elements are required for the movie, look at the script breakdown sheets for lists of what you need. Because you already broke down the script into categories, it should be pretty easy to start collecting the props and wardrobe on the list.

Although we shot the exterior scenes in the town of Chardon, Ohio, we still needed the cooperation of the store owners. With their assistance, we dressed each store in a 1950s style with borrowed elements from antique shops, friends, and custom-made set dressing.

- Production design will make the difference between an amateurish film and a professional film. Invest time in dressing sets and locations so they are not only appropriate to the story, but also visually interesting. Make backgrounds as realistic as possible by incorporating visually interesting items, shapes, and colors.
- Work closely from the storyboards so you know what areas of the set need to be dressed. Dress only what the camera will see to save money and time.
- Discuss production design with the director of photography so that color selections and textures work in conjunction with lighting and camera angles.
- Avoid shooting against white walls AT ALL COSTS. They are boring, are flat, and look cheap. If you have to shoot in a small apartment or a location with white walls, consider adding plants, fake trees, or posters (make sure you have the rights to use them in your movie).

- White walls are very difficult to expose because they reflect so much light. Consider painting walls a light to medium gray so they fall off in the background. The director of photography can easily add light to brighten up gray walls or throw a colored light to break up the background much easier than with white walls.
- Contact local interior designers for decorating advice and suggestions on where to get inexpensive set dressing. Also call local construction companies and ask them who decorates their model homes. They might not only be up for the challenge of dressing movie sets, but also have great contacts to get inexpensive furniture and set dressing elements.
- Think out of the box. Good production design doesn't have to be expensive. Use local resources like garages, attics, thrift shops, and even stores looking to get rid of old inventory to dress the set, clothe the actors, or provide props.

The contributions of the production design and art departments are both vastly underrated and underappreciated on most independent films until the day of the shoot arrives and the director realizes how sparse the background looks. When producing a low-budget film, bring the proper art department people onboard early, communicate your vision, and give them a budget to go out and begin collecting set-dressing elements, props, and wardrobe.

DIRECTOR'S NOTES

The production design of a movie is incredibly important in creating a realistic environment for the characters, especially in a period film like *Time and Again*. We spent a lot of time making sure that everything in every shot was of authentic 1950s look and feel. In some instances, like the diner, we didn't have to do too much work, but other sets, like Awanda's trailer, were dressed from the ground up.

Often, simple things like old dishes, a blanket, and old pots and pans work wonders. We tried to find a few authentic items like radios and clothes to put in the background that really sold the time period.

Ultimately, we spent less than $250.00 on all the props and set dressing in the movie, finding free or really cheap objects in thrift shops, borrowing from friends, and sometimes making our own props. Doing the production design for *Time and Again* wasn't difficult; it just involved doing a little research, seeking out good deals, and having fun in the process!

PROPS

Props are objects or items that an actor physically touches or handles in a scene.

- Begin collecting props as soon as you finish the script to avoid the rush of searching days before you go into production. There will be many other things for you to worry about.

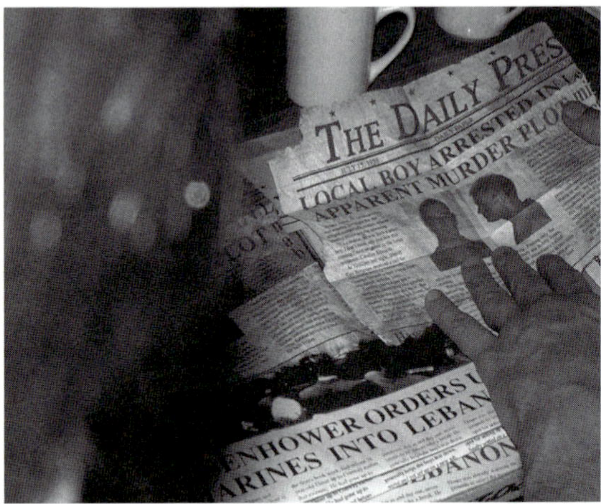

I created the 1958 newspaper on my computer and then asked a local newspaper printer to donate a roll of newsprint. Using a blueprint printer, I printed three copies of the newspaper, just in case something happened to one of the props.

Awanda's diner dress came from a rental shop in Cleveland. For a very reasonable price, I was able to rent almost 20 complete outfits, simply by asking.

- If you're producing a period film, do the necessary research to ensure that the props are appropriate to the time period. Be aware of even the smallest details.
- Go through the script and make a list of props mentioned in the script (which you should have already done when you broke down the script), then assemble a list of items that could be used to dress the set. Work off the list and pass it around to people and contacts you know to see if they have any leads.
- Delegate responsibility to the property master, whose job it is to research, collect, and possibly make the necessary props for the film.
- Props can be acquired inexpensively from thrift stores, garage sales, Internet auctions, and even family and friends. Ask around—you'd be surprised what you can find.
- Keep a variety of spray paints on set in case props need touching up during the rigors of shooting.
- It's a good idea to keep a master list of the props you borrow from people so that at the end of production, you know to whom the props belong.
- Some more expensive props may require proof of insurance.
- If you damage any props that you borrowed, be sure to offer to either repair or replace the prop, at the owner's discretion.
- When assembling props, be sure to tag each one with the scene number and day of production so it's easy to store and locate each prop when you need it.
- Approach a store and ask them if you can borrow merchandise as props. Give them a credit card number and pay them if the prop is damaged and not sellable.
- For physically demanding scenes in which props can be broken, consider acquiring two or three replacements.

WARDROBE

Wardrobe is the clothing actors wear in the movie. Wardrobe can be as simple as jeans and a T-shirt or as elaborate as an 1800s French ball gown.

- Do your research on the Internet, at the library, or simply by talking to people knowledgeable about the time period your story is set in, and select wardrobe that is appropriate to the time.
- Try to avoid white and black colors. They present an exposure problem for the director of photography. Also avoid tight patterns such as tweed. If you are shooting on video, the patterns

will create a rainbow moiré interference effect on the television screen that can be distracting to the viewers.

- Make sure all actors try on and size their wardrobe well before you begin shooting to allow time for alterations.
- If stunts are involved, secure multiple sets of the same wardrobe in the event that a piece is damaged or torn. If wardrobe is supposed to look torn and dirty, like Bobby Jones's wardrobe, make sure blemishes are consistent from one article of clothing to the next.
- Make sure that the wardrobe fits in a way that allows the actor full range of motion. If the wardrobe is too tight, or doesn't fit right, it may tear during a shot.
- Clean and press wardrobe after every shoot and take care of every article of clothing . . . put it on a hanger, hang it up, and don't wad clothes up and throw them in a box.

DIRECTOR'S NOTES

In searching for appropriate wardrobe for *Time and Again*, I looked in the phone book under "costumes" and found Chelsea's Costumes, a terrific costume shop with thousands of costumes in Cleveland.

I spoke with the owner about our project and explained how we were working with a limited budget. She really got excited about what we were doing and offered us a flat rate to rent all the wardrobe we needed for the film. We borrowed Awanda's costume as well as wardrobe for dozens of extras.

Other wardrobe came from other places. Brian used his own clothes for Bobby Jones's outfit and we borrowed the Sheriff uniform from a friend of mine.

I was really surprised at just how many resources were available to us in finding appropriate period attire.

- Remember that you can make creative costumes out of existing clothes by layering or sewing different garments together to create different looks.
- Remember that the wardrobe department is also responsible for jewelry, accessories, shoes, hats, gloves, and anything the actor wears.
- Contact local seamstresses to help you design and create custom wardrobe. Often, local fabric stores know people in the community who enjoy sewing and may be able to give you references.
- As you locate and assemble the wardrobe, pin a tag to each garment that lists the actor it's for, the scenes the garment is to be used in, and which day of production it is to be used.
- Wardrobe continuity is extremely important, so take a Polaroid or digital photo of each actor in their wardrobe each day to make sure their look is continuous throughout the shoot.

- Actors should not be responsible for their own wardrobe. In Hollywood, SAG (union) actors are paid extra money if they bring their own wardrobe to the set. Even in instances in which the clothes may be as simple as jeans and a T-shirt, there should be two sets of the same wardrobe and the wardrobe needs to be maintained for its continuity. The actor shouldn't have to worry about his wardrobe, he has his own job to perform.

BUILDING SETS

Finding a location such as a laboratory or space ship interior can be both challenging and cost-prohibitive, so in many instances, building a set piece is the most reasonable course of action.

Constructing sets allows filmmakers unprecedented control over the layout, design, and style of the set, including the ability to design the color and texture of the walls, ceiling height, and floor plan and to create wild, or removable, walls to allow better camera access. Designers can design the layout of the set so it works to complement the actors' blocking, giving the director much more flexibility than working on a traditional location. Open-ceiling sets allow the director of photography to rig lights from behind and over the top of set walls, granting a greater degree of control over the look of the movie.

One factor in crafting realistic sets is the need for believable set dressing. Small details such as furniture, aging the walls, and details in photos and artwork on set will all help sell the realism of the set.

The crew built a shuttlecraft cockpit for my first feature film, *Clone*. The set was built using cardboard, masking tape, and Christmas lights and cost less than $60.

In finding a location to construct the set, consider empty warehouses or stores, gymnasiums, convention areas, or any high-ceilinged area with a floor that can withstand the wear and tear of construction and filming.

Remember that building a set doesn't have to be expensive. Creative thinking and looking at available resources are the best way to start.

After rigging the lighting, we transformed our cheap set into a realistic shuttlecraft cockpit.

- If you're looking for a location to build the set in, landlords of vacant commercial properties may be willing to give you a space for free or for a heavily discounted rate if you plan on using it for only a week or so. Just make sure that the location still has utilities such as power and running water. Empty grocery stores, shopping malls, and strip malls are great places to look. Look into any empty factory buildings. There is plenty of room to work and the circuits are wired for heavy power usage.
- Make sure that the rental space has a loading dock or is otherwise accessible to trucks so that you can bring lumber, set dressing, and camera equipment.
- Check the power and circuit configuration in the building to ensure that it is able to support the electrical draw of the lighting gear.
- When budgeting for set construction, consider the cost of truck rental, cost of materials, helping hands to load and unload the materials, rental of the property where you'll be building the sets, utility bills, flooring, cleanup, portable toilets if needed, dumpster rental, and possibly a generator for power.
- Listen to the ambient sound outside the building. Warehouses or gymnasiums aren't designed for the acoustics needed for film production. Avoid buildings near freeways or heavily trafficked areas.
- Sets can be inexpensively built using flats, a four- by eight-foot sheet of plywood stood on end and braced with two-by-fours. The flats can then be painted or wallpapered to create the walls of the set. The flats can be moved during production to allow placement of the camera in places otherwise impossible in a real location.
- Think about the floor and ceiling of the set. Building only walls will limit the potential camera angles. To build an inexpensive floor, consider buying carpet remnants or inexpensive carpet squares from a local carpet store. Use carpet tape to secure the carpet temporarily but safely to the floor.
- Consider hiring a local construction contractor to assist in building the sets. Although you may want to try it yourself, a professional touch will make the set believable on camera. If the scene requires an elaborate set piece, consult a local architect for help. Don't be afraid to ask these professionals to donate their time if you're on a tight budget. You may be surprised at their willingness to help.

- The use of furniture pads, normally used by movers to wrap furniture, is a great way to reduce sound on a location. Hanging packing blankets (also called sound blankets) on the back of the set walls will help reduce exterior ambient sound.
- When constructing the set it must be not only aesthetically pleasing, but technically functional as well. Be mindful of the placement of lights and how lighting and grip equipment can be rigged on the set.
- Creating a brick facade or stone wall can be simply achieved by using textured panels attached to the flats. These panels are lightweight and look very convincing. Although some hardware stores may have them, it may be easier to find them at a theater supplier.
- Create convincing exteriors outside of windows by adding greenery and plants. For a sky effect, consider taking a large light blue bed sheet of fabric and lightly spray paint clouds. A small section of fence may also help obscure the background.
- Always make sure the set is safe and secure. Use sandbags to weigh down flats, use safety cables when rigging lighting, and be sure the set can withstand the rigors of film production.

SET DRESSING

Set dressing is the decoration of the set, including wallpaper, plants, furniture, and any objects that an actor does not touch during the scene. Set dressing is important in establishing the tone of the scene and establishing the realism of the setting.

- Use storyboards to help prepare the design of the set and figure out how much of the set needs to be dressed.
- I know I said it before, but I'll say it again: DO NOT SHOOT AGAINST WHITE WALLS! Dress the set with furniture, wall coverings, tapestries, posters, and pictures (provided you have the rights to use them). If you can't hang anything on the walls, use light to create the shadows of blinds or an outside tree branch to break up the solid color. This is especially true if you're shooting in an apartment or house with white walls and little wall dressing or wallpaper.
- Although it depends on the director's vision, it is often better to have a background that is slightly darker than the actor's flesh tones. It's easy to light a dark background to make it brighter than it is to work with a bright or white background.
- Research the time period to ensure that everything in view of the camera represents the time frame of the story.

The set dressing in Bobby Jones's bedroom came from a bunch of electronic junk and an antique radio I borrowed from a friend. With a little creativity, it was easy to re-create the 1950s for next to no money.

- Work closely with the director of photography when you are designing the look of the set. Colors, patterns, and brightness values of the set will be very important to consider when the director of photography is designing lighting and camera placement.
- Design your plan for dressing the set during the location scout and work everything out on paper. Once you get to the set on the day of production, the production design team should simply unload the truck and set everything up . . . not figure out what to do ten minutes before it's time to roll the camera.

DIRECTOR'S NOTES

Set dressing is important not only from an artistic standpoint, but also for practicality.

A great example in *Time and Again* is when Bobby Jones looks into the basement of his father's house and sees him painting the figurines. In real life, the location we shot at didn't have a basement, so instead of moving the entire crew to another location, we faked it where we were. I noticed that the home owner's garage door had a window that looked like a basement window, so we raised the garage door high enough to bring the window up to six feet. We then built a simple frame out of saw horses and two-by-fours and laid a sheet of plywood across the top so it was propped up against the garage door, just under the window. Then, we took grass, mulch, a few branches, and a couple shrubs and built a fake ground. The actor, Brian Ireland, then climbed on top of our little set and, with a tight camera angle, looked as though he was at ground level looking down into a basement. The effect took less than an hour to rig and looked spectacular on camera.

Think outside the box when planning shots and remember that no matter how makeshift, jury-rigged, or cheap it looks on camera, all that matters is that with proper framing, good lighting, and convincing acting, you can sell practically anything.

This simple and zero-cost approach was effective and easy, taking only a little imagination and available resources.

- Shooting on location will allow you to use the existing dressing of the location; however, if you shoot on a soundstage or on a built set, there is virtually free license to create whatever look you want. Building and dressing a set can be extremely cost prohibitive, so think carefully about windows and window dressings, furniture, wallpaper or paint, rugs, and floor style.
- Plants, especially fake *Ficus* trees, are great to break up a solid wall or add an interesting visual element to an otherwise drab background.
- Fabric is a cheap way of dressing drab walls, floors, furniture, and windows. Purchase inexpensive material from a craft store, or buy ends at a discount. Be sure to coordinate the fabric's color and pattern with the actors' wardrobe and production design.

When Bobby was kneeling on the ground watching his father through the bedroom window, in reality, the actor, Brian, was on a piece of plywood covered with dirt looking into a partially-open garage door. Little did the audience know. . . .

- If you can't hammer nails or use regular push pins on the walls of a location, try using straight pins. They are so small that the hole isn't noticeable, yet strong enough to hold up material or set dressing.

CREATING A TIME PERIOD

Cars, props, and wardrobe from a different time period can easily be obtained by seeking out collectors, reenactment groups, and even museums. For *Time and Again* Adam Kadar and I used the Internet to figure out where all the antique car shows were around northeast Ohio. We visited nearly a dozen shows in the month before we went into production. Armed with a flyer detailing the production and what we were looking for, we approached and spoke with hundreds of car owners who were displaying vintage 1950s cars in an effort to sell them on the merits of providing their cars for the film.

Quantus Pictures Inc.

Motion Picture Production Company

Thank you for your interest in showing off your car in the short film, "The Day Bobby Jones Came Home." This project will run the international film festival circuit to promote Cleveland filmmakers and the resources we have in Northeast Ohio. The story takes place in the late 1950's and as a result, we are looking for several vehicles from that era to serve as set pieces.

Although we will call you with more specific information, below is listed the dates, times and locations for each of the shoots that require period cars:

Saturday, July 13, 2002 in Chagrin Falls, Ohio **1:00pm-7:00pm**
We need several cars to be parked on the street and in driveways.

Sunday, July 21, 2002 on Chardon Square **6:00pm-midnight**
We need several cars to populate the square. We will be closing the square for the evening and would like to have cars both driving in front of the theatre and parked in parking areas.

Sunday, August 4, 2002 on Stillwell Road in Huntsburg **8:00am-noon**
We need several "used" vehicles to drive down the country road, passing up a hitchhiker.

About the Film: "The Day Bobby Jones Came Home" is the story of convicted murderer Bobby Jones who has the chance to exonerate his name by jumping back ten years earlier to the day before he allegedly committed the murder that sentenced him to a lifetime in prison. Falling in love with the sexy diner waitress Awanda in his old home town, Bobby uncovers the true murderer, only to learn that Awanda is the victim. Framed by the very evidence he left during his relationship with Awanda, the police arrest and convict the innocent 15-year-old Bobby Jones, creating a paradox that will haunt Bobby Jones to his death.

About the Director: Jason J. Tomaric has directed and produced several productions including television commercials and music videos for clients such as McDonald's and RCA Records. Having recently won five national Telly Awards, Tomaric's most well-known work is the feature-film, "One" that premiered in Cleveland's lavish Palace Theatre.

About the Writers: Written by Jason J. Tomaric and internationally-renowned writer Bob Noll, Bob Noll now teaches script writing at several venues including John Carroll University and the Cleveland Film Society. After working in Los Angeles for several major studios, Bob Noll is the recipient of dozens of international awards and enjoys worldwide publishing success of hundreds of scripts.

About Quantus Pictures, Inc.: Quantus Pictures is a nationally-award winning Cleveland-based production studio whose clients include McDonald's, Hitachi, RCA Records, and many others. With dozens of television commercials, short films, and feature-length motion pictures, Quantus Picture's mark of excellence is known industry-wide.

This document is intended for reference only and is not intended as a legal binding contract.

Letter to car owners.

We used dozens of 1950s cars in *Time and Again* for free, because we got the owners excited at the prospect of being involved with a movie.

As we walked around the car show, we wrote down the names and telephone numbers of car owners who were interested in participating in the production. Adam then contacted them a few days later, inviting them to the set to establish that we are professional and legitimate. We knew exactly who was going to arrive on each shooting day with which car. In an effort to control how many people arrived with cars, we did not provide a blanket invitation to everyone.

The result was over 75 1955–1957 cars that established the time frame for the film. Although there was no compensation, the vehicle owners were all happy to show off their prized possessions for the camera.

- If authentic extras are needed, try calling a reenactment group, especially for military scenes in which costumed extras who understand the protocol from the era are needed. Often, reenactment groups can also provide props and even vehicles.
- Car shows are a great place to find owners of old or unique vehicles. Many owners love to show off their cars, provided the scene won't put the car at risk of being scratched or damaged. Some vehicle owners may wish to be placed under the production company's insurance policy.

UNIT 3

Production

Craft Services/Catering	Cast and Crew	Make-Up/Hair	Directing
i. Coffee and breakfast are set-up 30 minutes before call-time, location is unlocked and secured.	i. Cast and Crew begin arriving based at their call times and are directed to the appropriate parking areas. 1st Assistant Director walks everyone through the set before the crew begins unloading equipment in designated staging areas.	i. Make-Up and Hair departments set-up and begin prepping the actors. If the hair and make-up needs are complicated, the artists and the actors may need to arrive early before the rest of the cast and crew.	i. The director meets with the entire cast and crew, talks about the scenes to be filmed, and runs a rehearsal with the cast in front of the crew, so everyone understands what occurs in the scene.

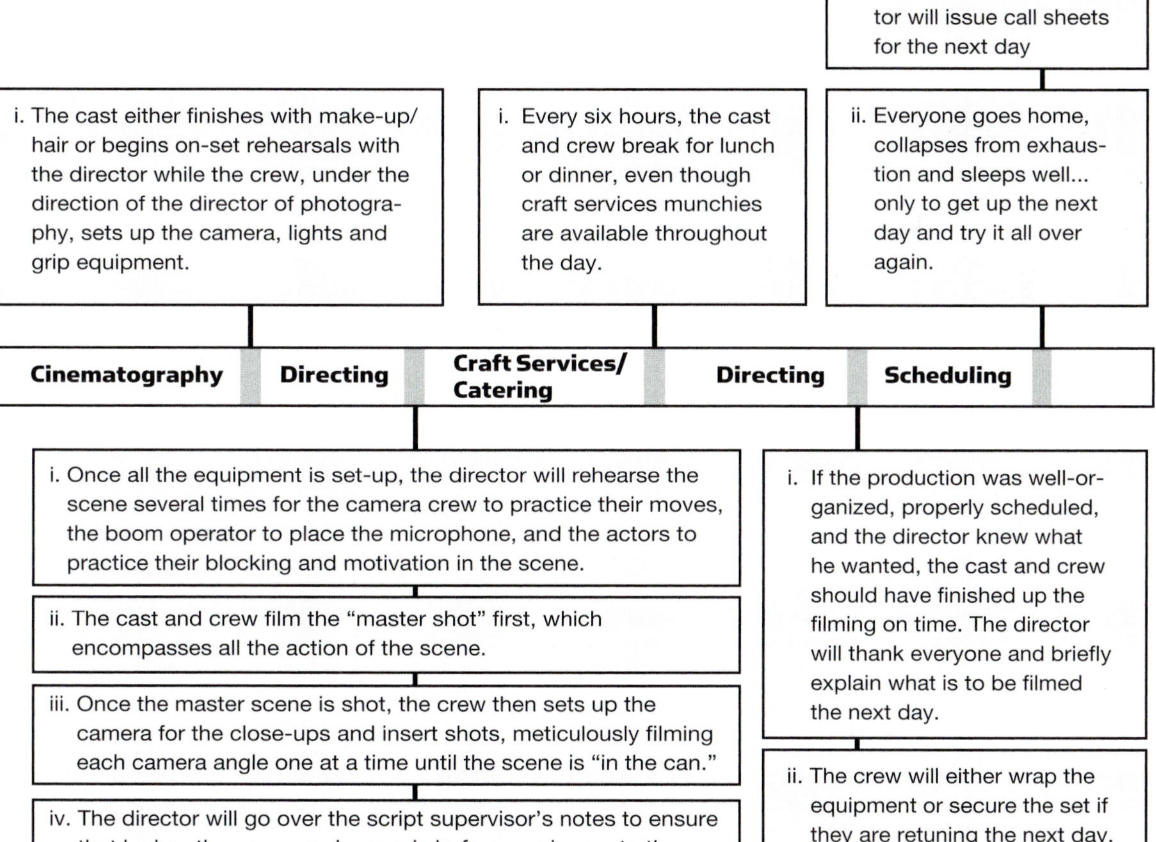
i. The 1st Assistant Director will issue call sheets for the next day
i. The cast either finishes with make-up/hair or begins on-set rehearsals with the director while the crew, under the direction of the director of photography, sets up the camera, lights and grip equipment.
i. Every six hours, the cast and crew break for lunch or dinner, even though craft services munchies are available throughout the day.
ii. Everyone goes home, collapses from exhaustion and sleeps well... only to get up the next day and try it all over again.
Cinematography
Directing
Craft Services/ Catering
Directing
Scheduling
i. Once all the equipment is set-up, the director will rehearse the scene several times for the camera crew to practice their moves, the boom operator to place the microphone, and the actors to practice their blocking and motivation in the scene.
ii. The cast and crew film the "master shot" first, which encompasses all the action of the scene.
iii. Once the master scene is shot, the crew then sets up the camera for the close-ups and insert shots, meticulously filming each camera angle one at a time until the scene is "in the can."
iv. The director will go over the script supervisor's notes to ensure that he has the coverage he needs before moving on to the next scene.
i. If the production was well-organized, properly scheduled, and the director knew what he wanted, the cast and crew should have finished up the filming on time. The director will thank everyone and briefly explain what is to be filmed the next day.
ii. The crew will either wrap the equipment or secure the set if they are retuning the next day.

CHAPTER 12

Production

INTRODUCTION

Once all the preparations have been made, it's time to begin production. Production is the process of physically making the movie, once all the elements are in place. Production begins once the camera rolls on set, either in the studio or on location, and continues until the final shot has been shot.

Production can be divided up into two categories:

- **Principal photography:** Principal photography is the shooting of any scenes that involve the main actors. The majority of the movie is principal photography and involves the director and the first unit crew, that is, the primary director of photography, department heads, and crew.
- **Second unit:** Second-unit photography is a separate, smaller crew headed up by a second-unit director and second-unit DP that shoots insert shots, establishing shots, plates for digital effects, special effects shots, stunts, and any other sequences that do not involve the main actors. Shooting second unit allows the first unit crew to focus on the performance and maximizes the actors' time to be working on set instead of waiting around for complicated set ups to be completed.

When it's time to enter the production phase, every department should be clear on what they need to do each day, what elements and equipment are needed, and what each person's job is. Every aspect of the production should be ready to go and no creative idea has been left undiscussed or unplanned.

GETTING READY FOR PRODUCTION

Shooting a movie is a very demanding yet exciting activity that is the result of months of work and preparation. When getting started in the production phase of a movie, be ready for what awaits you!

- **Long hours:** Shooting a movie often leads to long, tiring hours. Be sure to eat healthy food and get enough sleep before the production begins. You'll need as much energy as you can muster. Also be sure to eat well. Avoid sugary junk food from the craft services table; eating good meals will help carry you through the day.

- **Stress:** Be prepared for problems and stressful situations on set. The better organized you are in preproduction, the easier it will be to overcome problems as they arise on set. Remember Murphy's Law: If something can go wrong, it will go wrong. Assume there will be problems and keep a professional, level head so you can work through issues when they arise. It's easy to feel overwhelmed and stressed out.
- **Keep organized:** The secret to a smooth-running production is to be as organized as possible during the entire shoot. From keeping equipment organized to keeping the office paperwork in order, always maintain a clean, safe work environment.

A DAY ON SET

Stepping on set the first day can be a really intimidating experience, especially when the cast and crew are looking to you, the director, for advice and guidance. Begin the production day by going over ground rules for that day of shooting. The first assistant director should point out where the restrooms are, what parts of the set are off limits, where the trash is, where craft services are, where the designated parking is, and all other location-specific details. Then, once everyone has gotten his or her morning coffee, go over the production schedule with the cast and crew, and walk them through the scenes you are going to shoot. Explain what the scenes are and how they relate to the overall story, where they will be filmed, and how they fit into the production schedule. If the entire crew understands the shooting schedule, they will be much more invested in the day of shooting, feeling a part of the creative process rather than grunts moving and setting up equipment.

After the general overview, run through the first scene in its entirety with the actors so that everyone can see the blocking and flow of the scene. After this overview, briefly run through the camera angles and how you plan to shoot the sequence. Once everyone understands the setups for the scene, the crew should begin unloading the equipment, prepping the set, and getting ready for the first setup.

While the crew is rigging lighting and camera gear, meet with the actors and go over the motivations for the scene, refine the blocking, and rehearse the details of the scene. Talk about specific moments and describe what scenes came before the scene you're shooting and what the following scene is to help the actors understand where they are in the story arc. Then, the actors should visit the hair and makeup artists for any touch-up work needed.

There are instances in which the actors may need to arrive before the crew if elaborate hairstyling or makeup is required. In *Time and Again*, Jennie was always on set an hour and a half before everyone else to get her hair styled by Key Hairstylist, Deb Lilly.

Once the camera and lights are set up and the actors are ready, bring everyone on set for a camera rehearsal, allowing the director of photography to see how the actors look on camera, the second assistant cameraman to double-check focus marks, the director to adjust the performances or blocking, the production sound mixer to set the audio recording levels, the boom operator to set the microphone position, the art department to look over the set one last time, and the actors to get into character.

Once all departments are satisfied, go for the first take.

The first assistant director will call for quiet on the set and will give the command to call camera, roll sound, and mark the shot. After the second assistant cameraman marks the shot with the clapboard, you are free to call action.

Be sure to let the camera run for a few moments before calling action and after calling cut—this extra footage will provide pad for the editor to work with when cutting the film.

During the take, watch the performances carefully on the monitor and look for authenticity, realism, and emotion from the actors. Be aware of how the actors move around the frame and how well all the technical elements play together.

The crew shoots Bobby's approach into the playground. Every scene was carefully planned before we even arrived on set. The result was that each day of shooting was completed on time and on budget.

Does the moment feel real? Are the actors over- or underacting? Does the blocking seem real and motivated? Is the scene full of subtext, character, and driving story elements? Watch carefully and make mental notes of what to change or adjust for the next take.

Once you call cut, go directly to the actors and talk to them about their performance. Be encouraging and suggest different approaches to take if you'd like to change a performance. While you are talking to the actors, the first assistant director should be talking with the director of photography about the shot. Was it in focus? Was the frame clean of any stray equipment, microphone booms, and crew members or were there any other problems that necessitate another take? The 1st AD will also ask the same of the production sound mixer. Were there any problems with the audio—trucks or airplanes in the background, poor sound levels, actors turning away from the microphone?

After the director talks to the actors and the 1st AD talks to the crew, the AD briefs the director, who then decides if he wants another take. If yes, the crew immediately resets and gets ready to do the process all over again. The director will do as many takes as he needs and within the time the shooting schedule allows.

After the first setup is complete, the director then directs the crew for the second camera position. This process continues until the scene is complete.

Normally, shooting is slow in the morning and picks up pace as the day progresses. It is not uncommon for the production to fall behind schedule by lunch time, which will require you to reassess the shooting schedule and possibly cut shots out of the scene to save time on set. This difficult task can be avoided by carefully preplanning the day in preproduction, rehearsing the actors, and making sure the crew knows what is expected before the day of shooting arrives.

- Make sure everything is planned out on paper before stepping onto the set. All storyboards should be finalized, actors rehearsed, and camera angles planned. Remember that the production process is about executing the plan that you built in preproduction.
- Make sure camera angles are concise and camera coverage overlaps so that the editor has options in the editing room. A script supervisor will keep track of which parts of the scene are covered by which camera angle.
- Make sure the camera follows the actor's actions and the actor motivates the camera's movements. Rehearse every camera move to ensure the actor, dolly, focus puller, and boom operator hit their marks before rolling on a take.
- Do a complete rehearsal with the actors for the crew before setting up equipment so everyone on set understands what is happening in the scene. Go over general camera angles and how the scene is to be shot.
- Be mindful of the rules of composition (see Cinematography chapter) when placing the camera and determining angles and movement.

- Think about how the shots will be edited together while figuring out optimum camera angles on set. A smart director shoots for the edit.
- The camera operator should always communicate with the boom operator so she knows where the frame is BEFORE rolling. This will minimize the microphone boom drifting in and out of the shot.
- When shooting a camera setup, consider shooting another size frame (i.e., a long shot, medium shot, or close-up) of the action from the same angle. While this doesn't require a repositioning of the camera, it will provide the editor the option of intercutting closer and farther shots of the same action.
- Before each new camera setup, discuss the details of the shot with the crew. Good communication is always key to a smooth-running set.

Jennie and Brian rehearse the moment when Bobby discovers the ring on the floor of Awanda's trailer. Rehearsing the action in a scene for the entire crew before shooting helps the production process flow smoothly.

- Be mindful of on-set continuity as the camera positions change. Are props, set dressing, and even actors where they are supposed to be from one shot to the next?
- Productions always go slower early in the day. As the hours wear on, filming usually has to pick up pace because the production is running behind schedule. Move quickly and efficiently from the beginning of each day to avoid the mad rush at the end.
- Have a backup plan if exterior scenes are canceled due to weather. Always have a backup interior scene to film so the cast and crew can change locations and continue shooting.
- Make sure every crew member knows his on-set duties. If a crew member has nothing to do, he should ask his department head if she needs help. There is always work that needs to be done on set.
- Keep the set clear of equipment. Organize lights, grip gear, and electrical cables. This will make cleanup easier at the end of the day and make getting out new gear easier.
- Make sure breaks are allotted for eating.
- When working on set, practice on-set safety by securing cables and riggings and maintaining an environment that minimizes accidents.
- Ensure that every crew member has the day's script, call sheet, and shooting schedule.

SAMPLE PRODUCTION SCHEDULE

4:00 AM—The UPM arrives on set, opens the set, and lets craft services in to set up and prepare breakfast and coffee for the crew.

4:30 AM—The crew arrives and makes a beeline to the craft services table for coffee.

4:45 AM—The 1st AD welcomes everyone to the set and establishes rules and guidelines for working at this location, parking information, location of restrooms, first aid, shoot schedule, and any other important notes.

5:00 AM—The crew begins to unload the equipment and prep the camera, lighting, and sound for the first setup.

5:30 AM—The actors arrive and go to have their makeup applied and put on wardrobe.

6:30 AM—The lighting and camera are set up for the first shot. The director runs through a complete rehearsal of the scene for the actors and crew.

6:40 AM—The first shot of the day is taken. The crew continues to shoot.

10:30 AM—Six hours after call time, the crew breaks for lunch.

11:30 AM—After an hour, the crew returns to work.

4:30 PM—12 hours after call time, the crew wraps and begins to pack up the production equipment. The 1st AD issues call sheets for the next day.

ORDER OF ON-SET COMMANDS

Before every take on a sync-sound production, there is a series of commands that ensures that the set is quiet and every department is ready to roll. This helps keep everyone on track with what is happening.

1st AD
"Quiet on set, please!"
"Camera ready?"

Camera operator
"Ready."

1st AD
"Sound?"

Audio mixer
"Ready."

1st AD
"Actors?"

Actors
"Ready."

1st AD
"Roll sound."

Audio mixer
"Sound is rolling."

Second assistant camera
"Scene 46a, Take 4."

1st AD
"Roll camera."

Camera operator
"Speed."

Second assistant camera
"Marker."
The 2nd AC then carefully closes the clapboard before pulling it out of the shot. The camera operator may then need to reframe the shot after the clapboard is removed. Once the shot is reframed, he says . . .

Camera operator
"Set."

Director
"Action."

SAFETY

Safety is the single most important practice on set and should NEVER be compromised. When shooting, minimize liability by running an organized, safety conscious set.

- Always bring a fire extinguisher and first-aid kit on set. During the morning meeting, the 1st AD should point out where they are located and where to go in the event of an emergency.
- List the contact information for local police departments, fire stations, and hospitals on the call sheet, so in the event of an accident, everyone knows where to go.
- When working with firearms or pyrotechnics, the armorer and pyrotechnician must have a safety meeting to go over safety practices when working with firearms and explosives.
- Make sure cables are neatly coiled on the ground, are not stretched across the set, and are taped to the floor in high-traffic areas.
- Make sure C-stands, lights, and gobo arms are rigged either high or low so pointy ends aren't at eye level.
- Whenever rigging overhead lights or grip equipment, always tie a safety line in case a light loosens and falls.
- Make sure all weight-bearing stands are weighted down with sandbags.
- Never overload circuits, power strips, or cube taps.
- Use dollies or hand trucks to move heavy pieces of equipment.
- When using ladders, have someone to assist, and never use a ladder that is too short for the job.

Overall, take your time, slow down, and think about what you're doing on set. The injury or death of a crew member is never worth making the production schedule.

DIRECTOR'S NOTES

The first time I ever visited a professional set, I was shocked to see how many people were standing around. It seemed as though only a handful of people were actually working, while the rest congregated around the craft services table. What I later learned is that the people standing at crafty had already performed their jobs and were waiting for the camera crew and director to complete a series of takes so they could rush in and set up for the next take.

If correctly organized, production is an extremely methodical, calculated process, with each person understanding his or her job and helping the machine move forward. Every camera setup is meticulously lit, the camera is prepped, the makeup and hair are touched up, the set is tweaked, props are placed, and a myriad of other processes occur for EACH AND EVERY TAKE.

This type of organization and on-set rhythm is how movies get finished on time and on budget.

The crew shoots the windmill. Although it looks massive in the shot, the actual set piece was less than 12 inches in diameter. Using a wide-angle lens and a smooth dolly movement helped us create a million-dollar-looking shot for nothing.

ORGANIZATION OF SHOTS

Movies are shot in a very orderly, organized manner, and each camera shot is categorized so it is easy to reference.

- **Scenes:** Scenes are parts of the story that take place in the same location and time. Breaking a script into scenes makes it easy to schedule and shoot similar scenes. Scenes are always numbered.
  - **Setup:** Every time the camera moves to a new location or changes the angles, a new setup is created. Setups are marked with a letter within each scene. For example, Scene 45b is the third camera angle in Scene 45. (Scene 45 is the first setup and is usually the master shot, Scene 45a is the second camera angle, Scene 45b is the third setup, and so on). If you run out of letters, start over, but double up on the letters, Scene 45aa, Scene 45bb, and so on.
  - **Take:** The take is the number of times each setup is recorded. A shot can be taken numerous times because of technical issues, focus problems, changes in performance and blocking, or sound issues.

This method allows each shot to have its own unique reference. Use this reference through postproduction to ensure easy access to the footage.

CHAPTER 13

Acting

INTRODUCTION

A tremendous amount of work goes into the production of a movie, although much of that work is invisible to the audience. Location scouting, insurance, securing permits, and equipment are not as noticeable as on-screen components such as wardrobe, props, cinematography, and, most importantly, acting.

Choosing good actors who can convincingly play a range of emotions is the most important quality of making a movie, next to having a great script.

TIPS FOR THE DIRECTOR

Communicating with actors requires a finesse that will help the actors find the emotional and mental state needed to play a moment properly. Although the basics of acting seem simple, crafting the details of a performance requires a special level of trust and communication between the director and the actors.

- Explain to the actors what production is like: slow, tedious, and repetitive. The more prepared they are for the experience, the better they'll be. This is especially the case when working with inexperienced actors. Painting a picture of the realities of production will help them pace themselves and maintain a strong energy throughout the shoot.

Jeanie Lalande plays the teacher in *Time and Again.*

- Make sure the actors have their lines memorized before stepping on set. This will allow you to craft the subtleties and nuances of the scene.
- Always give actors feedback on what they did correctly and what they need to change. Never begin another take without giving the actor something to work off of. Remember that as a director, you are their only lifeline.
- Help the actors develop a purpose, or objective to attain, during the course of the shooting. In *Time and Again*, Awanda's purpose during the porch scene was to get Bobby home in bed.
- Always help the actors stay RELAXED on set. Keep actors sheltered from any problems and issues on set. The more relaxed the actor, the better the performance.
- Avoid saying phrases like "Just act natural" or "Just be yourself." These phrases don't give any meaningful insight or direction to the actor.
- Be specific in your direction. "Sheriff, when Bobby approaches, don't step back. Look him straight in the eye. It's a challenge. Which of the two of you is in command of this moment? He thinks he is. You're letting him know he's not. It's a power play."
- Don't be negative when asking an actor to change a performance, but rather, put a positive spin on it. Don't say, "I don't want you to say that line so loud," rather, say "Let's try it again, but this time, try the line a little softer. I think it would be more effective in this moment because . . . ." NEVER say what they did wrong; *suggest* a way they could do it *differently*.

- Encourage actors to remain in character, even when the camera isn't rolling. The more comfortable they are in their role, the more convincing and real the performance will be. Set a place aside for the actors to go to between setups so they can practice their lines and prepare for the next moment.
- The only person an actor should get advice from is the director. If crew members or other cast members feel free to give helpful acting suggestions, it will only undermine your relationship with the actors.
- Avoid foreign dialects or accents unless an actor can speak them convincingly.
- Be aware that working with children or animals increases the time and effort needed to get the shot.
- The more you rehearse, the better the on-set performance. Help the actors prepare not only their lines, but also their character motivations.
- After auditions, consider hosting a social event with both the cast and the crew to give everyone an opportunity to get acquainted with one another before you get to the set. You will find a tremendous improvement in quality and camaraderie.
- Help the actor understand where the character was emotionally before and after the scene you are shooting. Because movies are shot out of order, it is important to establish and discuss the character arc of how a character got to this scene and where they are going after the scene.

- Respect the fact that acting can be an emotionally stressful and trying process, especially with difficult scenes. Be sensitive to the actors' needs and always be supportive.

ACTIVITIES

Part of being able to act a moment in a scene properly is to understand how real people react to similar events in real life. Try these simple exercises to hone your ability to identify realistic performances.

Activity 1

Pick a public location such as a shopping mall or a restaurant and watch how people interact with others. Can you tell what kind of a mood a person is in? How long did it take for you to figure it out? What subtle body language did you pick up on? How can you direct an actor to convey an emotion using the same subtle body language instead of dialog?

Activity 2

Select a scene from the *Time and Again* script and choose two actors to play Bobby and Awanda. Direct the scene so the actors play the scene with two varying subtexts. Some examples of subtexts are:

The cast of *Time and Again.* From left to right, Bob Darby, Jason J. Tomaric, Jennie Allen, Brian Ireland and Paula Williams.

One of the characters is late to an important meeting.
One of the characters is tired from working all night.
One of the characters is concerned about a sick friend.
One of the characters is thinking about their upcoming birthday party.

None of these examples describe a particular emotion, but rather a situation that conjures up an emotion. It's easier for an actor to react to a situation than to play "happy" or "sad." Part of getting a good performance from an actor is to set up a situation and let them play the moment.

Activity 3

Because acting is about relaxing and trust, it's important to trust and feel confident in your fellow actors. Stand in a circle and place two actors in the middle. One actor should put on a blindfold and relax for a moment before falling backward. The second actor should catch him or her. The purpose is to relax and trust. If you can trust an actor in this exercise, then you can trust him or her with your innermost feelings when in front of the camera.

Questions

- What makes bad acting in a movie? Can you find an example?
- How is emotion conveyed through body language?
- Why, in scenes in which actors act well, does it not look like acting at all?
- How, in real life, can you tell if someone is lying? What are the visual and verbal cues?
- How do music, cinematography, and editing affect the acting?

TIPS FOR THE ACTOR

Like any other position on set, acting is a job and the actors are expected to do their part, especially when potentially thousands of dollars and precious time are resting on their ability to deliver.

- **Understand the character's history.** Remember that we are all the sum of our experiences and just as we have a history, so does the character. A movie is nothing more than sharing with the audience a small slice of this person's life. Understand where the character is coming from and what life experiences have shaped this person. Do research on the character's education, characteristics, hobbies, quirks, friendships, and problems and speak with people who have had experiences similar to those of the character to build a complete, multilayered person in front of the camera. Although the director will give you direction, it is your responsibility to develop the character in line with the director's vision and be prepared to perform, in character, every time, and without hesitation.

DIRECTOR'S NOTES

None of the principal actors in *Time and Again* had ever acted before. This was their first experience on a movie set and their first opportunity to play a role. I was very lucky to have found inexperienced actors who were able to deliver. Their maturity, outlook on the project, and life experiences all contributed to their on-camera abilities and attitude on set. Not all filmmakers will be as lucky to find such talented novice actors.

Remember that acting is a skill that takes a long time to develop. For some people it comes naturally and others require years of schooling and training to hone and perfect their skill. Beware of actors who overuse techniques and rules of thumb to play a character. Unless their ability to play the part comes from their heart, the result will be an academic, flat performance. However, using technique can make a good actor great. Learn to hone your intuition and understand what makes a realistic performance so you can effectively work with your actors and achieve the best results.

- **Listen.** Listen to the director . . . very carefully. The director is the guide to the story and will tell you how the character should react and what your motivation and subtext are for each scene. The director is also the only person on set who knows how all the other elements will come together to support the performances, from music and sound effects to the editing and digital effects. Don't be afraid to ask the director questions. The actor–director relationship is very important to creating a living, breathing character on the screen.
- **Relax.** The set can be an intense, stressful place, but you must not transmit this tension to the screen. Be prepared on set and focus on the moment. Learn to forget the crew, equipment, and camera and create a bubble of real life in the middle of the on-set hustle and bustle. If necessary, ask for a quiet place to focus on your character while the crew is setting up the next shot.
- **Memorize the lines.** Knowing the lines allows you to focus on the other details of performance and keep the moment real. Don't waste the crew's time by coming to the set unprepared. You are an actor and your job is to arrive on set with lines memorized, just like the property master's job is to arrive with all the props. The production will run longer and you will only add to the tension if you show up unprepared.
- **Know the objective.** Talk to the director and make sure you're clear about what the character's goal is in each scene. What does he want and what is he doing to attain it?

Bobby and Awanda.

DIRECTOR'S NOTES

After I cast *Time and Again*, I got the entire cast and crew together socially several times even before we read through the script or talked about the characters. Having dinner together, going bowling, and ice skating were great ways to allow everyone to get to know and feel comfortable with one another.

Filmmaking is a challenge because you're asking actors to bare their souls in front of people they've known for only a few weeks. If the process is too rushed, the performances will suffer.

By allowing Brian, Jennie, Bob, and the rest of the cast and crew to mingle and socialize, it made our time working together smooth and effortless. By the end of the production, we had all become great friends and were all saddened to have to part ways.

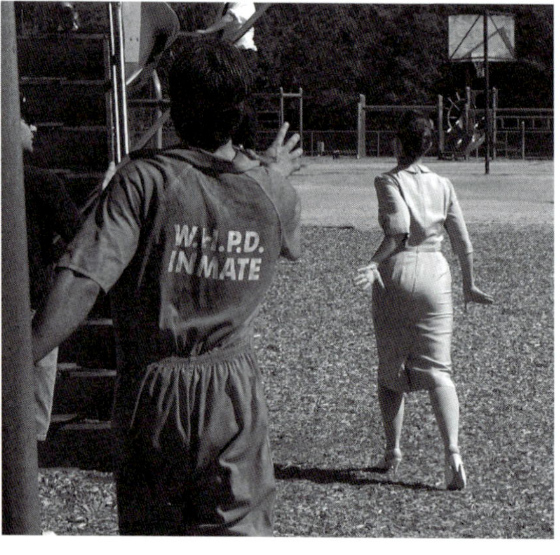

Know where the character is coming from in the previous scene and where he is going in the next scene. If you don't know, then ASK!

- **Act the subtext.** Acting isn't about reading lines; the dialog is a symptom of the deeper feelings and drive of the character. Act for the subtext, or deeper meaning, not the dialog. Ask yourself WHY the character is saying a certain line, what is the underlying motivation for this comment, and is that motivation the real driving force behind the movie?
- **Know the story.** The process of making a movie means shooting it out of order. When shooting a scene, know where, how, and why it fits in the overall movie. Understand the complete plot and character arc so that when you're asked to begin filming Scene 46, you should know what your character's behavior, feelings, and motivation are in Scenes 45 and 47. When the editor edits Scene 46 together with Scene 45 (which you may have filmed a month later), the transition of performance must be seamless.
- **React, don't act.** Be open and spontaneous to what happens next in the scene. Don't anticipate action or your performance won't be realistic. A good actor simply reacts to the events occurring in the scene, in much the same way that we all react to events in everyday life. I don't know when the doorbell will ring, so when it does, I REACT accordingly.
- **Know the business.** If you want to work in the entertainment industry, you have to understand how it works. This knowledge comes not only from books, but also from talking to agents, production personnel, and

other actors in the industry. Know what's expected of you and what procedures you need to follow to get work.

An industry standard headshot and resume.

- **Learn your craft.** Much like the medical or law fields, acting and filmmaking require years of training and study of the craft. Always strive to learn more and perfect your craft. Take acting classes, attend seminars, involve yourself in community theater, read books, watch interviews with successful actors, and talk to working actors.
- **The camera sees everything.** Acting for the stage and the screen are completely different crafts. A screen performance, in which your image will be blown up 40 feet tall, requires subtlety to convey volumes of emotion. Learn to internalize your performance. Be the character but don't act the character. The difference will be a strong, subtle performance.
- **Don't tell the crew what to do.** There's nothing more annoying than an actor who tells a cinematographer how to light or the sound person where to put the boom. Your job is to act. Period.

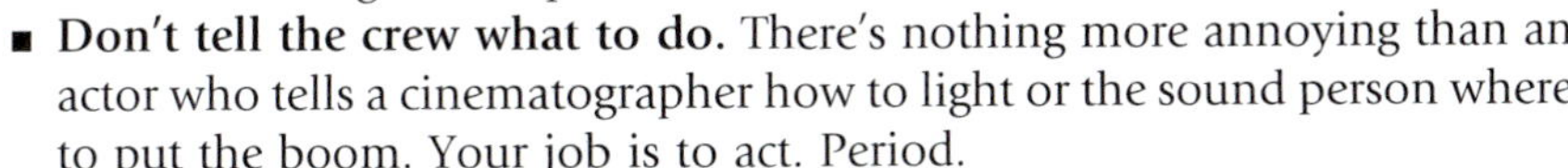

- **Be positive.** Movie production is a long and tedious process and the better the cast and crew's attitude, the smoother the shoot will go. Be pleasant to work with and don't have an attitude. No one likes egos, especially egos from actors. The crew arrives much earlier and leaves much later than you do. They work hard and become very frustrated with egocentric actors. Remember that everyone in the production process is equally important.
- **Headshots.** Headshots are eight-by-ten color photos of you, usually from the shoulders up. Find an excellent photographer who can capture the essence of you—your look, personality, and character. Your headshot is the first and usually only thing a casting director will see and it's important to make the best impression!

SUBTEXT—THE SECRET TO A KILLER PERFORMANCE

When people talk to each other, the words that come out of their mouths do not necessarily reflect how they are feeling. But, the words are a symptom or result of how they feel. True acting isn't based on the words a character utters, but is driven by WHY she says those words. What is MOTIVATING those words?

For example, you may run into an old friend at a restaurant that you haven't seen in years. Although you may exchange greetings, ask how he or she has been, and express an interest in seeing him or her for lunch to get caught up with each other, the scene would be played very differently if you secretly hated that person. What if you found out that person stole from you? Or was cheating with your boyfriend or girlfriend? Although the dialog is pleasant, the subtext is anger. Acting the subtext will add additional layers of realism to the performance.

Part of creating multilayered subtext is having a strong character backstory. Understand what is driving the character to act certain ways, say certain things, and react to different situations.

In *Time and Again*, Awanda's subtext was that she was a woman who used her looks to sleep with many men. Although she was beautiful on the outside, inside, she was a lonely person looking for a man who would love her for her personality, not her body. When she met Bobby Jones, at first she saw him as another physical conquest, but, as the story progressed, she found herself attracted to him as a person. This driving subtext can be seen in every scene and motivates the way Awanda behaves and what she says around Bobby Jones.

Actor Brian Ireland pulled moments in his performance from past life experiences.

- **Network.** Meet people. Talk to everyone. The more people you know and the more your name is known, the more likely you will be remembered if a part comes up. Attend parties, plays, industry events, and classes to build a group of people who can support you and help you achieve your acting goals.

ACTING TECHNIQUES

Acting techniques are tools that help the actor convincingly play a character in a situation. Whereas there are several acting methods, a skilled actor understands each of them and may employ the techniques taught in each method depending on the demands of the scene.

The Stanislavsky system

Before movies became an entertainment mainstay, actors worked on stage, where performances involved reciting lines of dialog, using very "external techniques." Gestures were broad and sweeping, performances never explored the true emotions of the character, and the actors played characters no deeper than the dialog written on the page.

This all changed when Konstantin Stanislavsky, born in 1863 in Russia, developed an acting method that, for the first time, took actors beyond the page and provided them with tools to explore the real emotional subtext of their characters. By exploring how to control and manipulate seemingly intangible human traits such as feelings and emotions, he devised one of the most influential techniques of modern acting.

In the "Stanislavsky system," actors must develop and feel every emotion their character is feeling. Unlike previous methods in which actors simply "acted" the emotions, in Stanislavsky's approach, actors actually "feel" the emotions, creating organic life within moments, psychological realism, and emotional authenticity. The result is a true, multilayered performance through which the actor can introduce subtext and behavioral subtleties that take the character to a new layer of realism.

Actor Jennie Allen worked as a bartender, which helped her play the role of a waitress.

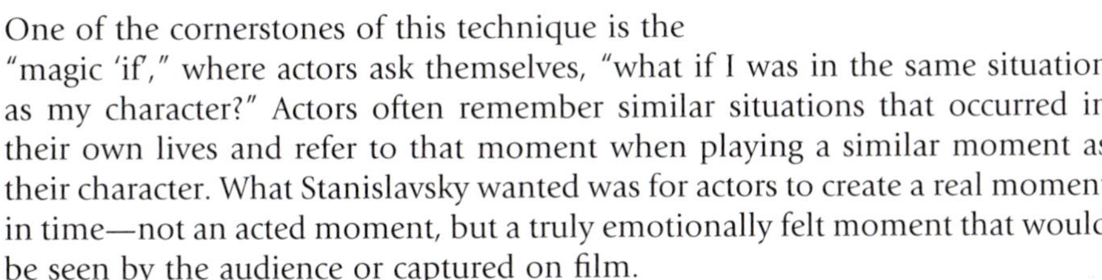

One of the cornerstones of this technique is the "magic 'if'," where actors ask themselves, "what if I was in the same situation as my character?" Actors often remember similar situations that occurred in their own lives and refer to that moment when playing a similar moment as their character. What Stanislavsky wanted was for actors to create a real moment in time—not an acted moment, but a truly emotionally felt moment that would be seen by the audience or captured on film.

This approach is considered the foundation of modern television, stage, and movie acting. Stanislavsky's technique evolved into what is considered "method acting" today.

The Meisner technique

Whereas in the Stanislavsky system actors create life within moments, the Meisner technique, developed in the 1930s by Sanford Meisner, encourages the actors to use a method called "Substitution." If the actor is playing a character who walks into his house and finds that his mother died the night before, the actor may not have had that experience of his mother dying to draw from. The Meisner technique allows the actor to substitute that experience for another, similar experience that the actor actually had in his life. Perhaps the actor walked into his house and found his dog had died. Although the situation isn't the same, the actor is substituting a similar moment he experienced to motivate his performance on screen.

An important aspect of the Meisner technique involves repetition. Repetition exercises minimize the emphasis on the spoken word and focus on the nuances and subtext of how the words are being spoken. These exercises help the actor craft in-the-moment subtleties of body language and inflection in the performance.

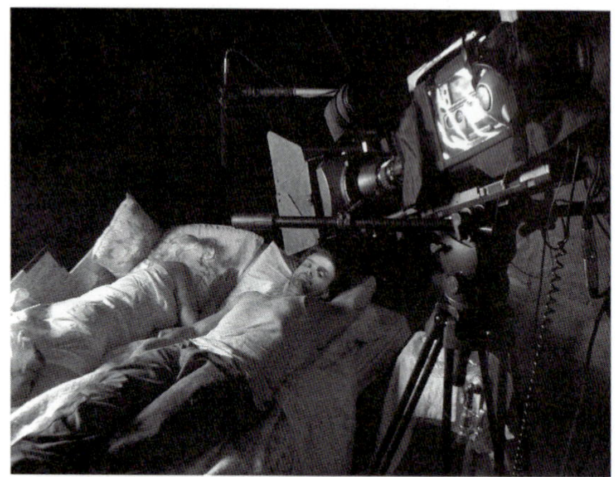

The bedroom scene was especially challenging for the actors because it was shot in a garage. Their bed was a piece of plywood and a blanket.

The Chekhov technique

Russian-born actor Mikhail Chekhov developed a variation of the acting technique in the 1920s. Rooted in the Stanislavsky technique, Chekhov's "dual-process" approach taught actors not only how to create life within the moment (first process), but also to understand how to portray that moment within the actor's realistic surroundings of the movie set, in front of an audience and in front of cameras and lights (second process). As deep as the actor is in her character, the actor is still subconsciously aware of her surroundings and must consider them when acting.

One aspect of Chekhov's approach is the "psychological gesture," which is a physical or verbal cue that a character expresses under pressure that reveals his heart and soul. To reach this psychological gesture, an actor must understand the character's breaking point and the personality aspects that will come out as a result of that pressure. The gesture quantifies the character's inner need in the form of an external action. The actor uses the gesture subtly as a way of refocusing the performance internally.

Supporting characters such as the waitress played by Mary Slowey help add realism to the story.

BACKSTORY

A play, story, or movie is nothing more than a short glimpse of a part of a character's life in a moment of conflict. The audience does not have the luxury of knowing the character from birth, so personality and behavioral traits, quirks, likes and dislikes, and temperaments must be derived during the short time the audience watches the character in action. An actor who plays a character must understand the character's life up to the point the story takes place. This is called the "backstory."

Backstory is critical to a performance because people operate on many levels, each level determined by our past. For example, a man may react when provoked in a bar fight differently if:

1. He grew up in a poor neighborhood in a single-parent family. His father is in prison for murder and his mother is a drug addict who has resorted to a life of crime to support the family, or . . .
2. He grew up in a wealthy house where money was no object. His father is an attorney and his mother a congresswoman.

When creating a character's backstory, determine:

Actor Brian Ireland waits between takes.

- How was the home life? What was the character's relationship with parents, siblings, and extended family? What conflicts were there?
- How was the character in school? What was the best memory of school? The worst memory? Was the character teased? Was he or she popular? An outcast? How did this affect the character later in life?
- What is the character's job history? Is he or she frustrated at work? Ambitious? Lazy? Always waiting for the big break?
- Who are the character's friends and enemies?
- How did the character get to the point at which the story begins?

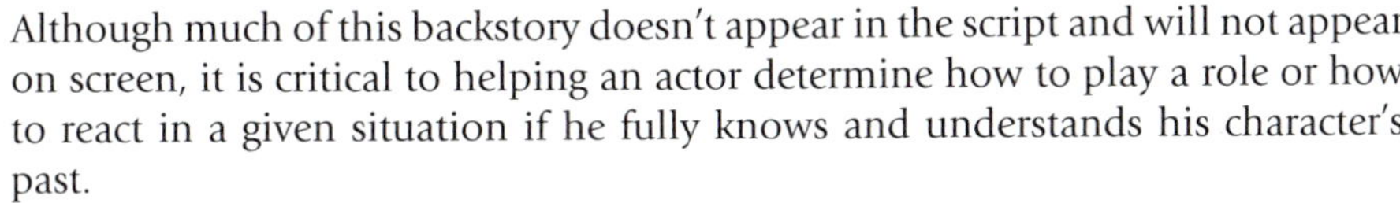

Although much of this backstory doesn't appear in the script and will not appear on screen, it is critical to helping an actor determine how to play a role or how to react in a given situation if he fully knows and understands his character's past.

Write out the backstory for every character in the story. Create a detailed character profile as if you were writing the character's biography. In addition to broad points, create a variety of specific moments (scariest moment, happiest moment, a moment when the character experienced death) for the actor to refer to when on set.

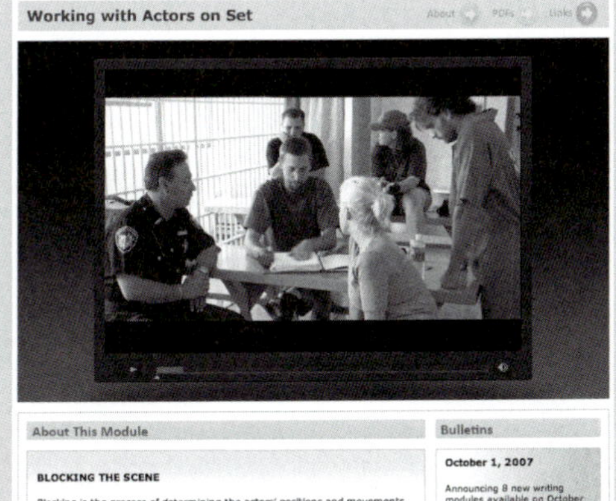

GO BEYOND THE BOOK

Learn how to effectively communicate with actors on set. Hollywood acting coaches, directors and actors share valuable tips and secrets to help you get the best performances out of your actors.

Check out the directing modules at www.powerfilmmaking.com.

CHAPTER 14
Directing

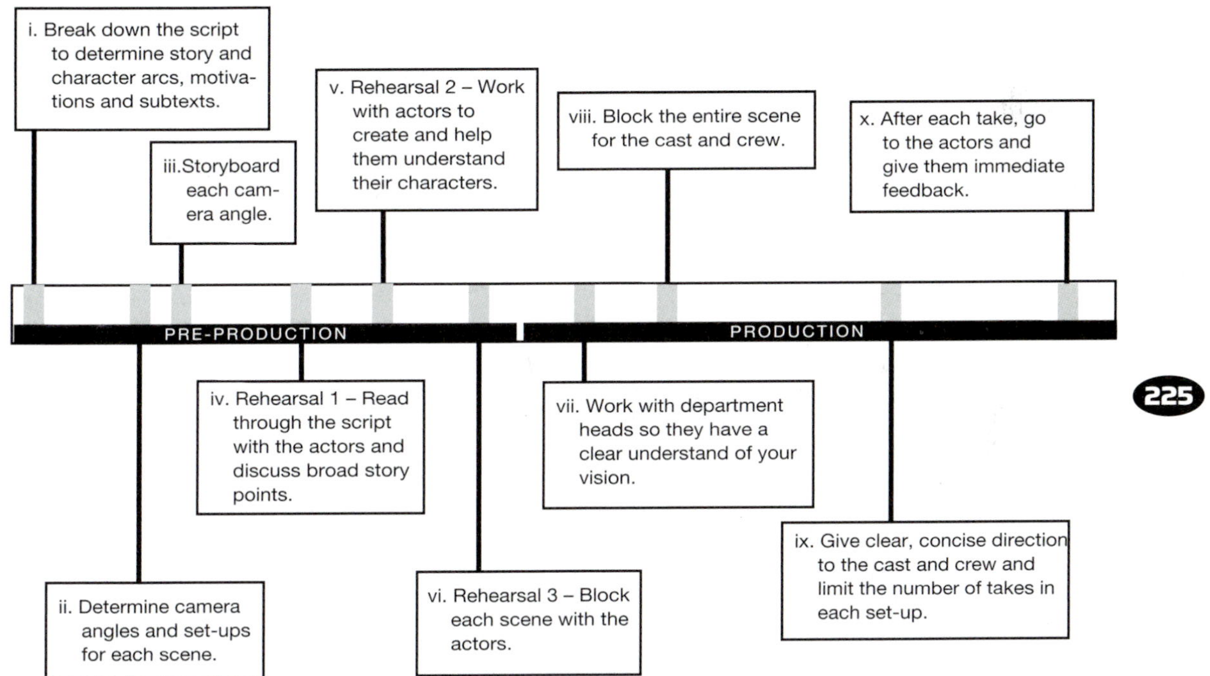

i. Break down the script to determine story and character arcs, motivations and subtexts.
ii. Determine camera angles and set-ups for each scene.
iii.Storyboard each camera angle.
iv. Rehearsal 1 – Read through the script with the actors and discuss broad story points.
v. Rehearsal 2 – Work with actors to create and help them understand their characters.
vi. Rehearsal 3 – Block each scene with the actors.
vii. Work with department heads so they have a clear understand of your vision.
viii. Block the entire scene for the cast and crew.
ix. Give clear, concise direction to the cast and crew and limit the number of takes in each set-up.
x. After each take, go to the actors and give them immediate feedback.
PRE-PRODUCTION
PRODUCTION

INTRODUCTION

The director is the master storyteller of the movie with two primary jobs. The first is to read the script and develop a strong mental image of how the movie will look, sound, and feel. By researching other movies, studying art, traveling, and reading, the director develops the style, pacing, and tone of the movie.

The second part of her job is to communicate her vision to the cast and crew during preproduction, production, and postproduction, helping direct the cast and crew's artistic and technical skills. The ideal director knows exactly what he wants, is able to communicate clearly and effectively, and maintains a positive, creative environment for everyone involved.

I am directing the extras on Chardon Square. When I arrived on set, I knew how I wanted to shoot the scene. I had spent dozens of hours working out my shot lists, actor blocking and lighting schemes. As a result, the day went smoothly and I got every shot I wanted.

Often glamorized, a director's job is rarely simple. The degree of organization necessary to coordinate with actors, cinematographers, editors, sound designers, costume designers, hair and makeup artists, production designers, producers, and writers is incredibly essential to producing an on-time, on-budget project.

Most importantly, remember that the director is a director, not a dictator. Direct the cast and crew toward the vision and allow each person to add his or her own talents to the mix.

DIRECTING DURING PREPRODUCTION

The director's role during preproduction includes three main areas of focus: study the script to determine the tone, theme, and style of the movie; rehearse the actors so they can play convincing characters based on the director's vision; and work with the crew as they prepare the technical and artistic elements of the movie.

Reading the script

As a director, either you will direct a script that has been written by another writer or you may have written the script yourself. In both instances, it is essential to become intimately familiar with the story before moving into preproduction with the cast and crew.

If you are given a script, read the script enough times so you have a complete understanding of the story arc and how every individual scene ties in with the greater story. Figure out how each scene needs to be paced, how each scene is going to start and stop, and what story elements need to be conveyed in each scene by writing notes to yourself in the margin of each page. For example, if a scene foreshadows a future plot point, the director's note for that scene may read "scene necessary to foreshadow John's theft of the car at the end of the story by establishing his need to steal paper clips." Each scene should have notes on the character's objective and the scene's overall purpose written in the script. As you read through the script, make sure every scene tightly drives the story forward and consider cutting any scenes that are superfluous.

Once the story plot points are mapped out, identify the story's deeper meaning, subtext, and overall theme so you understand how every scene and every moment supports and develops toward that theme. Most good scripts have several layers of meaning, and it's the director's job to identify these because they will be the foundation for the actors' performances. For example, in a story whose theme is how family is stronger than worldly hardship, one scene may be about loss, whereas the next may be about vindication. Understanding the themes of each scene and how it ties into the overall theme is critical in directing the performances, style, and pacing of the movie.

Once you've read and identified the plot points and subtexts, begin studying the personality traits, motivations, subtexts, and histories of each of the characters and develop a clear understanding of why a character behaves the way he or she behaves in each scene. This is the foundation for beginning to work with the actors. Unless you know each character's role in the story, how can you expect to direct the actors? I do this by taking a blank sheet of paper for each character, listing each scene number along the side if the paper, and listing the motivation and subtext of the character in each scene. The description is usually only a few words, like, "Awanda's goal is to take Bobby home. All she can think about is sex," or "Bobby wants to go to Awanda's trailer so he can get washed up. He has no intention of doing anything else." Understanding what each character wants in each scene is critical in directing the actors and giving them the guidance they need.

If you wrote the script yourself, you should already have a good idea about the motivations, plot, and character arcs. Beware, however, because you may be so familiar with the story that you may miss plot holes or confusing areas because of your deep familiarity with the subject. Try to read the script with fresh eyes as if you are an audience member seeing the movie for the first time.

Going through the script and breaking down each of these elements is important because, invariably, the cast and crew will ask you questions like:

- What is this scene about? How does it fit into the scene that came before and the scene that comes next?
- What is my character's motivation, or reason for acting this way, in this scene?
- What is the driving subtext of this line of dialog? Why am I saying this? How should I say this line and what is my character implying by saying this line?
- How would you like the lighting and cinematography to serve the theme?

Determining coverage

The next step is to go through each scene and envision the actors' blocking and the camera angles and positions. Rarely at this stage does the producer have any locations locked, so although it's impossible to block out specific moves, you can still determine where and when you want a long shot, a master shot, close-ups, and medium shots. The goal is to arrive at the number of setups, or times the camera has to move to a different position, for each scene. This will help determine the rough shooting schedule and number of days needed to shoot the movie.

A common approach to blocking the camera positioning of a scene is:

- Always shoot a master shot that covers all the action in the scene from the beginning to the end. Even if you run out of time or encounter prob-

Write down the shots you envision for each scene. This should ideally done before the budget and schedule are determined.

lems that prohibit you from shooting any other angle, you will always have the entire scene in a master shot. For example, if a couple is having dinner at a restaurant, the master shot includes the two actors, the waiter, and the table in the shot for the entire scene.

- Plan for medium shots of each character. Especially in a dialog scene, plan a single or over-the-shoulder shot of each actor. In our sample scene, there would be three medium shots: one of the man, one of the woman, and one of the waiter.
- Plan for any insert shots. Inserts are shots that cover action already covered in the master shot, but are closer and draw the audience's attention to an action or detail. For example, an insert shot may be of the man pouring wine into the woman's wine glass or a close-up of the woman's hand as she temptingly caresses her wine glass.
- Once you determine the basic coverage of the scene, write down any special dolly, steadicam, handheld, or jib arm shots. In this example,

we may want to shoot a dolly in from a two-shot of the actors into the waiter as he arrives, breaking up a tense moment between the dining couple.

I like to draw vertical lines through the scene with a pencil and ruler to identify how much of the scene will be covered by each camera setup. I then write the setup name in the margin next to each line.

The result will be a shot list of the scene that lists each camera setup. For example:

- Master shot of entire scene
- MS OTS (medium shot, over the shoulder) of the man
- MS OTS of the woman
- Insert of the woman's wine glass
- Dolly into waiter

Once the shot list is developed, sit down with the director of photography and first assistant director to build a rough shooting schedule and determine whether the budget will allow for all the proposed setups. Be prepared to consolidate or reduce the number of setups during this initial process. In the low-budget realm, it isn't uncommon to cut any complicated camera moves like dolly, crane, or jib shots.

During the location scouting process, take the shot list and determine the actors' final blocking, camera position, lighting options, and technical requirements before committing to the location. Once a location is secure, plan the final blocking and make any necessary adjustments to the shot list, so when you go into rehearsals with the actors, you already know how they will move and what the frame will be.

Storyboarding

Once each scene is broken into a shot list, the next step is to sketch each setup in a comic book form and indicate specific framing, camera moves, and actor movements. These sketches are called storyboards.

Storyboards are used to previsualize the action that occurs within each frame and convey the director's vision to the cast and crew. By thinking about the shots in advance, the crew is better able to prepare and plan the shooting schedule, art direction requirements, and lighting and camera needs and, most importantly, the director is able to judge the pacing, movement, and structure of the story before getting to the set. Remember that revising shots on paper is a lot cheaper than revising shots on film. Use the storyboards on set as a reference for the cast and crew as to how the scene will be shot and ultimately pieced together. The alternative to previsualizing the movie with storyboards is arriving on set with no one on the cast or crew knowing what the director wants or how a scene is to be framed, lit, or dressed. Time will be wasted and the director may not get the shots he wants because he will be worrying about how to

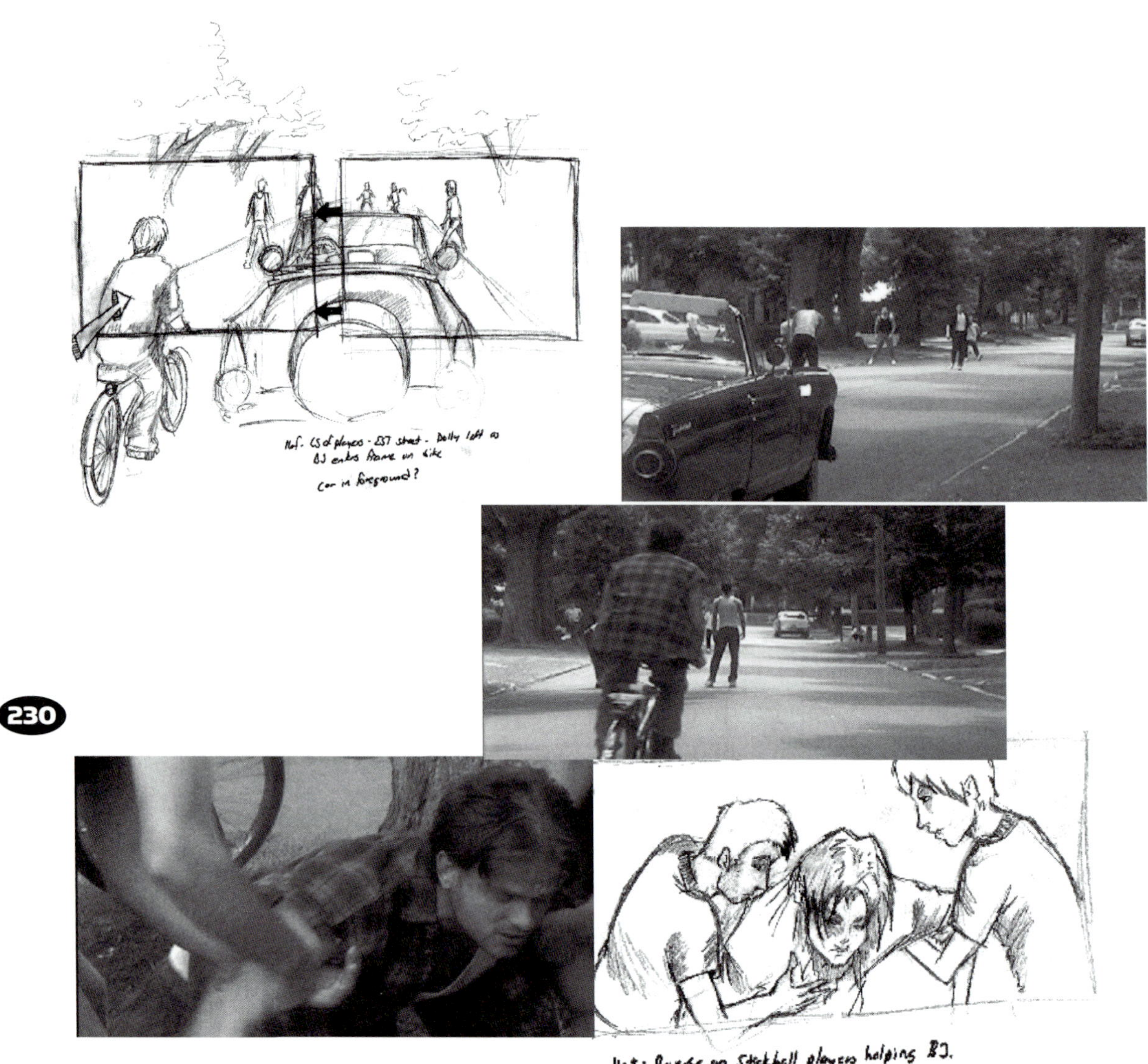

cover the scene with the camera rather than focusing on perfecting the performances.

Be careful, however, not to be so heavily reliant on the storyboards that you can't deviate from them if there's a change on set that is out of your control. Oftentimes, productions run over schedule because of technical, scheduling, or weather-related issues, and the director is forced to cut shots and even entire sequences. Flexibility in adapting the storyboarded shots makes it easier to adjust to the continuing demands of the shoot.

- The purpose of storyboards is to convey to the cast and crew actor blocking and camera positions.
- It's important to establish what the shot size and framing of subjects is within the frame. The reader should be able to determine if the shot is a long shot, medium shot, or close-up.
- Include important set, set-dressing, prop, and wardrobe information in each frame.
- Convey movement of subjects and objects in the frame with single, bold arrows.
- Convey camera movement with 3D arrows.
- Label each shot with a brief description of what is happening in the shot, and even lines of dialog. A well-done storyboard should incorporate all elements of the script so that it reads like a comic book. Pictures represent the visuals, and sound and dialog are written below each frame.
- When representing different characters, draw a simple characteristic to differentiate one character from another, i.e., a hat and necktie for the lead male character and a bow and dress for the lead female character. Storyboards don't have to be great works of art . . . just tools to convey the framing of the object or subject within the scene.
- Try drawing the scene first on blank paper, then draw the frame box around the action you want. Sometimes, it's easier to storyboard this way than to draw the shot within predrawn frames.
- Spend extra time storyboarding any shots that incorporate digital effects. Consider working with the digital effects artist to develop any digital effects shots so that they are properly shot and framed for their post needs.

Once complete, storyboards should be copied and distributed among the department heads.

Example of a close-up.

Example of a medium shot.

Example of a long shot.

I also find it valuable to post a spread of the storyboards on an empty wall of the production office and on set so everyone can readily access and see them.

Although many filmmakers create storyboards by hand, there are a number of 2D and 3D programs that make rendering storyboards easy. For creating 2D storyboards, check out a program called "Storyboard Artist," and for 3D boards, "Poser" and "DAZ Studio."

REHEARSING ACTORS

The director's primary job on set is to work with the actors to get the best performance for the story. This process begins long before the cameras roll, during rehearsal. Once the actors are cast, the director begins to help the actors craft their character's history, motivations, and subtexts so they can play their characters realistically during the time of their lives in which the movie takes place.

When working with actors, try a three-rehearsal process:

Rehearsal 1—Understanding the story

For the first rehearsal, assemble the entire cast together for an informal meeting. This is the first time the actors are meeting each other, so providing snacks and drinks and creating a relaxed atmosphere is a great way to break the ice and allow the actors to get to know each other. Once you feel comfortable, assemble everyone and pass out a copy of the most current draft of the script. Begin the rehearsal by thanking everyone and introducing them to your vision.

Tell the cast:

- What inspired the idea for the movie
- How you envision the style, pacing, and feel of the story
- What the main theme is
- How you view the overall feel of the performances

Once you establish the overview of the story, introduce each actor to his or her character with a brief introduction and description of how you envision the character. Once you get through the main and supporting cast members, begin the read-through of the script.

The read-through involves the actors reading the lines of their own character. Choose an actor with a small part in the script to read the narrative directions. Take this time to listen carefully to how the dialog and pacing sound during the read, taking notes about where the story lags, where dialog feels unnatural, and any other ideas that come to mind. Do not interrupt, but listen to the entire read-through from the beginning to the end.

The first rehearsal is about describing the story, characters, and plot points in broad brushstrokes. This is not the time to delve too deeply into each character,

Quantus Pictures Inc.

Motion Picture Production Company

PRODUCTION STORYBOARDS

Production: "The Day Bobby Jones Came Home"
Director: Jason J. Tomaric
Director of Photography: Jason J. Tomaric

Date: June 20, 2002
Producers: Jason J. Tomaric & Adam Kadar
Storyboards by: Fredrick Allison Jr.

Scene: 16 (Bobby Jones approaches stickball game and sees his younger self)

16m - XCU of BJ's eyes - tilt up to forehead. Scar appears

16n - MS of YBJ as batter swings bat, striking YBJ in head. YBJ goes down

Quantus Pictures Inc.

Motion Picture Production Company

PRODUCTION STORYBOARDS

Production: "The Day Bobby Jones Came Home"
Director: Jason J. Tomaric
Director of Photography: Jason J. Tomaric

Date: June 20, 2002
Producers: Jason J. Tomaric & Adam Kadar
Storyboards by: Fredrick Allison Jr.

Scene: 16 (Bobby Jones approaches stickball game and sees his younger self)

16o - LS as Bobby Jones, hits tree

16p - Reverse/RXN of stickball players rush to BJ - police car pulls up in BG.

Quantus Pictures Inc.

Motion Picture Production Company

PRODUCTION STORYBOARDS

Production: "The Day Bobby Jones Came Home"
Director: Jason J. Tomaric
Director of Photography: Jason J. Tomaric

Date: June 20, 2002
Producers: Jason J. Tomaric & Adam Kadar
Storyboards by: Fredrick Allison Jr.

Scene: 16 (Bobby Jones approaches stickball game and sees his younger self)

16u - Sheriff pulls up and exits car - MS
(exit screen right)

Quantus Pictures Inc.

Motion Picture Production Company

PRODUCTION STORYBOARDS

Production: "The Day Bobby Jones Came Home"
Director: Jason J. Tomaric
Director of Photography: Jason J. Tomaric

Date: June 20, 2002
Producers: Jason J. Tomaric & Adam Kadar
Storyboards by: Fredrick Allison Jr.

Scene: 16 (Bobby Jones approaches stickball game and sees his younger self)

16 v- sheriff approaches BJ. BJ walks to camera, (see scor)
looking at Young BJ.
16v (con't) sheriff arrests BJ.

their arcs, subtext, or motivation. Talk in terms of how the film will look cinematically, what the themes of the movie are, even the music style and what the moral of the story is.

Once the read-through is complete, ask the actors what they thought, answer any questions they may have, and determine what weak spots the script has. Listening to the actors' feedback on the first read-through is an outstanding opportunity to gauge how well the story unfolds, especially considering that the actors are reading the material for the first time, are unbiased, and have significant interest in making sure the movie is done as well as it can be done.

At the conclusion of the first rehearsal, ask:

- What parts of the story and script dragged?
- Did every scene contribute to the overall theme of the story?
- Which actors immediately understood their character and which will need more help?
- Does each actor seem committed to the project?
- Are there any strengths the actors have that can bring a unique depth to their characters?

After the first rehearsal, have the actors read and reread the script on their own time until they have a concrete understanding of the story points and their character arc. This will help build a strong foundation for the second rehearsal.

Rehearsal 2—Creating the characters

Whereas the first rehearsal introduces the actors to the basic story, theme, and style of the movie, the second rehearsal helps the actors delve deeper into their characters by crafting the backstory and subtext of their characters with the director.

A truly exceptional exercise for helping create each character's backstory involves seating the cast in a circle around two chairs. One chair is for the actor who must always remain in character and the other is for the director who plays the role of a psychologist. The director takes each actor through his character's life by asking the actor questions that help shape memories of past events like, "Tell me about your first day of school" or "Tell me about the moment in life you were the most afraid." The questions the director asks should help develop events in the character's life that motivate his actions during the time of the story. For example, in a scene in which a character watches a man get run over by a car, consider creating an event in the character's life that explores how he copes with death, say the death of his father. Even though the father's death isn't mentioned in the script, the director can reference this backstory on set when directing the actor.

During this exercise the director can help create these events by asking questions like:

- Let's talk about the day you learned that your father died. What were you doing when you found out? How did you feel as soon as you heard the news?
- Do you remember the day of the funeral? What were you thinking about as you sat in the back of the car on your way to the cemetery? How did you react when you saw the casket for the first time?
- What was the first time your father's death really hit you? What were you doing? How did his death change you?

Although this is primarily an improvisational exercise for the actor, the director steers the "session" the way he wants, guiding the actor through the development of his character with the type of questions he poses.

Performing this exercise in front of all the actors allows everyone to build their character's backstory into the other character's backstories. In the case of *Time and Again*, Awanda and the Sheriff's pasts have a direct influence on how they behave with each other in the story.

The objective of this exercise is twofold. The actors understand their character's personality, history, and motivations and are now able to develop the characters on their own. The second benefit is that the director can reference these prebuilt memories on the set when directing the actors. For example in the scene in which the character sees a man getting hit by a car, when the director is directing the actor's reaction, he can mention, "Go back to the day that you learned that your father had died. Feel the numbness you felt at that moment for this scene." This gives the actors a real, tangible moment that is true to the character.

Andrew's portrayal of Young Bobby Jones was both convincing and moving, especially when he finds Awanda's body. We discussed this moment often during rehearsals.

After the second rehearsal

Now that the actors have an understanding of their characters with the blessing of the director, they are free to research their roles, study the script, and apply what they learned on their own time. The actors can meet with the director individually to craft any finer points of the character or discuss specific moments, working out the subtext and motivation for specific scenes.

Rehearsal 3—Scene specifics

The third time the actors and director get together is to block the actors' movements for each scene. Plan movements, discuss camera angles, and work out natural blocking until each scene feels kinetic and fluid. Because this rehearsal rarely occurs on set, the director needs to explain and translate the blocking in a way so that it will work on the actual set. Start with major scenes and work through to the medium scenes so the actors understand how minor scenes connect the main story beats.

Some questions to tackle with the actors:

- Discuss each character's intent and goal for each scene. What is his objective? Does the character obtain his objective or does he fail?
- Even though the actors are playing the words written in the script, work out what each character is *really* trying to say. Define this subtext for each character in each scene.
- Discuss any themes or subplots in any given scene so the actor understands how the scene fits into the greater story.

This rehearsal is a great time to discuss where the characters are coming from emotionally in the moments before the scene and where they are headed in the scene following. Avoid working on the emotional context too heavily as the actors should remain fresh for the day of shooting.

By the end of this rehearsal, each actor should feel comfortable with how to play each scene. This blocking combined with the research each actor has done on his character will greatly help the actors feel extremely comfortable when they arrive on set.

Overrehearsing

Every director has a different style of rehearsing actors. Some directors prefer light rehearsals so the first time actors truly perform is on set in front of the camera. Other directors prefer to rehearse every emotion and every moment beforehand. The decision on how to rehearse should be based on the nature of the story, the experience of the actors, and the director's experience. In Hollywood movies, actors rarely rehearse. They prepare for the role on their own time, arrive on set, act, make adjustments based on the director's feedback, and go home. For less experienced actors, more rehearsal time may help boost their confidence on set.

Scenes that involve stunts or digital effects need to be carefully rehearsed and blocked until they are done correctly. Bring the animator or stunt supervisor on set to help ensure that the blocking will work in the editing room and on set. Working out logistics, safety, and blocking in a rehearsal space is a lot cheaper than losing expensive time on set. The more prepared you are in preproduction, the smoother production will run.

Learn additional tips on directing actors, rehearsing actors, working with extras, and directing on set at www.powerfilmmaking.com. Visit the section on Directing.

Exercises during rehearsals

There are a number of exercises that you can use to help an actor develop the subtext and motivation of his role. Use these exercises sparingly and only in an instance in which the actor is having difficulty finding his or her character's motivations.

- **Gibberish exercise:** In this exercise, the actors should perform a scene as written, but instead of saying the lines of dialog, they should speak gibberish. The purpose is to help the actors convey what their characters mean instead of what they are saying. Try this exercise if the scene is flat and the actors are having difficulty playing the subtext or if the scene is in the actor's nonnative language.
- **No words:** During rehearsal, the actors should convey their objective and the theme by playing the scene only through their actions. For example, if a wife has learned that her husband has cheated on her, during a scene in which she's making breakfast she may be unsuccessfully try to hide her betrayal. Even though the words on the page are about going to a party that night, her actions speak differently. Use this exercise to craft this physical subtext by removing the dialog.
- **Act the subtext:** This exercise is designed to help the actors identify and understand the subtext of a scene. Instead of playing the scene as written, for example, the breakfast scene, the actors should play the raw subtext. How do the character's really feel? In the previous example, the actress playing the wife would play the scene angry, upset, and betrayed and make no attempt to hide or conceal her feelings.

It was always important for us to sit down and review the plan for how I wanted to shoot each scene. Although this work was done in advance, this little refresher helped get everyone on the same page.

If you've properly rehearsed, worked with the actor to develop the backstory, identified the subtext of each scene, discussed the character's motivations, and set up where the character is coming from emotionally in the previous scene and what his objectives are, then let go and let the actor do what he does best. Remember that good actors are artists who simply need to be directed in the right direction so they can play a convincing role, not dictated to and hand-held by the director through every bit of minutia.

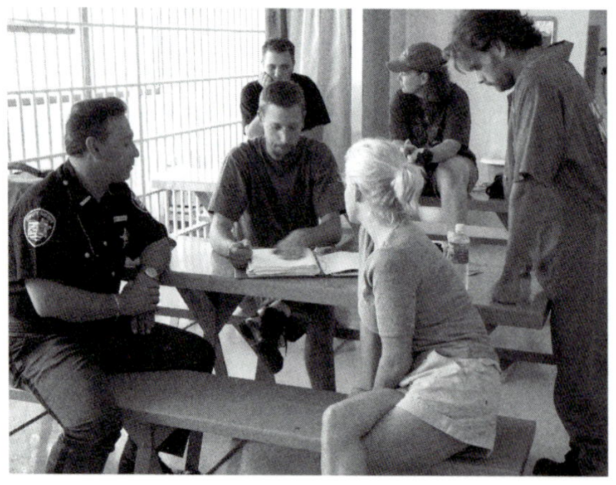

WORKING WITH THE CREW DURING PREPRODUCTION

The director's role is critical during the preproduction phase of the movie, as she makes important decisions about actors, production design, cinematography styles, and locations. The director's vision and ability to focus a creative team toward her vision are essential in keeping the production on time, on budget, and a pleasurable experience for everyone.

On a low-budget production, the director assembles main crew positions, such as the director of photography, production designer, producer, casting director, actors, and composer, himself, unlike larger productions on which the line producer assembles most below-the line crew members. For more information on finding and hiring the crew, go to the Crew chapter.

The daily demands of preproduction can be extreme for the director as she is pulled by the needs of the cast and crew. Dozens of people from different departments will be asking hundreds of questions a day, questions that often require immediate answers. It can be very overwhelming unless you have done your homework in advance and can be clear about what you want. You should be able to give concise, decisive answers and direct each department in the right direction. Waffling or changing your mind will only cost time and money, make your crew frustrated, and maybe even make them lose their confidence in your abilities.

Conversely, don't be too dictatorial. Moviemaking is a collaborative effort and everyone involved is an artist with a unique talent or specialty. A good director will recognize these talents, give a direction for the crew to go in, and then step back and let them do their job. These artists will infuse their own experiences and skills into their work and feel a greater sense of pride than if the director walks them through every step.

The director's duties during preproduction include:

Studying the script

- Determine story plot points, theme, and story arc.
- Plan the visual and storytelling style of the movie.
- Build the shot list and storyboard.

Rehearsing with actors

- Discuss the theme of the movie with the actors.
- Help actors build their character's backstory, motivations, and personality.
- Rehearse blocking and pacing.

Working with the crew

- Scout locations and determine blocking.
- Work with the director of photography to determine the visual look and feel of the lighting and shooting style.
- Work with the production designer on set dressing, wardrobe, and props.
- Help develop the shooting schedule.
- Coordinate with department heads.

ACTIVITIES

Activity 1

Objective: Learn to determine coverage.

Activity: Write a simple two-page script and think about what types of camera shots you might like to use to cover the action. When would you want to use a long shot? A dolly shot? A close-up? Then illustrate what the camera will see from each set up, in much the same manner as a comic book artist illustrates a story. Draw each frame and label what is happening in the shot.

Activity 2

Objective: Learn how to interpret a script for an actor.

Activity: Select a scene from a play or a movie that you haven't seen before, and discuss what the scene is about and why the characters are in this moment of the story. Once you know the style and approach you'd like to take, you can begin creating the character profiles and backgrounds and then block the actors in a convincing way. Produce the script as a play, focusing on the actor's performances.

Activity 3

Objective: Learn how to place critical action within the frame of the camera.

Activity: Write a simple one-minute scene and rehearse your actors and their positioning. Then videotape the scene *without cutting*. Shoot the scene as many times as necessary until all the critical moments in the scene make it to the screen.

Activity 4

Objective: Create a constant action through shooting and editing together multiple camera angles.

Activity: Write a short scene that involves one actor performing a task, then shoot the scene with 8–12 different camera angles. Edit the shots together to create a continuous flow from one shot to the next, without any jumps in time or space. The final result should look as though the actor seamlessly performed the task and it was covered by 8–12 cameras scattered around the set.

DIRECTING DURING PRODUCTION

The director's primary responsibility on set is to the actors, coaching, guiding, and supporting their efforts. In addition to this main responsibility, the director must wear several other hats, all of which involve coordinating the efforts of all departments.

- The director works with the actors on set and helps them achieve the best performance to serve the story and the director's vision.
- The director works closely with the director of photography in determining the look of the lighting, camera placement, camera movement, and framing of each shot.
- The director works with the production designers to approve and make minor adjustments to the set, wardrobe, makeup, hairstyles, and props.
- The director works closely with the first assistant director to stay on time and on budget.

Blocking the scene

Blocking is the process of determining the actors' positions and movements around the set.

- Use gaffer's tape to set T-marks to identify specific starting and stopping points for actors.
- Set marks on the floor to determine where the camera should stop and start if a dolly or crane is being used. This helps the camera operator correctly frame the shot consistently in each take, the 1st AC consistently pull focus to keep the actors sharp, and the dolly grip time out the speed and stopping position of the dolly with ease.
- Before going for a take, rehearse the entire cast and crew to make sure that the blocking works for performance, lighting, and sound.
- Good blocking feels natural and motivated. Remember that the actors need to have a reason to move throughout the set.
- I block out a scene as early as the location scout, because before I commit to a location, I want to make sure it works for the actors' movements, as well as camera and lighting placement. Although there are small refinements on the day of the shoot, the rough blocking has already been determined early in the preproduction phase.

Blocking a scene isn't only about the actors' performance, but about affording the camera the most interesting angle, finding the most aesthetically pleasing part of the set to shoot, factoring in lighting and sound requirements. As a result, the more experienced a director is in how the technical side of production works, the more effective he will be at blocking a scene so it works well for all departments.

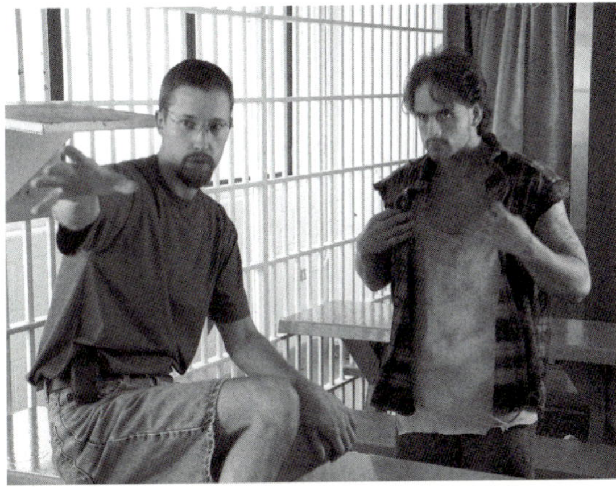

In the scene in which Bobby sees Awanda, I directed Brian where his eye line should be and where Awanda's final position is behind the bars. Jennie (Awanda) was in hair and makeup and was unable to be present for the shot.

Remember that all this work should have been done during preproduction. When the cast and crew arrive on set, the day should be about carrying out the details of the plan, not figuring things out for the first time. The more time you spend preparing in preproduction, the more smoothly the shoot will go.

Directing actors

Directing actors is the primary function of the director. Work closely to help them understand where their characters are at any given point in the story so that they can deliver a believable and realistic performance.

All too often, directors are technically adept and understand where to place the camera and how to work with the crew but they do not know how to speak with or work with actors. Few directors have ever acted and, thus, lack the understanding of the actor's process.

- Take acting classes or audition for a play to help your understanding of what the actors are going through on set and how to communicate effectively with them. Learn what it's like to be directed and what type of feedback and guidance you need to play your role.
- Learn acting theory and terminology. Working with actors effectively means speaking their language.
- Most first-time directors will direct the actors with a surface direction such as "Act happier" or "Scratch your head when you say 'I don't know.'" These directions don't give the actor anything to work off of and limit their ability to craft a real performance. Instead, give the actor a subtext to work from, such as "You are really attracted to this girl and every time she looks at you, you're afraid she notices the rash on your forehead. Because you're so afraid of rejection, try to subtly cover your forehead up. In reality, you're drawing even more attention to it, making the moment even more uncomfortable for the two of you."
- Make sure that every actor is sure of his or her character's objective in the scene. What does the character want? What are his or her goals? Does he or she achieve those goals? Let's say that the scene is about a mother asking her little boy how his school day was. Although he's telling her about his math test, he's secretly trying to sneak cookies from the cookie jar behind her back. This objective makes the scene not about math tests, but about the little boy talking about math tests to keep his mother from seeing him steal cookies.
- Make sure that the actors' blocking, or positioning during a scene, is motivated and makes sense. In real life, people only approach another person or an object if there's a reason to do so. Make sure the characters have a reason to move.

Brian and I would shoot simple moments together. I found that the strength of our actor-director relationship led to some really honest performances.

- Remember that actors are artists and enjoy practicing their art. Give the actors a general direction and let them craft a performance. Treat the actor/director relationship as though you were both on opposite ends of a football field and you run to meet each other at the 50-yard line. It's a creative collaboration with each side respecting the other.
- Be open to feedback from your cast and crew. Remember that filmmaking is a collaborative process that involves many artistic people, each of whom is probably very passionate about his or her work. Listen to them, but . . . when it comes time to make a decision, stand firm.
- Set a positive tone on set and treat everyone with respect. Your attitude will trickle down through the cast and crew.
- Take time to get to know your cast before you go into production. The better the relationship and the stronger the trust level, the more inclined your actors will be to open up and deliver a real, heart-felt performance.
- Take time to rehearse and discuss the script BEFORE getting on set. Give the actors solid direction in terms of where their characters are in the arc of the story, what the characters' goals are in the scene, and what their relationships are with other characters. Discussing this beforehand gives the actors time to prepare.
- Even though working on set is stressful, take the time to communicate with your cast in a slow, concise manner. Remember, you're the only person who can see the big picture and everyone is looking to you for guidance, so organize your thoughts and present them in a simple, direct way.
- Never demonstrate what to say or how to do something. Asking an actor to mimic the way you say something kills the art of acting and will turn the actor off to you.
- Help the actors block out and ignore the camera, crew, lighting, and boom microphone so they can delve deeply into their roles and not perform for the crew.
- Give actors something to do during a scene. Most people never stand and stare at the person they're talking to. Most conversations are held while one person or both people are busy doing something: washing dishes, changing a flat tire, or looking through papers. Directing this type of business will help make a performance more real.
- Inexperienced actors are more likely to overact than underact. The result is a showy, theatrical, and ultimately unconvincing performance. If this is a problem, talk to the actors in simple terms and help them internalize the moment by acting the subtext rather than the dialog itself. Allowing actors to improvise the dialog in the scene can also help.
- If an actor is having a difficult time with a particular moment, help him remember a similar moment in his own life he can draw upon for reference.
- Because you are shooting your movie out of order, it's important to help the actors understand where their characters are coming from in the story

and where they are going. Always set up the scene so that it's clear how this scene relates to the overall story.

- Try to minimize the number of takes in emotional scenes to avoid overtaxing the actors. The more takes you do, the more you risk stale, overrehearsed performances that will lack spontaneity and real emotion.

Directing the subtext

Directing actors is all about understanding what happened in the character's life up to the point the story takes place. One common mistake of first-time directors is that they direct the moment without any regard to the history, circumstances, and personal trials and challenges in the character's life that may affect his behavior in the moment. For example, when I am teaching a class, to the casual observer who doesn't know me, I am simply a teacher, but my behavior in the moment is shaped by many other influences in my life. Earlier that day, I got in a fight with my significant other, my car broke down and I'm concerned about how much it will cost to fix, I'm also worried about if my friend will show up to drive me home from work, and I'm hungry. All these short-term factors will influence my behavior as I stand in front of the class and give the day's lecture. The subtle nuances of my behavior will automatically come out because they are motivated by these other thought processes in my mind, not because I was directed to "act like I have something on my mind." In this case, I actually do.

I remember that Bob (Sheriff Karl) and I had an extremely difficult time arriving at the right emotional intensity for the moment when he learns that young Bobby committed the murder, so we discussed the Sheriff's backstory, which helped Bob find the inspiration to play the moment. What could have been disastrous ended up being a minor issue, because we spent the time in rehearsal developing the backstory and subtext of each character.

When directing actors, describe for them other outside factors that may be influencing their behavior in the scene. The more layers, and the more a character feels these undercurrents of thought and emotion, the more realistic and subtle a performance will be.

This can be called the subtext of the scene. Although the character is doing one thing, her actions are motivated by another. For example, if you were shopping at the mall and you ran into a high school bully you haven't seen in years, you may exchange pleasantries, talk about your career and life after high school, and maybe even throw out an offer to have lunch to get caught up on old times. Although this seems like a civil conversation on the surface, the undercurrent may be one of hatred, as old memories are conjured up of when the bully shoved you into the lockers and beat you up. You may be secretly happy he's been unemployed and divorced two times. This subtext drives the actor's performance and it is important to understand this when directing.

Always know what the character wants in each scene. Although they might not say it through the dialog, the actors should have a clear objective of their characters' goal . . . what they want to achieve by the end of the scene. A well-written scene will always introduce an obstruction that prevents them from achieving the results they want. This conflict is what makes for good drama.

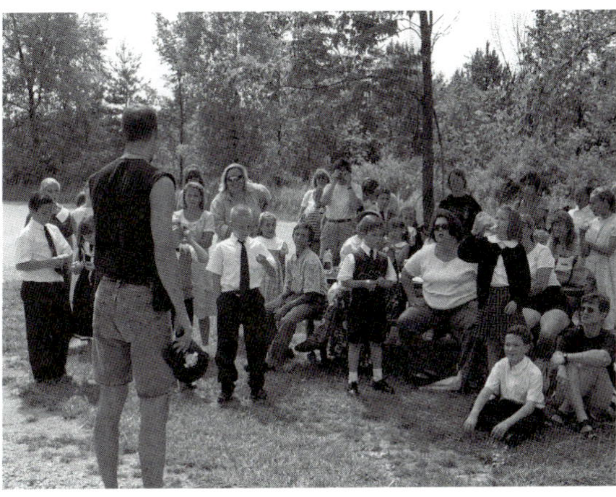

Working with kids requires specific, simple direction. I told them to pretend like they lost their voices. They could play, run around, and move their mouths, but they could not say anything, allowing our production sound engineer to record the actors' dialog cleanly.

Directing extras

In Hollywood movies, the job of directing the extras usually falls on the first assistant director, but in independent movies, that job will probably fall on the director. Extras are nonspeaking actors who work in the background of a scene to bring life, movement, and a sense of realism to the set. Extras are the other patrons in a restaurant behind the main characters, they are the passersby on the street and the people sitting around our characters in the movie theater. Extras add production value, scope, and size to the movie.

When I was shooting *Time and Again,* we had nearly 200 extras from the schoolchildren, to the people in the diner, to the townspeople on the square outside the theater. Everyone was willing to work for free simply for the experience of being in a movie and really helped add to the realism of the scene.

Finding extras can be as easy as looking to your local resources:

- Try contacting local theaters, schools, and university theater programs. Many aspiring actors are willing to work for free simply to get the chance to be in a movie.
- Avoid shooting in high-production towns like Los Angeles or New York. These cities attract people who are looking to make a living as actors and it is more difficult to find people who are willing to work for free than in nonproduction towns.
- Providing food on set is a great way to help attract extras.

Working with extras is similar to working with the principal cast.

- Be as concise as possible as to what each extra needs to wear and bring to the set. On larger budget movies, the production provides hair, makeup, and wardrobe for the extras, although this may be cost-prohibitive on lower budget projects.
- Be sure to provide an area on set to hold the extras between takes. This area needs to be off the set and out of the way of the crew.

The extras outside the theater and all along the town square were actors from the Geauga Lyric Theatre Guild. Organized by Stacy Burris, they not only added life to the scene, but graciously volunteered their time.

- Make sure you have appropriate restroom facilities to accommodate the number of extras working on set.
- When directing extras, explain to them the nature of the scene and what type of atmosphere they need to create in the background.
- If necessary, give groups of extras specific direction for blocking, or something you would like to see them do, especially if their action is happening directly behind the principal actors.
- Beware of extras who try to draw attention to themselves. Move them to the back, out of sight of the camera. Good extras should make the background invisible to the audience.
- Extras should never talk during a take even if they appear to be making noise or speaking on camera; they should always mime the action so sound editors can put the sound of the background in later.
- Always be supportive. Many extras have never had any experience shooting a movie and are probably volunteering their time. Always thank them and let them know when they do a good job.

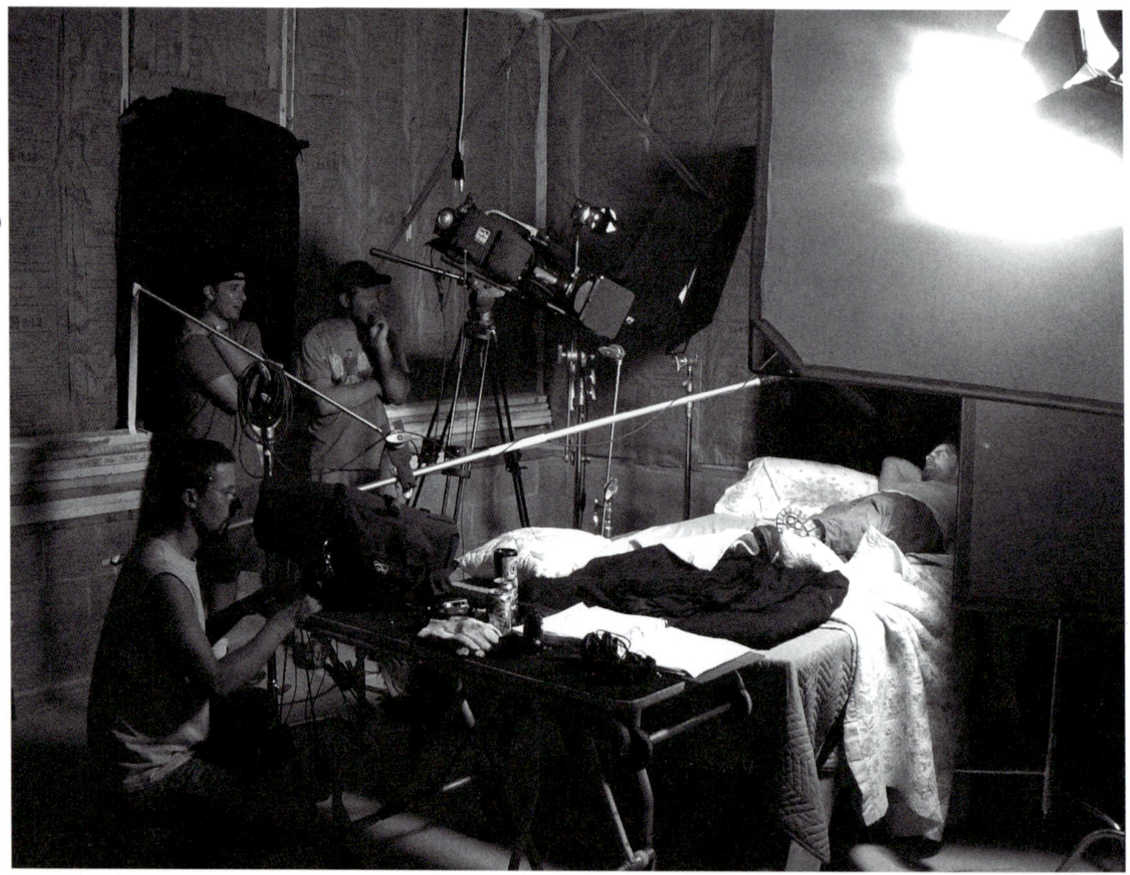

The "bedroom" in Awanda's trailer was really a sheet of plywood resting on two sawhorses in my garage. Part of my job was to help Brian and Jennie understand the environment their characters were in so they could effectively play their roles.

- Make sure each extra signs a release form before stepping on set.
- Keep a mailing list of the extras so when the movie is finished, you can notify each person of how to see the film.

Balancing acting with the technical tools

When the audience watches a movie, they experience a complete soundtrack, sound effects, digital effects, color correction, and editing style as well as the actors' performances. Unfortunately, actors and crew members on set do not have the luxury of seeing or hearing all these elements when the scene is being filmed. It is therefore important for the director to paint as complete a picture as possible for the cast and crew of what the audience is going to be seeing and hearing in the theater so the actors can give a performance that works in conjunction with all those elements.

For example, when I was directing Brian in the opening title sequence of *Time and Again*, I asked him to play the scene as if the crushing exhaustion of the prison break met the overwhelming sense of freedom of being outside, bathed in warm sunlight in the calm, serene wheat field. His objective was to play the scene with two motivating factors: fatigue and his basking in his new-found freedom. Cinematically, I chose to shoot the scene with wide, sweeping vistas and used warm, soft lighting to convey to the audience that this place is safe.

Although this is how we filmed the scene, the audience got a very different sense when they saw the final scene, complete with sound design and music. Although the look of the scene was warm and comforting, it had a foreboding and eerie overtone that came from the musical score. Using instruments that conveyed a sense of strangeness and creepiness, I was able to instill an emotional response in the audience using techniques other than the acting. The final result is a scene that, whereas Bobby is tired and content in the field, the audience gets that there is something wrong with this picture . . . that something is going to happen, unbeknownst to Bobby Jones.

Sound effects, cinematography, music, and digital effects can create these overtones, with each aspect adding to the drama of the scene. Acting is only one part of this "dramatic pie." For the director to create a strong scene, he has to understand how all these elements are going to be used in advance so that when he directs the actors, he can tailor the performance so it works when all the other elements are added.

When directing the cast and crew on set, explain to them what the music is going to sound like over the scene or what sound effects will be added. The more complete a picture the cast has of the final story, the more fitting their performances will be.

Directing the crew

Directors come in two varieties, the kind that is technically gifted, but has a hard time working with actors, and the type that is great with actors, but feels

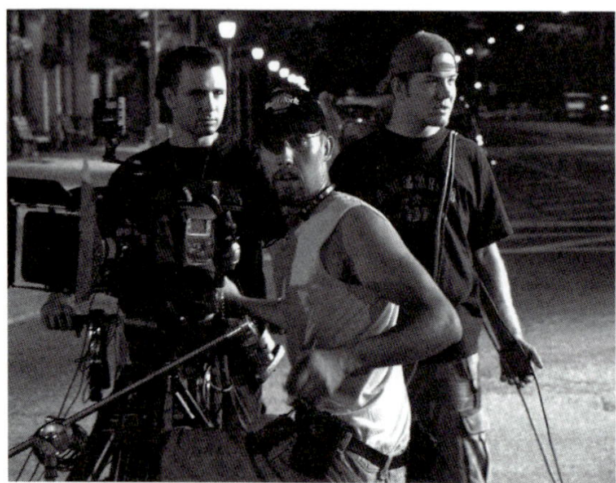

Producer Adam Kadar, Grip Tom Clack, and I prepare to shoot Bobby's approach to the theater.

out of place with the technical side and the crew. Although a director's primary responsibility is to the actors, the more she knows about the role of the crew and the technical aspect of filmmaking, the better her understanding of the available tools will lead to a quality film.

Working with the crew is much like working with actors. Crew members are artists in their respective crafts and need direction on how their contributions fit into the director's vision.

- Sit down with the department heads and talk about your vision and what you're looking for both for the entire movie and in each scene.
- Communicate clearly. You may feel like you are oversimplifying a concept, but in reality, walking through every detail is critical in helping the crew understand what you want.
- Have daily meetings with the department heads to get updates on where they are at and what changes need to be made.
- Work closely with department heads so that the work they are producing is in line with your vision.
- Be clear about every element needed in the scene. From the storyboarding and breaking down of each scene, the department heads have a clear idea of what is required in each scene so they can properly prepare. For example, if a set needs to be dressed and the storyboards indicate that the camera angle will favor only one wall, then the set dresser need be concerned with dressing only that single wall.
- Encourage communication between department heads: DP and set dressing, makeup and wardrobe, and so on.
- Consider renting a production office so all department heads can work out of the same office. The closer everyone is, the smoother the operation will run.
- KNOW WHAT YOU WANT! Do not show up on set without having a strong vision of what you want. Tell the cast and crew what you are looking for in a scene. Do not second guess yourself or rely on the crew to tell you what to do. This is the single biggest complaint from crew members about first-time directors. The director is the ONLY person who knows how to tell the story.
- Be clear in explaining your vision to the crew, especially department heads who need to translate your vision into physical reality.
- Don't try to do everything yourself. Surround yourself with people who know their jobs and do them well, and let them do it! Directors who try to wear too many hats are taken away from what should be their primary focus—the actors.
- Listen to the advice you receive from the crew, especially if they are more experienced than you.

- If you are in doubt, always hire a good, experienced cinematographer who can guide you through the process, help you with setting up shots, and even give you guidance with the actors.
- Balance the attention you give to both the cast and the crew. Remember that your first obligation is to the actors. The first assistant director will manage the crew, but you still need to know what you want from them.
- Hire a good crew and let them do their jobs. You shouldn't have to worry about the sound levels or if there's enough light in the scene. Trust that your crew will do the best they can so you can focus on the job of directing.
- Always run through the scene with the actors once for the crew so they can see how the scene plays. Doing this before each new scene will help the crew understand what each setup covers in the overall scene.
- Stay calm and positive. Your attitude will determine how the entire set will run. If you're stressed, the cast and crew will feel it!

Directing the camera

In addition to directing actors, the director must also direct the camera. Although many of these duties can be shared with the director of photography, the director must understand how to break a scene down into shots, where to place the camera, and how the shots will cut together in each scene.

One technique I use to plan my camera shots is to plan camera angles that mimic where an observer would be compelled to look during a scene. As I block the actors, I take note of where my natural human tendency is to look. If I feel the need to look at a character's face in a certain moment, odds are I will need to cover him in a close-up. If I am pulled to stand back and watch an entire action unfold, I will think about covering that part of the scene in a wide shot.

I always think of my camera as being like a member of the audience, almost voyeuristically catching a normally fleeting moment.

The camera is really an extension of the audience, so treat it as such. Pretend as though you were taking an audience member by the hand as the scene unfolds around you and walking him or her to different parts of the set to experience the action unfolding. What would be the best vantage point to see the action? Where would the audience member stand? How close or how far would he or she be? All these answers can translate directly into the positioning of the camera.

Although every filmmaker would like to have dynamic dolly and jib moves in his or her movie, the practicality of low-budget filmmaking prohibits too many extreme camera setups.

- When shooting a low-budget movie, always shoot the following shots:

- ○ **The master shot**—The master shot is a wide shot that covers the entire action of the entire scene. Even if you didn't shoot any other angles, the audience would be able to understand what the scene is about. The master is the universal safety shot and can always be cut to if there's a problem with any other shots or if you run out of time on set.
- ○ **Close-ups**—Move the camera in and frame up each actor in a close-up single shot and run the entire scene from beginning to end. Direct the actors not to overlap their lines with each other because that will be done in the editing room. Make sure their eye lines are as close to the lens as possible so the audience can see the actor's face.
- ○ **Insert shots**—Insert shots are close-up shots of objects or actions within the scene that draw attention to that action or can be used as a cutaway. In a restaurant scene, a cutaway is a close-up of a woman playing with her wine glass or a close-up of a man checking his watch. These insert shots will be invaluable in covering up editing and shooting mistakes later.
- ○ **Cat-in-the-window shot**—These shots are usually of unrelated people or objects in a scene that can be cut to at any time during the scene. In our restaurant scene, it's a shot of a waiter waiting in the corner of the room, watching our couple dine. This shot got its name because filmmakers would actually shoot a cat sitting in a window, regardless of whether it had anything to do with the scene. These unconnected shots save the editor in the event there is a continuity problem or an editing issue. An editor will cut one of these shots into a scene to help bridge what could be a jarring edit, jump cut, or lapse in continuity. Always shoot a couple shots like this for each scene.

- Work with an experienced line producer or first assistant director to determine how long it will take for each camera set up. Many first-time filmmakers underestimate the amount of time it takes to set up a shot and subsequently end up running over schedule.
- If you're confident that you can shoot the basics to cover the scene, then you can consider adding specialized moves like a dolly or jib shot. Beware that setting up dolly track and a jib arm is very time intensive, requiring time not only to set up the equipment, but also to rehearse, set starting and stopping positions, pull focus, and coordinate with the actors and boom operator.
- When planning camera angles, think about what you want the audience to learn from each angle. There needs to be a reason the camera is positioned and framed in a certain way.
- Aside from the master shot, a scene is told through a number of different shots. Not every shot needs to tell the complete story. For example, in a conversation scene, dedicate one shot to focusing on one character's close-up. Then, reposition the camera to cover the other actor's close-up. In the editing room, you will then have the option of cutting to either character and can make that creative decision then.

- Shooting on set is about options. Be sure to shoot as much coverage as you can from each of your camera setups.
- Work closely with the director of photography. In Hollywood movies, producers would often pair new directors with the most experienced, seasoned director of photography they could find. If you hire a good DP, she will help you determine proper camera placement.

Directing problems

There are a number of problems that plague a first-time director.

- **Overshooting:** Directors who aren't confident in their plan tend to overshoot a scene from too many angles, wasting time and falling behind schedule. Take the time in preproduction to walk through the coverage of each scene so when you arrive on set, you are confident in the number of camera angles you need to cover the action properly.
- **Indecisive direction:** The director who constantly looks to the crew for help in directing a scene is a director who doesn't know what he wants. This is the most dangerous situation to be in because you end up in a boat with no captain. As a director, take the time to sit down and map out what you want, not only for each scene, but for the entire story. The

There are so many problems to juggle when on set that the director rarely has enough time to think about his shots. The more prepared he is arriving on set, the happier he will be leaving the set.

cast and crew appreciate a director who knows what he wants to do, even if he is wrong sometimes.

- **Lack of communication:** Many directors may have their vision in their head, but have a difficult time effectively communicating it to the cast and crew. Often, directors fear that they will sound stupid and simplistic when they explain what they see, but an effective director will communicate as clearly as possible what he wants to have happen. Remember that the cast and crew have no idea what the director is looking for and need everything spelled out in as much detail as necessary for them to do their jobs.

DIRECTING DURING POSTPRODUCTION

Once a movie is complete and enters the postproduction phase, the director is usually exhausted and may be disappointed with the results of the footage. It's rare in the independent world for a director to have achieved her exact vision due to time and budget restrictions. By this point in the process, it is best for the director to find a fresh editor who isn't familiar with the movie to bring an objective eye to the project. The director should sit down with the editor and talk about her vision and the tone, style, and pacing of the movie and then leave the editor to assemble a cut of the movie on his own.

Many directors are afraid of losing control of the film by turning it over to an editor. Holding the reigns too tightly is a mistake because the director is carrying a lot of baggage; she knows what scenes she likes, what scenes didn't turn out; she knows what performances were difficult to get, what shots were time consuming to shoot . . . each shot is full of emotion, blood, sweat, and tears. This emotional attachment makes it difficult for the director to separate herself from the footage to assemble the shots objectively into a cohesive, well-paced story. The editor doesn't have this emotional connection to the material and is confronted with the task of looking at the available footage and assembling it in a way that best serves the story. The director should allow him the time to do this while he relaxes and clears his mind so when an assembly cut is ready, the director can view it with fresh eyes.

- Communicate your vision to the editor in the same manner as you would with an actor. Discuss each scene, what you want it to accomplish, how you envision the tone, style, and pacing.
- Be open to ideas and suggestions from the editor. He is seeing the footage with fresh eyes and may have a perspective you haven't considered yet.
- Relax and let the editor do his job. You're probably tired and emotionally charged from the shoot itself, so take the time to get away from the project and clear your mind while the editor builds the first assembly cut.
- After the cut is finished, work with the editor to refine and tweak the edit until you are happy with the pacing and flow of the story.

- Confer with others to get objective opinions throughout the editing process, but be careful which advice you listen to. Everyone will have an opinion, but not everyone will be right.

Refer to the postproduction chapters for more information on the editing process, working with composers, adding digital effects, and the audio postproduction process.

GO BEYOND THE BOOK

Check out the companion DVD and watch the Directing video to see my approach to directing *Time and Again*.

The Director's primary job is to work with actors. Check out the directing modules at www.powerfilmmaking.com and listen to Hollywood directors, actors, producers and acting coaches as they reveal valuable techniques for helping you direct the best performances from your actors.

The Directing modules include:

- Rehearsing Actors
- Working with Actors on Set
- How to Direct Actors
- Working with Extras

LEICA DICOMAR
13x OPTICAL ZOOM ϕ82mm
f=4.2~55mm 1:1.6

CHAPTER 15

Cinematography

INTRODUCTION

Cinematography is the art of lighting and photographing a scene. Much like photography, which involves taking single photographic images, cinematography refers to cinema or a series of moving images over time.

Cinematography can be broken down into two different, but very related categories: lighting and the camera. One aspect of the director of photography's (also known as the DP or cinematographer) job is to create the look of the movie through the lighting. By coordinating with the grip and electrical department headed by the key grip and the gaffer, the DP lights each set not only to meet the photographic requirements of the medium he's shooting on, but also to create a mood that complements the story.

The second element of the DP's job is to understand the camera, how it operates, where to place it, how it should move, which lens to use, and how to frame the action for the best emotional and logical impact.

The camera we used to shoot *Time and Again*, the JVC-GY-DV500, a professional miniDV camera.

WORKING WITH A DIRECTOR OF PHOTOGRAPHY

The director/DP relationship is very powerful and extraordinarily unique. With the director working with the actors and crafting the story, and the DP responsible for crafting the look, emotion, and movement of the story through lighting and the lens, communication and mutual understanding between the two are key.

When it comes time to hire the DP, consider the following tips to help you find the best, most qualified person:

- Contact local film commissions, post an ad on craigslist.org or any crew web site, and ask for online links to web sites or DVD demo reels. When you begin looking at DP reels, look at:
  - Are the shots well framed and motivated by the story?
  - Does the lighting have a style that positively contributes to the story? Does the picture look professional? Are there any shots that are over- or underexposed?
  - How does the camera move? Are camera movements necessary and do they contribute to the story, or are they frivolous?
  - Does the cinematography pull you into the story?
- Meet with prospective DPs to see if your styles are compatible. Look at her demo reel and talk to her about her approach to lighting a scene. Discuss your story and see if it resonates with her. Much like auditioning an actor, your quest to find a cinematographer lies not only in your comfort level with her craft, attitude, and professionalism, but also in her ability to work with you to fulfill your vision.
- Once you choose your DP, sit down with him and show him scenes from movies that you like the look of. Gather various examples of styles, camera movements, and lighting that you'd like to see in your movie and listen as the DP explains how to approach these styles. You both should be on the same page as to the style and look of the movie, enabling the DP to determine the equipment needed for the production. Discuss:
  - **Camera movement:** Are you looking for static setups? Tableau shots? Handheld, documentary-style shots? Dolly or crane moves? Steadicam? How are you looking for the camera to interact with the environment and the set?
  - **Lighting:** Are you looking for flat (1960s Technicolor), colorful (*Amélie*), black and white (*Schindler's List*), or monochromatic (*Minority Report*) lighting or lighting tinted with rich shadows (*The Matrix*)?
  - **Style:** Do you want a documentary (*Babel, Traffic*), poetic (*Amélie*), or dramatic (*Titanic*) style?
  - **Editing:** How will the movie be cut together? Are you using long shots? Quick, rapid MTV-style cuts?
- While discussing these elements, an experienced DP will be able to help you balance your vision with the realities of production, scheduling, and equipment availability. Listen to her . . . she will be your greatest asset on set.

The key to a successful collaboration between the director and the DP is open communication of ideas, thoughts, and technical approaches to realizing the director's vision. Never hesitate to ask questions and always understand the complexities of achieving your vision. Most neophyte directors could benefit by partnering with an experienced DP who can help with the blocking, framing, and pacing of the movie.

SHOOTING STYLES

Before shooting a movie, discuss the visual style of the film with the DP. Look at the tone, feel, and theme of the movie to help craft the appropriate look. Some common styles include the following:

Dogme 95

The principle behind Dogme 95 is to empower independent filmmakers to make movies that focus exclusively on the art without the hindrance of technique. The Dogme 95 principles dictate that:

- Filmmakers must always shoot on location. No sets can be used.
- The sound and picture must always be produced at the same time. There can be no alterations in the sound or picture in production or postproduction.
- The camera must always be handheld. Dollies, tripods, cranes, or any other camera-support equipment may not be used.
- The image must be acquired with only natural light. No lighting instruments of any kind can be used.
- No superficial action such as murders, weapons, or explosions can be used. The drama must come from the actors and their performances.
- No genre-specific themes like horror or sci-fi.
- No temporal or geographic alienation.
- Film format must be Academy 35 mm.
- The director must not be credited in the movie.

Adhering to these principles allows the filmmaker to obtain a "Dogme Certificate." Although this style requires little to no equipment, the result is usually amateurish. If you have any intention of producing a commercially viable movie, I would strongly avoid using this style. I find that filmmakers without resources, or who are lazy, tend to use the Dogme 95 principles as an excuse for why their film is technically inferior.

Cinema Verité

The cinema verité style of shooting often incorporates a handheld camera that appears to capture the action spontaneously. Contrasted by highly refined and carefully rehearsed camera moves, the cinema verité style creates an ultrarealistic feel to the characters and the setting. Even though it may seem random, this style of shooting is very carefully planned, lit, and rehearsed so as to appear impromptu. Examples are *Babel* and *Traffic*.

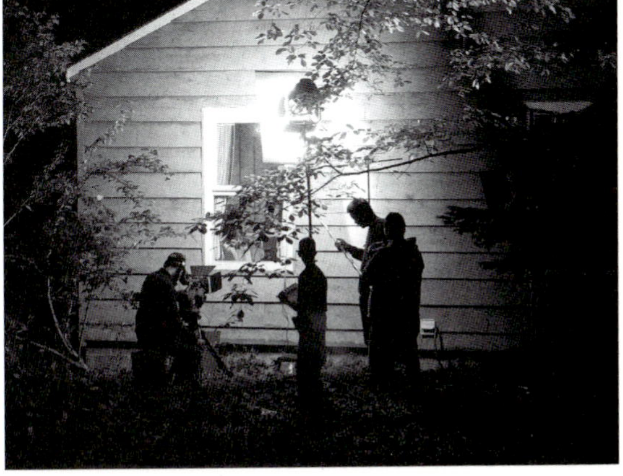

I chose a polished style of shooting for *Time and Again* that incorporated strong camera angles, subtle dolly moves, and a very clean aesthetic.

Polished

Films with a polished style incorporate very deliberate and controlled camera movements, precise lighting, and carefully choreographed blocking. Films like *Schindler's List* and *Titanic* represent the typical Hollywood style of shooting. Every frame is carefully planned and expertly shot. Although this style can be more time consuming and expensive to attain, audiences equate this style more closely with professionally produced cinema.

The roving camera

Pioneered by the television show *NYPD Blue*, the roving camera style mixes the polished and cinema verité styles of shooting. With well-lit scenes and tight blocking, the camera frame tends to roam around the scene, catching snippets of action, obscure reactions, and insert shots through foreground elements, in reflections, and through other abstract means. Although it appears easy to replicate this style, the roving camera style is extremely difficult to attain correctly and can look amateurish if not done properly. Even though much of this style appears to be handheld, a loose-headed tripod is often used to create the controlled, fluid style.

THE CAMERA

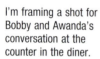

The DP's primary tool is the camera. Regardless of whether the movie is being shot on film or digital video, a firm understanding of how the camera works and how to frame is the key to achieving Hollywood-quality results.

- NEVER, NEVER, NEVER use any automatic camera functions like auto-focus, auto-white balance, or auto-iris. You're an artist! Don't let your tools tell you how your shot will look; instead, control your equipment to get the look you want.
- ALWAYS, ALWAYS, ALWAYS use a tripod unless the story requires otherwise. Shooting hand-held may be quicker, but the results will always be amateurish. You never want your audience to be pulled out of the story by a shaky camera.

I'm framing a shot for Bobby and Awanda's conversation at the counter in the diner.

Operation of the camera can be broken down into two categories: the way the camera and its settings function and choosing where to place the camera and how to approach the framing of a subject.

First, let's review how the camera functions by introducing the most powerful part of the camera: the lens.

CHOOSING THE LENS

The lens is the single most powerful tool in your arsenal. Although there are lots of film-look software programs available, a mastery of the lens is the best way to create a motion-picture-quality look. What's really exciting about the lens is that it works the same in every camera, whether it's a disposal camera from the drug store or an expensive Panavision 35 mm film camera. The principles we're going to identify are all a matter of optics and the way that light interacts with the lens.

Before we start, we need to understand that there are two types of lenses: prime lenses and zoom lenses.

Prime lenses

A prime lens has a fixed focal length. The lower the number, for example 12 mm, the wider the angle, and the higher the number, such as 120 mm, the closer the lens brings the subject. Typically, prime lenses come in a set from which the director of photography will choose the ideal lens for the desired field of view and depth of field for the shot.

Prime lenses have fewer pieces of glass for light to pass through than zoom lenses, which results in a sharper, crisper image. Prime lenses are often the choice among directors of photography, especially when shooting a movie that will be projected or shot under low light conditions or when a shallow depth of field is desired. Although primes are more expensive to rent than zoom lenses and require more time on set to change, the results are well worth the cost and effort.

Many professional camcorders accept 35 mm, ⅔-inch bayonet-mounted interchangeable lenses, giving the director of photography the opportunity to use primes. For cameras that have the lens built in, 35 mm adapters can be attached to the front of the camera and accept 35 mm lenses. Despite the advantage of obtaining a look closer to that of film, the amount of light lost through the adapter requires up to four times more light on set to obtain the same exposure than if the scene were photographed without the adapter.

Zoom lenses

Zoom lenses feature variable focal lengths because of additional pieces of glass added to the lens. The majority of video cameras feature noninterchangeable zoom lenses and offer greater flexibility and ease of use. Although they are faster when setting up a shot, zoom lenses are not ideal for high-quality motion picture usage because the increase in glass panes in the lens reduces the amount of light that reaches the film plane.

Zoom lenses are much faster to use in the field and cut back on the time needed to interchange primes, although the lens reduces the sharpness of the image and requires slightly more light than primes for the same exposure.

DIRECTOR'S NOTES

The biggest secret to making Hollywood-quality movies lies in the lens you choose and how you use it. Many filmmakers spend thousands of dollars on high-format cameras, quality lighting equipment, and camera-support equipment, never realizing that if they use a cheap lens, the potential clarity and sharpness of the recording format will never be fully utilized. The quality of the optics, especially in high-resolution formats like HD or 35 mm film, will make a substantial difference in the quality of the image. Rent the highest quality lens you can find, even at the expense of being able to afford the best recording format.

THE FIVE RINGS OF POWER

Every lens has five basic controls that the director of photography can manipulate to obtain the best technical and artistic image. Professional cameras with better optics afford a wider range of control than consumer or prosumer camcorders, and having a firm understanding of these five controls will help improve the image of even the cheapest camera.

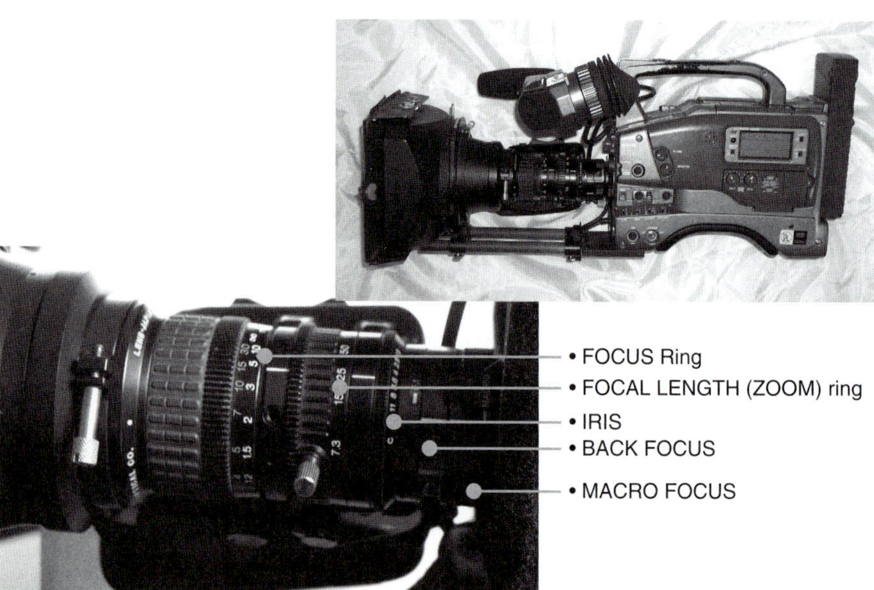

The JVC GY-DV500 camcorder I used to shoot *Time and Again.*

Ring 1—Focus

The first control of the lens is the focus ring. The focus ring adjusts a piece of glass to focus light entering the camera from a certain distance onto the film plane or CCD. You may have noticed the first assistant cameraman in behind-the-scenes videos of Hollywood movies, measuring the distance from the lens to the actor with a tape measure. He marks these measurements on the camera so he knows the precise focus setting for each of the actor's blocking marks.

If focusing using a zoom lens, zoom all the way in on the actor's eye, set the focus, then zoom back to the proper focal length. This ensures that the actor is in the sharpest focus and eliminates the need to measure the distance from the actor to the lens.

Pulling focus

Setting your focus once at the beginning of a setup works, provided neither the actor nor camera moves. In situations in which one or both move, the first assistant cameraman must "pull," or adjust the focus, during the shot to ensure that the actor remains in sharp focus throughout the shot. Pulling focus is a very important skill that takes years to master. The trick lies in the fact that a lens measures distances logarithmically, not linearly. If an actor stands 50 feet away from the lens and walks 2 feet toward the lens, the first AC needs to rotate the lens barrel a little bit. If, however, an actor is only 10 feet from the lens and walks 2 feet toward the lens, the first AC must rotate the barrel almost one-fifth of the way around. This may seem easy, but when the DP chooses a long focal length, the first AC may have a depth of field that is only an inch deep, making it challenging to keep the actor in a zone that narrow.

Follow focus units are designed to help the first assistant cameraman pull focus. The two marks on the white ring identify the focus positions necessary to keep the actors in focus.

If it's necessary to pull focus on a shot, use these simple steps to maintain focus throughout the shot:

1. Make sure the director is happy with the actor's blocking, then use colored gaffer's tape to mark the actor's starting and stopping positions.
2. If the camera is on a dolly, mark the starting and stopping points of both the camera and the dolly positions.

WATCH A RACK FOCUS

These four stills are taken from the opening sequence of *Time and Again*. In this shot, neither the camera position nor the focal length changed. Rather, I racked focus from the wheat in the foreground to Brian, who was about 250 feet away. The lens was set at 175mm at an *f*1.8.

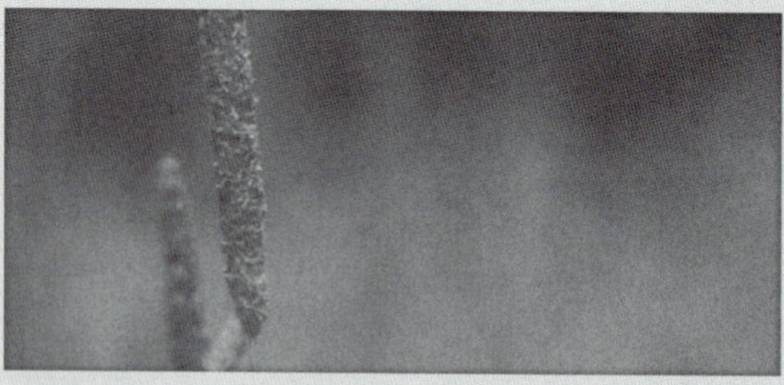

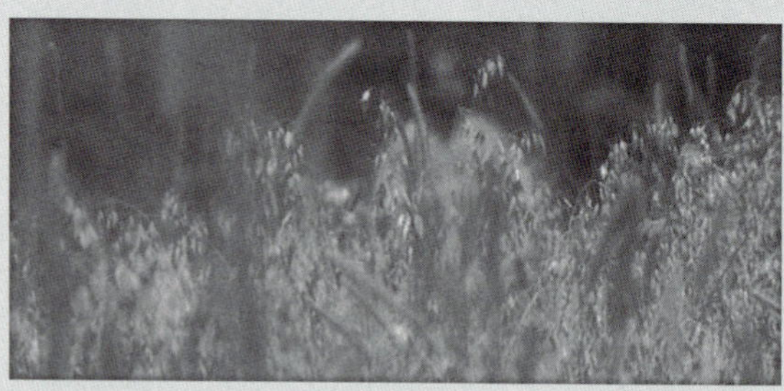

3. Move the camera and the actor to the first position and set focus. The first AC will put a piece of white tape around the focus ring of the lens and mark that focus setting using a thin line. Then move to the second position, set the focus, and mark that as the second mark on the lens.
4. Rehearse the action several times to ensure that the actor, dolly grip, and first AC are all in sync with each other.
5. Shoot the scene and keep a sharp eye on the monitor to make sure the entire shot is in focus.

Pulling focus can result in remarkable Hollywood-like images, but also requires careful preplanning and execution on set.

- Remember that the longer the focal length, the shallower the depth of field and the more difficult it is to keep the subject in focus.
- Combining camera moves with moving actors will require additional time to block the action, set focus, and properly pull the focus for the shot.
- Using 35mm lens adapters on HD cameras allows the use of 35 mm prime lenses and the desired shallower depth of field that emulates the look of film cameras; however, because of the way the optics work, the distance markings on the 35 mm lenses are inaccurate, making focus pulls even more difficult.

Ring 2—Focal length

The focal length is the measurement (in millimeters) from the optical center of the lens to the film plane (the film itself or, if you're using a video camera, the CCD). Zooming is the process of changing the focal length. Zooming out shortens the focal length and zooming in lengthens the focal length. Remember that prime lenses have fixed focal lengths.

WHAT HAPPENS WHEN YOU CHANGE THE FOCAL LENGTH?

Shorter focal length (zoomed out)	Longer focal length (zoomed in)
Deeper depth of field	Shallower depth of field
More, exaggerated depth	Flatter image
Farther from subject	Closer to subject
Perception of faster time	Perception of slower time

- **Shot size:** Changing the focal length has a huge impact on the look of your image. The most obvious is the difference in shot size. Longer focal lengths bring the audience closer to the subject, whereas shorter focal lengths give us a very wide shot. Changing the focal length also affects the depth of field. Believe it or not, the change in size isn't the primary reason most DPs change the focal length of the lens, but rather they want to create a shallower depth of field or exaggerate or flatten the depth of a shot.
- **Depth of field:** The depth of field is the zone in front of the lens in which objects are in focus. Changing the focal length, the exposure, and the distance of the subject from the lens can control the depth of field. Lengthening the focal length (zooming in), opening the iris, and moving the subjects close to the camera lens are three ways to create a shallow, or small, depth of field. Shortening the focal length (zooming out), closing the iris, and moving the subjects away from the camera lens are all ways to create a deep depth of field. Whereas the focal length determines how big the depth of field is, the focus determines where the depth of field is. Moving the depth of field from one subject in the foreground to a subject in the back-

This shot (left) was taken with a 7.5 mm, or a short, lens. Notice that everything in the shot is in focus and the background appears sharp and deep. You can judge the distance between the actors and the trees in the background. The iris was set at *f*11, so closing the iris helped add to the deep depth of field. The camera is only about 15 feet away from the actors.

This shot (right) was taken with a 120 mm, or a long, lens. Notice that the shot brings the audience much closer to Brian, although the camera is actually about 50 feet away from him! Shooting with the long lens gave us a very shallow depth of field, which threw the weeds in the foreground and background out of focus, drawing our eyes to Brian. It also flattened the shot so we can't really tell how far away the weeds in the distance are.

ground is called racking or pulling focus. The farther apart the subjects are and the shallower the depth of field, the more effective the technique.

- **Depth:** The second change in the image when shortening or lengthening the focal length is depth perception. A short lens (short focal length) will exaggerate the distance between objects in the foreground and background. Increasing the focal length will flatten the image and the viewer won't be able to determine visually how far apart the foreground subject is from the background image.
- **Time:** One side effect of using a long lens to flatten out a shot is the illusion of slowing time. If an actor were to start walking toward the camera from a distance of 200 feet, and you were to shoot him or her with a long lens, the resulting image would be so flat that it would appear as if the actor wasn't moving forward at all. This creates the illusion of time slowing down, because the character doesn't seem to be making any forward progress. Fight scenes, on the other hand, are usually shot with short lenses, because the increase in depth adds to the intensity and exaggerates the motion of the actors.

ACTIVITY

If you look into the zoom lens of a camera while you zoom in or out, you can actually see the pieces of glass moving closer or farther apart. The farther apart the pieces are, the "longer" the lens, or the longer the focal length. An easy way to remember this is that telescopes have very long housings designed to separate the pieces of glass, thereby getting very close to an object.

Ring 3—The iris: exposure

Any optical instrument, whether it's a camera or an eyeball, has a certain limit to the amount of light it is capable of seeing. In order to regulate the light to the optimum range, an iris or aperture can be opened or closed. In a camera, the size of the iris is measured in *f*-stops.

Mathematically, an *f*-stop is the number of times the distance across the lens opening must be multiplied in order to arrive at the lens focal length. Therefore, *f*-stops represent the ratio between the lens opening and the lens focal length:

f-stop = focal length/lens opening.

When a lens iris is set at *f*4, the diameter of the lens opening must be multiplied by 4 to arrive at the lens focal length; when it is set at *f*2.0, the diameter of the iris opening must be multiplied by 2 to arrive at the focal length.

This ratio results in the oddity that the smaller the *f*-stop number, the more OPEN the iris is, and the larger the *f*-stop number, the more CLOSED the iris is.

The *f*-stop scale on every camera lens is:

1	1.4	2	2.8	4	5.6	8	11	16	22
		More open				More closed			

Practically, understand that opening the iris by one *f*-stop DOUBLES the amount of light let into the lens. Closing the iris by one *f*-stop HALVES the amount of light let into the lens. The engineers who designed early optics wanted each *f*-stop to represent either a doubling or a halving of light, so the resulting *f*-stop numbers happened to be fractions instead of whole numbers. For example, if a camera were set to *f*5.6 and we open the iris to *f*2, we would be increasing the amount of light by 8*x*. Why? Opening the iris from *f*5.6 to *f*4 doubles the light being allowed through the lens, then *f*4 to *f*2.8 doubles the light again (to 4*x*), and then *f*2.8 to *f*2 doubles it again (from 4*x* to 8*x*).

As is the case with the focal length, changing the iris has a variety of other effects. Not only is the amount of light let into the lens affected, so is the depth of field. The MORE OPEN the iris, the SHALLOWER the depth of field. The MORE CLOSED the iris, the DEEPER the depth of field. Many cinematographers will choose their exposure setting first, based on the resulting depth of field and will light the scene for that particular exposure setting.

The proper way to expose a shot in video, when using prosumer and professional camcorders, is to use zebra stripes. Zebras are diagonal lines displayed in the viewfinder over any overexposed area of the shot. Zebra stripes are only a visual indicator in the viewfinder and are not recorded to tape. Set your exposure so that you barely see any zebra stripes on your subject (unless you want to overexpose it intentionally). This will ensure that your subjects fill out the contrast range of the camera. It is always important to have at least one part of your frame be at or near the 100 percent exposure area.

Ring 4—Macro focus

Lenses are designed to focus incoming light onto a CCD or film, but there's a limit to how close an object can be to the lens and still remain in focus. Most lenses aren't able to focus on anything within a couple feet of the lens, making extreme close-ups impossible. Manufacturers found a solution by introducing another piece of glass in the lens that gives the user the ability to focus on objects within a couple feet of the lens. This is called "macro focus." The macro focus function is virtually invisible on consumer cameras because the camera automatically switches from standard focus to macro focus whenever an object gets too close to the lens. Professional cameras, however, have a separate ring on the lens that allows the operator to set the macro focus manually.

The beauty of macro focus is that it exhibits the same changes in depth of field and perceived depth as standard focus. Using this technique and convincing miniatures you can rescale objects to appear large by working close to the lens and using the macro focus.

Ring 5—Back focus

Lenses are either permanently built into the camera body or designed to be interchangeable. The problem with swapping lenses between camera bodies is that each lens needs to be calibrated so the image is properly focused onto the film plane of the host camera. Because each camera is built differently and the CCD is set either closer or farther to the lens, each lens has a back-focus adjustment used to focus the image squarely on the CCD.

The back focus should be set each time a new lens is mounted on the camera. Although a qualified engineer should calibrate the lens, it's possible to set the back focus using a back-focus chart.

ACTIVITY 1

Take the camera outdoors and frame a small object (a water bottle, picture frame, etc.) in the foreground and an object in the background (a tree or a car). Using a short focal length (zoomed all the way out) and moving the camera so the foreground object is framed within the frame, study how the distance and focus between the foreground and the background objects are affected. Then, zoom all the way in (lengthening the focal length), and physically move the camera backward far enough to frame the foreground object at the same size as when you were close. Look at how the distance and focus change between the objects now that you're shooting on the long end of the lens.

- How did the depth of the shot appear to change when you shot the objects on the short end of the lens vs the long end of the lens?
- What benefit is there in shooting with a long lens? A short lens?

ACTIVITY 2

Shoot an object using a close-up shot, medium shot, and long shot, but shoot it in a way that reveals the object without ever revealing what it is until the long shot. Practice proper composition and framing so that each object is properly placed in the frame. Try different objects and different reveals, using the camera to tell a story about the object. For example, begin with a frame full of mud. The frame cuts to reveal a muddy tire. Cut to a car, caked in mud. Cut to an open field torn up by the car. It was off-roading. Learn to reveal the story with a series of consecutive cuts, prompting the audience to ask more and more questions that lead up to the reveal.

LENS CARE

Always take care of the lens by keeping it free of dust and scratches. Carry a can of compressed air to blow away dust that collects on the lens. If the compressed air isn't enough, use a camel hairbrush available from a local photography shop to lightly brush away the dust. As a last result, use a lens tissue and lightly wipe debris off the lens, careful not to scratch the lens coating.

Use a flashlight to check the lens at the beginning of each setup to ensure the lens is clean.

DIRECTOR'S NOTES

One of the easiest tricks to creating a Hollywood-quality look is to work with a shallow depth of field as often as possible. The 35 mm cameras used to shoot Hollywood movies have a much larger film plane than most prosumer video cameras that utilize 1/3 inch CCDs. Larger film planes mean shallower depth of field.

To mimic the look of a 35 mm film camera, follow these basic steps:

- Use the long end of the lens (zoom in) and move the camera forward or backward to set the proper frame. Remember that the longer the focal length, the shallower the depth of field.
- Open the iris as much as possible. The more open the iris, the shallower the depth of field. Consider picking up some ND (neutral density) filters to force the iris open.
- Slow down the shutter speed. This will also make for a shallower depth of field.

When I shot *Time and Again*, I almost exclusively worked on the long end of the lens, even in wide shots. The result comes really close to mimicking the depth of field attained on 35 mm film cameras.

CAMERA SETTINGS

There are a number of camera settings that can influence the look of the image. The director and DP should carefully discuss each setting in advance so they are clear about what the look of the movie should be and how to achieve it.

Shutter speed

In film cameras, the shutter is a rotating disc with an opening that allows light to pass through it to expose each frame. The wider the opening, the longer each frame is exposed, resulting in greater motion blur. Narrower shutter angles create a sharp, staccato look like the opening scene in *Saving Private Ryan*, when Allied forces attack the beaches of Normandy.

In video cameras changing the shutter speed has the same effect, but the "shutter" is a digital function that controls how long the CCD registers light for each frame.

The shutter speed is usually set to an angle of 180, or half the exposure time of a frame. For a more film-like look when shooting video, consider shooting with a slightly faster shutter speed.

- Maintaining the same visual look when changing the shutter speed requires compensating by either opening or closing the iris. For example, if you change the shutter speed from 1/30 second to 1/60 second, the light hitting the CCD is being cut in half. You must either double the amount of light on set or open the iris one *f*-stop to compensate.
- Think carefully about working with a faster shutter. You may need to add more light to expose each shot adequately, and additional lighting fixtures will add to the equipment budget.

Gain

Gain is to video the way film speed is to film cameras. Gain is a setting that electronically boosts the sensitivity of the CCD, making it more sensitive in low-light situations. The downfall, like using faster film, is that the resulting image is grainier and noisier.

Gain is used primarily in documentaries and newsgathering situations in which it's impossible to light, but grainy images are acceptable to the viewing audience. If you're shooting a narrative film, avoid using gain at all cost, because the image degradation is irreversible. If you want a grainy, contrasty image, filters and plug-ins in the editing room allow you more flexibility and control over the look.

White balance

Different light sources have different colors and, although difficult to see with the naked eye, are painfully evident to the camera lens. For example, tungsten light has a warm orange color, fluorescent light has a green hue, and sunlight at noon on a cloudless summer day has a blue hue. As a result, objects lit by these light sources are tinted, resulting in the need to correct for the tint.

This process, called white balancing, involves holding up a white card under the light source illuminating the set, zooming in on it so that the card fills the frame, and then pushing the camera's manual white balance button. Doing so tells the camera that the light falling on (and reflecting off) the white card should be viewed as white. The camera will then adjust the colors in the shot by removing the tint so the light from the source appears white. For example, if you are shooting a living room scene lit by table lamps and you white balance to tungsten, the lamps will not cast an orange light, but a white light.

The entire diner scene has a subtle orange tint (top), which helped create a 1950s look. I white balanced through a ¼ blue gel to warm up the image.

For Bobby's flashback sequence (bottom), I white balanced through a ½ orange gel to create deep, rich blues in the scene.

Avoid using either the camera's auto white-balance feature or the preset white balance settings. These auto-settings are calculated in the factory for specific color temperatures and rarely match the actual color of the light you're shooting under.

There are also ways to cheat the white balance to tint the overall look of the shot. Instead of white balancing to a white card, as is standard, place a lightly colored gel over the lens and then white balance to a white card. This forces the camera to remove the color of the gel to make the white card appear white. When you remove the gel from the front of the lens, the shot will be tinted the opposite color.

You can see examples of this in *Time and Again*. In the trailer scene, we white balanced through a slightly blue gel, resulting in a warm, orange-tinted shot. In the courtroom flashback, we white balanced through an orange gel, which tinted the shot blue. Do not use a deep-colored gel and overtint your shot because once the color information is gone, it cannot be replaced. Unless you're confident in using this trick, it is always better to tint your image during the editing process, in which you can always change or undo the effect.

COLOR TEMPERATURES

Why is it called color temperature when it has nothing to do with the heat of the light source? In the late 1800s, British physicist William Kelvin heated a block of carbon (called a black body) that glowed in the heat, producing a range of different colors at different temperatures. It first produced a dim red light, increasing to a brighter yellow as the temperature went up, and eventually produced a bright blue-white glow at the highest temperatures.

The temperature of the carbon black body then identified the corresponding wavelengths of light, hence the term color temperature. An example of this is tungsten. The color of light emitted by a tungsten filament is equal to the color of light emitted from the carbon when it is heated up to 3200 Kelvin. Hence, the color temperature of tungsten is 3200K and has nothing to do with the heat temperature at which the tungsten filament burns.

The Kelvin scale is a temperature scale at which zero starts at −273.15 degrees Celsius, also known as absolute zero, a temperature so cold that all molecular activity in matter stops.

Color temperature chart	
Blue sky	28,000K
Summer sky	9600–12,000K
Partially cloudy	8100–9500K
Summer shade	8000K
Light summer shade	7100K
Average daylight	6500K
Overcast	6000K
Midsummer	5800K
HMI	5500K
Average noon	5400K
Fluorescent	5000K
Late afternoon	4500K
Early morning	4400K
Hour after sunrise	3500K
Tungsten	3200K
Half-hour after sunrise	2500K
Sunrise/sunset	2000K
Candle flame	1900K
Match flame	1700K

Table 15.1 Aspect ratios for common film and video formats

INTENDED ASPECT RATIO	SIZE	DESCRIPTION
16 × 9	.3775 × .2123	Digital CCD Area
16 × 9 (2.40:1)	.3775 × .1579	Digital CCD Extended Area for Anamorphic
1.37:1	.404 × .295	Regular 16mm Camera Aperture
Various	.486 × .295	Super 16mm Camera Aperture
Various	.980 × .735	35mm Full Camera Aperture
2.40:1	.825 × .690	Anamorphic Projection Aperture
1.85:1	.825 × .446	35mm 1.85:1 Projection Aperture
2.40:1	.945 × .394	Super Panavision 35mm Extracted Area for Anamorphic Projection
1.33:1	.792 × .594	35mm TV Transmitted Area *(SMPTE recommended practice)*
	.713 × .535	35mm TV Safe Action
1.78:1	.945 × .531 (16 × 9)	4-Perf Transmitted Area
Various	.980 × .546	Panavision 3-Perf 35mm Camera Aperture
1.78:1	.910 × .511 (16 × 9)	3-Perf Transmitted Area
2.29:1	2.072 × .906	65mm Camera Aperture
2.20:1	1.912 × .870	70mm Projection Aperture *(Panavision Super 70mm)*
2.40:1	1.912 × .797	Extracted for 2× Projection

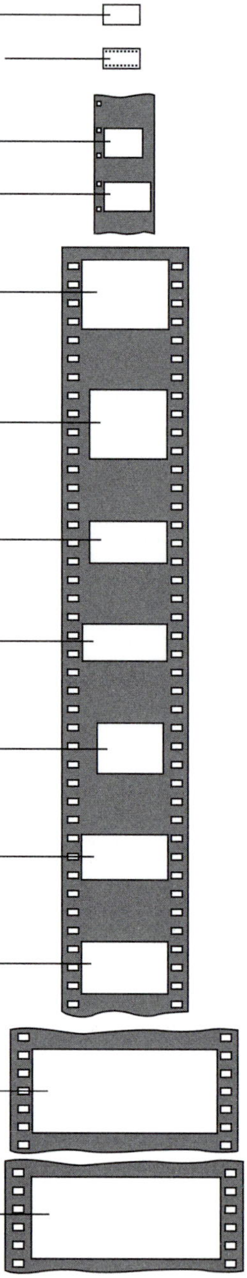

WORKING WITH THE FRAME

The biggest difference between amateur and professionally produced movies is how shots are framed. With an almost limitless number of possibilities as to where to place the camera and how to frame up a shot, a careful eye and some forethought will greatly improve the professionalism of your movie.

Although this sounds simple and mundane, the audience sees only where you point the camera. Especially in the low-budget realm, creative camera angles and careful framing can help sell limited locations, basic production design, and even simple lighting.

Aspect ratios

The aspect ratio is the ratio of the width of the frame to the height of the frame. Referred to as a dimension such as 16 × 9 or 4 × 3, the aspect ratio refers to the shape of the frame, not the size.

Film and video formats have different aspect ratios that are chosen for creative and technical reasons. Most filmmakers will agree that shooting with a wider aspect ratio more closely mimics the human eye's area of view and is more aesthetically pleasing.

Converting from one format to another can create problems because the aspect ratios may not match. Letterbox and pan-and-scan techniques are used to overcome differing frame shapes.

Letterbox

Converting one film/video format to another can be challenging, especially when the aspect ratio of the two media is different. In this instance, a 1.85:1 35 mm film frame is wider than an NTSC 4:3 television frame, so one possible option is to reduce the 35 mm frame so that it fits inside the NTSC frame and to fill the top and bottom areas with black. Although it may seem as though the top and bottom of the frame are cut off, the letterbox format allows the viewer to see the entire 35 mm frame.

Pan and scan

Many distributors and broadcasters do not want to use the letterbox format, so instead, the pan-and-scan technique is utilized. This process involves blowing up the 35 mm frame so that it fills the NTSC frame. Because the 35 mm frame is wider than the NTSC frame, the sides of the picture are cut off, losing up to 40% of the image. Critical elements in the movie may be lost outside the NTSC frame, therefore the 35 mm frame can be shifted left and right to "reframe" in order for critical objects to appear.

RULES OF COMPOSITION

There are a number of guidelines that help the cameraman best utilize the area of the camera frame. Although these guidelines can easily be compromised,

A letterbox preserves the 35mm aspect ratio when it is converted to NTSC.

Unlike letterboxing an image, cropping cuts off almost 40% of the 35mm frame.

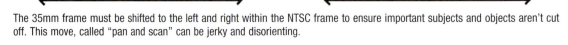

The 35mm frame must be shifted to the left and right within the NTSC frame to ensure important subjects and objects aren't cut off. This move, called "pan and scan" can be jerky and disorienting.

they provide the most aesthetically pleasing look and should be heavily considered. From classic paintings to modern motion pictures, you'll begin to notice these conventions used again and again.

- **Rule of Thirds:** The Rule of Thirds is designed to help the camera operator determine where in the frame to place important objects. Instead of centering a subject, always frame the subject a third from either side of the frame or a third from the top or bottom. Here's how it works: Place an imaginary tic-tac-toe board over the frame and place the subject on one of the lines. For example, frame an actor's eyes one-third from the top of the frame, or when shooting a sunset, place the horizon one-third from the bottom of the screen. Whereas these examples demonstrate framing of horizontal elements, this same concept applies to the placement of vertical elements. If there is a single tree silhouetted against the setting sun, the tree should be placed either a third from the left or a third from the right of the frame, never centered.

- **Lead room:** Not only should an operator frame for an object or subject, but also for the action of the subject. If an actor were to look directly into the camera lens, he should be centered in the frame with his eyes a third from the top of the screen. If the actor were to turn his head frame right, pan right to allow room for him to look into. The more drastic to the side the action is, the more lead room must be provided.
- **The 180 Rule:** If you and I were standing on set, we would be able to see every object in the room, know the geography of the room, and have a sense of spatiality. The audience, however, sees only what the camera sees, and when the camera shoots a series of close-up shots, the geography of the room and the objects in it are never fully revealed to the audience. Take, for example, two people facing each other, talking over a restaurant table. If you're standing on the set, you know they're facing each other. But if the only camera coverage is two single close-ups, it is possible to misplace the camera so that it looks as though the two people are looking in the same direction, incorrect as it may be.

The 180 Rule prevents this geographic confusion from taking place. In order to apply this rule, draw a line, called the line of action, between the two subjects, as though you were connecting the dots, except that this line extends infinitely in both directions. The rule specifies that the camera must remain on one side of the line of action to prevent a geographic conflict that confuses the audience as to the placement of the subjects and objects on the set. You can choose any camera angle, any distance from the actors, any lens type, and any camera height, provided the camera always remains on the same side of the line.

As is the case with many rules, there are three exceptions when the camera is allowed to cross the line:

(a) In the first exception the camera cuts to a shot while on the line. In the instance of a car chase, a shot on the line could be a point of view of a driver, or a car could drive over the camera, or, if placed on a bridge, the camera could shoot directly down onto the cars driving underneath. Once we establish a shot on the line, the camera is free to either return to its original side of the line or cross to the other side for the duration of the scene.

(b) In the second exception the camera crosses the line during a dolly or handheld shot. If the camera dollies across the line of action, then the audience is watching as the camera crosses, preserving the geographic layout of the set. If the camera crosses, the next shot must occur on the same side the camera ends up on.

(c) In the third exception the line of action crosses the camera. For example, if two actors are seated at a table and one of the actors stands and walks across the frame, then the line has effectively moved across the camera. The next shot must be taken from the new position unless one of the above-stated exceptions is applied.

Remember that the 180 Rule is a guide you can use to determine where to put the camera for the next shot. Regardless of whether you followed the rule or used an exception, the next shot must always take place from the correct side of the line to avoid confusing the audience.

- **Eye line:** When shooting a dialog scene between two actors, place the camera close to the line of action so the actors are facing the camera as much as possible, with their eye line just off the side of the lens. A common mistake committed by many new filmmakers is to place the camera too far away from the line of action, framing a profile shot instead of a full-facial shot. The more an actor faces the camera lens, the greater the audience will emotionally connect with him.
- **Headroom:** Headroom is the distance from the top of the actor's head to the top of the frame. If you follow the rule of thirds and always place the actor's eyes a third from the top of the frame, then the headroom should automatically fall into place.
- **Background:** Make sure the background is free and clear of any distracting elements like plants or phone poles that, if improperly framed, appear to grow from the actor's head. Using tools to throw the background out of focus will draw the audience's attention toward the subject of the shot. Think and preplan the background of every shot from an art direction, set-dressing, and color standpoint so the background serves to tell the story.

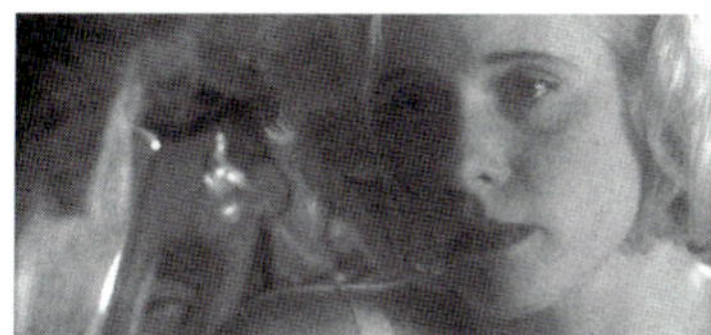

Camera: CU on Awanda

In this frame, Awanda is looking FRAME LEFT at Bobby who is looking FRAME RIGHT.

Line of action

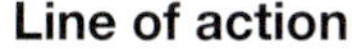

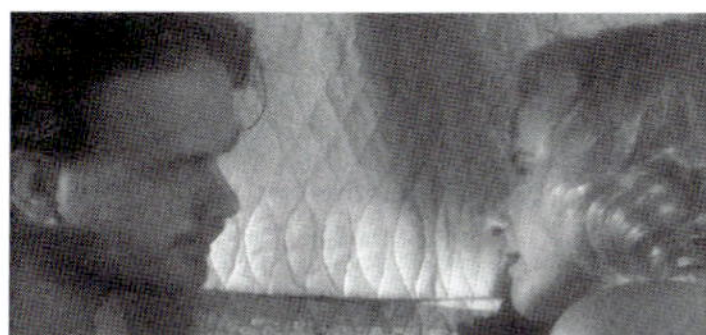

Camera: Master shot of Bobby and Awanda

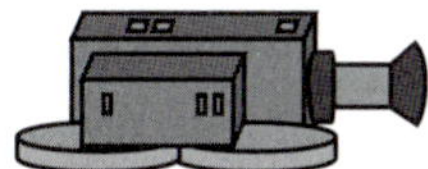

In this frame, Awanda is STILL looking FRAME LEFT at Bobby while Bobby looks FRAME RIGHT.

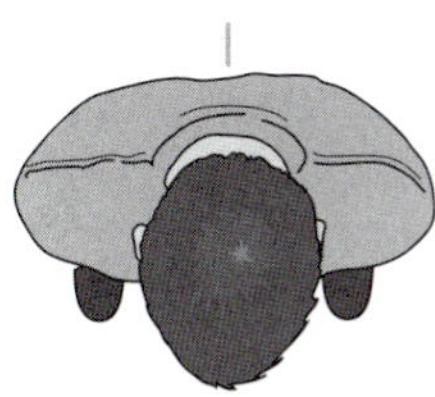

By crossing the line of action, this shot of Bobby WILL NOT edit correctly with the shot of Awanda because both Bobby and Awanda are looking FRAME LEFT! Editing them together will make it appear as though they are facing the same direction.

Camera: CU on Bobby

In this frame, Bobby is STILL looking FRAME RIGHT.

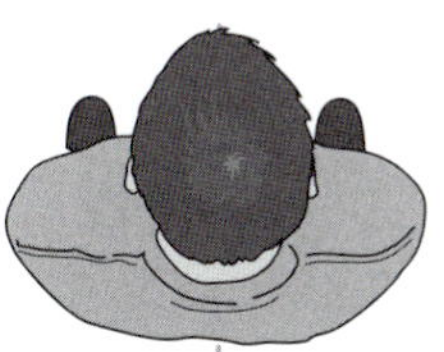

This shot was framed through the controls of a tractor. By using a shallow depth of field, the foreground was thrown out of focus, yet the tractor still framed Bobby. The background element in the frame is a wheat field. The foreground and background elements both help make the shot more visually interesting.

In *Time and Again*, whenever a shot was framed, we looked at the background very carefully to make sure it accurately portrayed the 1950s. We added props or set dressing to help sell the illusion and were always mindful of the colors and textures, making sure the frame was as rich as possible.

- **Foreground:** Add depth to shots by shooting through foreground elements. Fences, objects on a table, plants, and even shooting through car windows all add several layers of depth to a shot and can help frame a subject. Always think in terms of what the background, midground, and foreground elements are in a shot.

A great example of using the foreground occurs in *Time and Again* when Bobby Jones leaves the wheat field and is walking around the barn behind the house. The shot was framed through a piece of farm equipment that was thrown out of focus, helping to draw the audience's attention to Bobby Jones.

If you have access to a dolly, consider opening a scene by dollying from behind an object or slowly dollying in front of, or through, a foreground element. These subtle techniques help add production value and make for interesting shots.

- **Balance:** Always make sure that elements in the frame feel balanced. Look at the rough shape, color, and brightness of the primary objects in the shot and make sure they complement each other in the frame.

DIRECTOR'S NOTES

Don't be afraid to cheat! In many instances, I would frame up a shot and decide that it needed a little more spice to make it interesting. Provided it didn't interfere with the continuity of previous shots, I would add elements in front of the camera lens to provide an interesting foreground to shoot through, or we would move and finesse the set dressing in the background, always taking time to scrutinize the frame before rolling off a take. Sometimes small changes like moving a plant into the frame or removing artwork from the wall that competes for the viewer's attention can make a big difference in the balance and feel of the shot.

Don't be afraid to experiment and, provided you have the time, make each shot a masterpiece that you could print, frame, and hang on the wall.

SHOT TYPES

Communication between the director and the director of photography starts by understanding the size of the frame and how the actors will look in the frame. Below are the most common frame types and examples of what they look like.

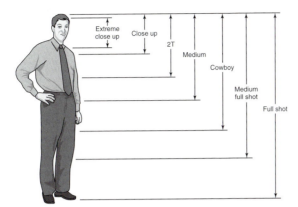

- **Establishing shots** are wide shots, generally to show the audience where the following scene is taking place. These shots serve to set up, or establish, the location.

- **Master shot** is a wide shot that covers all the action of a scene from the beginning to the end. Usually a simple shot, master shots sometimes incorporate a dolly move to keep them from being stagnant. Master shots always include everything the audience needs to see to understand the scene.

- **Full shot** is a full head-to-toe body shot of the actor.
- **¾ or Hollywood shot**—The frame cuts the actor off at the knees. This shot is not used often in modern cinema because cutting off a subject at the joints is considered bad composition and looks awkward.

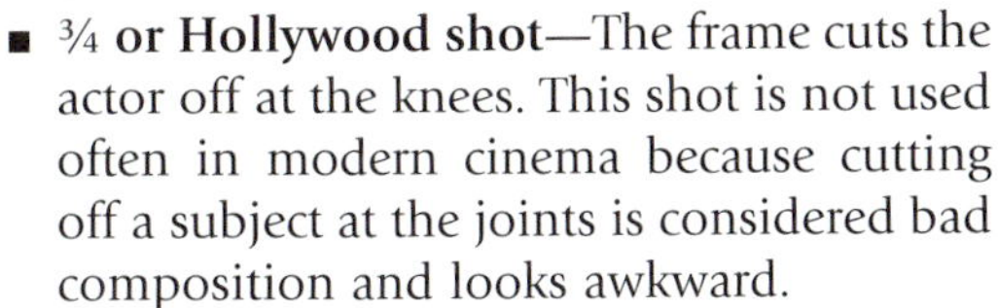

- **Medium shot**—The medium shot is the most common shot and frames the actor from midtorso to his head.

- **Two shot**—Two actors, usually standing next to each other. A two shot has two actors in the frame. A three shot has three actors in the frame and so on.

- **Walking two shot** is a two shot, except that the actors are walking during the shot. They can either stop or start or be walking when the camera rolls.

- **Standing two shot** is a lock-down shot in which neither the camera nor the actors move.

- **Reversal**—A shot in which two actors are facing each other, across a dinner table for example, and the camera cuts from a medium shot of one actor to a medium shot of the other actor, hence "reversing" the shot.

- **Over-the-shoulder shot** (OTS)—A medium shot of an actor over the shoulder of another actor. An OTS shot frames one side of the shot with the back of the actor's head and shoulder. As a general rule, the audience should see only one ear of the actor facing away from the camera.

- **Close-up**—A tight shot framing an actor's head and shoulders, the close-up focuses the audience's attention on an actor's facial expression and is a very powerful frame, but should be mixed in with a variety of other shots to keep the sequence from feeling claustrophobic.

- **Deep focus**—A shot in which all elements in frame are in focus. Also called a "deep depth of field," this can be achieved by using a short focal length (zooming out) and closing the iris.

- **Shallow focus**—A shot in which only certain objects in the frame are in focus. You can achieve a shallow depth of field by lengthening the focal length (zooming in) and opening the camera's iris.

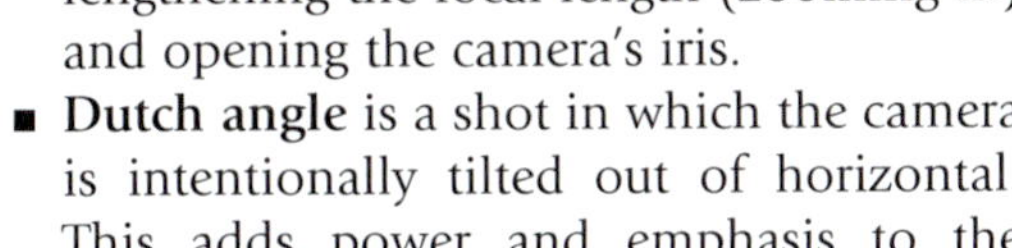

- **Dutch angle** is a shot in which the camera is intentionally tilted out of horizontal. This adds power and emphasis to the shot.
- **Panning** is horizontal movement of the camera on its axis, usually while on a tripod.
- **Tilting** is vertical movement of the camera on its axis, usually while on a tripod.
- **Pedestal**—Vertically raising or lowering the camera. This term is used in television production. On a film set, the term is "boom up" or "boom down," when using a pneumatically controlled dolly.
- **Tracking shot** is a shot that involves moving the camera laterally, side to side.
- **High shot** is a shot in which the camera is positioned above the subject and is shooting down, making the subject look inferior.
- **MOS**—Short for "mit out sound" (German), which identifies a shot recorded without sound.

- **Montage**—A series of shots interwoven with transitions to show the passage of time.

WORKING WITH A PRODUCTION MONITOR

One of the most critical tools on set is a properly calibrated production monitor. Although expensive (a good field monitor will cost between $800 and $1200), professional monitors offer calibration tools so the image displayed on the monitor is exactly what is being recorded.

This is especially important when shooting in a digital format in which the director and DP tend to light and expose the shot based on how the image looks on the monitor.

The process for properly calibrating a monitor is as follows:

1. Connect the monitor to the camera and, through the camera's settings, activate the color bars. Color bars are used to ensure that all the video devices through the production chain are properly calibrated. Always view the monitor in a dark room or in a low-light environment to ensure proper calibration.
2. To set the luminance, or brightness, of the monitor, look for the three vertical gray bars in the lower right portion of the color bar chart. You'll notice that the left bar is black, the middle bar is dark gray, and the right bar is light gray. Adjust the brightness on the monitor until the two bars on the left appear as black and the rightmost bar is barely visible.
3. The next step is to adjust the contrast. Look at the white square in the lower left corner of the color bar chart and turn up the contrast until the white begins to bloom into the surrounding boxes. The contrast is properly set when the edges of the white box are sharp and defined.
4. Professional monitors have a "blue-only" mode that turns off the red and green cathode ray tubes, displaying only blue. If your monitor doesn't have a blue mode, try placing a 47b blue gel over the monitor so it filters out all colors except blue. Adjust the chroma (color) setting until the two outside bars match the same brightness as the bars below them. When properly calibrated, the two bars should appear as one.
5. To adjust the hue (phase or tint), adjust the setting until the two inner bars match in brightness to the bars directly beneath them. It may be necessary to readjust the chroma and hue together, as one will influence the other.
6. The monitor will be properly calibrated once top and middle bars match each other in the first, second, sixth, and seventh columns.
7. Turn off blue mode and know that the image you're seeing is true and accurate.

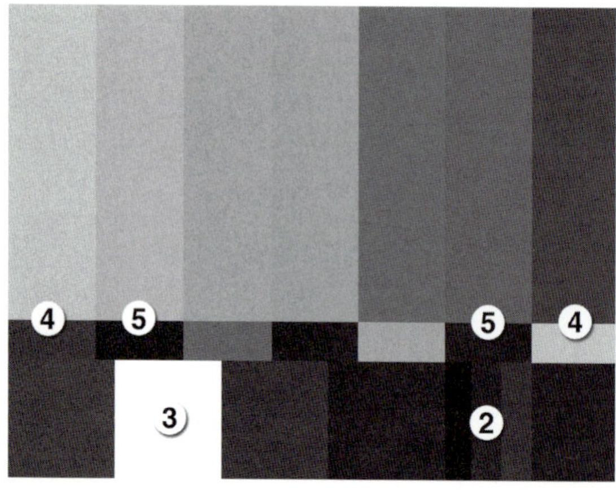

LIGHTING

Lighting is as important to crafting the emotional tone of the scene as the actors' performance. One of the most common mistakes made by independent filmmakers is either neglecting the craft of lighting all together or, even worse yet, using light simply as a way of illuminating the subject enough to expose the shot.

Properly lighting a shot is, by far, the best way to achieve a big budget, Hollywood-quality look. Good lighting can enhance limited set design and art direction and truly make the difference between an amateurish and a professional movie.

One of the most common lighting techniques and the foundation of most lighting setups is called three-point lighting, which utilizes three different types of lights:

Key light: The key light is the main source of illumination on the subject and is generally placed about 45 degrees off the camera line. Off-setting the key creates shadows on the face and brings out depth and dimension. The harsher the key light, the more pronounced the shadows. The more diffused the light, the softer the shadows.

Fill light: The key light will create shadows, and the "fill" is used to fill in some of those shadows without adding so much light that the shadows are completely lost. Fill lights can either be the ambient light on set or be added with something as simple as a bounce board. Remember that the fill light is never as strong as the key.

Rim/back light: Positioned so that it is almost facing the key light, the back light is a very subtle accent that brings out the actor's shoulders and back of head, separating him from the background.

Although the three-point lighting technique is a classic approach to lighting, there are many variations that can be used to help create a high-quality look, even on a low budget.

- **Always place the camera and the key light on opposite sides of the actor's eye line.** In the traditional three-point lighting demonstration, the actor is almost always facing the camera. Unfortunately, actors rarely look directly into the camera, but rather off to the side of the lens, usually at another actor, which affects the placement of the key light. The trick to placing the key light is to determine the actor's eye line, or the direction of his gaze. If the camera is on one side of the eye line, then place the key light on the other side so the key light will illuminate the far side of the actor's face. This technique brings out the depth and details of his face, while allowing the fleshy part of his cheek to fall slightly into shadow. This will help frame his eyes, nose, and mouth while creating a sparkle in his eye, called an eye light.

Rim/Back Light: Lightly edges the shoulder and head from the background; usually faces the key light
Subject
Key Light: Main source of illumination; positioned about 45° off the center line of the camera
Fill Light: Fills in some of the shadows cast by the key light, but not all; positioned about 45° off the center line of the camera, opposite the key light
Camera

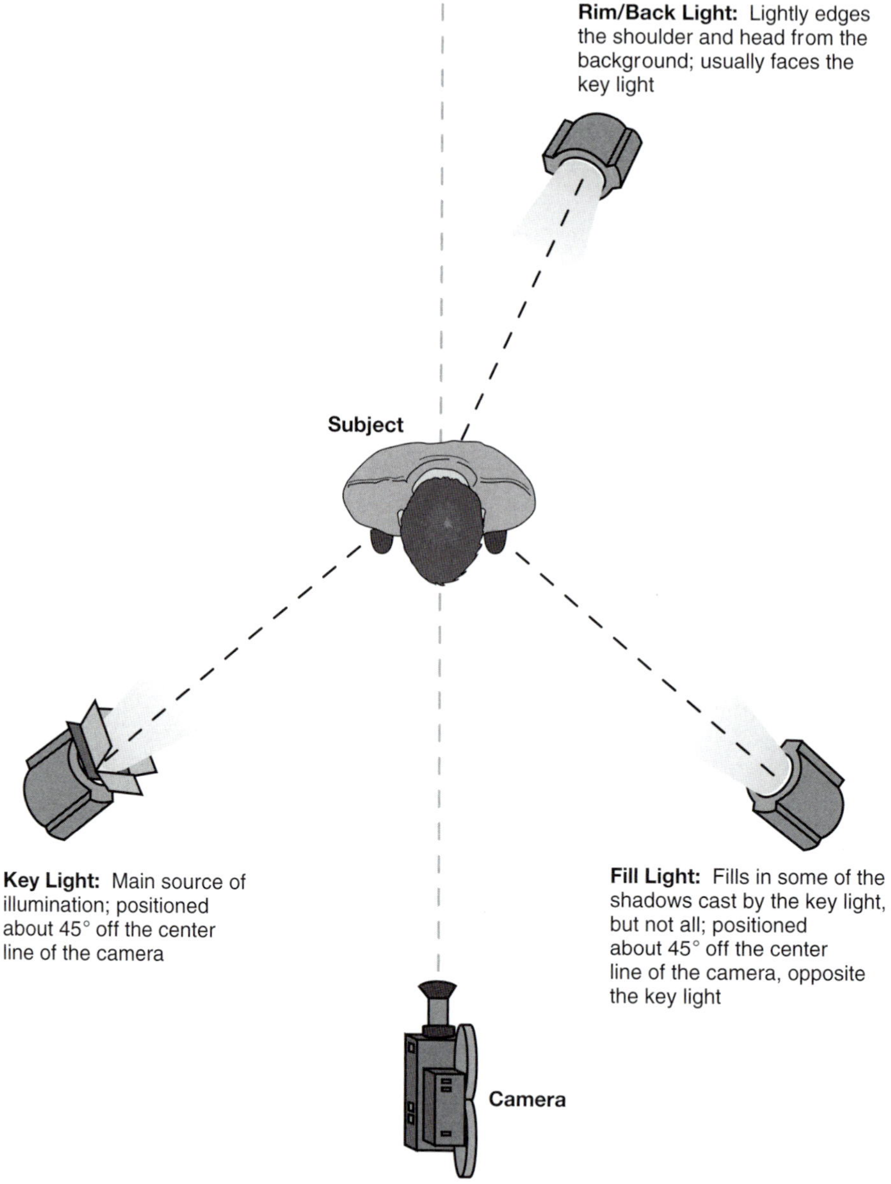

- **Light the actor brighter than the background.** Try lighting the actor at least one *f*-stop brighter than the background to help her pop out of her surroundings. One big problem in independent films occurs when the actors and set are so evenly lit that there is no sense of depth within the frame. Lighting the actor and blocking any spill off the background is a great way to guide the audience's eye to what you want them to be seeing—the performance.

- **Use reflected light.** When most independent filmmakers approach lighting, their natural tendency is to aim a light directly at the actors. Try bouncing the light off a reflector, a piece of white foam core or bead board to soften the light. Applying this technique to the key light is especially helpful when shooting an actor's face. The light will be much more natural and flattering to the actor.

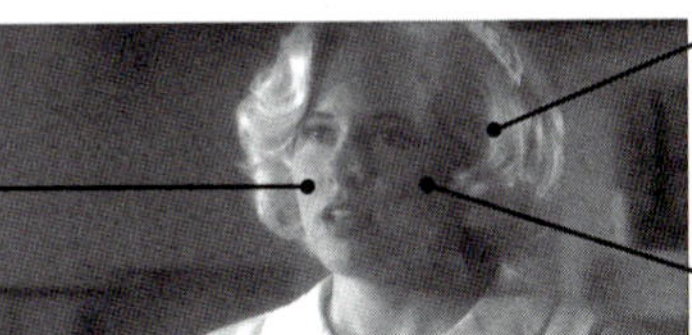

Key light: We used a 1200-watt HMI, which is equal to a 5000-watt tungsten light, through a 4 × 4-foot silk diffusion to soften the light.
Back light: We used a 250-watt Lowel Pro light to accent Awanda's hair.
Fill light: We used a white bounce card to fill in some of the shadows created by the key.

Working with shadows

It would make sense that lighting a subject would involve directing a light at the subject and turning the light on. Although this approach works some of the time, it results in harsh shadows and usually creates an unnatural look.

Good lighting creates shadows, provided those shadows are in the right place. In real life, we are able to determine depth and distance because we have two eyes that work together, each one seeing an object from a slightly different angle. When our brain puts these two images together, we are able to see depth. This process, called triangulation, helps us determine the distance between objects or the distance from an object to our face. Incidentally, the closer an object is to our eyes, the more depth sensitive we are. The farther away it is, the more

difficult it is to determine depth. For example, if you hold your finger at arm's length and move it 12 inches toward your face, your brain will detect that change in distance much more than if a friend, standing 100 feet away, moves his finger 12 inches closer to you. It is for the same reason that it is difficult to tell how far away stars are relative to each other. The angle from the stars to our left eye and the stars to our right eye is so narrow that we can't tell how far away they are from us, or from one another.

Unfortunately, a camera doesn't have depth perception because it only has one "eye," the lens. In order to create depth, you have to create shadows through the use of good lighting.

There are good shadows, called internal shadows, and bad shadows, called external shadows. External shadows are created when a light casts a harsh shadow of the subject onto another object, drawing the audience's attention to the presence of the light. Internal shadows are cast by the subject onto itself, resulting in contrast. For example, lighting one-half of an actor's face will not only cast a shadow of him on the wall, resulting in an external shadow, but also cast a shadow on the other side of his face, an internal shadow. He casts a shadow onto himself. Good lighting technique avoids distracting external shadows, but uses internal shadows to give a sense of depth and dimension to a shot.

The transition between the bright and the dark sides of a subject's face is called the "wraparound." A harsh, distinctive line between the bright and the dark sides of a subject's face is called a hard wraparound, whereas a soft transition from dark to light is a soft wraparound. Famous female movie stars of the 1940s and 1950s look glamorous because of soft wraparound.

- You can create a soft wraparound by reflecting light off a white piece of foam core (available at most home improvement stores), walls, or other reflective surfaces. The larger the reflector area and the closer to the subject, the softer the wraparound.
- If you need to break up an empty wall behind the subject, try taking a piece of foam core and cutting out the pattern of a window frame, a random shape, or the pattern of Venetian blinds. Place this "cookie" in front of the light to cast a patterned external shadow onto the back wall to help break up the monotony. Try cutting some small tree branches and mounting them in front of a light to cast the shadow of branches or leaves on the set. The closer the cookie is to the light, the softer the shadow cast on the set wall.

- Another great way to break up the background is to focus a light onto the wall, then use a flag to cut off the top, bottom, or sides of the light. The result is a smooth grade from light to dark. I like to set my camera frame and grade the wall directly behind the actor's head so the darker part of the wall helps his face stand out.

Notice in these still images taken from *Time and Again* that no matter what the shot, the key light is offset to the side of each subject, creating a light and a dark side of the face, with varying grades of wraparound. Good cinematography and lighting create contrast on either side of the subject's face; the amount of contrast is dependent on what you want the scene to look like artistically.

Four examples of wraparound.

The qualities of light

Light has a number of attributes, each of which can be controlled to create the desired look on screen.

- **Falloff:** Falloff is the distance light travels before its brightness severely drops off. Focused lights tend to have greater falloff than soft, diffused sources. Falloff is important when working in tight locations such as an apartment, where lights with a long falloff will overlight the background walls. Fluorescent lights, like Kino-Flos, have very fast falloff.
- **Color:** The color of the light is measured by its color temperature. It's important to match the color temperatures of the lights when shooting. For more information, please refer to the color temperatures section in this chapter.
- **Brightness:** The brightness is how much light a fixture generates and is measured in foot candles or watts.
- **Wraparound:** Wraparound is the transition from light to shadow on an actor's face. Harsh direct lights have a small wraparound, whereas large, soft sources have a greater wraparound.
- **Specularity:** Specularity is the intensity and color of highlights on a subject. An example of a highly specular source is a bright spot on a bald actor's head created by the rim light.

LIGHTING TERMS

Baby—a 1000-watt light
Blonde—an open face 2000-watt light
Brute—a 225-amp, DC-powered arc light
Deuce—a 2000-watt light
Junior—a 2000-watt light
Mickey—an open face 1000-watt light
Midget—a 500-watt light
Redhead—a 1000-watt light
Senior—a 5000-watt light

Lighting a scene

1. Look at the existing ambient light. In the ideal situation, the director of photography would be working on a pitch black soundstage and have complete control over all the lighting and reflective surfaces. Unfortunately, on location, you will be forced to contend with windows, sunlight, overhead lights, and reflected sources, so planning your lighting to work *with* these ambient sources will greatly improve the look of the film. The worst ambient light sources are nondirectional, even light. Although there may be plenty of light, if it is evenly spread or diffused on the set, the result is a low-contrast, flat look. Use locations that have a directional ambience such as windows on one side of the room or focusable spotlights in the ceiling. The more directional the ambience, the easier it will be to control.

2. Determine the direction of the light. Referring to three-point lighting, thenext step is to determine the position of the key light. The secret to placing the key light is to watch the blocking of the actors, determine the camera's position for each setup, and then think about light placement. Once you know where the camera will be placed for each setup throughout the scene, place the key light so that it works for each angle. For example, in the trailer scene between Bobby Jones and Awanda, the light was coming in from the side of the trailer, so that no matter where the actors were, as long as they were positioned along the length of the trailer, the window light would always serve as the key. Try to think ahead so that the key light's position will work for each camera position in the scene. Storyboards are helpful in preplanning the camera positions.

The crew lights the garage for Bobby and Awanda's bedroom scene.

3. Determine the amount of fill light needed to balance out the key light. Once the key light has been placed, look at the amount of fill light you may want to add to increase or decrease the contrast ratio. Remember, the less fill you have, the more contrast, and the more dramatic the shot will look; the more fill you add, the less the contrast ratio and the flatter the lighting will be on the subject. Adding a fill light source could be as simple as reflecting a light onto a white bounce card or using a softbox.

4. **Add rim light if necessary.** Determine if you need a rim light to help separate the actor from the background. Make sure the rim light is motivated by a light source that the audience can see in the shot, either a window or a lamp in the background, and for realistic lighting designs, try to keep the rim light very subtle and not overly harsh.

5. **Add accent lights to the set, if necessary.** Once the actors are lit, look at the scene and determine if any accent lights are necessary. Does the background need any splashes of light? Or perhaps the wine glasses on the table may benefit from a kicker to help them sparkle. While adding accents like this, don't forget to also include shadows, because good lighting stems from both light and shadow.

For more information on lighting, camera movement, and framing, check out the Cinematography modules at www.powerfilmmaking.com.

Working with a single light source

Many times, especially when working outdoors, you only have one light source with which to work: the sun. Although this may seem like a limitation, the sun is the most powerful light source available and can be easily reflected, bounced, and diffused to move, shape, and craft the light to serve the needs of your shot.

In working with the sun, treat it in the same way you'd treat the key or rim light. The only difference is that you need to move the subject and camera to position the sun in the ideal location.

There are two ways to approach shooting using the sun as the primary light source:

- **Use the sun as the key light.** Position the actor so the sun is illuminating the far side of the actor's face, opposite the actor's eye line. This is much easier to do before 11:00 AM and after 2:00 PM, when the sun hangs lower in the sky. Avoid shooting near noon, because the sun tends to cast shadows on the actor's brow, creating deep, cavernous shadows over the actor's eyes. Use a bounce board to fill in some of the shadows, especially if the sun is too direct.
- **Use the sun as a rim light.** Position the actor so the sun is positioned behind him or her, then use a bounce board or reflector

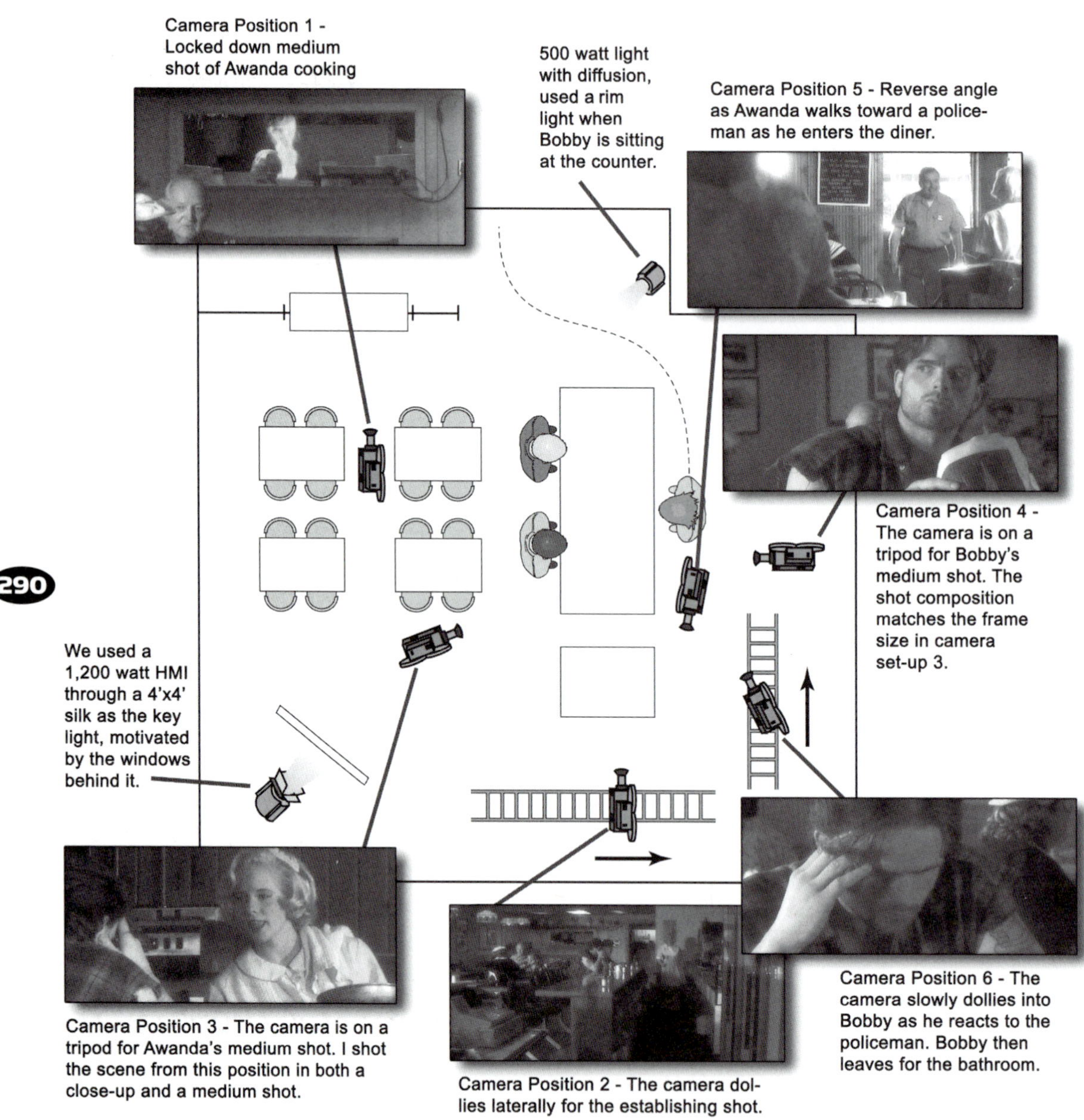
HOW WE LIT AND SHOT THE DINER SCENE
Camera Position 1 - Locked down medium shot of Awanda cooking
500 watt light with diffusion, used a rim light when Bobby is sitting at the counter.
Camera Position 5 - Reverse angle as Awanda walks toward a policeman as he enters the diner.
Camera Position 4 - The camera is on a tripod for Bobby's medium shot. The shot composition matches the frame size in camera set-up 3.
We used a 1,200 watt HMI through a 4'x4' silk as the key light, motivated by the windows behind it.
Camera Position 3 - The camera is on a tripod for Awanda's medium shot. I shot the scene from this position in both a close-up and a medium shot.
Camera Position 2 - The camera dollies laterally for the establishing shot.
Camera Position 6 - The camera slowly dollies into Bobby as he reacts to the policeman. Bobby then leaves for the bathroom.

HOW WE LIT AND SHOT THE PLAYGROUND SCENE

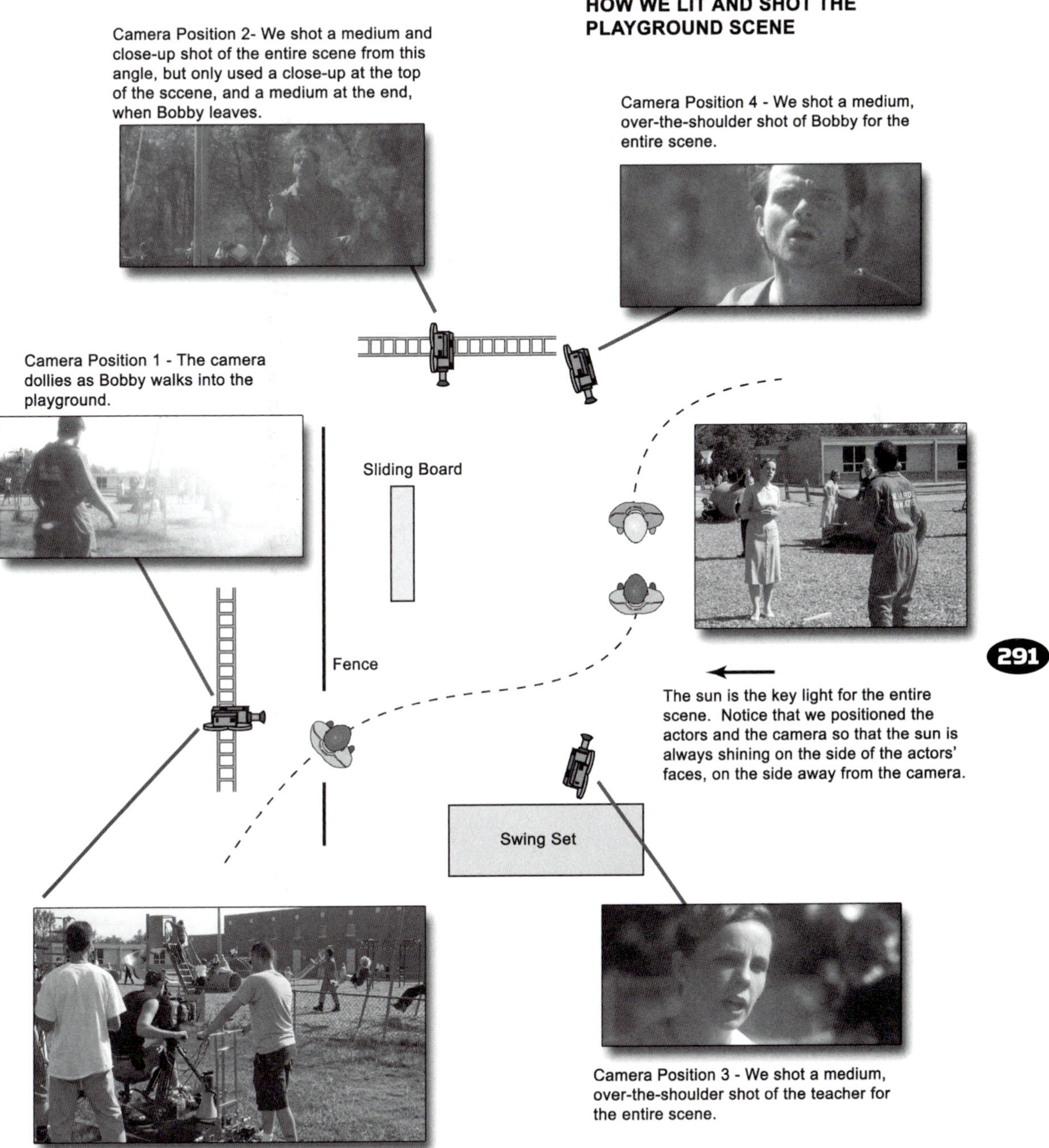

Camera Position 2- We shot a medium and close-up shot of the entire scene from this angle, but only used a close-up at the top of the sccene, and a medium at the end, when Bobby leaves.
Camera Position 4 - We shot a medium, over-the-shoulder shot of Bobby for the entire scene.
Camera Position 1 - The camera dollies as Bobby walks into the playground.
Sliding Board
Fence
The sun is the key light for the entire scene. Notice that we positioned the actors and the camera so that the sun is always shining on the side of the actors' faces, on the side away from the camera.
Swing Set
Camera Position 3 - We shot a medium, over-the-shoulder shot of the teacher for the entire scene.

HOW WE LIT AND SHOT THE PRISON BREAK SCENE

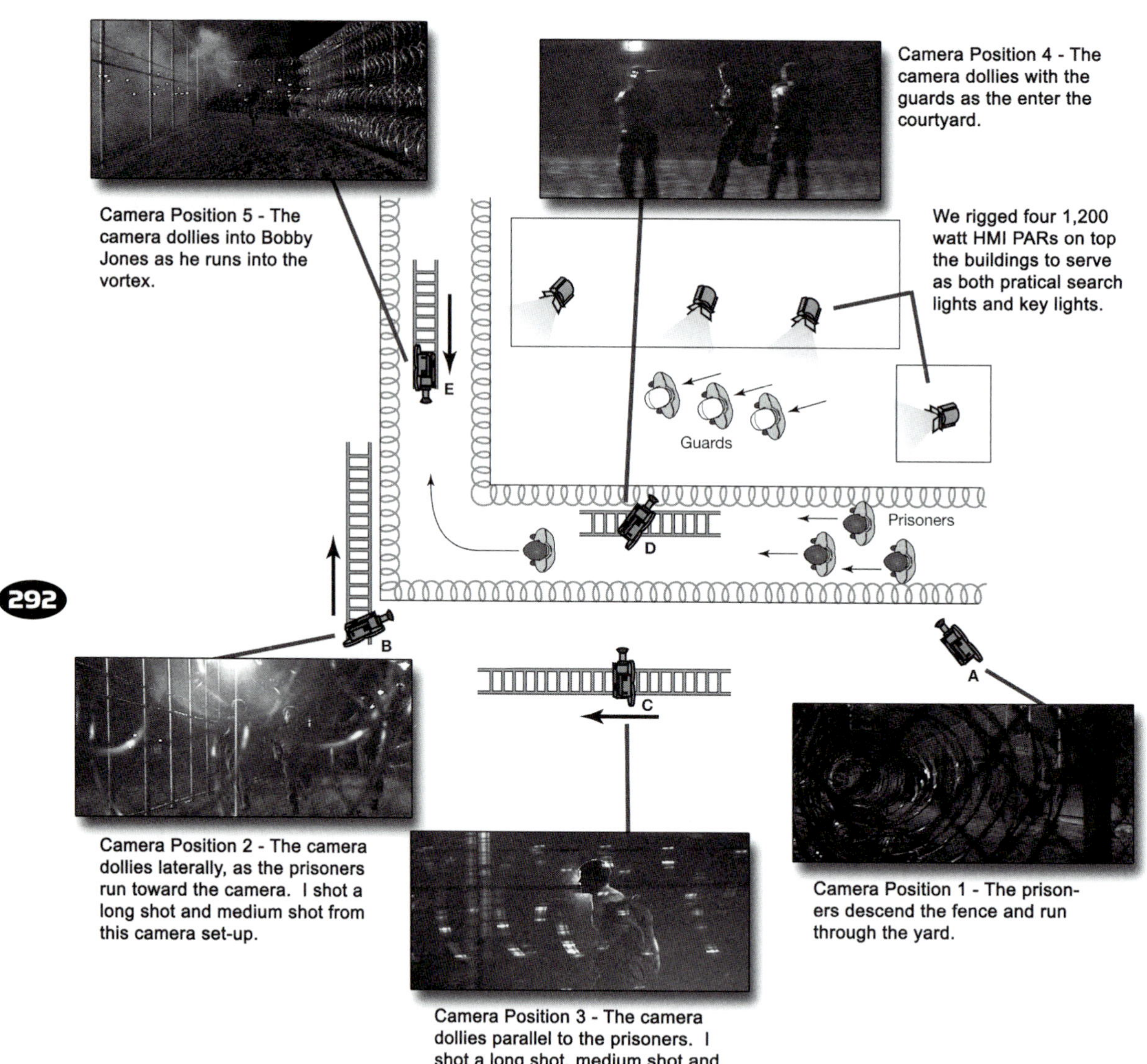

Camera Position 5 - The camera dollies into Bobby Jones as he runs into the vortex.

Camera Position 4 - The camera dollies with the guards as the enter the courtyard.

We rigged four 1,200 watt HMI PARs on top the buildings to serve as both pratical search lights and key lights.

Camera Position 2 - The camera dollies laterally, as the prisoners run toward the camera. I shot a long shot and medium shot from this camera set-up.

Camera Position 3 - The camera dollies parallel to the prisoners. I shot a long shot, medium shot and close-ups from this position.

Camera Position 1 - The prisoners descend the fence and run through the yard.

HOW WE LIT AND SHOT THE TRAILER SCENE

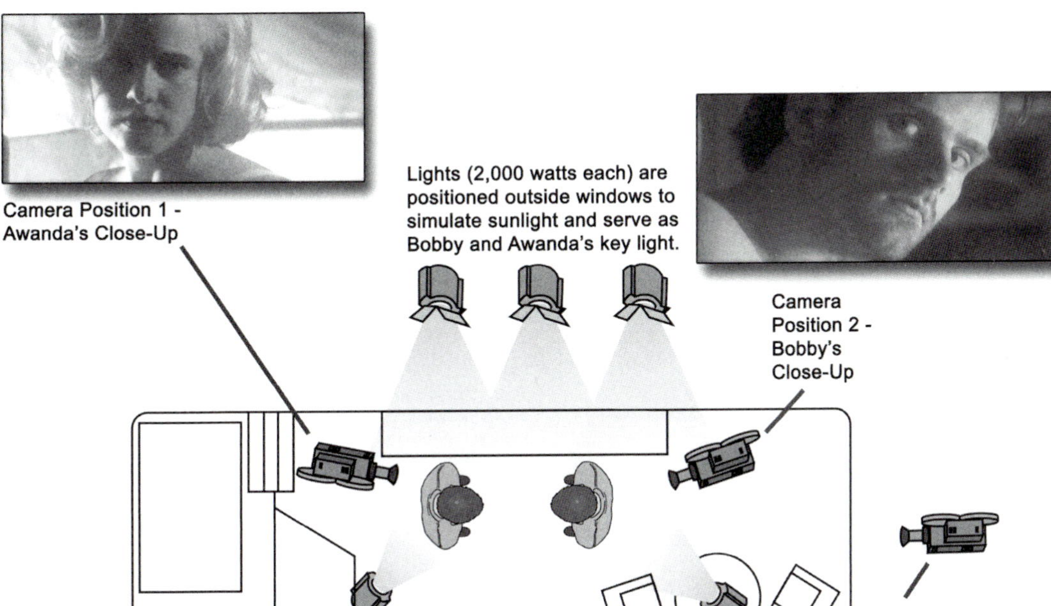
Camera Position 1 -
Awanda's Close-Up
Lights (2,000 watts each) are positioned outside windows to simulate sunlight and serve as Bobby and Awanda's key light.
Camera Position 2 - Bobby's Close-Up

Rim Light (250 watts), with diffusion is focused on the back of Bobby's head, helping edge him out from the background.

Rim Light (250 watts), with diffusion is focused on Awanda's hair, adding a glow. This light is motivated by the open window behind her.

Camera Position 3 - We placed the camera outside the trailer and removed a window to get a clean establishing shot of the entire scene.

293

to bounce the sunlight as the key light. I would recommend using a silver reflector available at most camera stores.

There are a number of low-budget approaches to working effectively in sunlight:

- Obtain foam core or bead board to reflect sunlight and create a softer light on the subject.
- Use mirrors to reflect direct sunlight onto the subject. The more mirrors you use, the brighter the light.
- If you need to soften the sunlight directly, consider renting a silk stretched across an 8 × 8-, 12 × 12-, or 20 × 20-foot frame that is rigged over the actors. Because these professional tools can be expensive to rent or purchase, consider building a frame out of 1.5-inch PVC pipe and then using a white bed sheet or shower curtain to serve as diffusion, softening harsh sunlight on your subject.
- When scouting a location, look at the sun's position to determine the best placement for the actors and the camera, then make sure the background works for that blocking. It may be necessary to choose a location based on the optimal sun position.

Guide to building a cheap softbox

Softboxes are large enclosures around a light that soften the light while preventing spill all over the set. Professional softboxes can cost almost a thousand dollars, but there is an inexpensive way to build your own. All you need is an open face light (try a 500- or 100-watt Lowel light) and four 2 × 3-foot sheets of foam core. Using a utility knife and gaffer's tape, build a four-walled tunnel that is tapered toward the light fixture so that the small opening of the box can neatly fit over the light's barn doors. The wide opening of the softbox can be as large as you like. Secure the softbox to the barn doors using grip clips, and cover any light spill with black wrap (black-coated aluminum foil that can be purchased at www.filmtools.com). On the open end of the softbox, tape a piece of diffusion across the entire opening.

GETTING THE FILM LOOK

Film has such a rich, textured look that many filmmakers work hard to mimic that look when shooting video. Here are some tricks to creating a film look for your video.

- **Shoot in 24p.** Film cameras capture in 24 frames per second. For a long time, video cameras were locked into capturing 60 fields per second because of technical restrictions of the NTSC format. With the advent of high-definition video, camcorders are able to capture true 24 progressive frames per second, mimicking the look of film.
- **Use a shallow depth of field.** The second major component in achieving a film look is to shoot on cameras with the largest CCD. The bigger the

CCD, the shallower the depth of field and the more film-like the image will look. Most movies are shot on 35 mm film, which, because of the large frame size, yields a very shallow depth of field. Even in wide shots, the background can be in soft focus. Because video cameras use very small CCDs, force a shallow depth of field by shooting on the long end of the lens, opening up the iris and slowing down the shutter speed.

- **Fill out the contrast range of the camera.** Film has a greater latitude than video, which equates to much richer blacks and more details in highlights; it's important to light the scene with as much contrast between the bright and the dark areas as the format will allow. Always make sure there is a perfect black element and a perfect white element in the frame.
- **Shift the gamma curve.** The gamma curve (brightness of the midrange values) for video-acquired images is much more linear than that of film. In postproduction, shift the curve to more closely reflect the gamma response of film.
- **Move the camera.** Controlled camera movements are typical of high-budget Hollywood productions, so the more you can move the camera with dollies, jibs, and cranes, the higher the production value.
- **Filters.** Consider using a Tiffin ¼- or ½-grade Pro-Mist filter to soften highlights. Film tends to bleed overexposed elements into surrounding objects, whereas highlights in video are often sharp and crisp. Using softening filters will help soften the effects of overexposure in the frame. Pro-Mist filters were used in *Time and Again* throughout most of the 1950s scenes. Look at the scenes in the diner and in Awanda's trailer and you'll see how the background windows are softened and appear very film-like.

SHOOTING THE SCENE

When it comes time to shoot a take, look over the shot in the viewfinder or on a monitor to double-check framing, the actor's blocking, focus, and set-dressing elements. Be sure to rehearse each shot to ensure everyone in the cast and crew is clear on what they are doing. This communication is essential, especially in complicated shots.

- Make sure you have complete coverage of important scenes from multiple angles. Be sure to cover the entire action of a scene from beginning to end from each camera angle, then choose which one works best in the editing room. Always remember, it's easier to cut a shot than it is to need it and not have it.
- Treat the camera as though it's an actual member of the audience that you're taking around your set. Show them exactly what you want them to see. If ever in doubt as to where to put the camera, think about what you want the audience to focus in on and position your camera accordingly. Your camera angles should reflect our own positioning as observers within the set watching the action unfold.

The crew sets up the next shot in Bobby Jones' jail cell.

- Watch continuity carefully to ensure that objects, characters, and movement are consistent from shot to shot. This is the job of a script supervisor, to watch and log continuity issues like the amount of milk in a glass, or an actor's hand position on the steering wheel, so it remains the same during the course of shooting the scene. The better the continuity, the easier it will be to edit the scene.
- Take your favorite movie scene and storyboard it, shot by shot. Study WHY the filmmaker made certain choices about camera placement, lighting, and timing. Then try to replicate those shots at home with a video camera and friends.
- Always carefully check the frame before you start shooting for stray production equipment, soda cans, garbage, or even crew members. Also, make sure there are no bizarre objects such as light poles or trees positioned behind your actors in a way that makes it look as though they were sticking out of the actor's head.

- The best way to learn about camera coverage is not only to do it, but to follow in the footsteps of the people who are doing it right. Study cinematography in movies and try to determine the placement of lights and why certain camera angles were chosen.
- Let the camera roll for several seconds before the director calls "action" and after he yells "cut." This padding can always be trimmed in the editing room, but may prove invaluable for transitions or fade-outs.
- Always keep good logs of the shots taken on set. Camera logs are forms on which you record the shot number and description, the focal length and exposure settings of the lens, and any comments. These logs are invaluable when editing, saving a tremendous amount of time when searching through the rough footage.
- Be precise with every camera angle and shoot each shot with the intention of covering a particular action. Remember that each scene is a combination of camera shots and not every shot has to cover the entire scene in its entirety.
- Always shoot the master shot first, covering the entire action of the scene from beginning to end. Then, move in for close-ups and coverage. If, for some reason, there is a problem later in the day, at least you have the master shot to fall back on.
- The best way to learn cinematography is to be a good editor. Practice shooting several small sequences and then edit them to see what shots work and what shots don't.
- Think of creative angles that accentuate the performances. Unique shots are fine provided they support the story and the characters. The cinematography should NEVER draw attention away from the performances.
- When covering a scene, shoot a variety of long shots, medium shots, and close-ups. Remember that the more variety an editor has to choose from, the more dynamic the scene will feel on the screen.
- Never set the camera up and have the actors perform in front of it. Involve the camera; move it around the set and treat it like an audience member. What does the audience want to see? What is happening in the scene that would motivate the audience to look in a certain direction? Think about this if you're ever in doubt as to where to place the camera on set.

KEEPING ORGANIZED

Each day of shooting will yield dozens of shots, takes, and setups. It is critical to organize and track each shot carefully so that each shot can be easily located in postproduction.

Using a clapboard

The first step in organizing shots is to mark each take with a clapboard. Clapboards serve two purposes. The first is to identify the name of the production, the shooting date, the director and director of photography, which roll of film or video tape you are shooting, the scene, the setup and take, any filters used, and whether the take has recorded audio.

The second purpose of the clapboard is to assist the editor in syncing the audio to the visuals if the audio is being recorded on a separate unit. You cannot record sound directly to film, because film is designed only to react to light. As a result, a separate audio recording device is required, usually a Nagra (reel-to-reel analog recorder), DAT (digital audio tape) recorder, or digital hard drive recorder. Technology has progressed to the point where audio engineers record the sound from the set directly to a laptop computer.

Although technology is progressing, it is still necessary to sync, or line up, the audio with the visuals . . . hence the clapboard, which provides a visual sync indicator to the editor. For each take, once the sound recording device and the film camera are rolling, the second assistant cameraman verbally speaks the film title, scene, setup, and take. It sounds like this, "*Time and Again*, Scene 45 apple, Take 3 . . . marker." Then he claps the clapper. This action provides a visual cue for the editor so he can line up the sound of the clap with the visuals of the clap. Once synced up, the rest of the take should line up and remain in sync.

- **Recording audio into the camera:** It is not necessary to clap the clapboard because the audio is already synced to the visuals. When marking this type of shot, the second AC need simply to hold the clapboard from the top, with his hand covering the clapper.

- **Recording sync sound:** When recording audio into an external recording device, it's critical to clearly mark each shot by clapping the clapboard. The second AC should always place the clapboard in frame with the clapper open and ensure the camera has a clean view of the slate.

- **Recording MOS (mit out sound):** If recording with no audio, the second AC should place her hand between the clapper and the clapboard. This indicates to the editor that there is no audio associated with that take.

- **Tail slate:** There may be instances when it's easier to mark the end of a take rather than the beginning. The second AC indicates a tail slate by holding the clapboard upside down and marking the shot and then quickly turning the clapboard right side up so the editor can read the information.

Camera logs

When you're shooting on set, use camera logs to keep track of the details of every shot. Usually filled in by the second AC, the camera logs are used to track the scene and shot numbers, description of the shot, camera settings, and a rating for each take. Camera logs are beneficial in the editing room because they enable the editor to quickly and easily find the best takes from each tape. The same information is written on the clapboard, so each shot should match the camera log. Although it may seem like a lot of work on set, tracking the shots will save a tremendous amount of time in postproduction.

Script supervisor

The script supervisor's primary function on set is to maintain the internal continuity of the production by watching the script and logging any deviations in performance by the actors. The script supervisor's duties on set include:

- Making sure everyone on the cast and crew has a current version of the script.
- Taking detailed notes during each take so as to maintain strict continuity from one shot to another and from one scene to another, including dialog, actors' blocking, screen direction, and even camera information such as lens type and iris setting.

Camera Log

Production: Date: Page:
Studio: Logs by:
Director: Location:
Director of Photography: Scene:

☐ Day ☐ Night
☐ Dusk ☐ Dawn
Weather:

Filters:
Effects:
Notes:

SHOT #	DESCRIPTION	F-STOP	FOCAL	RATING

- Coordinating with the second assistant camera to make sure each shot is properly marked on the clapboard and coordinating shot markings with the sound department.
- Lining the script by drawing vertical lines through each scene to identify which part of the scene is covered by each camera angle.
- Producing production reports that include the continuity logs; the time the production started and stopped; the times of the first shot, last shot, and meal breaks; a breakdown of the pages, scenes, and minutes that were shot that day; as well as the numbers of takes and retakes.

The script supervisor is a vital position to have on even the lowest budget movie sets.

GO BEYOND THE BOOK

Watch *Time and Again* on the companion DVD and study Jason's lighting and framing choices. What would you have done differently?

Learn valuable lighting techniques, how to choose a lens, framing, camera movement and much more in the Cinematography modules of www.powerfilmmaking.com.

Listen to Hollywood experts as they reveal tricks of the trade to obtaining a professional look with both light and lens.

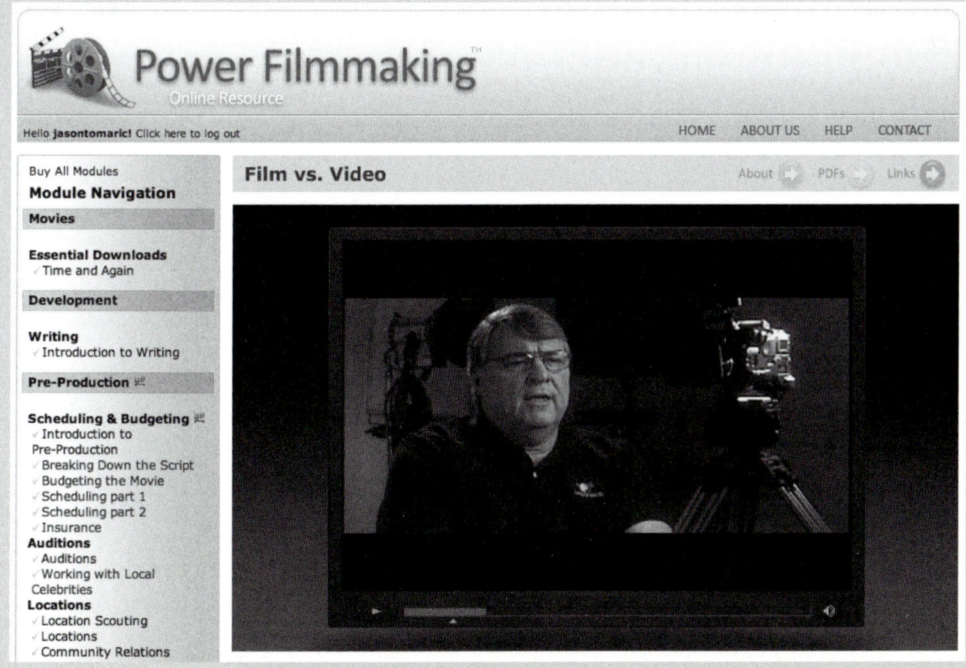

10

CHAPTER 16
Audio Recording

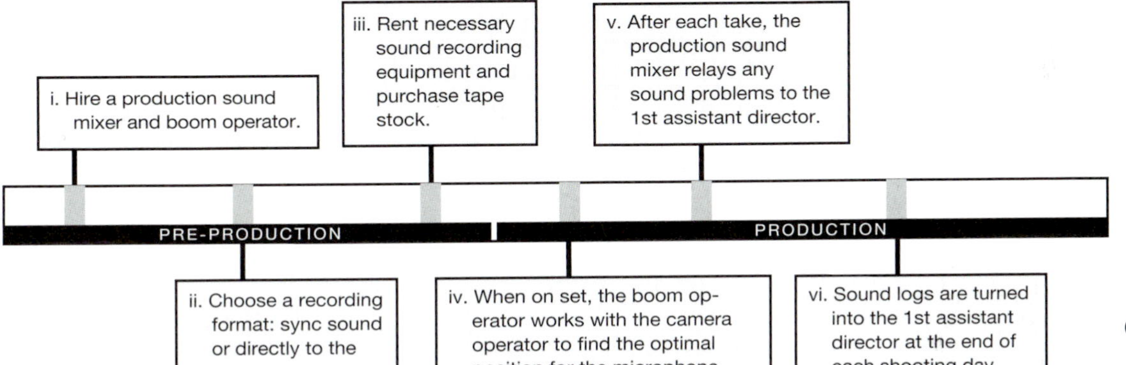

i. Hire a production sound mixer and boom operator.
ii. Choose a recording format: sync sound or directly to the camera.
iii. Rent necessary sound recording equipment and purchase tape stock.
iv. When on set, the boom operator works with the camera operator to find the optimal position for the microphone.
v. After each take, the production sound mixer relays any sound problems to the 1st assistant director.
vi. Sound logs are turned into the 1st assistant director at the end of each shooting day.
PRE-PRODUCTION
PRODUCTION

INTRODUCTION

Audio is the other 50% of the movie-going experience and requires very special attention. Good audio in a movie isn't nearly as noticeable as bad audio, which can ruin a great film and take the audience out of the story. The seemingly simple approach to audio recording is really an art.

Sound is nothing more than changes in air pressure that originate from a vibrating source. The stronger the waves, the louder the sound. These waves are measured in increments called decibels, or "db" for short. A decibel is the smallest amount of change in a sound wave that our ears are capable of detecting. In much the same way that film has a range of sensitivity to the brightness of light, sound recording devices have a range of the volume of sound they are capable of recording. For analog recording devices, this range is around 70 db. For digital recording devices, the range is greater, at 100 db, from the quietest sound capable of being detected to the loudest sound.

So whereas the amplitude of the wave determines the volume of the sound, the frequency determines the pitch. Measured in hertz, or Hz, the lower the frequency, the lower the pitch of the sound, and the higher the frequency, the

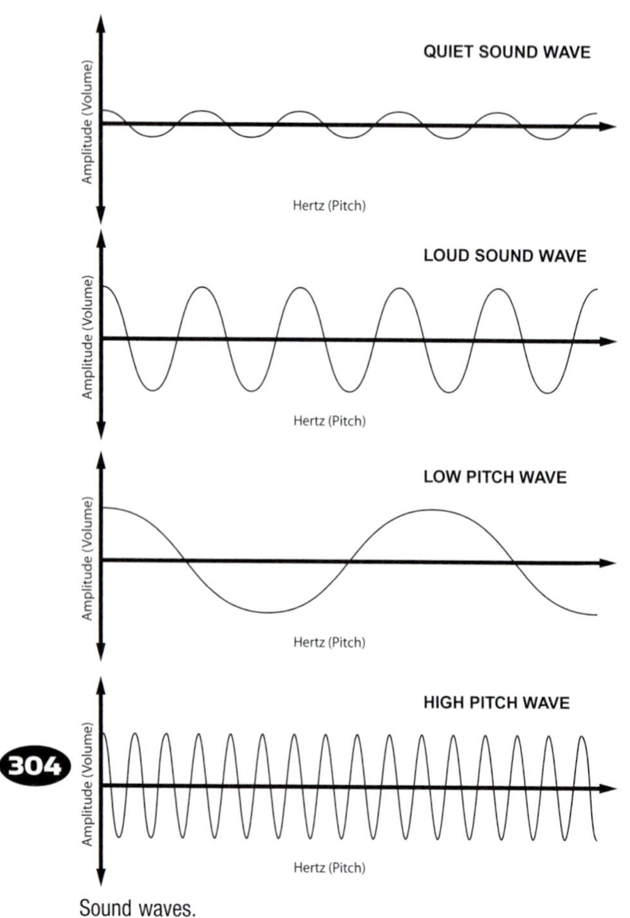

Sound waves.

higher the pitch. Human hearing can detect sounds as low as 20 Hz and as high as 20,000 Hz, although this ceiling is reduced as you get older.

The goal in recording a strong signal-to-noise ratio is to use as much of that dynamic range as possible, without exceeding it.

ANALOG VS DIGITAL

Sound travels in sinusoidal waves that move the pickup device in a microphone. The microphone then converts these waves into an electronic signal, which is then recorded onto the recording device. In early days of recording, the sound waves were recorded in a way that preserved the true curve and all the nuances of the sound waves. This type of recording, called analog recording, results in rich, textured audio. Tape cassettes, records, and reel-to-reel recorders are all analog formats.

The analog signal is recorded by capturing the signal and using magnetic heads in the recording device to position magnetic particles on the tape into a pattern. Playback heads read the position of the particles and reconstruct the signal. Because particles can be oriented in any one of an infinite number of ways, the analog signal can be recorded with great detail and warmth. Despite the richness of the sound, analog recording's major setback is the loss of quality each time a copy is made. This is called generational loss and it occurs each time a copy of a copy is made. Each time a copy is made, the recorder copies the position of each particle to a new tape, although a certain amount of unavoidable error is introduced and the particle's position is close to the original, but not identical. The result is degraded signal that further randomizes each generation.

Digital recorders sample the audio wave thousands of times per second and convert the resulting signal to a binary code so that instead of recording particles in one of an infinite array of patterns, they record them in one of two: 1 or 0. The higher the number of samples, or the sample rate, the higher the audio quality. The result is a sound signal that can be broadcast and copied without loss because any error added can be easily detected and corrected. The major downfall of digital recording is that recording devices do not capture the true sinusoidal wave, but break it down into a number of samples, resulting in what many audio experts describe as a loss of warmth and presence.

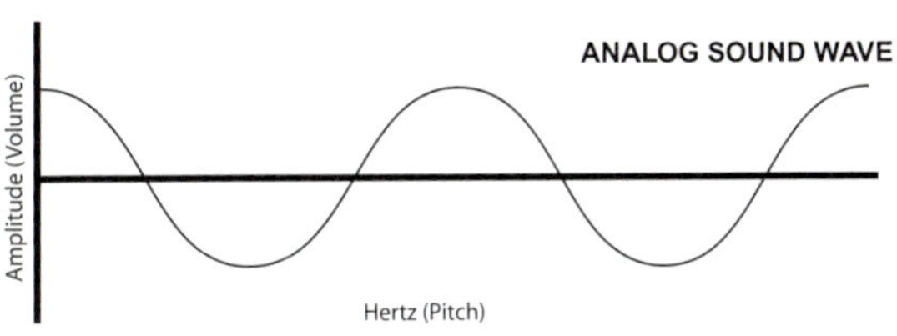

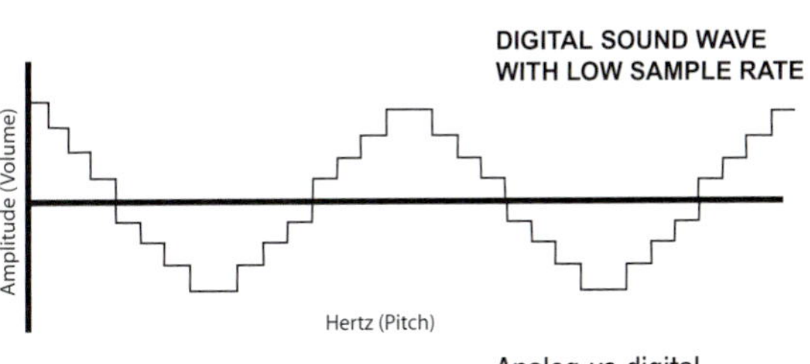

Analog vs digital.

Whereas the sample rate is the number of samples per second, the bit depth is the amount of data recorded in each sample. A bit is the smallest, most basic amount of data, which in binary is a 1 or a 0. An 8-bit data stream will have 8 bits, or 10010101. Sixteen-bit, which is the most common bit depth for digital video recorders, has a data stream with 16 bits, or 1010010100110101.

Common sample rates and bit depths in the recording industry are:

Telephone: 8 kHz (8000 samples per second)
MPEG/PCM compressed audio: 11.025 and 22.050 kHz
CD: 44.1 kHz (44,100 samples per second) at 16 bits per sample
MPEG-1 audio (VCD, SVCD, MP3): 44.1 kHz
DV: four tracks of 32 kHz (32,000 samples per second) at 12 bits or two tracks of 48 kHz (48,000 samples per second) at 16 bits
Digital TV, DVD, DAT: 48 kHz
DVD audio, Blu-ray, HD-DVD: 96 or 192 kHz

Advances in increased sample rates have made digital sound recording comparable to the quality of analog recording and an industry standard.

MICROPHONE TYPES

There are a variety of microphone types, each one designed for a specific purpose.

Omnidirectional

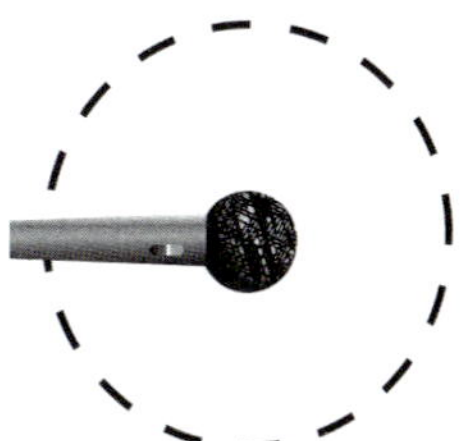

Omnidirectional microphones have a pickup pattern that captures sound in all directions, making them ideal for recording ambient sound. Omnidirectional mikes should not be used to record dialog because they record too much of the surrounding ambience, making it difficult to hear the actors' lines clearly. Omnidirectional mikes are usually inexpensive and can be found at your local electronics or video supply store.

Cardioid

Cardioid microphones have a heart-shaped pickup pattern that is more sensitive to sounds in front of the microphone than to the sides. Cardioid mikes are usually used for singers, public speakers, and reporters when the mike can be placed three to six inches away from the mouth. Any farther and the vocals begin to lose their presence. Because of this limited proximity, cardioids are not the best choice for recording dialog.

Shotgun

Shotgun microphones have a narrow pickup pattern of 5–25 degrees and are designed to record sound from an optimal range of one to four feet. Shotgun microphones are ideal for recording on-set dialog because the narrow pickup pattern helps reduce ambience on the set, helping the spoken word stand out in the recording.

Lavalier

Lavalier mikes are clip-on mikes with a very tight cardioid pattern used for on-camera interviews in which it is acceptable to see the microphone in the shot. Usually clipped to a necktie or lapel, the mike should ideally be placed over the subject's sternum so that it picks up not only the voice, but also the low-end resonance from the chest cavity. Lavalier microphones work best when they are within one foot of the subject's mouth.

PREPPING AUDIO

The location scout is the time when the director and her key department heads look at a potential location to determine whether it will work creatively in the story and technically for the production.

Part of determining the feasibility of a location is to listen for any sound problems that may exist and figure out how, if possible, to reduce or eliminate them. Sound sources that may cause problems when recording audio include:

- **Air conditioners or air handling units.** The blowers, although they may be quiet, emit a broad-spectral sound that is nearly impossible to remove in postproduction. Take the time during the location scout to figure out how to turn off all air handling systems.
- **Refrigerators and appliances.** Often the bane of location sound mixers, appliances cause intermittent hums in the background that change tone and intensity when the microphone is repositioned during setups. Figure out how to turn the fridge and freezer off, and as a tip, leave your car keys inside. Then no one will leave until you remember to turn the fridge back on. I remember when we were shooting at the Chester Diner for *Time and Again.* There was a long row of coolers for deli trays and various pastries that would have wreaked havoc on our sound, especially considering that we only had two days to shoot the coverage we needed. Knowing in advance that these coolers would cause problems in any shots for which

we needed to record sound, we contacted a local grocery store manager who let us move all the food out of the diner's coolers into theirs. We were then able to turn every appliance and cooler off, put fake food inside the coolers, and save the audio for the scene. This only goes to show that a little preproduction can save you major headaches in postproduction.

- **Sirens.** Note the locations of hospitals, fire stations, and police stations and whether they are active around your location. Sirens and alarms not only ruin your audio, but also cause major time setbacks as you wait for ambulances, police cars, and fire engines to get far enough away so you can resume shooting.
- **Schools.** Check to see if there is a school nearby and determine if the children and school buses passing by in the morning and afternoon will disrupt your audio.
- **Airports.** Is there a nearby airport and, even more importantly, is your location within the arrival or departing flight path? If so, calculate the time between flights and schedule your shots accordingly. The script supervisor will keep you aware of how much time you have before the next flyover.
- **Freeways.** Listen for highly directional ambient sources like freeways. Although it may sound quiet on location, pointing the microphone in different directions will change the volume and tone of the ambience and make it very difficult to match from one shot to the next in the editing room. If you have a choice, shoot away from freeways, intersections, and roads.
- **Beaches.** Although the beach has a romantic allure for filmmakers, it almost always signals immediate death for the audio track. The directional crashing of waves is nearly impossible to filter out of the recording mix, and changes in the microphone position will make the change in the sound of the ambience abrupt and disruptive to the audience.
- **Camera noise.** The camera itself can be a source of noise. From the sound of the magazines to lens motors, the operations of the camera are loud enough to be picked up by a microphone. Use a barney or a thick padded blanket draped over the camera to muffle some of the camera noise.

DIRECTOR'S NOTES

Consider this: you, as a director, are scouting houses for your next film and you find the perfect location. It matches your vision, the colors and layout are perfect, and you can practically see your characters moving through each room. The big problem is that it's next to the freeway. So, no matter where you are in the house, you can hear the cars. If you choose to shoot in this house, you may later learn in postproduction that the audio you recorded on set is unusable because of the changing volume and tone of the freeway ambience. The sound engineer tells you that the only option is to ADR, or rerecord the actor's dialog. So, at a rate of around $100/hour, you spend dozens of hours with the actors re-creating the performance, timing, and emotion of each and every line of dialog, racking up a bill into the thousands.

At this point, the dialog sounds great, but you then learn that you need to re-create the Foley (the sounds the actors make while interacting on set). So the sound engineer spends countless more hours rerecording footsteps, movement of props, and clothing rubbing together to rebuild what you should have recorded originally.

So dozens, possibly hundreds, of hours later and thousand of dollars in the hole, it suddenly seems like that exquisite house, although artistically perfect, wasn't a good technical choice to shoot in. Perhaps it would have been better to have chosen a house that might not have been as artistically perfect, but that was at least away from the freeway.

ROLE OF THE SOUND TEAM ON SET BEFORE ACTION

When working on an independent film, a lot of attention is spent rehearsing the actors, setting up the lights, tediously blocking the camera, and making sure that makeup and hair look good. Unfortunately, sound doesn't seem to get the same attention and time the rest of the departments receive. Although the audio is half the movie-going experience, the boom operator always seems to be the last person to rush in as the director is about to call action, struggling to find a position that doesn't cast shadows while he's being prodded by the first AD to hurry up. The result is unspectacular sound that eventually comes back to haunt the filmmaker later in postproduction.

The proper way to achieve high-quality sound on set is for the boom operator and production sound mixer to be in constant communication with the rest of the crew to determine the best possible position from which to record sound.

1. As the director is rehearsing the scene for the cast and crew, the boom operator should be watching the blocking, taking note of the positions of the lights and camera in order to determine the most optimal position to place the microphone in the set. Ideally, the shotgun microphone should be one to four feet away from the actors, always pointed at the chest of the person speaking, and positioned about 45 degrees above their heads. The microphone should move with the actors so that the actors are always facing it. Because the shotgun microphone has such a tight pickup pattern, it's easy for the actors to move in and out of the microphone's range, so the boom operator must constantly adjust the position of the boom for optimum recording.
2. Once the boom operator has located the ideal microphone position, she needs to ask the camera operator what the frame is in order to determine the amount of headroom in the frame. She then places the microphone above the actors and slowly lowers it until it appears in the shot so she knows how close the microphone can be to the actors before it breaches the frame.

3. The boom operator then determines how he will move relative to the actors' blocking so that his microphone remains at a consistent distance and always points at the actors' chests. He must always be aware of the positions of lights so as not to block any light or cast shadows on the actors or the set.
4. Once in place, the boom operator will wait until the director is ready for a camera rehearsal. During this rehearsal, the production sound mixer will set the levels for the recording based on the actors' delivery and any final blocking alterations are made.
5. The sound department is ready and awaits the first AD's call for a take.
6. After the director calls cut, the boom operator confers with the first AD and notes any problems with the audio and then waits for the director and first AD to decide whether to pursue another take.

Learn more about proper audio recording techniques from industry professionals at www.powerfilmmaking.com.

RECORDING TO THE CAMERA

There are two ways to record audio when shooting with a digital camera. The first is to plug the shotgun microphone directly into the camera, and the second is to record the audio to a separate recording device.

If you are recording the audio directly into the camera, you will need:

- Shotgun microphone
- Boom pole
- XLR cable
- XLR splitter

If you want the production sound mixer to have more control over the audio, plug the microphone into a sound mixer and then from the sound mixer into the camera. This will free the camera operator from the pressure of having to monitor the audio levels while watching the frame during a take. Usually, with this configuration, the audio mixer should be able to generate a 0-db tone that is used to set the camera's input levels to −20 db. After the camera input level is set, put a piece of tape over the gain levels so no one accidentally changes the levels. From that point, the production sound mixer will monitor and adjust the levels of the incoming sound source from his mixer.

SYNC SOUND

Sync sound means that the audio is recorded to a device other than the camera. When recording sync sound, the microphone is plugged into an audio mixer that is then run into an external recording device. The recording device's independence from the camera gives the boom operator the freedom and flexibility to move around the set, untethered from the camera.

Used in film production because audio can't be recorded onto film, and used more often on high-definition productions, recording sync sound offers a variety of benefits and drawbacks for the filmmaker.

- Sync-sound recording allows the sound recording device to be placed anywhere on set, giving the boom operator and production sound mixer greater flexibility and range of motion around the set.
- Recording sync sound shifts the burden of monitoring the audio levels from the camera operator to the production sound mixer. This allows the camera operator to focus on the frame.
- Running the microphone into the camera yields very few choices as to the recording format of the incoming audio. For DV and HD cameras, audio is recorded at 48 kHz, 16 bits. Sync-sound recording devices offer a wide variety of sample rates and bit depths, allowing the filmmakers to record very high quality sound.
- Many new Flash media-based recording devices allow instantaneous recording, playback, and transfer of sound files by shifting from tape-based recording to recording onto digital media.
- Several sync-sound recording devices record multitracks that allow the use of multiple microphones on set, each with its own channel. This gives the editor the option to choose between separate microphones to build the best audio track. Using multiple microphones while recording into the camera requires that the multiple feeds be mixed down to two channels, making it impossible to separate later.
- One drawback of sync-sound recording is the cost of the recording device. Some common recording devices are:
  - **Nagra**—Nagra is an older, reel-to-reel analog recorder that was popular for its high sound quality and durability. Nagras were the primary recording tool used on set prior to the advent of digital recording technologies.
  - **MiniDisc**—This format is a small recordable disc housed in a plastic casing. Developed for the consumer market, the MiniDisc never caught on in professional applications because the sound was overcompressed. This compression makes it a poor choice for location-based audio recording.
  - **DAT**—Short for "digital audio tape," this format is a standard in professional audio recording and is still used on set today. Recording to inexpensive tapes, DAT recorders are inexpensive and durable, although adverse weather conditions may affect the contact point between the tape and the recording heads and cause audio dropouts.
  - **Digital**—Digital recorders record directly to a hard drive and record reliable, high-quality audio. Digital recorders allow the user to play,

seek, transfer, and delete individual clips instantly and offer a wider range of compression and audio formats.

- Recording sync sound requires the editor to line up the audio and visuals manually in the editing room. Although this process is not difficult, it is time consuming.

BOOM HANDLING TECHNIQUES

The boom pole is used to suspend a microphone over the actors on set. Although using a boom pole seems easy, there are a number of techniques that are used to reduce boom-handling noise and improve the quality of the recorded audio.

- After the microphone is placed in the shock mount, tape the XLR cable to the end of the microphone-end of the boom pole, alleviating any pressure or stress on the microphone. Be sure to allow enough slack so the microphone can be tilted up or down depending on the angle of the boom pole.
- Tightly coil the XLR cable along the length of the boom pole so it doesn't move or rub against the boom pole. The end of the cable should hang from the back end of the boom pole.
- When holding the boom, lock your hands in position as if your hands were glued to the boom. Do not move, twist, or rub your hands against the boom during a take because the microphone will pick up handling sounds.
- When holding the boom during a take, extend your arms straight above your head, as though you were hanging from a tree limb. This relieves muscle fatigue and helps keep the boom parallel to the top frame line, minimizing the risk of clipping the corners of the frame.
- Always point the microphone at the actor's chest and hold at a 45-degree angel in front of the actor, moving with the actor so the actor never falls outside the pickup pattern of the microphone.
- Never put the microphone in anyone's face.
- If you ever need to change the boom's position during a setup, notify the production sound mixer in the event that he needs to recheck the sound levels.
- When recording a scene in which the actors are walking, or there is complicated blocking, consider taking off your shoes to minimize the sound of your footsteps.
- When not in use, place the boom in the corner. Do not lay it on the floor or against a wall as it can fall, or be stepped on, damaging the microphone.
- Always wear headphones when operating the boom to ensure optimal placement of the microphone and to listen for any noise that could disrupt a take.

- Remember that changing the distance from the microphone to the subject is a much bigger problem than changing the distance from the subject to a light source. Maintain an equal and consistent distance between the microphone and the subject for optimum sound quality.

RECORDING WITH A SHOTGUN MICROPHONE

Most dialog on set is recorded using a shotgun microphone, a highly directional microphone that is usually suspended over the actors using a boom pole. Shotgun mikes are the best for isolating dialog spoken by the actors and their movements while reducing the ambient sound.

Shotgun microphones can be purchased for $500–$2500 from Audio-Technica, Sennehiser, and Neumann or rented from an equipment rental company. In addition to the shotgun microphone, you will also need a shock mount, which suspends the microphone in a series of rubber bands to minimize boom-handling noise, a zeppelin or wind sock to place over the microphone to reduce

BUILD AN INEXPENSIVE BOOM POLE

Professional boom poles can cost up to $1000, but why spend that money if you can build one for less than $100? A terrific, low-budget boom pole can be constructed from a telescopic paint roller extender available at a hardware store. Then purchase a paint roller handle that will screw onto the end of the pole. Unscrew the roller from the handle and screw a shock mount (you can pick one up from a music/audio store) to the handle. Now you have a homemade boom pole. Don't think it will work? Listen to the audio in *Time and Again* . . . we used one!

Shock mount.

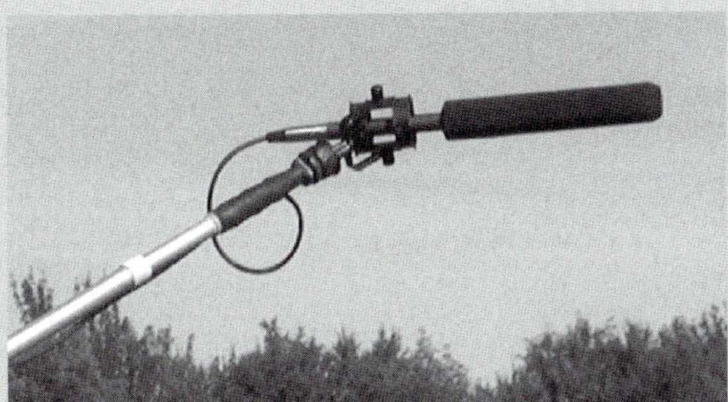

Microphone mount.

wind noise, and a boom pole. Boom poles can be made inexpensively, or they can be rented. Be sure to have plenty of XLR cables on set not only to ensure enough distance between the camera and microphone, but also for backup in case one of the cables goes bad. Run the shotgun directly into the camera or external recording device and be sure to monitor the audio with headphones from the recording source. If you're recording the audio to the camera, plug the headphones into the camera. If you're recording to an external recording device, listen to the audio from the device.

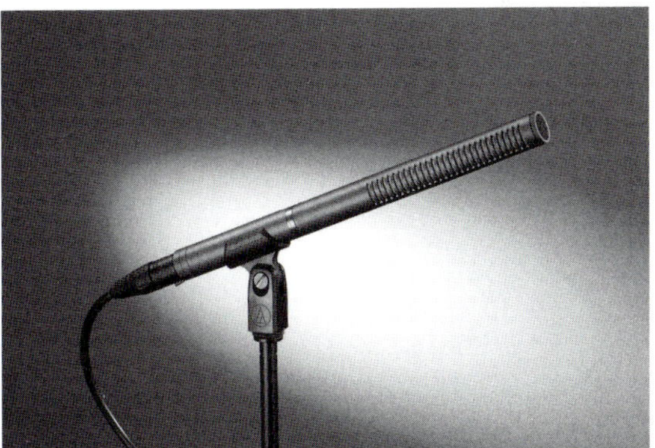

Shotgun microphone.

USING LAVALIERS

Lavalier microphones are outstanding for recording interviews for documentaries or news, actors for corporate and industrial videos, and actors on stage. Although they can be used in film production for long shots, lavalier microphones are not the best choice for recording on-set dialog because the need to

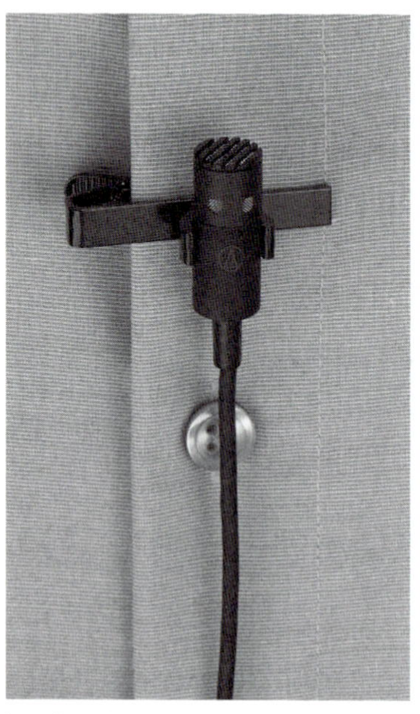
Lavalier microphone.

conceal them in an actor's wardrobe increases the chances the fabric will rub against the microphone and ruin the audio. Concealing the wire leading from the microphone to the camera may also interfere with the actor's performance. The best way to record on-set dialog is with a shotgun microphone suspended over the actors with a boom pole. Use lavaliers sparingly and only when you have no other option.

Lavaliers are best used in the following situations:

- Lavaliers allow the recording of audio in big, wide shots, and in moving shots in which it's difficult to place a shotgun microphone, or when the actors' movements make it difficult to record the dialog.
- Lavaliers can be placed closer to the actor's mouth in high-ambience locations, helping to improve the sound quality by increasing the signal-to-noise ratio.
- Use them when interviewing a subject or shooting a corporate video in which it is acceptable for the microphone to be seen.
- Use them in closed, cramped quarters such as in a car, when positioning a shotgun microphone is impractical. A common trick for recording sound in cars is to mount a lavalier mike above the sun visor of each actor and run the mike cable into a separate DV camcorder on the floor. Although separate from the main camera, which can be placed anywhere in or out of the car, this sync-sound rig produces surprisingly good results with minimal syncing efforts in the editing room.
- Where ambience is too loud, such as on a beach, using a lavalier microphone will help reduce ambience that a shotgun will more than likely pick up. A conversation between characters on the beach can be recorded using a little bit of audio trickery and careful art direction. Try running a lavalier mike up the pole of a beach umbrella and drilling a tiny hole on the side of the pole to stick the mike through. Place the umbrella close to the actors so they fall within the one-foot pickup pattern. The mike will pick up the dialog while reducing the ambience, which will be added in later.
- Lavaliers are sometimes used when actors are far away from the camera and positioning a shotgun microphone is impossible. Be aware that intermixing audio recorded by a shotgun and a lavalier will yield very different sounds and could prove challenging to edit.
- Although lavalier microphones record strong dialog, they will not pick up ambience and an actor's interactions with his environment as well as a shotgun mike. Often, using a lavalier requires additional Foley work in postproduction to fill in the sounds that weren't recorded on set.
- One challenge of using lavaliers is that they are fixed in one position on an actor's body, so when the actor turns her head, her voice may trail off as she talks away from the microphone.

In general, I would not recommend using lavalier microphones to record dialog. The issues of hiding the mike, avoiding the rustling of clothing, inconsistencies with proximity to the actor, and problems in postproduction make it a useful tool in extreme situations, but not a substitute for the ever-useful shotgun microphone.

WIRELESS MICROPHONE SYSTEMS

Wireless systems use a transmitter connected to the end of a microphone to send the audio signal to a receiver mounted on either the camera or a sync-sound recorder. Wireless systems free the boom operator from the confines of being tethered to the recording device by XLR cables and allow microphones to be mounted on actors or sets without unsightly cables. Although beneficial, wireless systems are prone to a number of problems.

Some of the benefits of working with wireless systems:

- The number of cables running to and from the boom microphone, camera, or sync-sound recorder is reduced.
- They allow wireless lavalier mikes to be inconspicuously placed on the set or on actors.
- The production sound mixer can be located anywhere on or off set so long as he is within the range of the transmitter.
- The boom operator has the freedom to move and place the microphone anywhere without worrying about tripping on cables.
- They save setup time by reducing the need to rewire and restring XLR cables from the microphones to the production sound mixer.

Some of the drawbacks of wireless systems:

- All wireless devices are prone to picking up transmissions from other devices, especially radio stations and other wireless transmitters on similar frequencies. Purchasing high-quality UHF systems gives users the flexibility to change frequencies for cleaner audio.
- The wireless signal can be disrupted by large metal objects like fences, trucks, buildings, and power lines, which may introduce interference. This interference can be minimized by using fresh batteries in the unit and minimizing the distance between the transmitter and the receiver.
- Wireless lavalier transmitters may be difficult to hide on actors, but can be attached to their belt, thigh, or ankle using straps or gaffer's tape.
- The range of wireless systems can affect the quality of the audio. The greater the distance between the transmitter and the receiver, the weaker the signal.
- Wireless transmitters and receivers require a lot of battery power. Be sure to have plenty of extra batteries on set.

One of the most common types of wireless microphone is a wireless lavalier, which consists of a small fingernail-sized microphone attached to a transmitter via wire that the actor usually wears on his belt. The transmitter is a battery-powered unit about the size of a pack of cigarettes. The receiver is connected to the camera, usually with XLR inputs. With a range of about 50–1000 feet, depending on the quality of the mike, wireless microphones are mostly used for "walk and talk" scenes that would be difficult to record with a boom pole.

Always use headphones on set and listen for interference as the scene is being recorded.

AMBIENT SOUND

Ambient sound is the background noise of a location. For example, waves, seagulls, and wind are the ambient sounds of a beach, and traffic, horns, and people talking are the ambient sounds of a city street. Although ambient sounds are important in helping establish the location, they must be reduced as much as possible so that on set, the only sounds recorded are the actors' dialog and their movements. Ambient sounds are then added to the entire scene in post-production, helping add consistency to a scene. There are several techniques to help minimize the ambience. Most importantly, listen on set during the location scout to determine what sounds are present. Most often, the ambient sounds will be air conditioning units and refrigerators. Talk to the location owner about turning these off on the day on the shoot.

Interior locations are easier to control because the walls absorb much of the sound from the outside. Shooting outdoors makes controlling ambient sounds more difficult. If you're in a noisy location, bring several packing blankets (available from your local mover) and hang them on C-stands to create movable "sound walls" that can be positioned between the actors and the source of the sound. Place the sound blankets behind lights and the camera after all the equipment has been set up. If you're recording in a church or a large room with a lot of echo, try placing the packing blankets on the floor under the actors to absorb the sound. It is important to minimize the ambience as much as possible to save time and money in postproduction. If there is too much ambient noise, you may need to ADR the actors' dialog and then recreate the Foley and ambience. This is a time-consuming and expensive process that can be avoided by using these techniques on set.

WORKING WITH EXTRAS

There may be scenes that involve background actors or extras, such as a restaurant, bus station, auditorium, or any other public place. Although in real life you can hear the ambience of people talking, laughing, chatting on cell phones, arguing, and otherwise interacting with their environment, when you film that moment in a movie, filmmakers instruct the extras to ACT as if they are talking but to SAY NOTHING. The only sound that should be heard on set when the cameras roll is the sound of the principal actors delivering their lines and their interaction with the environment. The rest of the ambience is recorded later and mixed in during the editing process, giving the filmmakers control over the balance between background sounds and dialog.

A few years ago, I shot a short film called *The Overcoat* that featured a scene in a grocery store. In order to control the environment, we closed down the store on a Sunday night; populated it with extras; turned off the overhead music, coolers, and appliances; oiled the shopping cart wheels; and asked the extras not to make any sounds when the camera rolled. Although it seemed bizarre to see people miming their actions, it allowed us to record the actors' dialog cleanly and without competition from background noise.

Later, in the editing room, we added the sounds of people talking, squeaky shopping carts, tacky elevator music, beeping price scanners, bag boys loading up groceries, and a baby crying, among other sounds that added to the realism of the moment back into the scene. As a result, we were able to control the volume of each individual sound so nothing competed with the dialog. The result was a scene that appeared to be recorded in a busy, bustling grocery store.

SOUND LOGS

The production sound mixer should maintain complete and comprehensive sound logs, which list the audio take, the scene and setup, the timecode of each take, and any notes regarding the quality of each take. These sound logs will help the editor determine which take is best to use and aid in finding a particular take.

TIPS FOR RECORDING GOOD ON-SET AUDIO

- Choose locations that are as quiet as possible, away from freeways, airports, hospitals, police stations, and fire stations.
- When in the location, disable anything that makes noise, including refrigerators and air conditioners.
- Use a shotgun microphone to isolate and record ONLY the dialog from the actors and NEVER use the built-in microphone in the camera.
- Position the microphone on a boom pole above the actors at a 45-degree angle and aim the microphone at the actor's chest.
- The camera operator and boom operator should be listening to the audio over headphones to ensure maximum sound quality.
- Make sure that the audio levels average between –3 and –6 db on the audio meters and NEVER hit or exceed 0 db.
- Record with XLR (or balanced) cables only from the mike to the camera. Using unbalanced cables creates an antenna that picks up unwanted signals like radio stations.
- If there is a lot of ambient noise such as traffic, waves on a beach, or wind, try setting up several stands and hanging furniture pads or other thick material around the set to absorb some of the sound before it hits the microphone.
- At the end of the shoot, in each location, always record 30–60 seconds of the ambient sound of the location. Ensure the cast and crew stand perfectly still so the room tone is as pure as possible. This will come into play during the editing process, in which the room tone will be used under shots with no audio, or to fix problems with the ambience track.

CHAPTER 17

Hair and Makeup

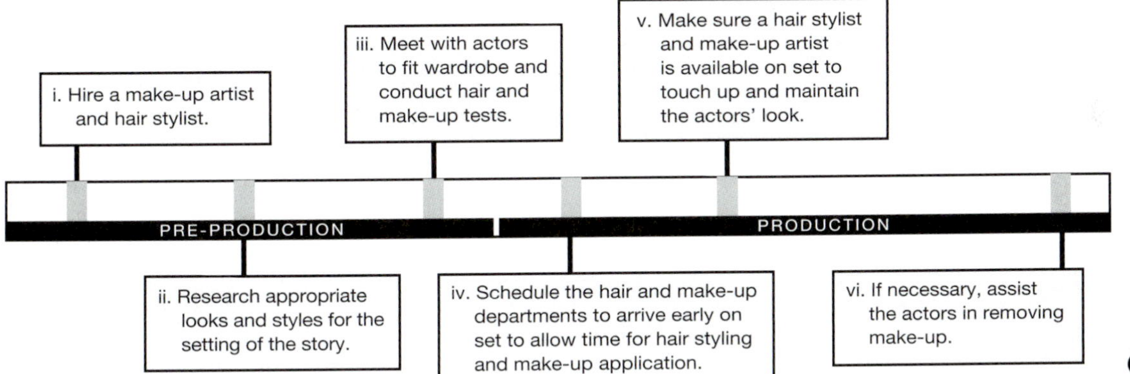

i. Hire a make-up artist and hair stylist.
ii. Research appropriate looks and styles for the setting of the story.
iii. Meet with actors to fit wardrobe and conduct hair and make-up tests.
iv. Schedule the hair and make-up departments to arrive early on set to allow time for hair styling and make-up application.
v. Make sure a hair stylist and make-up artist is available on set to touch up and maintain the actors' look.
vi. If necessary, assist the actors in removing make-up.
PRE-PRODUCTION
PRODUCTION

INTRODUCTION

Makeup and hairstyling are an essential part of making a movie, for both practical and technical reasons. Whereas the creative aspects are obvious, it is important for a hair and makeup artist to monitor the continuity of the actors' look as well as ensuring that the actors aren't shiny or sweaty or have hair that will draw attention away from their performance.

STRAIGHT MAKEUP

Straight makeup (or beauty makeup) is noneffects makeup designed to maintain the actor's flesh tones, minimize oil and shine that show up under production lights, and help facial features stand out on camera. Both male and female actors wear makeup that is usually applied by an experienced makeup artist at the beginning of each production day and touched up before every take. This ensures that the actor's look remains consistent during the course of the scene.

Most makeup is applied so the actor looks natural. Although we often think of plaster-faced news anchors or highly made-up fashion models, most movie actors wear makeup to look like they're not wearing makeup! The ability to create a natural look is difficult and often requires the skills of an experienced makeup artist.

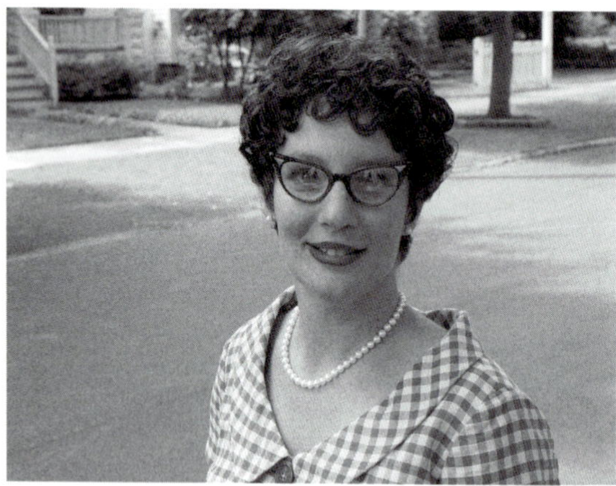

Actress Paula Williams' remarkable transformation into Martha Jones, courtesy of Hairstylist Deb Lilly and Makeup artist Jason Blaszczak.

Even elements like sweat and dirt must be carefully maintained by makeup artists to ensure that they remain consistent from take to take. The dirt on Bobby Jones's face from the prison to the school yard to the farmhouse was carefully monitored so it appeared the same, even though these three scenes were filmed within weeks of each other.

- Determine the work load during preproduction, the number of actors to be made up, the amount of makeup, and the complexity of the makeup, and then figure out how many makeup artists are needed.
- Discuss how much time is needed at the beginning of each day to apply makeup on the main actors and schedule call times for actors and makeup artists accordingly.
- Remember to factor the cost of makeup materials in the budget. Even though makeup artists may be willing to work for free, many will expect to be compensated for the cost of their materials.
- Discuss the look of the lighting with the director of photography. The color of the lighting, harshness, and wraparound and whether the light is a bluish outdoor light or warmer tungsten light will affect the look of the actors. Make sure the makeup complements the lighting.
- If there is time, consider testing the makeup on the actors before getting to set. This will save time if there is a problem with the colors chosen or the application process.
- Make sure there are adequate facilities and power for makeup artists and hairstylists to do their jobs on set. Although you may be shooting in a remote location, it is important that the artists have the resources they need.
- Once the actors' hair and makeup is done in the morning, it is important to touch it up for each and every take, requiring that a hairstylist and makeup artist be on set and ready to tweak the actor's look before the camera rolls.
- When producing a period film, hairstylists and makeup artists can help create a convincing and believable look for each character, but keep in mind that time needs to be factored into the schedule for them to do their jobs. In *Time and Again,* the actors spent two to three hours getting their hair and makeup done before they appeared on set.
- Take Polaroid or digital photos of the actors to maintain a continuous look throughout the production of the movie.

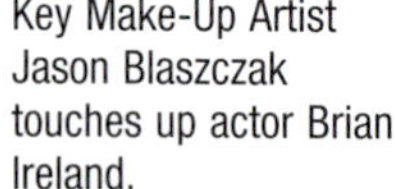

Key Make-Up Artist Jason Blaszczak touches up actor Brian Ireland.

MAKEUP TERMS

Straight makeup: The standard, noneffects beauty makeup applied to male and female actors.

Special effects makeup: Prosthetics, foam latex appliances, gashes, cuts, and bruises all fall under this category. Special effects makeup artists require special training to perform these types of effects competently.

Key makeup: The lead makeup artist to whom all other makeup artists answer.

DIRECTOR'S NOTES

Developing the look of the female characters was extremely important in creating a realistic 1950s film, so Key Hairstylist Deb Lilly and Key Makeup Artist Jason Blaszczak did a lot of research before *Time and Again* went into production. We studied 1958 hair styles and makeup trends and performed several tests on the actors to make sure that the look of our characters was accurate.

The two most striking changes were in Jennie Allen, who played Awanda, and Paula Williams, who played Bobby Jones's mother, Martha.

The platinum-blond hairstyle (that nearly ruined Jennie's hair) completely transformed Jennie into the Marilyn Monroe look I had always envisioned for the story. We worked to make sure that Awanda's hair would work with the pink waitress outfit, coordinating her look with the hair, makeup, and wardrobe departments.

Paula's transformation was even more incredible. Jason's makeup job and Deb's hairstyle were so different from Paula's normal look that Paula's own sister didn't recognize her. Unbelievably, Paula is not wearing a wig in the film!

These looks, while drastic in real life, appear as normal on screen and accepted as what these women would have looked like in July of 1958.

Jennie without makeup.

Awanda with makeup.

Paula without makeup.

Martha Jones.

BUILDING A MAKEUP KIT

If the production is so small that the budget doesn't allow for a makeup artist, consider building a small makeup kit to use on set.

A basic makeup kit can include:

- **Pancake**—Pancake is a powder that is tinted to match the skin tones and is used to reduce shine. There are numerous shades, so be sure to perform tests on the actors before arriving on set to ensure a color match. Pancake is applied over the entire face as a finishing makeup.
- **Greasepaint**—Extremely thick makeup used for theatrical applications that helps facial features stand out.
- **Concealer**—Covers imperfections of the skin, blemishes, acne, and circles under the eyes. After applying concealer to problem areas of the skin, apply pancake to cover and blend the makeup.
- **Powder**—Lighter than pancake and usually translucent, powder is used all over the face to reduce shine. Be sure to keep plenty of powder on set to keep sweaty actors looking dry.
- **Highlights**—Highlights are used to accentuate parts of the face by drawing attention to or away from facial features like the nose, cheekbones, or chin by creating fake "shadows." Use highlights to make a large nose appear smaller or to reduce the appearance of a double chin.
- **Blush**—Adds a touch of color to an actress' cheekbones.
- **Lip color**—Adds color to an actor's lips.
- **Lip gloss**—Adds a sheen to an actor's lips.
- **Eye liner**—Applied around the actor's eyes to bring out the shape and details of the eyes.
- **Mascara**—Applied to bring out the eyelashes.
- **Application tools**—Latex sponges, lip brush, powder puff, fluffy powder puff, cotton swabs.
- **Cold cream**—Used to remove heavy makeup while protecting and moisturizing the skin. Cold cream helps reduce damage to the skin caused by makeup.
- **Removers**—Makeup remover.
- **Miscellaneous**—Aprons, drop cloths, facial tissues, cotton balls, cotton swabs.

PROSTHETICS

Makeup prosthetics are foam latex appliances that are glued to an actor's body to create everything from simple special effects like burns, scars, and cuts to major makeup effects like turning an actor into a monster or alien. These appliances are created from a mold that is taken of the actor's face to ensure that the appliance fits correctly. Then, using the mold as a reference, the makeup artist is able to sculpt a foam latex appliance that will be painted and glued to the skin.

Foam latex is an effective material for appliances because it mimics the look and movement of human skin and muscle, is lightweight, and is able to "breathe."

It is advisable to hire an experienced makeup prosthetics artist if appliances are needed for the story. These makeup effects look terrific when they're done properly.

- When using makeup prosthetics, be sure to schedule enough time on set to allow the application of the makeup appliance.
- Talk to the makeup artist in advance to determine the cost of materials needed to produce the desired effect.
- In productions with a heavy effects work load, it may be necessary to bring numerous makeup artists to the set.

SPECIAL EFFECTS MAKEUP

Special effects makeup includes everything from blood to scars. These basic effects can be easily and inexpensively accomplished with common ingredients available from the grocery store.

DIRECTOR'S NOTES

Time and Again ends with the camera dollying out from Bobby Jones, who is kneeling in the prison yard about to die from a shotgun wound. Because of the length of the shoot and how long the audience would be staring at the wound, Jason Blaszczak created a wound that could be applied within an hour while the crew reset the shot.

The prison gave us only one night to shoot the entire prison break as well as the final shot, so we were racing against the sun to finish the scenes. Because of the time crunch, we couldn't wait for Jason to apply a complete makeup prosthetic, so he jury-rigged a shotgun blast makeup effect that worked well.

Thanks to tight scheduling, Jason's smart thinking, creative lighting, and Brian's terrific performance, we were able to convince the audience that Bobby was shot in the chest, making the end of *Time and Again* as powerful as I envisioned.

- **Fake blood**—Go to the grocery store and purchase corn syrup. Similar to maple syrup, corn syrup is clear to yellowish in color and has the consistency of blood. Mix a few drops of red food coloring and a dash of blue to make a deep red blood-like color.

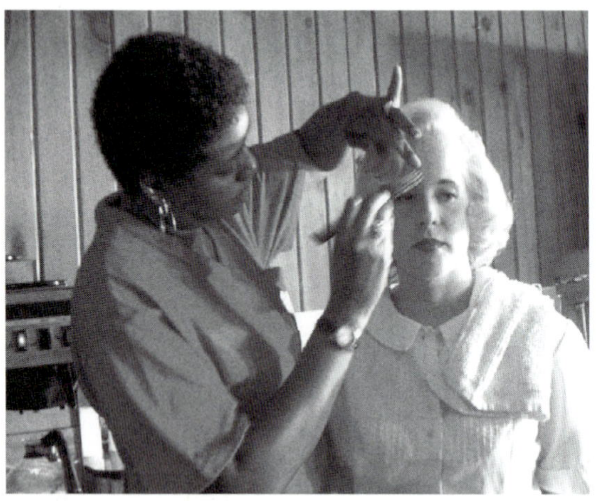

- **Scars**—Go to the grocery store and purchase unflavored gelatin. Mix one tablespoon of gelatin into a tablespoon of near-boiling water so it completely dissolves. Be sure to avoid any bubbles. Wait for the mixture to cool, and then apply it to the skin, building and molding it as needed. Be careful because the gelatin will cool and harden quickly. Once dry, apply regular makeup to match skin tones.
- **Sweat**—Try using baby oil in a spray bottle. The oil won't evaporate as quickly as water and provides a great sheen for the camera.

HAIRSTYLING

In addition to maintaining makeup needs, hairstyling is extremely important. Working with a professional hairstylist can add an artistic touch when creating the look of a character, establish a time period, and ensure hair continuity from one scene to the next. Be mindful of extras as well as principal characters. With a movie like *Time and Again,* each extra needed to have his/her hair styled by our make-up team before every shooting day. This made the 1950s era the story was set in look realistic.

In working with hairstylists, provide the necessary resources on set for them to work, including access to power, a trailer, tent, tables, makeup chairs, and mirrors. For *Time and Again,* Hairstylist Deb Lilly worked everywhere from bathrooms in nearby homes for the dirt road scenes to under tents in Chardon to process the nearly 100 extras for Bobby Jones's run through the town.

- When talking with a hairstylist, find out if the actor needs to go through any hair treatments prior to each shooting day. Jennie, who played Awanda, needed extensive sessions to dye her hair the platinum blond color that turned her into Awanda.
- When casting, notify the actors during the audition process if there are extensive hairstyle requirements, for example, if a man needs a buzz cut for a military role.

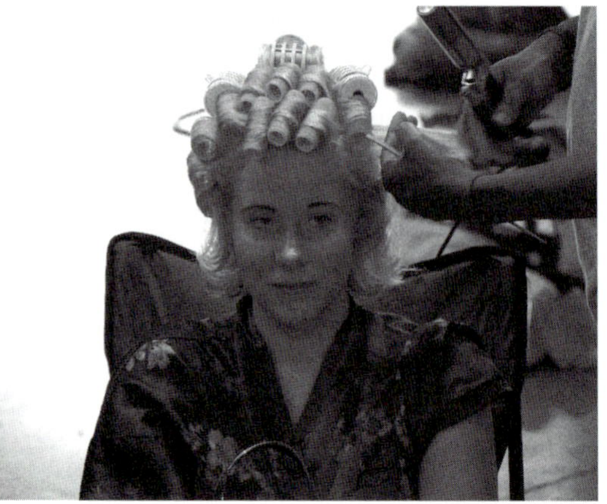

ACTIVITY

1. Purchase powder from your local drug store and shoot an actor both with and without makeup. Both men and women use powder when they're in front of the camera, mostly to absorb oil from the skin and reduce glare or shine.

2. Choose a time period for a movie and then research the appropriate styles of both hair and makeup. Determine what types of resources and the number of hairstylists and makeup artists that will be needed to implement the designs.
3. Contact a local makeup artist and ask for a demonstration of basic beauty makeup. Learn basic application techniques and video tape the results, both before and after.

Learn more about finding qualified hairstylists and makeup artists at www.powerfilmmaking.com.

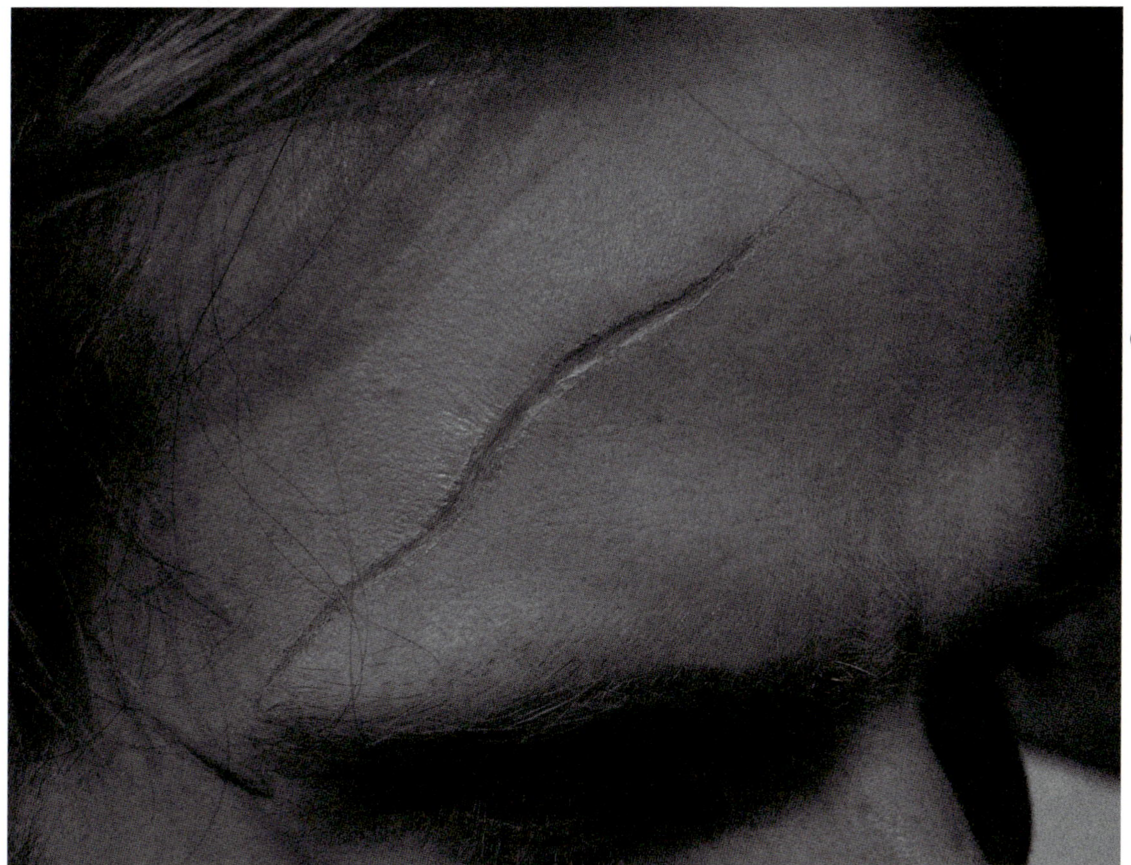

Bobby Jones's scar was a simple makeup effect that took less than ten minutes to apply each day.

CHAPTER 18

Craft Services and Catering

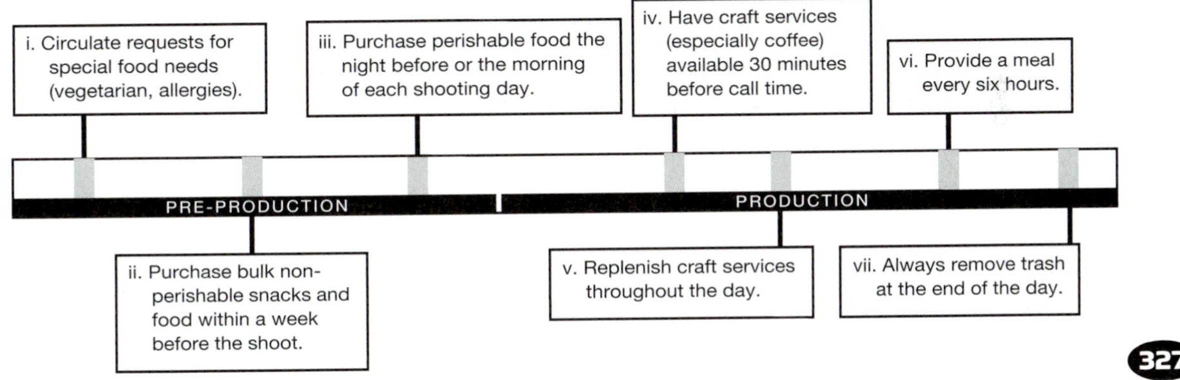

i. Circulate requests for special food needs (vegetarian, allergies).
ii. Purchase bulk non-perishable snacks and food within a week before the shoot.
iii. Purchase perishable food the night before or the morning of each shooting day.
iv. Have craft services (especially coffee) available 30 minutes before call time.
v. Replenish craft services throughout the day.
vi. Provide a meal every six hours.
vii. Always remove trash at the end of the day.
PRE-PRODUCTION
PRODUCTION

INTRODUCTION

The cast and crew of any movie will tell you that second to being paid, the availability of good food on set is one of the most important aspects of a movie production. Especially if the project is a low-budget project and the cast and crew are volunteering their time, providing craft services and catering is essential in not only keeping everyone's energy up, but also maintaining a positive morale on set.

When working on set all day, it's standard industry practice to provide a meal for the cast and crew every six hours. Although these meals can be as simple as sub sandwiches, pizza, or hot dogs, try to keep it healthy and you will have a happy, productive cast and crew that will have the energy for a whole day of shooting. Also provide a table of snacks and beverages available all day.

In producing an independent movie, craft services and catering will most likely be the most expensive line item on the budget. Do not cut back on the food for the set, especially if the cast and crew are volunteering their time. It is often said that if the cast and crew are well fed, they will follow the director anywhere.

Producer Adam Kadar was instrumental in negotiating with restaurants to secure free or heavily discounted food for the set. One day, he procured dozens of bagels from a local bakery, all by asking.

The food on set can be divided into two different categories: craft services and catering.

CRAFT SERVICES

Craft services are buffet-style snacks and drinks available to the cast and crew throughout the shooting day. Usually featuring an assortment of hot and cold drinks, fresh fruit, vegetables, candy, and snacks, craft services helps keep everyone going during long production days.

Usually a craft services crew member is hired to purchase the food in advance, bring the tables, and prepare and maintain the food during the course of the day, although on low-budget projects a production assistant can be assigned these duties.

When planning craft services, be aware of the shooting location and the weather conditions and plan the food selection accordingly. In general, most craft services items must be easy for the crew to grab and eat on the run.

BREAKFAST

Craft services usually arrives and is set up 30 minutes before call time, so any crew members wishing to eat breakfast can arrive early on set.

A typical breakfast spread includes:

- An assortment of bagels.
- Cream cheese, butter, and jelly in individual packs. Avoid purchasing jars as it can get messy.
- An assortment of donuts.
- An assortment of muffins.
- Fresh fruit: apples, bananas, pears, and peaches. Cut them into small, easy-to-grab pieces.
- Hot coffee with cream, sugar, nondairy creamer, coffee stirrers, and coffee cups. Consider bringing a coffee maker to the set, as coffee is the primary drink of choice throughout the day.
- An assortment of juices, especially orange juice and apple juice.
- Bottled water (lots of it).
- An assortment of cereal travel packs with milk. The crew can eat out of the box.
- An assortment of yogurt.

THROUGHOUT THE DAY

After breakfast, the craft services table is updated with new selections throughout the day. Common items include:

- Mixed nuts
- Trail mix
- Peanut butter and jelly
- Bread for sandwiches
- Potato chips and pretzels
- Raisins
- Fresh fruit
- A deli tray
- Raw vegetables
- Granola bars
- Chocolates and candies
- Chewing gum and breath mints

Also include a variety of hot and cold beverages throughout the day:

- Coffee . . . all the time
- Hot water and a variety of teas

A typical craft services table on set.

- Bottled water (try buying half-size bottles of water, since less will go to waste)
- Caffeinated and caffeine-free soda
- Juice

Approach local grocery stores and ask them to donate craft service items. Also be sure to check out large wholesale stores where you can buy bulk items inexpensively. Send a production assistant on a craft services run several days before the shoot for nonperishable items and have him or her pick up fresh food items the morning of each shooting day.

Here are some tips for setting up a craft services table on set:

- Craft services food should be easily accessible and easy to grab during the day. Avoid food that needs to be cut or overly prepped.
- Set up the craft services table near the set, but not so close that it is in the way.
- Be aware of bugs, wind, or animals that may disrupt the food, so pick a location where the food will be safe for the entire day of shooting.
- Have coffee ready three hours after call time and three hours after lunch, when the crew starts to slow down. Also have abundant coffee ready after dinner, especially if the shooting goes into the night.
- During the location scout, determine where power can be drawn for the coffee pot and toaster. Make sure the location owner has given permission to serve food on set and approves the designated location.

CATERING

Catering is the full meals served for lunch and dinner. Typically provided by a catering company or restaurant, catered meals consist of boxed meals or a buffet-style layout. Full meals should be served six hours after call time and every six hours afterward, based on standard industry guidelines. In fully paid union situations, cast and crew members are paid extra money if the meals are served late because shooting runs overtime.

Catered meals usually include a choice of two different entrees, one of which is pasta or rice; a salad; several sides; and a dessert. Bigger-budgeted productions can increase the selection of food to where a chef is brought on set to prepare custom meals for the cast and crew. Be sure to include a vegetarian entree for those people with dietary restrictions.

When I produced low-budget films, I negotiated with a local restaurant for a discounted rate not only to provide the food, but to bring the food to the set, set up the tables, and clean up afterward. This allows the crew to focus on the production, not on food preparation and cleanup. For *Time and Again*, for which the budget was limited, I was able to convince several restaurants to donate food, free of charge. I also approached grocery stores that donated beverages, condiments, plates, napkins, and utensils and even some sides like potato salad and cole slaw. If we weren't able to negotiate these deals, the producers and I would make big containers of pasta to bring to set, which is cheap and easy to prepare and provides a hearty meal.

Choose food that is healthy and energy-inducing. Remember that working on a film set is long, tedious work, so having good food on set will help maintain everyone's energy level and make for a much more pleasant demeanor on set.

When choosing catered meals, here are some suggestions that are both nutritious and inexpensive:

- Sub sandwiches (meat, tuna, and vegetarian)
- Pasta, either hot or cold; pasta salads
- Pizza (although not for every meal, please)
- Chicken
- Fresh salads

While shooting at the prison, we decided to cook up a late night snack for the cast and crew.

TIPS FOR ON SET

- If the location you're shooting at has a refrigerator, ask them if you can use it. Don't assume you can. Always clean it out at the end of each shooting day.
- NEVER, EVER serve alcohol on set, even if the actors are "drinking" in the scene. Every alcoholic beverage can be faked using diluted soda, juice, or food-colored water.
- Provide vegetarian options or any other special dietary requirements of the cast and crew. Send out an e-mail before production asking cast and crew members if they have any special requirements.
- When ordering food from a restaurant, contact the manager a week in advance to make all necessary preparations, including the number of people being served, types of food, delivery and pick-up information, time the food is needed, and cost.
- Be sure to bring plenty of garbage bags so you can dispose of your own trash yourself. Never use public trash cans or private dumpsters, unless you have permission to do so.
- Assign a production assistant the duty of picking up and maintaining the craft services table if you cannot afford a dedicated craft services company.

UNIT 4
Postproduction

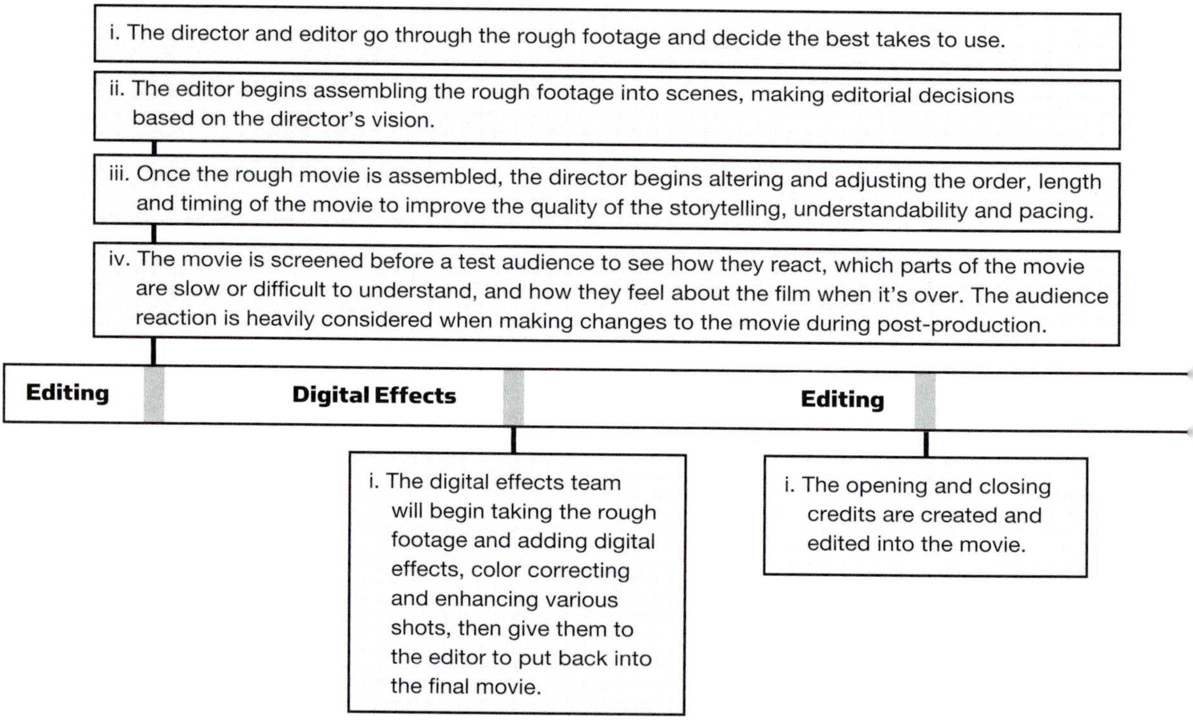

i. The director and editor go through the rough footage and decide the best takes to use.

ii. The editor begins assembling the rough footage into scenes, making editorial decisions based on the director's vision.

iii. Once the rough movie is assembled, the director begins altering and adjusting the order, length and timing of the movie to improve the quality of the storytelling, understandability and pacing.

iv. The movie is screened before a test audience to see how they react, which parts of the movie are slow or difficult to understand, and how they feel about the film when it's over. The audience reaction is heavily considered when making changes to the movie during post-production.

Editing | **Digital Effects** | **Editing**

Digital Effects

i. The digital effects team will begin taking the rough footage and adding digital effects, color correcting and enhancing various shots, then give them to the editor to put back into the final movie.

Editing

i. The opening and closing credits are created and edited into the movie.

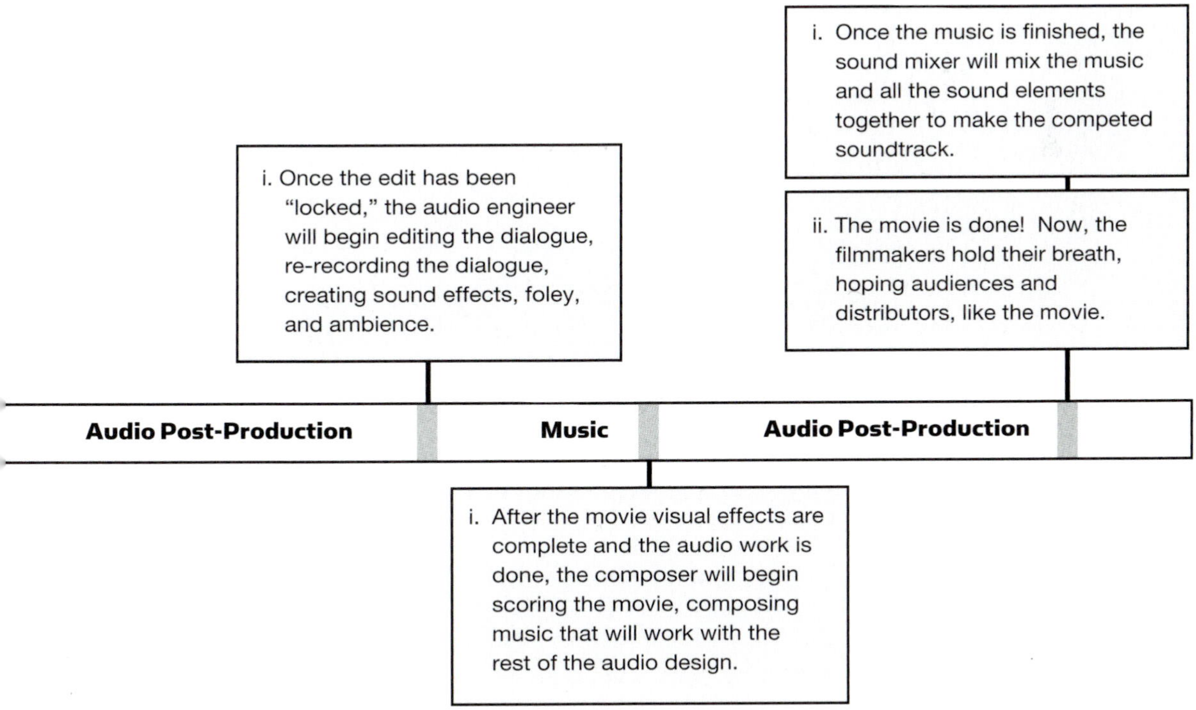

i. Once the music is finished, the sound mixer will mix the music and all the sound elements together to make the competed soundtrack.

ii. The movie is done! Now, the filmmakers hold their breath, hoping audiences and distributors, like the movie.

i. Once the edit has been "locked," the audio engineer will begin editing the dialogue, re-recording the dialogue, creating sound effects, foley, and ambience.

Audio Post-Production | **Music** | **Audio Post-Production**

i. After the movie visual effects are complete and the audio work is done, the composer will begin scoring the movie, composing music that will work with the rest of the audio design.

Bobby Jones / Roll 1
8-02-02
BJ. Woods Day1 Tape2
BJ. Woods Day2 Tape2
BJ. Farmhouse
BJ. Dirt Road - 1
BJ. Dirt Road - 2
BJ. Dirt Road - 3
BJ. 2nd UNIT
BJ. Trailer 1
BJ. Trailer 2
BJ. Trailer 3
BJ. Woods Day 2
BJ. Flashback
BJ - Tape 2
BJ. - Jail - 1
BJ - Jail - 2
BJ - B/A street 2
BJ. Diner - 1
BJ - Diner - 2
BJ. Diner - 3
BJ. home 1
BJ. home 2
B-Roll - B.J.
BJ. Bedroom
BJ. rough cut
Love 1
BJ. Woods Day 1 Tape 1
BJ. B/A street 3

CHAPTER 19
Editing

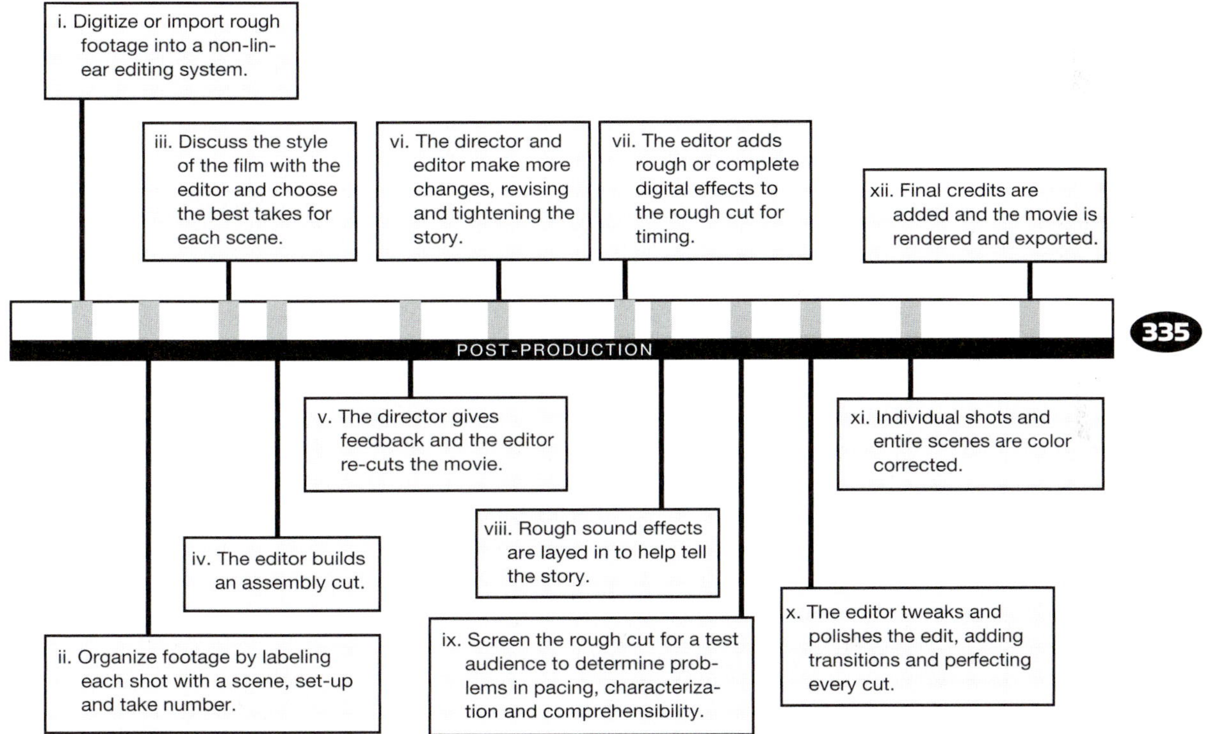

i. Digitize or import rough footage into a non-linear editing system.
ii. Organize footage by labeling each shot with a scene, set-up and take number.
iii. Discuss the style of the film with the editor and choose the best takes for each scene.
iv. The editor builds an assembly cut.
v. The director gives feedback and the editor re-cuts the movie.
vi. The director and editor make more changes, revising and tightening the story.
vii. The editor adds rough or complete digital effects to the rough cut for timing.
viii. Rough sound effects are layed in to help tell the story.
ix. Screen the rough cut for a test audience to determine problems in pacing, characterization and comprehensibility.
x. The editor tweaks and polishes the edit, adding transitions and perfecting every cut.
xi. Individual shots and entire scenes are color corrected.
xii. Final credits are added and the movie is rendered and exported.
POST-PRODUCTION

INTRODUCTION

Editing is the process of assembling a series of shots to form a logical sequence. Pacing, subtext, and the ability to convey emotion can be heavily influenced by decisions made in the editing room. A good editor must possess a strong sense of timing and an outstanding storytelling ability to assemble a logical, entertaining, and emotionally driven story from thousands of individual shots.

CONCEPTS OF EDITING

Filmmaking is the tedious process of shooting a scene numerous times from many angles using only one camera. When on set, always shoot "for the edit" by envisioning how every shot will be cut together. Ensure good continuity by directing the actors to perform each scene consistently in its entirety for each camera setup.

In the editing room, assemble the shots so the action in the scene appears to have occurred only once, yet creating the illusion that it was covered by multiple cameras positioned around the set.

RELATIONSHIP BETWEEN SHOTS

The process of visual storytelling, whether the medium is a comic strip, cartoon, or motion picture, involves juxtaposing images that have no real meaning by themselves, but have a greater meaning when placed with a series of other images.

Take for example the following shot: a young man runs down the sidewalk in busy New York City. This shot, by itself, means nothing. We cannot tell to what or from what he is running or even why he is running.

If we take a completely unrelated shot and edit it either before or after the shot of the young man running, it will give added meaning to the shot. For example: Let's edit a shot of a dog running before the shot of the man running. Even though the dog and the man do not appear in the same frame, the audience will automatically associate the two shots together and assume that the dog is chasing the man. Or, we could replace the dog with a shot of the sky, filling with storm clouds. The audience now thinks that the man is running to avoid the storm. Or, we could place the shot of a young woman waiting, looking at her watch. Now we're implying that the man is late for a meeting. No matter what shot we place before or after the man running, the shot is, after all, simply of a man running. It means nothing by itself, but stands to gain a greater meaning from whatever precedes or follows it.

A linear editing suite.

This is the basic principle of filmmaking, assembling a series of seemingly unrelated shots to tell a story. Shots edited together make a scene, and scenes edited together make a film. Don't try to pack every story element into one shot, but rather, let the collective power of multiple shots tell the audience what you want them to know.

EDITING SYSTEMS

A decade ago, editing was performed by linking two VCRs, one to play the rough footage and a second to record selected clips onto a blank tape.

A nonlinear editing suite.

A program was cut linearly, from the beginning to the end, limiting the editor's ability to make changes earlier in the program. Nonlinear editing frees the editor from this restriction by allowing the editor to edit any part of the movie at any time while preserving the integrity of the original footage. Sophisticated software brings a myriad of editing, titling, transition, and effects tools right to the desktop of your home computer.

Nonlinear editors work on the principal that rough footage is digitized, or converted into the binary language of ones and zeros, and stored on a hard drive. An editing program like Apple Final Cut Pro or Adobe Premiere is then used to assemble the clips into a logical sequence, add titles and transitions, color correct, and even composite clips together. The software isn't altering the original files on the hard drive at all, but rather creating a play list in much the same way a CD player can be programmed to play music tracks in a certain order. Just as the CD player does not affect the actual media on the CD, nonlinear editing systems reference but don't affect the clips on the hard drive.

As you edit a sequence, the editing program plays the marked sections of each movie file from the hard drive fast enough to appear continuous and seamless. If the editor changes a movie clip by changing the color or brightness or by adding any filters, titles, or transitions, the computer must calculate the changes and render new frames. Many of these effects can be rendered in real time, although complicated effects may require additional rendering time for the computer to play them. If this happens, the computer saves the newly rendered shot on the hard drive and plays it at the appropriate time in the sequence. For example, if Shot A dissolves into Shot B, the computer will play Shot A up to the dissolve, then it will play the new clip it made of the dissolve, then it will jump back to play what's left of Shot B. To the viewer, this process is seamless.

Editing map.

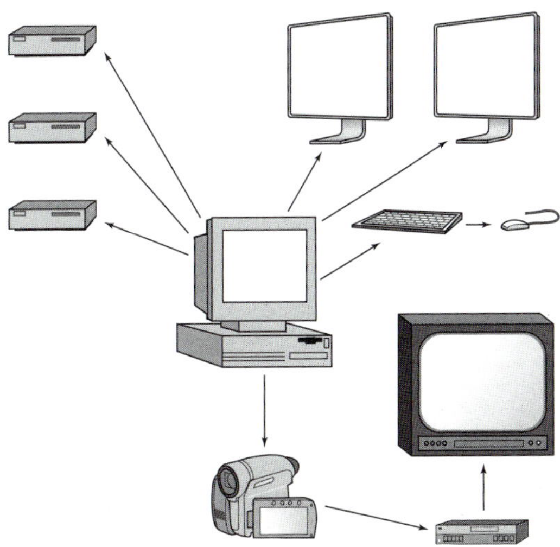

Because it is a nondestructive process, editors can undo, change, and alter previous edits at any time, in any part of the movie.

Some of the most common editing programs include:

Apple Final Cut Pro
Apple iMovie
Avid Xpress Pro

Avid FreeDV
Adobe Premiere Pro
Pinnacle Studio
Window's Movie Maker
Sony Vegas

THE EDITING PROCESS

Organizing your clips

It isn't uncommon to find yourself working with hundreds, possibly thousands, of individual shots. One key to editing productively is to organize your footage meticulously by naming and categorizing each clip. Each shot should have a numeric name, 16a-6 (Scene 16, Setup A, Take 6), and a brief description, "LS, dolly Bobby enters street" (long shot, Bobby enters street). Organizing the footage will make it easier to locate and identify specific shots throughout the editing process.

Before you begin editing, always familiarize yourself with the rough footage by watching all the source material and making any notes about outstanding takes.

Maintaining detailed camera logs on set is helpful when logging and organizing your footage. Here, the second assistant cameraman and script supervisor wrote detailed comments about each shot, problems encountered and the director's rating of each take.

The assembly cut

Once the footage is organized, begin assembling the selected takes into a rough edit of the movie. Usually built with very few edits and without inserts or close-ups, the assembly cut is a way of laying down the rough story points before working in the details.

- While editing the assembly cut, do not be concerned with audio, titles, music, insert shots, close-ups, sound effects, pacing, or timing. You're building the basic foundation of the story.
- Use the assembly cut to judge broad plot points, character arcs, and story beats. Serving much the same purpose as an outline or treatment in the writing phase, the assembly cut gives the director the opportunity to work in broad brush strokes while losing the least amount of work if sweeping changes need to be made.

It is common for the editor to begin the assembly cut even while the movie is still being filmed. This allows the director to see how the film is coming together, giving him the opportunity to shoot scenes differently on set, pick up missing shots, or grab an insert or reaction shot. At this stage, the editor usually works alone, althoughs she may have an assistant that helps digitize and prepare the footage for editing.

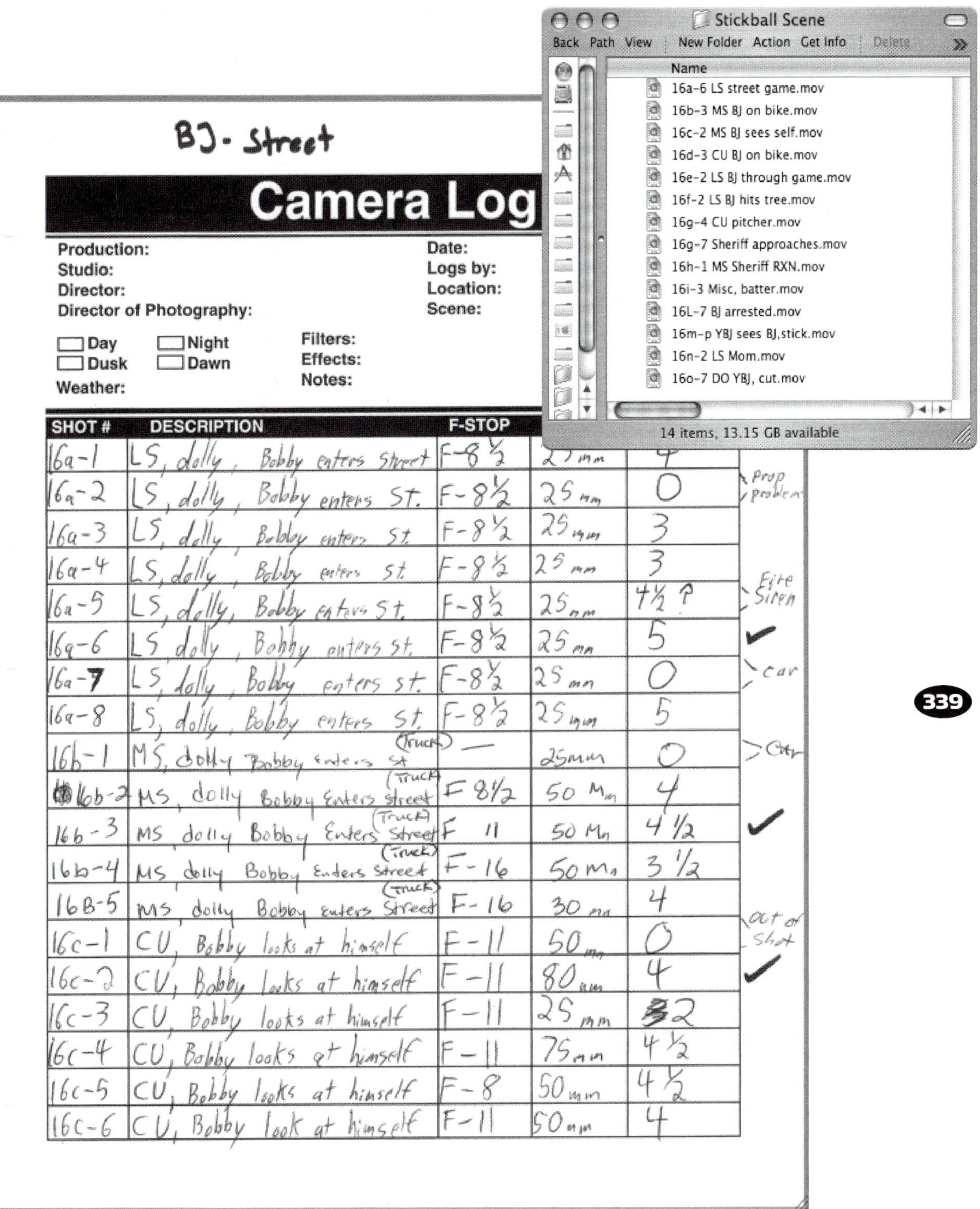

BJ - Street

Camera Log

Production:
Studio:
Director:
Director of Photography:

Date:
Logs by:
Location:
Scene:

☐ Day ☐ Night
☐ Dusk ☐ Dawn
Weather:

Filters:
Effects:
Notes:

SHOT #	DESCRIPTION	F-STOP			
16a-1	LS, dolly, Bobby enters Street	F-8½	25 mm	4	
16a-2	LS, dolly, Bobby enters St.	F-8½	25 mm	0	Prop problem
16a-3	LS, dolly, Bobby enters St.	F-8½	25 mm	3	
16a-4	LS, dolly, Bobby enters st.	F-8½	25 mm	3	
16a-5	LS, dolly, Bobby enters St.	F-8½	25 mm	4½ ?	Fire Siren
16a-6	LS, dolly, Bobby enters st.	F-8½	25 mm	5	✓
16a-7	LS, dolly, Bobby enters st.	F-8½	25 mm	0	car
16a-8	LS, dolly, Bobby enters st.	F-8½	25 mm	5	
16b-1	MS, dolly (Truck) Bobby enters st	—	25mm	0	Car
16b-2	MS, dolly (Truck) Bobby Enters street	F 8½	50 Mm	4	
16b-3	MS dolly (Truck) Bobby Enters Street	F 11	50 Mm	4½	✓
16b-4	MS dolly (Truck) Bobby Enters street	F-16	50 Mm	3½	
16B-5	MS dolly (Truck) Bobby enters Street	F-16	30 mm	4	
16c-1	CU, Bobby looks at himself	F-11	50 mm	0	out of shot
16c-2	CU, Bobby looks at himself	F-11	80 mm	4	✓
16c-3	CU, Bobby looks at himself	F-11	25 mm	~~3~~ 2	
16c-4	CU, Bobby looks at himself	F-11	75 mm	4½	
16c-5	CU, Bobby looks at himself	F-8	50 mm	4½	
16C-6	CU, Bobby look at himself	F-11	50 mm	4	

Editing window and camera log.

During this stage, the director sits with the editor to look at the footage and gives guidance regarding how he envisions the pacing, timing, and flow of the story. The director will then allow the editor to assemble the movie on her own, trusting his objective eye on the project.

Many novice filmmakers insist on sitting with the editor, directing each edit. This common mistake takes away not only the editor's creativity as an artist, but also the director's ability to make objective decisions as to how the film will cut together. The director has spent months, possibly years, working on the movie and knows every detail of the story. Subsequently, plot holes may be invisible to the director, who mentally fills the gaps with his knowledge and familiarity with the story. That's why working with an editor is so important. Editors come onboard the project later in the process and aren't exposed to the creative process during production. When they receive the footage, they can objectively build the story with the available shots.

The smart director will give the editor guidance and allow him to build the assembly cut alone. Once the assembly cut is finished, the director canwatch the film and give the editor notes as to what changes need to be made.

The rough cut

Once the assembly cut is finished, begin going through each scene one at a time and reediting it until you are happy with it. Review all possible takes, arrange and rearrange, tighten and move edits so that the final result features the best performances, emotion, pacing, and timing possible with the available footage. Add insert shots, master shots, and any footage needed to make the scene work on its own.

- Work your way through each scene in the assembly cut, but don't worry about music or sound design yet.

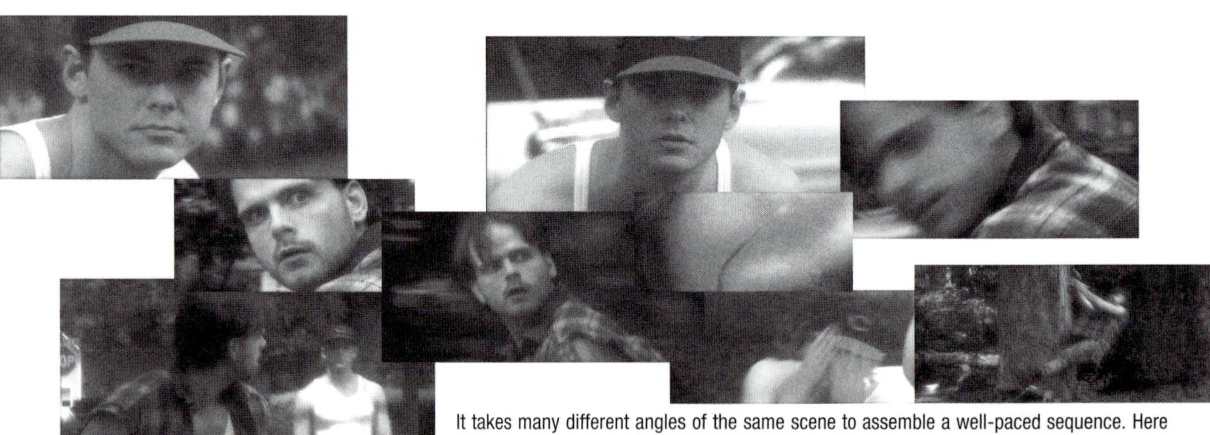

It takes many different angles of the same scene to assemble a well-paced sequence. Here are, in order, nine shots taken from the stickball scene of *Time and Again*.

- If a scene needs a digital effect, or the shot isn't yet available, edit in a blank title card that describes to the viewer what he will be seeing. Make this title card the same length as the real shot.
- Edit dialog scenes first to ensure that the conversations sound real, then focus on adding B-roll and cutaways. Scenes that are non-dialog-based are called action scenes and need to be driven by the pacing and timing of the visuals.

The assembly cut is usually the longest version of the movie, with all filmed scenes being edited into the movie. It is not uncommon for the rough-cut phase to last months, if not years. The Directors Guild of America rules give directors a minimum of 10 weeks after the completion of principal photography to build the first cut of a movie before the studio and producers are allowed to have input.

Programs like Apple Final Cut Pro give editors the ability to edit in any order they choose and to go back and make instant changes.

The working cut

Whereas the rough-cut phase is about working in each separate scene, the working cut is about getting those individual scenes to work together to produce a cohesive, well-paced story. During this phase, it is natural to run into problems with plot points, character arcs, and story pacing. Approach this edit with a creative, open mind and try different combinations of scenes, cut scenes, move scenes, and add transitions. You can also add rough music, important sound effects, voice-overs, and other audio elements to help develop the final feel of the film.

This is a good time to begin screening the movie and getting opinions from people who present a fresh perspective. Listen intently to their comments and pay close attention to any problems they have with confusing parts of the story, areas where the pacing lags, sequences that feel too long or too short, and character actions that don't seem motivated. Consider these comments and begin to tweak the edit to solve some of these problems.

If you plan on making a lot of changes to the working cut, consider saving a new version of the editing project on your computer. If you decide that the changes you made won't work, you can always return to the original edit.

The fine cut

Once all the problems have been solved, the story appears tightly paced, and the plot holes have been filled, go through each cut and perfect it to frame-accuracy, making sure each moment is the best it can be.

Once the fine cut is finished and approved, the movie is called "picture-locked," which means that no more changes to the timing of the film will be made. The movie is now ready to move on to audio postproduction.

EDITING TECHNIQUES

Editing an action scene

Action sequences refer to any scene that is driven by movements within the frame instead of dialog. When cutting an action sequence, ignore the audio tracks and cut the visuals together in a way that best suits the action, pacing, and flow of the scene.

Once the visuals are edited, begin piecing the audio clips together, cross-fading one clip into the next and adding sound effects, ambience, and music to pull the sequence together.

Editing a dialog scene

Editing dialog can be tricky, especially if the scene was shot at a location with a directional ambience that changes tone and volume from one shot to the next. Although removing distracting ambience like traffic, wind, or waves is nearly impossible, there are techniques to reduce the sudden impact of changing ambience from one shot to another. Here are a few tips:

- The most important factor in editing clean, ambience-free dialog is to shoot the scene in a quiet location.
- When shooting the scene on set, have the actors perform the scene as it should be played for the master shot. Then, when moving into close-ups of each actor, position the microphone so that it points toward only the actor who is on camera.
- When shooting close-ups, make sure the actors don't talk over each other's lines. In noisy environments, longer pauses between lines can help smooth the ambience in the editing process.

Let's say we have two characters, Dave and Jessica, talking at a restaurant together. Although the restaurant was relatively quiet, the microphone still picked up the ambience of outside traffic on the busy city street. Because of the blocking and microphone position, the ambience is louder behind Dave's shots than behind Jessica's.

Follow these steps to create a smooth, consistent dialog track:

1. Find the best take of Dave's close-up performance and drag it to track 1 on the timeline. Using the razor blade tool, slice out Jessica's lines as close to the beginning of her first word and as close to the end of her last word as you can, keeping as much of the ambience in the middle as possible. Delete Jessica's segments from the track, leaving an open space.
2. Mute track 1 and drag Jessica's close-up take to track 2. Use the same technique to carve out Dave's performance, leaving as much ambience at the head and tail of each of Jessica's lines.

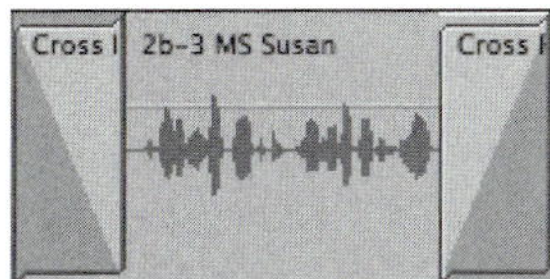

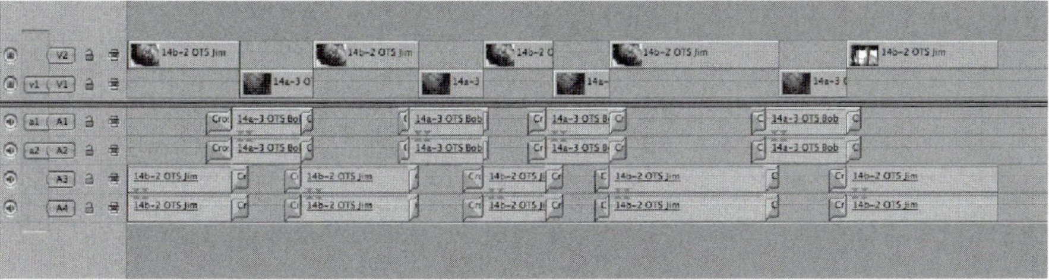

Editing dialog.

3. Keeping Dave's clips on track 1 and Jessica's on track 2, slide the clips together so the conversation sounds natural, even slightly overlapping the lines. Remember that people tend to talk over each other instead of waiting for the other person to finish speaking before responding. Mimic this pattern as you edit the dialog.
4. Create a cross-fade at the beginning and end of every clip. The cross-fade should start at the beginning of the clip and end just before the character begins speaking. At the end of the clip, begin the cross-fade at the very end of the last word to the end of the clip. The more of a pause the actors added between lines, the longer the cross-fade can be and the smoother the transition from one clip to another. As a note, make sure that cross-fades don't overlap each other, or you will hear a dip in the audio. Cross-fades should exist only under another clip.
5. By this point, the dialog in the scene should sound natural and the ambience should smoothly fade in and out while the other character is speaking.
6. Once the dialog has been edited and sounds natural, unlink the audio from its connected video clip. You can then change the in point and out point of the video without affecting the audio, enabling you to change when the video cuts from one shot to the next.
7. Now that the characters' close-ups have been edited, add insert shots or master shots to the third video track. Place each character's shots on one track, the master shots on another track, and insert shots on yet another track. This will make it much easier to make changes to the edit in the future.

EDITING TIPS

Some tips and tricks to keep in mind when you're editing:

- If you're the director of the movie, strongly consider bringing on an experienced, objective editor. No matter how good of an editor you think you

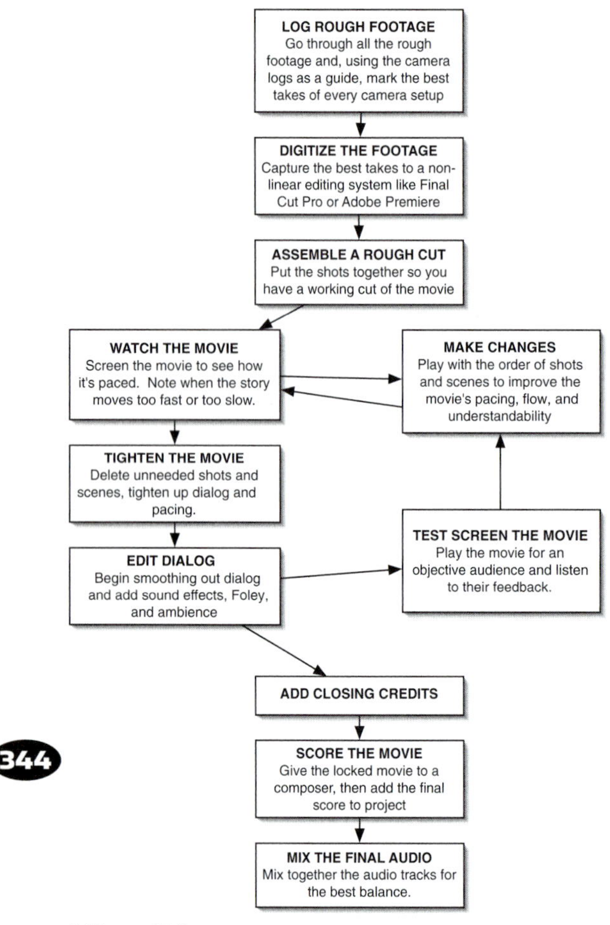

LOG ROUGH FOOTAGE
Go through all the rough footage and, using the camera logs as a guide, mark the best takes of every camera setup
DIGITIZE THE FOOTAGE
Capture the best takes to a non-linear editing system like Final Cut Pro or Adobe Premiere
ASSEMBLE A ROUGH CUT
Put the shots together so you have a working cut of the movie
WATCH THE MOVIE
Screen the movie to see how it's paced. Note when the story moves too fast or too slow.
MAKE CHANGES
Play with the order of shots and scenes to improve the movie's pacing, flow, and understandability
TIGHTEN THE MOVIE
Delete unneeded shots and scenes, tighten up dialog and pacing.
TEST SCREEN THE MOVIE
Play the movie for an objective audience and listen to their feedback.
EDIT DIALOG
Begin smoothing out dialog and add sound effects, Foley, and ambience
ADD CLOSING CREDITS
SCORE THE MOVIE
Give the locked movie to a composer, then add the final score to project
MIX THE FINAL AUDIO
Mix together the audio tracks for the best balance.

Editing guidelines.

are, NEVER cut your own film. You know it too well and will mentally fill in plot holes because you know the story so well.

- Make sure there is a clear reason for cutting from one shot to another, for example, a person enters the room or a character reacts to a particular line or action.
- If you're not sure about the exact frame to cut on, cut long rather than short.
- Ensure the edits smooth out the motion within the scene, giving the illusion that the scene occurred in real time and was covered by multiple cameras. This can be done by cutting on motion.
- Make sure that every shot you cut to is important to the story, remember that the audience is going to be looking for importance in any person or object you show on screen.
- Each scene should start and stop with continuing action to avoid a jerky "start–stop" sense while watching the movie.
- When faced with a continuity error, choose to edit for proper emotional continuity rather than physical continuity. Let the edits be driven by the content first, then technique.
- Keep establishing shots quick. Dwelling on them will serve only to slow down the story.
- Make sure that your edits are tight within a scene. Don't put pauses between lines of dialog. Try overlapping lines of dialog.
- Before fine-tuning the film, edit the entire movie in rough form and view it as soon as possible to see how the movie is paced.
- If a scene doesn't serve to push the story forward or is unimportant, then cut it out of the movie. Avoid falling in love with a shot so much that you're unwilling to cut it.
- When you finish editing your movie, put it away for a week or so and come back to it with a fresh eye before you make final tweaks.
- Once you have a strong rough cut, try watching the rough footage one more time to see if any unused takes may work better.
- Show the movie to an objective test audience and avoid being defensive. Rather, listen intently to their feedback and carefully weigh the validity of their suggestions.
- Remember that you can't make everyone in the audience happy.

Famed editor Walter Murch said it best when he described in his book, *In the Blink of an Eye*, in order of importance, the criteria used to determine an edit point.

1. **Emotion**—How does the edit make the audience feel in the moment?
2. **Story**—Does the edit drive the story forward?
3. **Rhythm**—Does the edit appear at a moment at which it feels it should appear?
4. **Eye trace**—Does the edit follow the audience's focus from one shot to another?
5. **Two-dimensional placement**—Does the edit respect and adhere to the 180 Rule?
6. **Three-dimensional space of action**—Does the edit respect the physical/special relationship between objects and characters in the scene?

ACTIVITIES

Activity 1: Using the footage on the accompanying disc, practice editing the stickball scene into a cohesive, logical sequence. Add your own music and sound effects. Try different edits of the scene, some longer, some shorter, and even try rearranging the order of the shots to see how it impacts and changes the feel of the scene.

Activity 2: Choose a scene from a Hollywood-produced movie and watch it frame by frame, studying why the editor cut from one shot to the next. Study where that edit was placed. Did it cut on motion? How did it help improve the pacing? Did the editor show more or less of the action than you would have? Why?

Activity 3: Produce a music video either using existing music or by shooting a band or single performer, then edit the music video together in a stylistic, creative way.

Activity 4: As a real-life exercise, when you find yourself talking in a group of three or more people, take note of who you're looking at and why you feel motivated to look at this person. What happens that makes you want to look away? Why do you hold your gaze?

If this moment were a scene you were editing, every time you shift your gaze should be an edit point between shots. Fluid editing should move the audience's attention from one shot to the next in the same way we would feel motivated to look at another person in a real-life conversation.

CONTINUITY

We have all seen movies in which two people are sitting on a couch talking to each other and in one shot, the guy's arm is on the back of the couch and in the other shot, his arm is across his lap. These errors, called "continuity errors," happen often on set and are embarrassing for the filmmaker. Continuity errors occur because scenes in a movie are shot out of order. For example, in a scene in which a man and a woman are having dinner, the first shot is a long master shot in which we see both the man and the woman and all the action of the scene.

The cast and crew will shoot the scene from the beginning to the end, multiple times, from this one camera angle until the director is happy with the shot. When they are finished, the actors leave the set and the crew repositions the camera for the man's close-up. The gaffer changes the lights, the set decorator redresses the part of the set that is visible in the new camera angle, and the production sound mixer repositions the microphone, just to name a few of the activities that occur between camera setups. Once the camera, lighting, audio, and set are ready, the actors return to the set and the director films the entire scene again, framing only the man in a close-up. After shooting several takes and making minor adjustments to the performance, the crew again moves the equipment, this time preparing for the woman's close-up. And the process begins again.

The editor must then take these three different camera angles and edit them together so that it appears as though they occurred once and that the moment was covered by multiple cameras. Continuity errors occur when the actors change their performance, either intentionally or by accident, or if crew members accidentally move a prop or a set piece.

346 The script supervisor, props and wardrobe crew, makeup artists, hairstylists, and set dressers take Polaroid photos of the set, hair, makeup, and wardrobe elements to ensure a consistent look from one shot to the next.

Avoiding continuity errors is the responsibility of the script supervisor, who notes the positions of people and objects and changes in dialog, camera coverage, or anything else that may not be continuous from one shot to the next. Even though the script supervisor is watching, there may still be a continuity error that he or she misses!

CUTTING ON MOTION

Imagine for a moment that you're filming a basketball game with 10 cameras positioned around the arena. Sitting behind a switching console, you are able to switch instantly to the camera with the best view of the action. Because the game happens in real time and occurs only once, your coverage of the game and choices of camera angles will be made in the moment, without much preplanning. The result is a kinetic, live feel that would be difficult to replicate, even with extensive rehearsals.

One of the reasons the action feels so real is that the edit point, the place where you would cut from one camera angle to another, usually falls in the middle of some action, a lay-up, a rebound, or a free throw. Even though you're cutting between 10 cameras, the editing isn't noticeable, because the action of the game ties all the camera angles together. For example, you may have a long shot of a player running up to the hoop and as he jumps up for a slam-dunk, you cut to a close-up of him in midair from under the net. His action of slam-dunking the ball bridges the two camera angles, making the cut almost invisible.

Unlike a basketball game, movies are shot with one camera. The point of editing is to cut together these multiple single-camera angles to create the same flow that you would have by shooting the scene with multiple cameras and switching live between them. This is the principle of cutting on motion: when editing two shots together, let the action in the scene bridge the edit point of the two shots. For example, if a character is sitting down in a chair and you want to cut from a medium shot to a close-up, cut from one shot to the next *as* the character is in the process of sitting down, *not* before she starts to sit down or after she already sat down. Cut on her motion of sitting. By cutting on motion, the flow of cutting from one camera angle to another will be much smoother.

MONTAGES

Montages are video collages. Using a variety of shots edited together with transitions, montages convey the passage of long periods of time by showing only the key moments of an event. For example, in a montage of an athlete preparing for a game, the montage may consist of the following shots:

- The athlete trains in the weight room and lifts only a little weight.
- The athlete runs through tires on the football field and collapses in fatigue.
- The athlete tries to catch a pass and misses.
- The athlete drinks a protein shake with friends.
- The athlete crashes at home on the couch after practice.
- The athlete gets yelled at by the coach.
- The athlete bench presses 185 lb quickly.
- The athlete tries to catch a pass and misses.
- The athlete practices alone on the field at night.
- The athlete does push-ups at home before bed.
- The athlete runs on the field.
- The athlete tries to catch a pass and catches it.

This montage, although consisting of only 12 shots, conveys the progression of the athlete in his attempt to win the big game. Montages can be powerful when the right images are used.

EDIT TYPES

There are a number of editing tricks used by professional editors to help stitch together unrelated shots into a smooth scene.

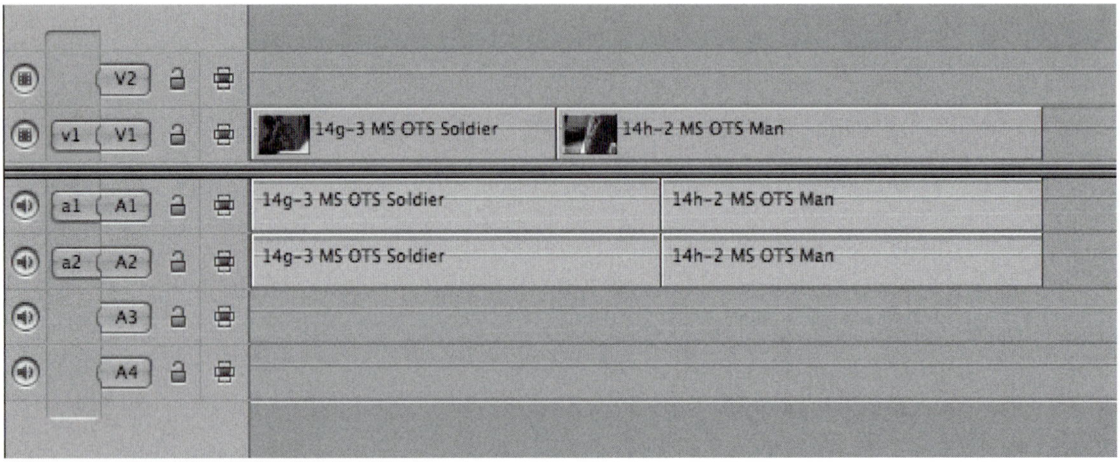

Example of an L-cut.

- **L-cut**—Also called a split edit, an L-cut is when the audio and visual cuts of two juxtaposed shots occur at different times. Used to help conceal the edit and improve the flow of a scene, L-cuts are primarily used in editing dialog.
- **B-roll**—B-roll is supporting footage inserted over the primary footage of a scene. In a documentary about a cookie company, the primary footage is an interview of a worker explaining the cookie-making process. While the interviewee is still speaking, the editor may insert B-roll shots of the actual manufacturing process. In a movie, B-rolls are also called cutaways or insert shots.

- **Jump cut**—A jump cut occurs when two shots of continuing action are edited together, but there is a discontinuity between the two shots. A jump cut is a jarring edit that draws attention to the discontinuity. Some jump cuts are intentionally used to add confusion to the scene.
- **Axial cut**—An axial cut occurs when the editor cuts from one shot to either a tighter or a wider shot from the same camera axis. Axial cuts can occur if the camera shoots a scene once from a short lens and then, without moving the camera, from a long lens, or if the camera physically moves toward or away from the subject without moving side to side.
- **Transitions**—Transitions are editing techniques used to segue from one shot to another.
- **Cross-cutting**—Cross-cutting involves cutting back and forth between two similar shots, for example, two medium, over-the-shoulder shots of a couple at a restaurant.
- **Cutaway**—A cutaway is a reaction shot that breaks away from the continuous action of a scene to show another person. Typically used to conceal an edit, the cutaway is a vital tool in covering continuity errors, improving pacing, and helping actors' performances.

- **Soft cut**—Whereas a hard cut places two shots back to back with no transition, a soft cut involves placing two shots together with a one- or two-frame dissolve.

USING TRANSITIONS

Transitions are ways of segueing from one shot to another. There are three basic types of transitions:

- **Cut**—The cut is the most common and simple transition, when the last shot ends and on the next frame, the next clip begins.

- **Dissolve**—A dissolve occurs when one clip fades out while the other clip simultaneously fades in. Dissolves imply a passage of time, especially when dissolving to an establishing shot or when used in a montage.

- **Wipe**—A wipe uses a shape pattern that moves across the screen to transition from one clip to another. One side of the wipe pattern is the first clip, and the other side is the second clip. Whereas wipes are fun and catchy to watch, they can be distracting to the viewer, drawing attention to the editing and away from the action on the screen. Wipes are commonly found in industrial videos, promotional and advertising spots, and wedding videos to transition from one picture to the next. Avoid using wipes in a narrative film.

Transitions.

COLOR CORRECTION

Shots in a movie may not match in brightness, contrast, or color, or they may not meet broadcast specifications. An editor can correct and alter the color and brightness values of individual shots to achieve an artistic look or for technical purposes.

- Always make sure there is a 0% black value (in PAL and digital formats; NTSC black value is 7.5%) and a 100% white value in every shot. Raising the black value lowers the contrast and washes out the image. Flat whites will look gray, but white values over 100% may flicker on a television screen.

- Use a waveform monitor to ensure the brightness values are within proper technical specifications. Use a vectorscope to monitor color balance and saturation.
- Correct the colors to match from one shot to the next in a scene. Often, changes in lighting, sun positioning, and cloud cover will affect the overall color palette of a scene, making it necessary to readjust the colors in each shot.
- Color correction can be used to simulate night time for scenes shot during the day, add a tint, soften the image, and enhance the colors in a scene or for any number of aesthetic techniques. In *Time and Again,* I warmed up the 1950s scenes with a light golden yellow tint and lightly softened the image.

TITLES AND GRAPHICS

When incorporating graphics and titles in a movie, there are a number of guidelines to follow to ensure the graphics appear as intended.

- **Safe action zone:** Most cathode-ray tube television sets and monitors display only 90% of the frame, with the other 10% projected off the edge of the screen. When framing a shot, be sure to keep all action within the 90% boundary of the frame.
- **Safe title zone:** Because 10% of the image is projected off the edge of the screen, any graphics and images are at risk of running into or off the screen edge. It's for this reason we use a second boundary marking 80% of the frame in which all graphics and text must be placed.
- **Lines thicker than three pixels:** In standard definition formats, horizontal lines thinner than three pixels will flicker on screen. Make sure all horizontal lines are at least three pixels thick.
- **Choose sans serif fonts:** In standard definition formats, serif fonts either flicker or lose their detail because of resolution limitations of the NTSC signal. When choosing fonts, select thicker sans serif fonts.
- **Color safe:** NTSC colors can bleed if they are oversaturated, especially reds and blues. Oversaturation is not a problem in high-definition formats.
- **Alpha channel:** When importing graphics to layer or composite into another video image, be sure to create the graphic with an alpha channel. This will make the background transparent so only the graphic appears.

The outer box represents the 90 percent safe action zone, and the inner, 80 percent box represents the safe title zone. Make sure all photos, text, and graphics appear within the safe title zone.

COMPRESSION

Imagine that you just moved to a new town, but you don't have a car yet. One day, you get a taste for orange juice, so you take your bicycle to the local grocery store and pick up a gallon of delicious, freshly squeezed, pulpy juice. As you stand in the checkout line, you realize that you have no way of transporting a gallon of juice home—your bicycle isn't big enough. So you return the gallon of OJ in favor of a small can of orange juice concentrate. This juice was filtered and processed at a factory so it could be compressed into a small container, where it also lost flavor and vitamin-rich pulp. You pay, stick the concentrate in your jacket pocket, and head home, where you add water to restore the concentrate back to a gallon. Although you still end up with a gallon of orange juice, the concentrate has been filtered and reduced in quality to make it more transportable.

Digital video works the same way. In its raw form, video is beautiful, full of detail, with bright, vivid colors. Unfortunately, uncompressed standard definition video is around 30 MB per second, and high definition is closer to 300 MB per second. The cost of managing such a high data rate would drive up the cost of camcorders, computers would need to be faster with better data throughput, and drive-space requirements would increase significantly. Because of the impracticality of transporting raw video, engineers developed a way of compressing the video and reducing the file size by averaging some of the detail and color information. This is done by special algorithms called "codecs" (codec stands for "compressor/decompressor").

Much like the process the factory used to compress orange juice, codecs serve to compress digital audio and video for any number of applications, and there are several of them. A few examples of codecs include:

- **MPEG-2:** The standard codec used in DVD players. Designed for high-quality NTSC and PAL video, this compressor is vastly superior to preceding analog, VHS formats.
- **Sorenson, H-264, and Flash:** These are all different codes used for compressing video for the Internet. Specially designed to maintain high quality and low file sizes, these codecs are ideal for downloadable and streaming videos.
- **DV-NTSC and DV-PAL:** The revolutionary standard-definition, digital video codec used in popular standard-definition consumer and prosumer DV formats.
- **HDV:** The new, ultracompressed high-definition consumer format. Recorded to tape, this codec uses extremely high compression resulting in motion artifacts and degradation in dark regions of the frame.
- **HDCAM and DVCPRO:** These are both professional, high-quality high-definition codecs.

When choosing the right codec for your project, be sure to research the pros and cons of each codec thoroughly.

CREDITS

Credits appear at the beginning and end of a movie and list all the people who worked on or contributed to the film. A cast or crew member's credit is the most important form of acknowledgment you can give.

The opening credits are reserved for the key cast and crew members as well as the production companies responsible for the film financing. The closing credits list all cast and crew positions, vendors, and those people the producers wish to thank.

- Make sure you include everyone in the credits. One good way of ensuring this is by going through the release forms. Extras are generally not listed in the credits unless they have been featured in some way on screen.
- Double-check the spelling of each person's name.
- Have fun with the look and design of the opening credits of the movie. Use font, size, animation, and color to set the tone for the story.
- Use Helvetica 8- to 10-point font for the closing credits. This is the optimum size for reading and speed.
- When you design the closing credits, type the credits in a page layout program like QuarkXpress or Adobe InDesign using a dual column format. Export the text as a postscript file and import it into Adobe After Effects. You can manipulate the credits just like a graphic and set them to scroll up the screen vertically at whatever speed you want. The results are professional and easy-to-read credits.

1ST ASSISTANT DIRECTOR KAILYNE WATERS
1ST ASSISTANT CAMERA RON FRANCISANGELO
2ND ASSISTANT CAMERA PAUL JANSSEN
GAFFER MARA EVANS
GRIPS JOHN P. LEEDER
HALLIE SHECK
DAVID KARGES
TECIA ESPOSITO
MATT HERZFIELD
TOM CLACK
SCOTT LEE
BILL IAMMARINO
KELLEN DARGLE
MATT FULLER
MARY ZALLER
DEIDRE LOOSZI
TROY THOMAS
DOLLY GRIP ADAM KADAR
ELECTRIC NATE SWIFT
JORDAN HALL
GT SANKOVICH
SKIP KELLEY

CHAPTER 20
Digital Effects

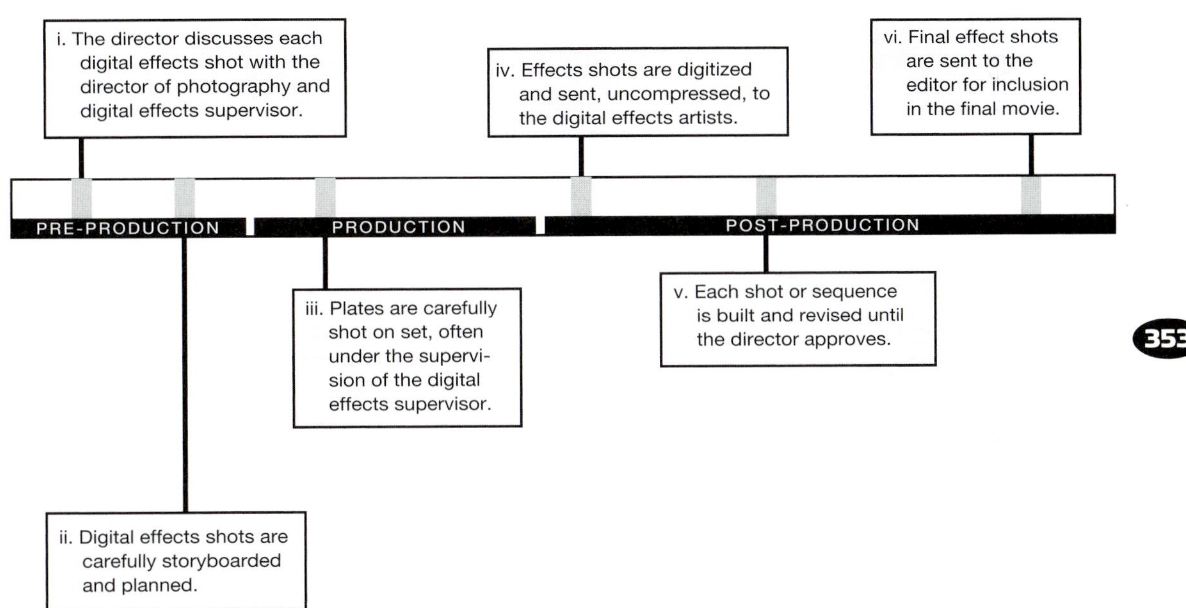

i. The director discusses each digital effects shot with the director of photography and digital effects supervisor.
iv. Effects shots are digitized and sent, uncompressed, to the digital effects artists.
vi. Final effect shots are sent to the editor for inclusion in the final movie.
PRE-PRODUCTION
PRODUCTION
POST-PRODUCTION
iii. Plates are carefully shot on set, often under the supervision of the digital effects supervisor.
v. Each shot or sequence is built and revised until the director approves.
ii. Digital effects shots are carefully storyboarded and planned.

INTRODUCTION

Whereas special effects are physical effects that occur on set, such as pyrotechnics, weather effects, miniatures, and forced-perspective sets, digital effects are created solely within the realm of the computer. Footage is either digitized and manipulated using sophisticated programs or created from scratch with every element being built within the modeling and animation software.

Digital effects can be organized into two basic categories: 2D compositing and 3D animation. Two-dimensional compositing is the process of using flat, or two-dimensional images, photographs, animation, film, or video clips and layering them into existing footage. Although the content of these images has depth, the images themselves are flat. Three-dimensional animation involves modeling,

The crew prepares to shoot an insert shot of Bobby Jones in the field when he sees Awanda. I realized we needed the shot well into the editing process, but with three feet of snow on the ground, our only option was to create the shot digitally. A local news station gave us permission to use their green screen.

applying textures, and lighting and animating a three-dimensional object in the computer so that it can be viewed from any angle creating, in most instances, a life-like, photo-realistic image.

Incorporating digital effects into your movie can yield spectacular results if the process is well organized. However, hasty shooting and adopting a "fix-it-in-post" attitude will cost both time and money.

- Before going into production, break down the script to determine how many and what types of visual effects are required. Which of these effects can be done mechanically or physically on set, which need to be second unit effects (i.e., miniatures, special set pieces, stunts, or pyrotechnics), and which need to be digitally rendered?
- To find a digital effects artist, contact your local film commission and ask for leads. There are also numerous production and postproduction facilities that have computer animation departments that may be able to help you. Other excellent resources are college and university art programs, many of which have a visual media department with computer animation classes. Students interested in breaking into the animation industry may be willing to create free effects for your film as a way of expanding their demo reel.
- Digital effects, when done well, are convincing and impressive, but if they are not executed properly or care is not taken to make them realistic, they will cheapen the quality of the production, drawing the audience's attention away from the story and to the bad effects work. Be sure to work closely with the digital effects artist during preproduction to plan the execution of each shot. If necessary, the digital effects artist should be present on set to make sure the lighting, camera angles, and framing are correct to ensure proper integration of the effects.
- Make sure you have the means to produce convincing digital effects. If at all possible, shoot both a scene with the visual effect plate (the shot that is the background for the composite) and a shot that could work without the digital effect. That way, if you run out of time or money or run into a technical issue, you have a backup option.
- Most importantly, make sure the story is strong enough to stand on its own and is not dependent on digital effects to carry it. Digital effects are often used as a crutch in films with weak stories.

COMPOSITING

Compositing is the process of digitally layering multiple flat images or video clips together to create the final shot. This handy technique can be used to replace the sky, add an image to a blank TV screen, place a map behind a

> **DEFINITIONS**
>
> **Visual effects** are created when animation, matte shots, composited elements, and computer-generated elements are added to live-action footage.
>
> **Physical effects** are those effects that are built and exist in reality, as opposed to computer-generated effects. Examples include models and miniatures, special makeup prosthetics, creatures and monsters, specialty vehicles (like the Batmobile), on-set tricks and gags, and special props.
>
> **Mechanical effects** include weather-related effects like rain, snow, wind, and hail, as well as pyrotechnics such as explosions, bullet hits, and car crashes.
>
> **Digital effects** include those effects created within the realm of the computer such as computer-generated monsters, environments, vehicles, and spaceships.

weatherman, or add any layer or source over another. Popular programs such as Adobe After Effects and Apple Motion are excellent tools for creating stunning visual effects.

The crew prepares the bike for a green screen shot. You can see the final shot in *Time and Again* when Bobby is riding on the handle bars in the long shot.

In *Time and Again*, the majority of the digital effects were composites. As an example, in the opening of the diner scene, the script described Awanda cooking and setting her food on fire. Because it wasn't practical or safe to use real fire on set, we shot Jennie's performance behind the stove first without fire. Called a "background plate," this shot was used as the foundation for the composite. To create the fire, I found some stock footage of a torch flame against a black background. Using Adobe After Effects, I was able to cut the torch flame out from the black background digitally and lay it over the background plate of Awanda in the kitchen. I then created a mask to crop off the top and bottom of the flame so it looked like it was behind the counter. The result is a realistic shot that tells the story and was safe to produce.

Composites can be used to add buildings to backgrounds, replace the sky, add images onto television screens, extend the set, mask elements out of the frame, and integrate any number of images and video into the shot. Compositing is a very powerful technique that adds production value to a movie.

- Compositing programs such as Adobe After Effects, Apple Motion, and Apple Shake are powerful, professional-grade applications that provide a tremendous array of compositing tools for the filmmaker. Although the learning curve on these programs is steep, there are a number of training

This frame is what we originally shot on set. This layer, called the background plate, will serve as the foundation for the composite. We will have to add the fire into this shot.

This frame is a stock video of a torch flame that will be added to the background plate. Compositing software like Adobe After Effects or Shake allows you to remove the background, especially if there's a large difference in color or brightness between the object and the background. In this case, the black background was easy to knock out.

This is the final composite of the two elements. Notice how the top and bottom of the flame have been cut off to give the illusion that the flame is behind the counter. We also cut out, or rotoscoped, the waitress so she appears to walk in front of the flame.

classes in major cities across the country. Even if you are working with a digital effects artist, understanding how the software works will help you better prepare for the integration of digital effects in your movie.

- Part of creating realistic and effective digital effects is to shoot high-quality footage. Make sure that the footage is properly lit and in focus and that all camera movements are smooth.
- Remember that compositing images and animation over locked down (nonmoving) shots is a lot easier than tracking, or following the camera motion to match the movement of the images to the movement of the camera. It may be faster to create 10 composites with a locked-down

camera than one shot with a moving camera, especially if you are on a tight budget.

- Effective preplanning and storyboarding can make for a smooth compositing process. All too often, beginning filmmakers shoot footage without worrying about how to add the digital effects, making it difficult for the animator to complete his job effectively. Work with the compositor or animator BEFORE shooting the footage and, if necessary, involve him on set to ensure that the footage you shoot can be used.

CHROMA KEY

Chroma key is a compositing technique that allows the animator to digitally replace a solid color (usually blue or green) background behind the actor or object with another image or film clip. Called "keying," chroma key is a great tool for placing the actor in environments that are impossible to create in real life. For example, in Star Trek, the windows of all the spaceship sets have green screens outside them that are replaced with a moving star field. Weathermen use the same technology; in real life they are standing in front of a green screen, but the chroma key system replaces the green with the weather map.

We used the chroma key technique in *Time and Again* to simulate Bobby riding on the handlebars of Awanda's bike. Because it was too difficult for the actress Jennie Allen to peddle with Brian on the bike, we brought the bike into a local news station (for free, of course) and set it up in front of their green screen in the weather department. Even though the bike was stationary, Brian and Jennie acted like they were actually peddling. We then digitally removed the green background and replaced it with a still photo of the dirt road using Adobe After Effects. Additional touches like lens flares from the sun, a little camera movement, and some color correction made a convincing shot that would have been impossible to do on set.

Here are some tips for shooting against a green screen:

- Choose either a green- or a blue-painted background. It will be easier to isolate and key because they are the opposite of human flesh tones. Make sure there are no traces of blue or green in the actors' wardrobe or the software will render these colors invisible to the background.

This is the original shot (left), with Brian standing in front of a green screen. We made sure to light him so the look of the studio footage matched the material we shot on location.

We replaced the green background with an image of the weeds next to the dirt road (right). By blurring out the background, and color correcting the shot, we were able to match it to the footage we shot on location.

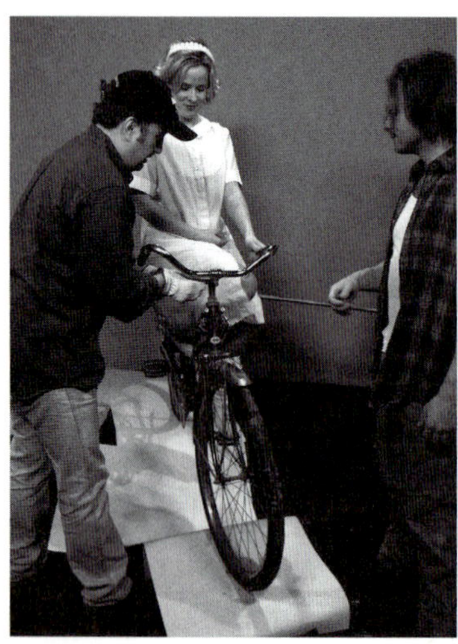

Prepping the bike and Awanda for the digital effects shot.

We shot Brian and Jennie riding the bike (which was stationary on set) and then composited the background plate of a dirt road. It would have been impossible for Jennie to peddle the bike with Brian on the handlebars.

- When lighting a green screen, it's critical to light the entire screen evenly. Avoid shadows of any kind. The more evenly lit, the better the key will be.
- If you need to paint a wall chroma-key green, use Rosco ChromaKey Paint, available from MarkerTek. The paint contains reflective particles that makes it easier for a compositing system to isolate and key out that particular color. If buying chroma-key paint is out of your budget, I find that neon green poster board works just as well, especially for close shots of actors.
- When shooting subjects or objects against a green screen, try to shoot in a video format with the least compression. Avoid miniDV and HDV codecs and consider shooting Digital Betacam, HD, or even Panasonic's

DIRECTOR'S NOTES

I created several digital effects in *Time and Again* to help cut production costs, by creating landscapes and set dressing and even by adding digital 1950s cars in the background. All the effects were free because I was able to use my limited experience in Adobe After Effects to create them on the Mac system at home.

Fire in the diner kitchen—I added the flame burning behind the counter in the diner digitally because using real pyrotechnics on set was too dangerous and would have cost too much money. In creating the digital fire, I masked off stock footage of a torch flame, so it appeared to be behind the counter, and even masked the waitress who walked in front of the flame, so it appears to be behind her. This effect took only a few hours to create.

Digital mailbox—As Bobby Jones rides his bike home, he passes a mailbox with his parents' names on it. Because we didn't have enough money to buy a real mailbox and create a sign, I decided to add it digitally. When it came time to create the mailbox, I simply walked up and down my street until I found a mailbox I liked. I took a few pictures with my digital camera, imported the pictures, and digitally cut the mailbox out from the background using Photoshop. I then created the sign with his parents' names and imported the final still image into After Effects. I then needed to add the image to a moving dolly shot, so I hand-tracked the image so that it matched the camera movement. Finally, I added a digital focus pull and color corrected the shot.

The town square—I really wanted a vast, sweeping shot of the 1950s town as Bobby left the diner, realizing his whereabouts for the first time. Because it wasn't possible to secure enough cars and shut down the town square for one shot, I created the entire shot digitally. I took my DV camcorder to the top of one of the buildings in town and rolled off a few minutes of footage. Then, using After Effects and Photoshop, I digitally painted masks to cover all the cars, while still retaining the movement of trees and flags. I then scoured the Internet for pictures of 1950s vehicles that matched the same lighting and angle as in my shot. After cutting them out from their background, I used After Effects to place them on the now-empty street and animated them moving down the road. After a final pass of color correction and softening of the entire image, it seamlessly matched the surrounding shots and convincingly showed off the town.

Digital picture frame—When Bobby Jones sneaks into his bedroom, he sees a picture frame sitting on the shelf. The photo was digitally added. The photo we needed to have in the frame wasn't ready at the time of the shoot, so I used After Effects to track the camera movement and insert the photo into the frame, complete with a reflection in the glass.

HDDVCPRO codec. Highly compressed footage is difficult to work with as the compression averages pixels together, resulting in large, blocky edges around objects.

- For the highest quality key, digitize the video footage into the editing system uncompressed.

THREE-DIMENSIONAL ANIMATION

Three-dimensional animation is the art of creating objects, setting lights, and moving a camera all within the virtual world of the computer. Programs like Maya, LightWave, and 3D Studio Max afford users the ability to create digital models of people, objects, and settings; stretch digitally created skins over the wire-frame models; add texture and interactivity with light; calculate the physics of how the objects move and interact within the environment; place lights; add cameras with real interactive lens functions; and render the final image to create realistic imagery.

Most Hollywood films use computer-generated imagery (CGI) in place of traditional hand-built models or old school tricks like matte paintings, forced-perspective models, and physical and mechanical effects. CGI is often cheaper and offers filmmakers limitless options in creating and manipulating the environment of the story.

In the low-budget arena, inexpensive software and a well-equipped computer can provide a myriad of options never before available to filmmakers. If the tools are available, high-quality effects can be produced inexpensively, although it still requires a lot of time to finesse and complete each effect until they appear real and can be smoothly integrated into the rest of the movie.

3D animation, like the shuttlecraft from my feature film, *Clone* are impressive, but very costly and time-consuming to produce.

CHAPTER 21
Postproduction Audio

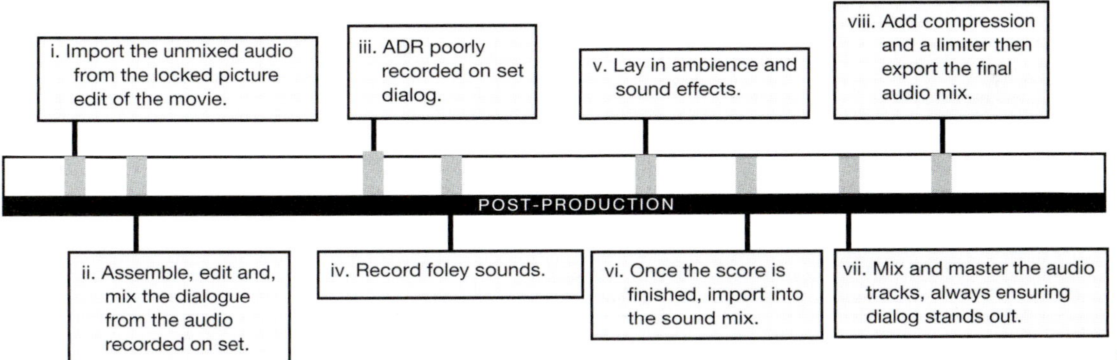

i. Import the unmixed audio from the locked picture edit of the movie.
ii. Assemble, edit and, mix the dialogue from the audio recorded on set.
iii. ADR poorly recorded on set dialog.
iv. Record foley sounds.
v. Lay in ambience and sound effects.
vi. Once the score is finished, import into the sound mix.
vii. Mix and master the audio tracks, always ensuring dialog stands out.
viii. Add compression and a limiter then export the final audio mix.
POST-PRODUCTION

INTRODUCTION

Once the visuals of a movie are edited, it's time to focus on editing the audio. Audio postproduction work includes rerecording dialog, mixing in music and sound effects, balancing the levels of each sound element, and making sure the audio is within the proper technical parameters for exhibition.

Considered even more important to the audience in making an emotional impact than the visuals, people can detect far more sound cues than visual images, making the sound design a very important, but often overlooked, aspect of the moviemaking process. Sound design, ambience, and music bring together the continuity of the movie by turning a series of choppy cuts into a fluid narrative. Creating the sound is a very creative job and good sound designers can bring the quality of a movie up to extraordinary new levels.

Before beginning work on the audio, be sure that you are completely finished editing the picture. Timing between shots should be locked, digital effects added, titles and transitions added, and the entire visual aspect of the movie finished. Locking the picture is important so the audio engineers know what sounds need to be created and mixed into the soundtrack. Reediting the visuals of a movie will throw all the audio files out of sync and require additional work to realign large portions of the movie.

Mike Farona works on the audio of "Time and Again" at the Neon Cactus Studios.

THE FIVE AUDIO TRACKS

Audio in a movie can be broken up into five different categories: the dialog, Foley, ambience, sound effects, and music.

Track 1—the dialog track

When recording audio on set, record the dialog with as little ambient sound as possible. This is especially important when producing a film that will be distributed internationally because the dialog track is often laid onto the master tape separately from the music and sound effects. This allows distributors in each foreign country to remove the English dialog track and record a new, translated track in the native language of the audience. The cleaner the dialog track, the easier it is to work with.

ADR

If the dialog is poorly recorded on set, it is possible to use a technique called ADR (automated dialog replacement) to rerecord an actor's dialog in a studio setting. To ADR a scene, an actor enters a sound booth, watches a monitor with the final cut of the movie rolling, and listens to the original recording from the set on a pair of headphones. The audio engineer will then cue up and repeatedly play each line that needs to be rerecorded one sentence at a time. The actor then recites the dialog to match the timing and emotional delivery of the original. Once the first line is recorded, is in sync, and is properly performed, the actor can then move on to the next line until the problematic dialog has been replaced. Once this process is finished, the audio engineer must EQ (equalize), or change the tone of the recording and add reverb to match the tone of the room in which the scene takes place. This process yields excellent audio quality, but is very time consuming and expensive and sometimes still doesn't match the original audio recorded on location.

- If you need to ADR problematic lines, be sure to ADR the entire scene. It is very difficult, even with the best software, to match the tone of dialog recorded in the studio with location audio.
- ADR is a very expensive and time-consuming process. For low-budget projects, it's smarter to choose locations where the sound can be controlled to avoid the ADR process. Even though the director may have to compromise his creative vision, at least the film won't go over budget due to unforeseen sound problems.
- ADR is a very tricky process and should be done in a professional sound studio with professional microphones. Avoid attempting ADR at home with a home editing system and a cheap microphone because much of

DIRECTOR'S NOTES

When we recorded the sound for *Time and Again*, we took great pains to make sure that dialog was cleanly recorded on set, making the audio postproduction process a breeze. The bedroom scene in Awanda's trailer was a notable exception. When we shot Awanda's angle, the set was quiet and we captured her sound flawlessly. When it got time to shoot Bobby's angle, the skies opened up and we recorded every bit of a typical Midwest thunderstorm over his lines.

Because I didn't have the money or the time to ADR the scene in postproduction, we took the sound of the rain falling on the roof that we recorded wild on set and laid it under Awanda's lines, making a continuous ambience throughout the scene. I then took the scene to Mike Farona at Neon Cactus Studios and, using sophisticated noise-reduction software, was able to practically eliminate the sound of the storm in the background. If you listen closely to the scene, you'll notice the actor's dialog is a little thin because the software had to remove a pretty wide range of sound frequencies to eliminate the thunderstorm.

Even though we ran into some problems, the available technology helped me fix a scene that could have been ruined.

the prosumer software doesn't allow the level of finessing required to match ADR'd dialog properly into a scene.

- Be aware that some actors are better at ADR than others. I found that actors who are musically inclined, especially drummers, are better able to match sync than those without a musical background. Less experienced actors can be more expensive because most audio studios charge by the hour.
- Remember that if you need to ADR a scene, you are replacing the original audio with studio-recorded audio. As a result, sound effects, footsteps, clothes rubbing, the handling of objects in a scene, and ambience, all need to be re-created and laid under the new dialog, adding to the postproduction budget.

We used the sound booth to record ADR and voice-overs for *Time and Again.*

Track 2—the foley track

Foley is the sounds of an actor interacting with his environment and includes footsteps, clothing rustling, doors opening and closing, and the handling of props. Often these very quiet sounds are virtually unnoticeable by the audience, but are critical in creating a realistic environment for the characters.

Scenes that use the audio recorded on set can benefit from Foley to sweeten sounds the microphone may not have picked up. Adding Foley sounds can help punctuate critical moments and can be easily done in the editing process.

Foley is especially critical when a scene is ADR'd. Remember that ADR is intended to replace audio that was recorded on the set, so in addition to the dialog, all the Foley sounds must be rerecorded and mixed as well.

Foley is usually recorded at special audio studios where the Foley artists watch the movie on a screen and use objects made of various materials, sizes, and shapes to record the sounds needed in the scene. Each sound is usually recorded separately and is then synced and mixed into the movie.

Foley sounds can be divided into several categories.

MOVES TRACK

Moves is the sound of an actor's clothing moving, rustling, and rubbing against other clothing and objects. It is virtually inaudible but critical in making the audio sound realistic. Foley artists use fabrics and materials similar to those of the actor's wardrobe and move with the actors on screen, recording the resulting sounds and mixing them into the movie.

FOOT TRACK

The foot track covers all the footsteps in the movie. Often, when dialog is rerecorded in ADR, it's necessary to add the sound of footsteps back in, matching the timing and pacing of each step. The Foley artist uses shoes similar to what the actor wore on a small square of floor that matches the make of the actual floor and mimics the movement, steps, and slides of the actor's shoes. She then mixes the foot track into the movie.

To record the foot track properly, try visiting a used clothing store and picking out pairs of shoes that match the shoes worn by the actors in the movie. Then, go to a flooring store and pick up a collection of wood, tile, marble, and stone floor samples that match the type of floor in each scene. It's also a good idea to have gravel, sand, grass, and concrete as well, if the scene calls for it. Position the mike two to three feet away from the floor sample, kneel on the floor with a shoe in each hand, and watch the movement of the actors. Try to hit the floor sample with the same rhythm and strength as the actors. Add reverb and EQ to the foot track and mix it into the scene.

SPECIFICS

Specifics are everything else beyond footsteps and clothing movement. Remember that you don't need to use the same object that appears on screen to create the sound. Part of the fun of creating the specifics track is creatively finding objects to mimic a similar sound.

Examples of the specifics track include the following:

Sound	How the sound is created
Bicycle riding over dirt road	Rustle hand in a thick paper bag of cat food
Horses galloping	Clap two coconut shells together
Bones breaking	Snap and twist celery stalks
Crackling fire	Twisting cellophane
Walking in leaves	Crushing egg shells
Bird's flapping wings	Pair of leather work gloves

Be organized before recording the specifics track. Make a list of the specific sounds needed for each scene, then gather the necessary objects you need to create the sound and record each sound effect separately so you can tweak them and mix them together later.

Track 3—the ambience track

Ambience is the sound of the environment. It's the sounds of waves, seagulls, and wind if you're on the beach; it's the sounds of car horns, people talking, brakes screeching, jackhammers, and radios playing if you're in New York City; and the sounds of copiers, phones ringing, background chatter, and music if you're in an office building. These ambience tracks add the final touch of realism to a scene and can be recorded on set, added using prerecorded sounds, or recorded anywhere after the fact in a similar location and laid down over the entire scene.

ROOM TONE

Ambience also includes *room tone*. Room tone is the background noise of the set you're shooting on. Even though it may sound very quiet, there are still signals being picked up from the microphone, whether they are sounds of the environment or simply the sound of the equipment operating. You can hear the difference the room tone makes by listening to a quiet clip both with and

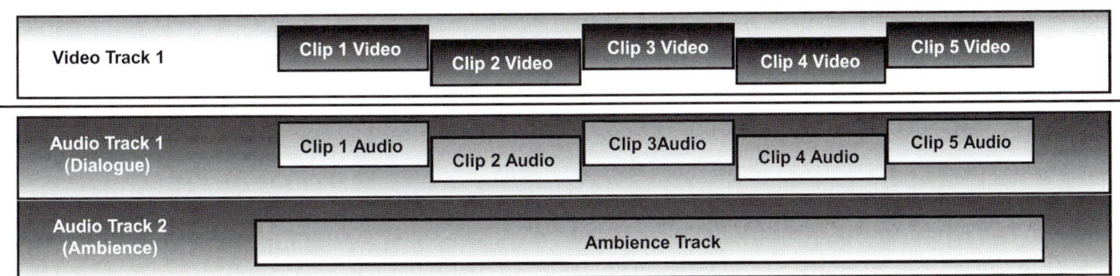

Add the ambience track under the entire scene to help cover the cuts between clips.

without the audio. Room tone is used to help bridge gaps between lines of dialog, in insert shots for which sound wasn't recorded, or to cover or conceal unwanted sounds.

One common way to record the ambience of a location is to record a few minutes on set. At the end of the shooting day, before you wrap production, ask everyone to stand still for a few minutes while the audio engineer records the ambience, or room tone, for at least a minute.

It may be necessary to edit the scene together and add room tone under some lines of dialog when there isn't any. Remember that the audience is more likely to notice a *change* in the ambience from shot to shot more so than they'll notice a consistent ambience track. Part of having room tone is so that it can be added to quieter shots for consistency. Once the room tone sounds consistent, then you can add the overall ambience such as people talking in the background of a restaurant or elevator music over the speaker in a store.

- When audio is recorded on set during a scene, the objective is to record only dialogue . . . the ambience is put in afterward. Because the ambience track is several minutes long, it will add cohesiveness to the scene, pulling the edit together.
- The objective is to mix the dialog and sounds of the actors interacting with the environment all by itself on set. The native sounds of the environment are added in the editing room, where more control can be exerted over these sounds.

SOUNDS OF THE LOCATION

After the dialog is properly mixed with the room tone and the background sounds consistent, it's time to add the actual ambience track to the scene. Most ambience tracks can be pulled from sound effects CDs or even recorded on a similar location. If I'm shooting in an office, I may visit an actual office and record the ambience of the environment for a few minutes and then take that recording and lay it under the entire scene. Or if I shot in a closed-down grocery store, I may visit a grocery store later and record several minutes of the ambience to add under the entire scene.

Ambience is a great way to add production value to your movie. In the instance of sci-fi movies, the sounds of a spaceship can make the cheapest cardboard sets seem much more realistic to the viewer. Let the sound complement the visuals.

Another type of ambience is called *walla*. Walla is the indistinguishable murmuring of people in the background of a scene, for example, other patrons in a restaurant. Designed to blend into the background, a good walla track is recorded in such a way that a listener cannot pick out any one conversation, allowing the principal actor's dialog to be heard clearly.

High-quality sound effects libraries have several walla tracks, or if you're on a budget, you can record your own walla track with friends or in an actual environment that matches the sound of your scene.

Track 4—the sound effects track

Programs like Pro Tools and Digital Performer offer a wide range of tools to help you deliver the best possible audio.

Sound effects are non-Foley sounds such as explosions, gunfire, car crashes, and monster noises. These can be collected from sound effects CDs, downloaded from the Internet, or created and recorded in the studio. Sound effects help to establish key events in the film and establish the environment.

Be wary of cheap sound effects CDs from record stores or the Internet. They are often poorly recorded and contain a lot of background noise, which will make it difficult to edit in postproduction. The cleaner the recording, the better the mix.

Sounds effects can be sweetened or enhanced using software plug-ins in popular editing programs. Reverb, EQ, pitch shifting, speeding up or slowing down, noise reduction, and compressing are all examples of filters that can be used to help integrate a sound effect into the soundtrack. Pro Tools is one of the most common audio-editing programs available, although editing programs like Final Cut Pro and Adobe Premiere offer comparable plug-ins with slightly less control and speed.

Track 5—the music track

The music is the composed orchestral score in the movie. For more information on composing music, go to the "Music" chapter.

MIXING THE AUDIO

When you are working in an editing program, I suggest creating a different time line to create a premix of each sound category. For example, one time line will contain only the dialog; the second is for Foley, the third for ambience, the fourth for sound effects, and the fifth for the music. This will not only help keep the potentially thousands of audio clips organized by category, but also help when it comes time to mix down the final audio. Using this process may even speed up your computer because large numbers of audio and video clips in a single project can slow down the system.

Audio mixing board.

When you are finished editing and mixing each sound category, open a new time line and import the mixed-down stereo dialog, Foley, ambience, sounds effects, and music tracks. You can then easily mix the tracks together to achieve the proper balance between them, all while making sure the audio never hits 0 db.

1. When you are mixing the five tracks, dialog must ALWAYS be the predominate and loudest of all the tracks. Even in the loudest battle scene in which music and sound effects drive the action, the dialog must always rise above the music and effects so the audience doesn't have to strain to hear what the characters are saying.
2. When mixing the dialog track, make sure that all the dialog, from shouting to whispering, falls between −6 and −3 db. Even though this doesn't match how the spoken word sounds in real life, movie dialog is roughly the same volume throughout so that the audience doesn't have to constantly ride the volume with the remote control in hand.
3. Play the movie while watching the VU meters. Every time the audio clips, or hits 0 db, use the rubber-band tool to isolate the part of the audio that peaks, and reduce the volume so it doesn't peak. You should be able to play through the entire movie and never hit 0 db.
4. Try applying a light compressor to the entire dialog track to bring up the quiet spots and crush the loud spots, making the dialog much more even. In addition, a limiter prevents the audio from hitting 0 db by bouncing the peaking audio away from 0 db, much like a giant spring. The harder the audio approaches 0 db, the harder it's pushed back down. Although a slight limiter is useful, heavily limiting peaking dialog causes distortion.
5. Once the dialog is ready, it's now time to choose which of the four remaining audio tracks will be brought into the mix. A common mistake that many novice filmmakers make is to muddy the soundtrack by bringing up the music, sound effects, ambience, and Foley so loud that they become indistinguishable. Unlike real life, in which we hear hundreds of different sounds all around us, movie audio is much more sparse and the audio that is put into the film strategically focuses the audience on what they should be watching in the frame. For example, let's say we have a scene on a busy New York city street where a woman is struck by a car and our hero rushes up to save her. Before she is struck, we hear the ambience of New York City, with the sounds of the cars passing by. We don't need to hear the Foley of her walking, or any substantial sound effects, so at this moment, the ambience is brought up. As she crosses the street, a single car horn blasts out at her. This horn must stand out from the rest of the ambience because it is coming from the car that will soon hit her, so we would bring up the sound effect of the horn over the ambience in the mix. Once the woman is struck by the car and our hero runs to her aid, we bring the ambience down to make room in the mix for our hero's dialog as he tries to save her and the music score that's fading in. At this point, we don't need the ambience of the city street. It's already been established and this moment in the scene is about our hero and the woman, not the surrounding traffic.

Mixing the sound effects, ambience, Foley, and music is like a dance. In any given moment, two tracks step forward while the other two are mixed down so they don't all compete with one another. Balancing the ever-strong dialog track, this approach to mixing yields clean, easy-to-listen-to audio that will not distract the audience, but draw it into the moment on the screen.

Once all the tracks are edited, add light compression and a limiter to the entire soundtrack and be sure to listen to the audio on different speakers to make sure that the mix is clear and clean.

Mix the audio in a properly designed sound studio. The acoustics are specifically designed so you can hear the broadest range of frequencies in as quiet a space as possible.

- Audio in a movie can be categorized into dialog, sound effects, Foley, ambience, and music. Be careful not to mix them too loudly, but in each scene, choose which of the five should take priority and make sure it stands above the other four. Dialog should ALWAYS stand above sound design or music.
- Make sure none of the audio elements exceed 0 db or the audio will peak and distort. Be careful when mixing your sound so you leave enough headroom for the louder scenes. The dialog, though, should be of the same volume during the entire movie so the audience doesn't have to strain to hear lines during quiet moments.
- If you're mixing the audio tracks together, be sure to listen to the mix through different speakers. Remember that some people will listen to your movie on an expensive home theater system, and others will listen on a small mono speaker 1970s fake wood-sided television with knobs to change channels. The audio needs to sound good on every system. When I produced *Time and Again*, I edited most of the movie on my Apple Final Cut Pro system and then took the final mix to a nearby audio studio to clean up several scenes. We listened to the mix on both $100,000 speakers and a pair of $20 speakers from the local electronics store. When the mix sounded good on each set of speakers, I knew we had found the correct balance.

M&E TRACKS

When a foreign distributor picks up a movie, they often require a DigiBeta or HD master tape with four tracks. Tracks 1 and 2 contain the stereo final mix of the movie audio, and tracks 3 and 4 contain a stereo mix of the music and effects, or M&E tracks.

M&E tracks are a complete mix of the movie audio minus the dialog, so that foreign countries can dub in the dialog in their native language. Keeping the various audio tracks separate makes it easy to generate an M&E track for distributors.

If you're planning on submitting your movie for distribution, be sure to keep the tracks separate during audio postproduction. If you don't, the distributor will require separate tracks and you will have to go back into the studio to remix the audio, racking up a bill for thousands of dollars in the process.

DIRECTOR'S NOTES

I had approached Mike Farona at the Neon Cactus Studios almost three years earlier for another film I had directed called *Clone*. We met at a party one night in Cleveland and began talking about my business as a filmmaker and Mike's business as a recording engineer of bands and live events. As we were both interested in getting into movie audio, we began to talk about my need for an audio studio to provide postproduction services for the film.

After meeting with Mike several times, I checked out the studio and he watched the rough cut of *Clone*, and we decided to work together. The arrangement was that Mike would do all audio postproduction services for free just for the experience of working on a movie. The result was a two-year collaboration that resulted in a film that won numerous international awards for artistic and technical achievement.

When I began working on *Time and Again*, I wanted to work with Mike again, but decided to perform the bulk of the audio work myself so as not to take advantage of his time and talents. Using Apple's Final Cut Pro, I was able to edit the dialog, sound effects, and music together into a 95% complete mix. I then converted the audio files to OMF and took them to Mike, where he was able to perform light noise reduction, clean up some problem scenes, and master the final audio mix. Within eight hours, the audio was finished and ready to go. We burned the final mix to a 48-kHz 24-bit stereo AIFF file and I took it to my Final Cut Pro system and laid it back into the movie. He agreed to do the work for free and, again, added a few more awards that we won for *Time and Again* to his shelf.

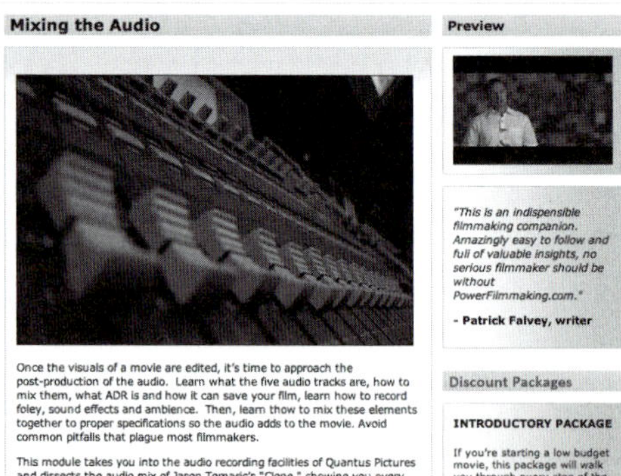

Mixing the Audio
Preview
"This is an indispensible filmmaking companion. Amazingly easy to follow and full of valuable insights, no serious filmmaker should be without PowerFilmmaking.com."
- Patrick Falvey, writer
Once the visuals of a movie are edited, it's time to approach the post-production of the audio. Learn what the five audio tracks are, how to mix them, what ADR is and how it can save your film, learn how to record foley, sound effects and ambience. Then, learn thow to mix these elements together to proper specifications so the audio adds to the movie. Avoid common pitfalls that plague most filmmakers.
This module takes you into the audio recording facilities of Quantus Pictures and dissects the audio mix of Jason Tomaric's "Clone," showing you every step of how to create the highest-quality soundtrack for your film.
This is a Masters Series Module
This module covers advanced topics pertaining to this subject matter.
Discount Packages
INTRODUCTORY PACKAGE
If you're starting a low budget movie, this package will walk you through every step of the production process. This package contains all the modules listed in black. For a DVD version of this package, visit www.directamovie.com.

GO BEYOND THE BOOK

Go into the studio and watch Mike Farona mix the audio for a feature film! Mike walks you through every step of the process from ADR to foley to the final mix.

Check out the Mixing the Audio module at www.powerfilmmaking.com.

CHAPTER 22

Music

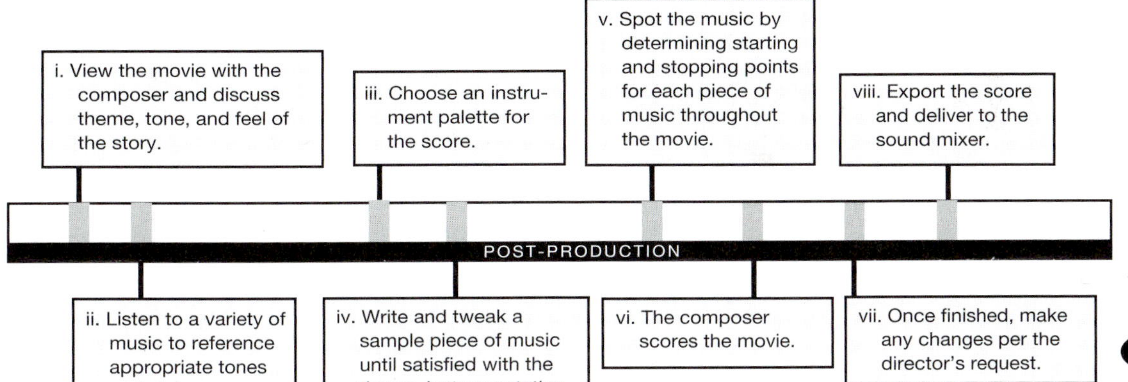

i. View the movie with the composer and discuss theme, tone, and feel of the story.
ii. Listen to a variety of music to reference appropriate tones and styles.
iii. Choose an instrument palette for the score.
iv. Write and tweak a sample piece of music until satisfied with the theme, instrumentation, and phrasing.
v. Spot the music by determining starting and stopping points for each piece of music throughout the movie.
vi. The composer scores the movie.
vii. Once finished, make any changes per the director's request.
viii. Export the score and deliver to the sound mixer.
POST-PRODUCTION

INTRODUCTION

Music is an important component of a movie and can help craft the feel and emotion of each scene. Considered the final dramatic player, the music is added after all the other dramatic elements, the acting, cinematography, sound design, and visual effects, have been completed. Music is also one of the most misunderstood and misused elements of the production, as first-time filmmakers will piecemeal music tracks without properly integrating them into the story.

Music needs to be directed in much the same way an actor does. The tempo, rhythm, timing, and phrasing of a musical score can be specifically written to bring out an emotion or feeling, filling in the last piece of the dramatic puzzle.

When I talk about directing the dramatic potential of a scene, I liken it to a pie that the director has to cut into pieces and divvy up among the departments. The actors get a piece, the cinematographer gets a piece, the sound designers get a piece; essentially, every department receives a piece. The size of the piece is entirely dependent on what the scene calls for. The final piece of the pie is reserved for the music, and for the music to be just right, it needs to be crafted so that it perfectly completes the drama and fits with the rest of the dramatic elements.

Music can be added to a movie from any one of several sources. The music can be originally composed for the movie, it can be published and copyrighted material that has been cleared by the copyright owner for use in the movie, or it can be stock music. Each type of music has its own benefits and drawbacks, from creative control to cost.

Stock music: There are companies that produce entire music libraries and license their unrestricted use to you when you purchase the library. You can use the music in any project you wish, from commercials to trailers to feature films, even if the project generates a profit. Once you buy the library, it is yours to use as if it were your own.

Music loops: Popular software programs such as Apple Soundtrack come with thousands of simple musical loops, melodies, and rhythms that you can combine in an almost infinite number of combinations to create an original piece of music. Much like buying stock music, you have the right to use the music in any production you wish, even if it generates a profit.

Original music: Local bands or artists who haven't been signed to a record label are usually willing to give you the rights to use their music in your film. It's free promotion for them and doesn't cost you anything. You can find local bands online or in any club that features local artists. Make sure that the CD recording is studio quality.

Composer: The best way to score your film is to have a composer write an original score specifically for the movie. While this a time-consuming process, the resulting music will fit exactly what the movie needs. Composers will often work for free if they feel that the movie will be a viable launching pad for their career. Composers can be found in collegiate music programs, in orchestras, on the Internet, and at churches. The best part is that you and your composer own the rights to the music at the end of the project.

Creating original music can be very time consuming, but the result is a musical experience that evokes the exact emotions a filmmaker wants from an audience.

Be aware of how music can change the overall theme of a scene. Although a particular mood may not be conveyed through the actors' performances, music can help add the underlying emotion, giving the scene its emotion. Play with different styles and emotions of music and see how it will give the scene a different look and feel.

STOCK MUSIC

There are a variety of companies that produce original music that give you the unrestricted rights to use this music in any production you like. You purchase the license to the music by buying the libraries that contain dozens of songs in dozens of styles, from classical and rock to action/adventure and jazz.

There are a number of benefits and drawbacks to working with stock music.

Benefits:

- It's easy to listen through the music library to find the perfect song for your movie, and when you find it, you know you already have permission to use it.
- The music is finished and ready to be edited into the soundtrack.
- Provided you legally purchased the library, you have the right to copy, distribute, exhibit, and profit from any production that has stock music.
- Many stock music libraries feature rich, orchestral sounds that are perfect for a movie soundtrack.
- They are quick to work with and are of great help in a time crunch.

Drawbacks:

- The music cannot be edited for timing or feel, although you can edit the music to shorten or lengthen it by slicing the sound file between verses or refrains or at the bridge.
- You are stuck with the melody and instrumentation of the music, which makes it difficult to adopt a musical theme for your movie. Most movies have a theme that runs throughout the movie as well as individual themes for the individual characters. The musical arc follows the characters along the story, changing as the characters change. With stock music, you only have one or two pieces of music with similar instrumentation and melody, making it difficult to maintain a recurring theme throughout the story.
- The music you use is not unique to your project. Because anyone can own a stock music library, your movie music may appear in anything from car commercials to industrial projects.

Ultimately, stock music libraries are terrific for television and radio commercials, industrial projects, and even short-form narratives for which you need music quickly and it doesn't need to fit to the action on the screen. If you're working on a feature film, I would recommend staying away from stock music, as the lack of flexibility may hurt your movie more than help it.

Check out some of these stock music libraries:

Digital Juice (www.digitaljuice.com)—They make a project called BackTraxx. It's a good library for the price and affords a wide selection of musical tracks.

615 music (www.615music.com)—This company offers orchestral stock music that is used in Hollywood movies and television series alike.

For a complete list of stock music companies, visit www.powerfilmmaking.com and check out the Music modules.

DIRECTOR'S NOTES

Even though I worked with a composer who wrote an original score for *Time and Again*, I still used stock music in a number of scenes. The diner is one example, in which the music playing over the radio in the background came from a stock library I bought from Digital Juice. I needed an upbeat 1950s rock-and-roll tune but didn't need it to change with the changing drama of the scene, so I ran it though a high-pass filter to make it sound a little tinny and then compressed it so it wouldn't detract from the dialog and main audio. The result was a great piece of music that sounded like it came from the radio. The even better part is that I had the rights to use it!

USING COPYRIGHTED MUSIC

If you like the soundtrack written by a Hollywood composer, or a popular artist, you can secure the rights by contacting the publisher (the publisher is always named on the CD case). Understand that the cost of leasing the rights to the song is dependent on the nature of your project, what the distribution plan is, how many copies of you movie will be distributed, and what the exhibition format will be (film festivals, theatrical, DVD release, foreign or domestic). These licenses are often very expensive, sometimes costing tens of thousands of dollars.

Most music rights are handled through the two following organizations:

ASCAP: www.ascap.com
BMI: www.bmi.com

Any work produced after 1920 is copyrighted and cannot be reproduced in any way without expressed written permission from the author, publisher, and copyright holder. This means you cannot add your favorite artist's music to your movie, even if it's ten seconds of a song, or use classical music or use an existing movie soundtrack.

Music written and performed before 1920 is in the public domain and can be used in your movie without any legal consequence. It's a difficult and time-consuming process to determine whether a composition is in the public domain, but visiting the Library of Congress is a great way to start.

When looking for works that are in the public domain, be careful of the following:

- **Classical music**—Although the written piece itself may be in the public domain, the performance of it may be copyrighted and cannot be used without permission of the musicians that performed it. If you have the written music, you can always perform the piece yourself or hire a musician to perform it for you under contract. You then become the owner of the performance and have the right to incorporate it in your movie. For example, Chopin's Nocturne No. 2 is in the public domain provided you perform it yourself or contract a pianist to play it. But using a recent recording by the Cleveland Orchestra would be illegal unless you secure permission from the orchestra and from the pianist who played it.

- **Pop music**—Permission must be secured from the publisher to use any portion of the music in a film or video production. A majority of music licensing is handled through ASCAP and BMI.

On a cautionary note, if your movie is picked up by a major film festival or a distributor, you will be required to show proof that you've obtained the necessary permission for all music, or the festival or distributor will refuse to exhibit your movie.

DIRECTOR'S NOTES

Do not use music in your movie without securing the rights from the copyright holder. Distributors will require you to provide proof that you have obtained the rights to a copyrighted piece of music before accepting your project. Many film festivals, especially the larger festivals, may also require similar proof. Remember that once you pick up a camera and begin to shoot, you are a producer who is making content. If you are looking to make a living as a filmmaker, you will be paying your bills with the money your movies and creative content make. People who steal movies and music are not only hurting the industry, they are also hurting you. One of the reasons the record industry has stopped paying for the development of new artists is because there's no money left to pay for new artists. Piracy of music and movies has seriously cut into the development funds that used to allow large media companies to discover and develop new talent like you! Support the industry you're trying to work in. Support yourself and protect your future. Don't encourage piracy of movies or music.

MUSIC LOOPS

A new alternative to working with stock music is working with loop-based music creation software. Programs like Apple Soundtrack, Adobe Soundbooth, and Sony ACID give you unlimited flexibility to create original music by providing thousands of sound loops. A loop is a simple recording of a beat, a rhythm, or a melody from hundreds of instruments that you can piece together to make a complete piece of music. These programs give you the freedom to change the tempo, pitch, and phrasing of the music by using complex algorithms to conform each recorded loop to your project settings.

Much like stock music, purchasing the software gives you the rights to use the music you write in any production you want, even if it makes a profit. Many of the programs even allow you to record your own instruments to mix into the score. You can even import the QuickTime version of your movie into Apple Soundtrack Pro so you can watch the movie while you score, ensuring that the score matches the pacing of the movie.

Although loop-based music creation software affords filmmakers a wide rage of options and creative flexibility, you're still limited to working with prerecorded loops. One excellent option is to lay down the basic percussion and rhythm tracks and then record live instrumentalists playing an original melody. By using a combination of techniques, it's possible to make a beautiful, original score that you have the rights to use in your movie.

WRITING ORIGINAL MUSIC

Working with a composer is a rewarding and challenging task. An artist in his own right, the composer must write each piece of music so that it meets the director's vision, serves the emotional subtext of the scene, and yet allows him to explore his own musical creativity.

Finding a composer

Finding a composer is easy; however, finding a composer with a compatible style, musical taste, and personality and the time to dedicate to your project can be difficult. There are plenty of ways to find a qualified composer in your area.

- **Internet:** With the advent of craigslist.org, community bulletin boards, and Google, searching the net will yield dozens of composers, small orchestras, and music aficionados in your area. If you live near a major city, I would recommend posting a listing on craigslist.org. The listing is free and you'll be surprised how many responses you'll receive.
- **Churches:** Many exceptionally talented musicians play at local churches every Sunday. Feel free to approach them after a service or call them during the week to discuss your project. I met my composer, Chris First, through a friend who attended a church Chris played at.
- **Universities:** Local universities often have music programs. Call the dean of the music program and ask to speak with a professor who might be able to refer talented students to you. If you live near Los Angeles or New York, several universities offer music courses specifically for writing movie music. Students will jump at the chance to have their work attached to a movie, even if it is independent.

Once you have a list of potential composers, take the time to meet and get to know them before deciding to work with them. Although their musical ability is important, it's even more important to find a composer with whom you feel comfortable working. Make sure the composer understands your vision, is excited about the project, and is willing to try new approaches if the current approach isn't working. The relationship between a filmmaker and a composer is a very special one, so be sure you choose the right person.

When working with the composer, remember that she is an artist as well and enjoys a certain creative freedom. As a director, paint the picture of what you want the music to accomplish and then allow the composer to do her job. Overdirecting the composer is a surefire way to limit the quality of the resulting score.

Working with a composer

Now that your movie has been locked and the dialog and sound effects are in place, it's time to begin working with the composer. It's important to have as complete an audio track as possible so that the composer understands what is happening in each scene and how to write the music so it works in conjunction with the existing sound elements.

- **The overview:** Sit down with the composer and watch the movie from beginning to end a few times and talk about the story, the character arcs, and the plot points to give him a solid idea of what the movie is about. Even thought the visuals are complete and the audio track is finished, you'll still be watching an incomplete film. Because the missing music will heavily influence the emotional tone of the story, it's critical for the director and composer to be perfectly clear about what the story is about. Talk about why you felt inspired to tell this story, what emotions you want it to stir up in the audience, and what the theme is. Understanding these intangibles is the first step in composing an appropriate score.
- **Musical tone:** Discuss how you envision the music's role in the movie as if the music were a character. What emotional support should it provide, how should it support the characters, and how much should it lead each scene? It doesn't matter if you understand music or not. As a director, you should talk about what the music should do emotionally in each and every scene. Give the composer a "motivation" for the music as much as you'd give each actor a motivation for his character. For example, in *Time and Again,* I talked with Composer F. William Croce about the scene in which Bobby Jones is walking through the wheat field during the opening title sequence. Even though the visuals establish a warm sunny day, I needed the music to imply that something was wrong by having an ominous, almost disconcerting, feel. Regardless of what the instrumentation is, the end result needed to be unsettling.
- **Choose the instruments:** After you discuss the overall feel of the music, think about the types of instruments you hear in the score. Orchestral instruments or synth sounds have an array of different tones and will heavily influence the sound of the score. Do you hear heavy percussion, light woodwinds, or emotional strings? Are the instruments native to a certain region of the world, or do you hear a traditional orchestra? I often spend hours with my composer listening to instruments from around the

world, either in her sample library or in other pieces of music, to find the perfect "voice" for the movie. The job of writing the first piece of music becomes much easier once you've selected your musical palette.

Once the composer and director share a common vision for the music, how it should sound, and what it needs to accomplish, it's time to begin planning the details of the score.

Spotting the film

An important step in the composing process is spotting the film with the composer. Spotting involves going through the movie and writing down when, to the frame, each piece of music needs to start and stop and then discussing what the music needs to accomplish during that time. At the end of the spotting session, the composer will know how much music is needed, where it goes, and what style of music is required.

I often sit down in front of my editing system and use the timecode as a reference as we scrub through the movie. The composer usually has a sheet of paper and I literally give him the starting and stopping timecodes for each segment that needs music. Sometimes the music needs to be only a few seconds and other times, the score will be seven or eight minutes long. For each piece of music, we discuss how it needs to fit into the movie, how it will carry the story.

For example:

01:01:34:12 to 01:02:07:25—Bobby Jones escapes from prison. Driving percussion, action, sense of urgency and fear. Heavy on drums, but not too brassy. Should crescendo to the point at which the vortex opens.

01:02:07:25 to 01:03:12:18—Bobby Jones exits vortex and enters field. Music suddenly shifts. Ominous, creepy. Something's wrong. Try synth strings and unusual sounds. Not too "in your face." Let music work in the background and support the scene.

By the end of the spotting session, you will have a list of the number of songs that need to be written for the movie so the composer can go off and begin writing.

- Be as clear and concise as possible about the starting and stopping points of each piece of music when talking to the composer. Tell her WHY the music is starting and stopping and what type of emotional feel you want the music to invoke. Explaining WHAT you want the music to do is sometimes better than trying to explain specifically what you want it to sound like.
- Be careful not to overscore the movie. Using too much music will hurt the movie by overdramatizing the action. Use music sparingly and carefully. Music in the right place will help a scene soar, but overscoring will

draw the audience's attention away from the scene itself to the music, defeating its purpose.

Sample scores

For larger, more complicated projects, I like to have the composer write a series of sample pieces that use different instrumentation and phrasing so we can find the right sound before beginning the actual work on the scene. Problems arise when a composer begins scoring a film and the results aren't what the director is looking for. This can be avoided by writing test scores before the actual scene work begins. My composer Chris First and I find this to be a very liberating process that allows us to try out a number of ideas, sounds, and styles before committing to using any one of them for the film.

Temp tracks

If there are two words that strike fear into the hearts of composers, they are "temp track." A temp track is a musical track the director edits into the movie using a preexisting movie score or classical music. Directors like temp tracks because it helps them see how music affects the movie in the editing room. The problem with a temp track is that the director often falls in love with it and asks the composer to replicate it—a difficult and very uncreative job. Most composers don't have the resources to re-create popular songs like Carmina Burana or Beethoven's Ninth Symphony, often favorite choices for many directors.

Composers would prefer that you leave all music out of the movie and allow them the creative freedom to write a score that fits the film. It's all right to listen to other music to get ideas or to share a feel you like, but don't lay it into the movie, fall in love with it, and expect the composer to write something comparable.

WORKING WITH MIDI

Most Hollywood movies employ orchestras and choirs comprising musical freelancers who are able to read the composer's music on their first read-through. These musicians and the recording facilities often cost hundreds of thousands of dollars a day, placing them well outside the financial reach of most independent filmmakers.

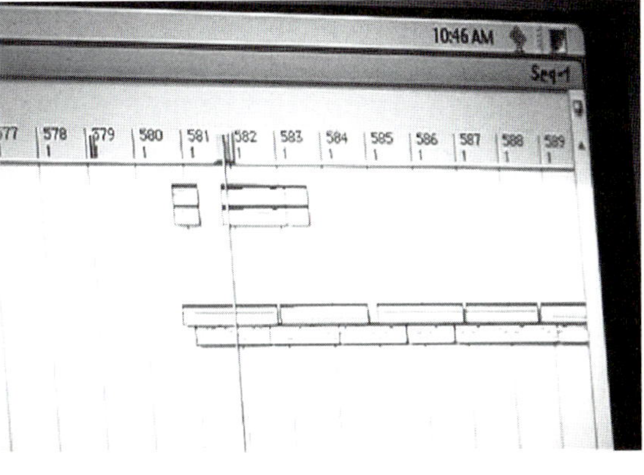

MIDI information records the duration, attack, and decay of each note hit on the keyboard. Then, by mapping a prerecorded sound to that key, the composer has an unlimited array of sounds at his disposal.

Fortunately, today's technologies give filmmakers access to original orchestral music through MIDI-based computer systems.

MIDI (Musical Instrument Digital Interface) is a computer interface that allows a composer to map various sounds, both prerecorded and digi-

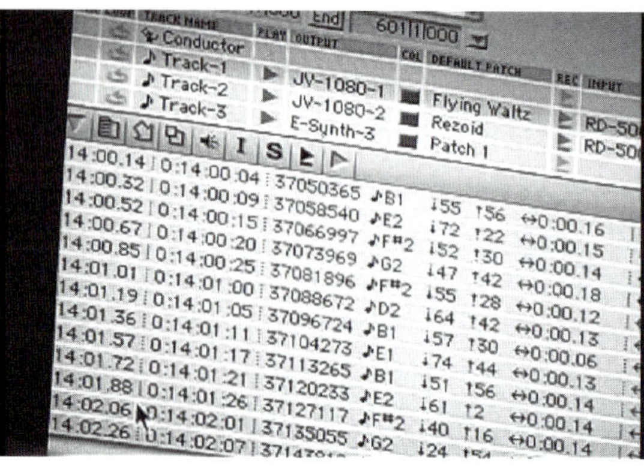

tally created in a computer, to individual keys on a keyboard. MIDI is the ideal alternative, providing realistic orchestral performances with less cost.

With a MIDI system, the composer can buy sound packages ranging from orchestral instruments to synth sounds to sound effects. Once loaded into the computer, he can program a certain sound set to his keyboard so, for example, if he were to hit a C key, it would play a recording of a violin playing a C note or a trumpet playing a C note. The sounds samples are also touch sensitive, so the harder a keyboard key is pressed, the stronger the attack on the instrument.

Instruments can be layered, much like audio tracks in Final Cut Pro, to build a massive orchestra or an array of sounds. Because it's nonlinear, any instrument can be changed at any time, tempos can be changed and pitch raised or lowered to meet the demands of the movie. MIDI is the best way to produce outstanding music for a fraction of the cost of recording it live.

In *Time and Again*, Fred Croce purchased several orchestral samples he used for the score. The result is a lavish score made up of real instruments, all mapped to the keys on the keyboard. Like Fred, most composers have their own composing suite and sound samples.

One added benefit of working with MIDI is the ability to load and sync the movie into the recording program. By importing the movie, the composer can write the music to frame accuracy.

FINISHING THE SCORE

Once the composer has finished writing the score and all changes have been made, it's best to output each piece of music separately as an AIFF file. If you're working in DV or HDV, output the files in stereo, 16-bit, 48 kHz. For HD movies, you can output stereo, 24-bit, 48 kHz. You can then either import the music into your editing program to mix into the final movie or give it to an audio studio so they can mix them together.

It may be necessary to add a compressor and some EQ to the music so it doesn't peak the levels. Refer to the instruction manual of your editing software for directions on how to do this.

- When the composer scores the movie, she should not adjust the volume of the music when scoring, but rather give the score to the audio engineer to mix it into the movie.

- A common problem in independent films is a music track that is too loud and overwhelms the dialog. Pull the music back in the final audio mix so that the dialog can be prominently heard.

ACTIVITIES

Materials

You will need a movie and a variety of music.

Activity 1

Pick your favorite movie and turn down the sound completely. Using different styles of music, classical, popular, or even other movie soundtracks, how can you change the mood of the scene?

- Can you make a normally happy scene seem scary?
- Can you diminish the intensity of an action scene by using a waltz?

Discussion

- How does the music change the mood and feeling of the scene?
- Does it matter if classical or pop music is used?
- If the scene was a simple conversation with no emotional overtones, how does the music add emotion to the scene?

Activity 2

Listen to a movie and how the music is used to accentuate the action on the screen, when the music is used, and when the director chooses not to use music. Pay attention to the instruments used and how intense or sparse the score is.

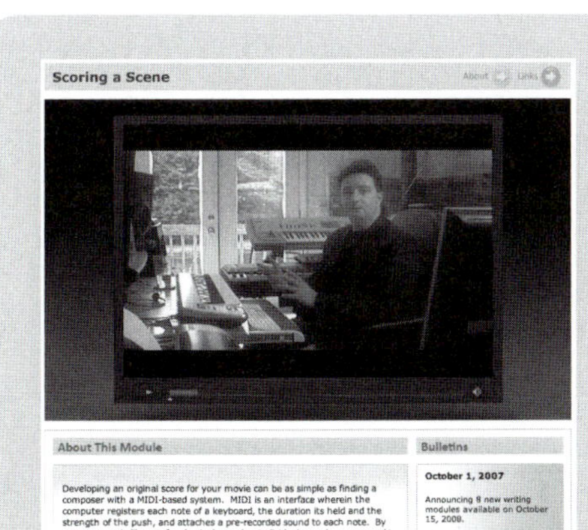

GO BEYOND THE BOOK

Watch as award-winning composer Chris First walks you through the process of scoring a scene from a movie. From choosing the instruments to building a MIDI system, Chris reveals his secrets in the Scoring a Scene module at www.powerfilmmaking.com.

UNIT 5
Distribution

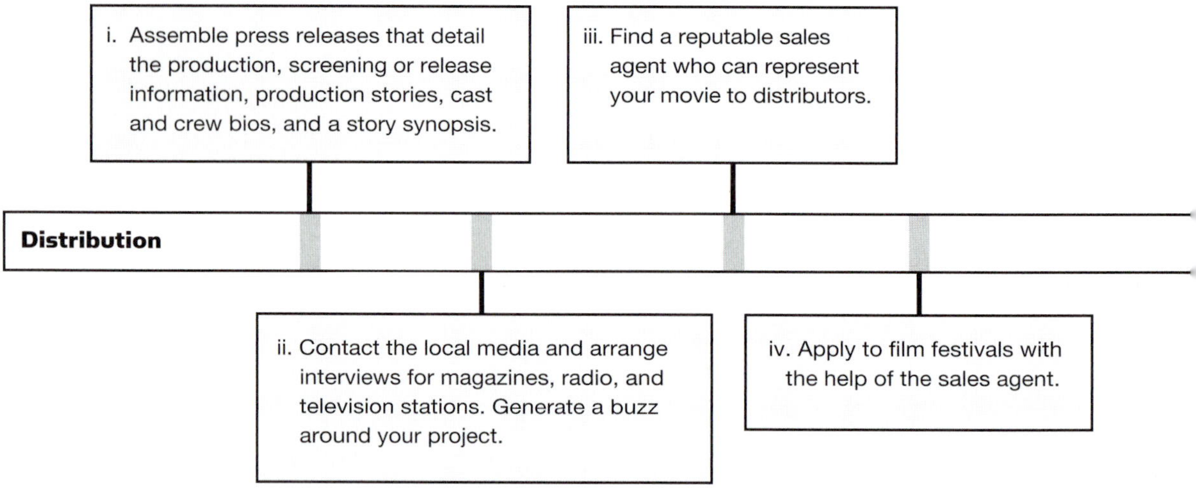

Distribution

i. Assemble press releases that detail the production, screening or release information, production stories, cast and crew bios, and a story synopsis.

ii. Contact the local media and arrange interviews for magazines, radio, and television stations. Generate a buzz around your project.

iii. Find a reputable sales agent who can represent your movie to distributors.

iv. Apply to film festivals with the help of the sales agent.

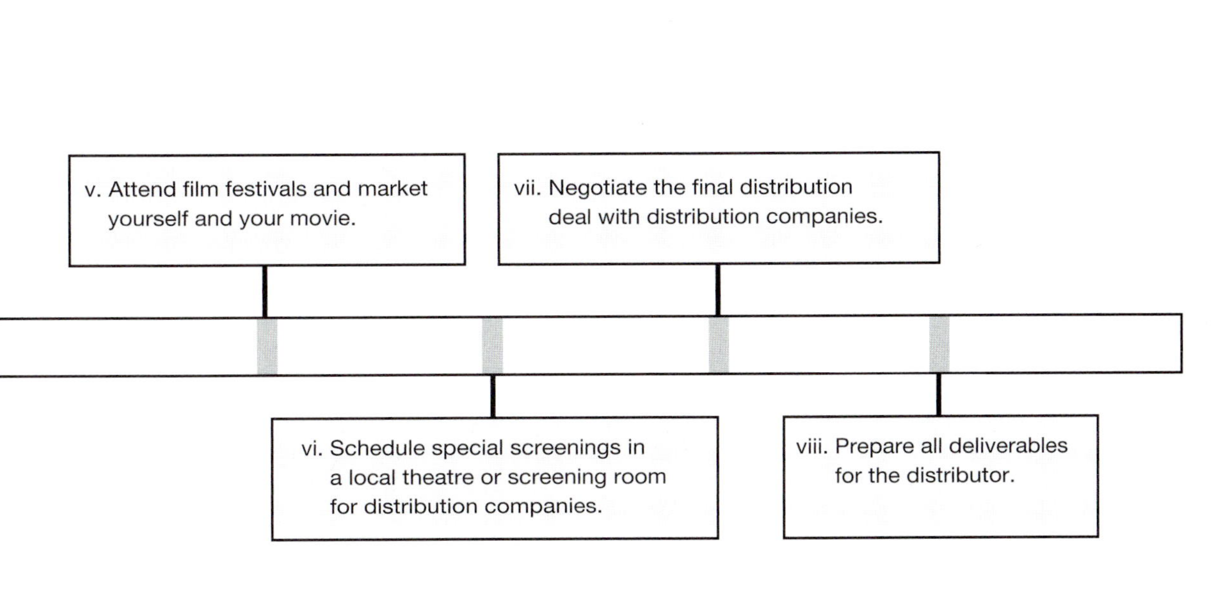
v. Attend film festivals and market yourself and your movie.
vii. Negotiate the final distribution deal with distribution companies.
vi. Schedule special screenings in a local theatre or screening room for distribution companies.
viii. Prepare all deliverables for the distributor.

DIGITALLY MASTERED
COLLECTOR'S EDITION
Time and Again
A JASON J. TOMARIC FILM
"A superbly-crafted suspense story!"
- Bill Martin, FOX News
WINNER OF 3 TELLY AWARDS
BEST DIRECTOR, BEST CINEMATOGRAPHER, BEST LOW BUDGET FILM
WIDESCREEN

CHAPTER 23

Distribution

INTRODUCTION

Distribution is the duplication, advertising, and promotion of a film to theatrical, television, or home video markets, both domestically and internationally. Securing foreign distribution is increasingly important due to the escalating worldwide demand for movies. Many distributors seek out new product at film festivals and film markets in search of quality films, in some cases, offering substantial advances.

Every filmmaker dreams of having his film premiere to a sold-out theater of excited, supportive moviegoers, but the reality is that very few actually get this opportunity. Distribution is a complicated and somewhat mysterious part of the process that most filmmakers seem to ignore until it's too late.

The process of making a movie is the same as the process of manufacturing any other product. Research the market, the audience, and what the distributors are looking for before you undertake a production. Most filmmakers spend massive sums of money and time on a movie only to discover that there's no market for it.

Smart moviemaking means figuring out a marketing and distribution plan before you begin preproduction.

- Call and set up meetings with domestic and foreign distributors and ask to talk to a sales rep.
  - Ask them what genres are selling and what genres they feel will be hot in a year. The horror genre is the best seller in the foreign market, is cheap to produce, and doesn't require big name actors in the cast.
  - Find out which actors you should approach to help increase the marketability of the movie. Which actors are bringing in the largest sales of independent movies in the foreign market?
  - Find out what format is the best. Do they prefer 35 mm film, or is an HD format acceptable?
  - What is the ideal length for the movie?

- What marketing materials should you begin to collect during production to help in the distribution of the movie?
- What are the average sales prices for the type of movie you're making? This will help as you calculate the budget and determine how much money you should spend.

DIRECTOR'S NOTES

Many filmmakers consider it a sellout to design a film around what distributors are looking for, rather than letting the movie stand on its own merits. Before you begin a production, you need to make a very important decision as to whether you want to make a commercial film or a film for art's sake. If you want to make a commercial film that gets distribution and makes a profit, you have to produce a movie that is a viable product in the world market. If distribution is of no interest to you and you don't care if anyone sees your movie, these guidelines do not apply to you.

The rules of producing and selling a movie are a lot like the rules governing the game of basketball. Each player must acknowledge and understand the parameters, the size of the court, the height and diameter of the hoop, the number of players on each side, and the time restrictions for an organized game to take place. Whereas some may find these rules limiting, many talented athletes have excelled at the game, even when playing within the guidelines. The same philosophy applies to the production of a movie, in that filmmakers must follow the distributor's strict guidelines governing the content, format, casting, and genre for the film to be commercially viable. Using a little creativity and talent, filmmakers can certainly succeed within a distributor's rules. Remember that the film industry is a business designed to make a product that sells and makes a profit.

So what are distributors looking for and how does a movie become a commercially viable product?

- **Who's in it?** The first question most distributors will want to know is what name actors are in the film. Recognizable names help sell the film to foreign distributors and command larger profits. Unfortunately, the stature of the actors involved overshadows practically every other aspect of the movie. If you want to sell a film and make good money, hire name actors.
- **What is the genre?** Horror and action films sell best in foreign territories because they're not overly reliant on translated dialog. These genres have a longer shelf life and are universally top-sellers in the global market.
- **How long is it?** Most movies need to be between 90 and 100 minutes long. If you're producing a low-budget movie, keep the length to as close to 90 minutes as possible to stretch the budget as far as possible.
- **Production value:** Quality cinematography, special effects, and production design are all important factors in helping sell a movie. Regardless of how low the budget it, all that matters is that the film looks expensive.
- **The buzz:** Movies with a bigger buzz tend to fetch higher dollar amounts. Be sure to drum up as much publicity as you can to attract distributors.

- Begin the marketing of the movie before you start production.
  - Build a web site that teases the audience and builds interest in the project. Post trailers and behind-the-scenes photos to build a buzz so that when the movie is finished, people will already be familiar with and anxious to see the film.
  - Take lots of publicity and behind-the-scenes photos during production. The distributors will ask for these to help promote the movie. They are also helpful to distribute to newspapers and magazines when critics write articles about the movie.
  - Get as much media coverage as possible during production. Newspaper clippings, television news stories, and magazine articles are all powerful ways of building a buzz around the film and attracting distributors.

FOREIGN DISTRIBUTION

Foreign distribution is the licensing of the film to theatrical, home video, and television buyers in over 65 countries. Most independent movies make more money in the overseas market than in the Unites States, which is why careful planning and casting are critical in making a film with the broadest appeal.

Most independent movies are picked up by a foreign sales company that serves as a middleman, brokering deals with individual distribution companies in each country. The foreign sales company does not replicate or distribute the movie itself, but markets the film to television stations, home video distributors, and theaters in foreign countries. The distributors in each country will pay a flat rate to the foreign sales company for the exclusive right to sell the film in that country, keeping the resulting sales and subsequent profits for themselves. The more recognizable the names and the more popular the genre, the higher that rate.

Foreign sales companies will sell films to international distributors at film markets. Held six times a year, these markets are high-profile events that may occur during notable film festivals. Using advertising, posters, and movie trailers, the distributors lure potential international buyers in an effort to showcase and sell off their library of films. Buyers include home video distributors, theatrical exhibitors, and television station owners looking to purchase programming for their companies.

There are six major film markets:

1. **American Film Market (AFM)** is held every November in Santa Monica, California, for eight days. Nearly 300 buyers attend the hotel-based market and can screen films on sale at local theaters.
2. **Cannes Film Market** occurs in May in Cannes, France, during the Cannes Film Festival. The festival is a showcase for screening films and the market is a venue for selling films.

3. **MIFED Market** occurs each October in Milan, Italy.
4. **MIPCOM** takes place in October in Cannes, France, and is mostly focused on television productions such as series and made-for-television movies.
5. **European Film Market** occurs in Berlin, Germany in February and runs in tandem with the Berlin Film Festival.
6. **Hong Kong International Film & TV Market (FILMART)** takes place in March and provides a sales opportunity for film and television programming.

Distributors will pay the costs of traveling and representing the film at these markets, although market costs and additional marketing expenses such as posters, trailers, and press kits will be taken out of the gross revenues generated by the movie.

If the movie is shot on 35 mm film, or the distributor chooses to transfer the movie to 35 mm film, the distributor may set up a screening at a nearby theater for potential buyers. Transferring a 90-minute digital movie to 35 mm film will cost on average $30,000–$90,000, depending on the lab and the quality of the transfer. This may be a necessary move to sell the theatrical rights to a movie.

Foreign sales companies usually require a filmmaker to assign them the rights to sell the film to all foreign (meaning outside North America) territories in all theatrical, home video, and television media.

- Do not try to market a film to foreign territories yourself. Part of the job of a foreign sales company is to collect the monies due to them from individual buyers. The larger the foreign sales company, the easier it is to leverage their position to make sure each distributor pays.
- The foreign sales company will also make sure that the movie is sent in the proper format and within proper technical specification as required by each distributor.
- The foreign sales rep will represent and pay for the up-front costs of marketing and promoting the movie, although these costs will be deducted from your movie's gross income.

DOMESTIC DISTRIBUTION

Domestic distribution is the licensing of the film to theatrical, home video, and television buyers in North America (United States, Canada, and Mexico). Unlike foreign distributors, domestic distributors will create the product, the artwork, and the marketing materials; replicate the product; and broker the distribution deals with stores in North America. Domestic distributors often have connections with large retail stores, video rental stores, and online stores and will push to sell large quantities of the movie through these outlets.

SOME FOREIGN DISTRIBUTORS

For a complete list of foreign distributors, please consult the Hollywood distributors directory from the Hollywood Creative Directory (www.hcdonline.com).

Alliance Atlantis

121 Bloor Street East, Suite 1500, Toronto, ON, Canada M4W 3M5
(416) 967–1174; www.allianceatlantis.com

Crystal Sky Worldwide Sales

1901 Avenue of the Stars, Suite 605, Los Angeles, CA 90067
(310) 843–0223

Curb Entertainment

3907 W. Alameda Avenue, Burbank, CA 91505
(818) 843–8580; www.curbfilm.com

Film Artists Network

P.O. Box 93032, Hollywood, CA 90093
(818) 344–0569; www.filmartistsnetwork.com

Fries Film Group

22817 Ventura Boulevard, Suite 909, Woodland Hills, CA 90093
(818) 888–3052; www.friesfilms.com

Miramax International

99 Hudson Street, 5th Floor, New York, NY 10013
(212) 219–4100; www.miramax.com

New Concorde International

11600 San Vicente Boulevard, Los Angeles, CA 90049
(310) 820–6733; www.newconcorde.com

New Line International

116 N. Robertson Boulevard, Los Angeles, CA 90048
(310) 854–8511; www.newline.com

Nu Image–Millennium Films

6423 Wilshire Boulevard, Los Angeles, CA 90048
(310) 388–6900

Show Case Entertainment

Warner Center, 21800 Oxnard Street, Suite 150, Woodland Hills, CA 91367
(818) 715–7005; www.showcaseentertainment.com

DISTRIBUTION CATEGORIES

Distributors specialize in one or more markets, be they theatrical, television, direct-to-DVD, or video-on-demand. The salability of your film and profit-generating potential will often dictate how much of a financial risk a distributor is willing to accept. Given that the distributor will pay the high costs of advertising and replication up front and will see a return only on the gross revenues makes many distributors choose the movies they purchase carefully. Subsequently, only those movies that have the commercial appeal will be considered for larger markets.

The primary markets throughout the world include the following:

Theatrical release: The film is released in theaters in the United States and in foreign territories. Independent films are rarely picked up for mainstream release, as screen availability is already extremely competitive among Hollywood films. Most independent films are released in small art-house theaters to small audiences who enjoy nonmainstream movies.

Home video: The most likely distribution outlet for low-budget, independent films, home video and DVD distributors sell the movie to video sales and rental stores.

Television: A sale to a television station or cable outlet can gross from $10,000 to $750,000 for the television rights of a film. Television sales can be divided up into broadcast, cable, pay-per-view, video-on-demand, satellite, and closed-circuit television (airplane screenings).

ATTRACTING DISTRIBUTORS

Attracting the attention and interest of a distributor is like trying to sell a book idea to a publisher. It's critical for the distributor to understand the value of the product and see a potential market for the film before agreeing to distribute it.

- **Make a poster for the movie.** Distributors who respond favorably to a poster are much more likely to view and consider purchasing a film. The poster should excite and engage the reader by painting an accurate picture of the tone and style of the movie. Consider hiring a graphic designer to design the movie poster professionally and have a small number printed at a local printer.
- **Produce a trailer of the film.** Distributors handle hundreds of films every year. Although they don't have time to watch every film, they can be enticed to do so after watching an engaging movie trailer. Editing a two-minute promotional trailer that contains the movie's best acting, dramatic, and action-based moments set to exciting music can generate excitement around the project. Be sure to include any recognizable actors, effects sequences, and any other shots that could help push a sale.

DOMESTIC DISTRIBUTORS

For a complete list of domestic distributors, please consult the Hollywood distributors directory from the Hollywood Creative Directory (www.hcdonline.com).

DreamWorks

1000 Flower Street, Glendale, CA 91201
(818) 695–5000; www.dreamworks.com

MGM (Metro Goldwyn Mayer)

2500 Broadway Street, Santa Monica, CA 90404
(310) 449–3000; www.mgm.com

Miramax Films

375 Greenwich Street, New York, NY 10013
(212) 941–3800; www.miramax.com

New Line Cinema

116 N. Robertson Boulevard; Suite 200, Los Angeles, Ca 90048
(310) 854–5811; www.newline.com

Paramount Pictures

555 Melrose Avenue, Los Angeles, CA 90038
(323) 956–5000; www.paramount.com

Sony Pictures Entertainment

10202 W. Washington Boulevard; Culver City, CA 90232
(310) 244–4000; www.sony.com

Twentieth Century Fox

10201 W. Pico Boulevard, Los Angeles, CA 90035
(310) 369–1000; www.fox.com

Universal Studios

100 Universal City Plaza, Universal City, CA 91608
(818) 777–1000; www.universalstudios.com

Warner Brothers

4000 Warner Boulevard, Burbank, CA 91522
(818) 954–6000; www.warnerbros.com

The Walt Disney Company

55 S. Buena Vista Street, Burbank, CA 91521
(818) 560–1000; www.disney.com

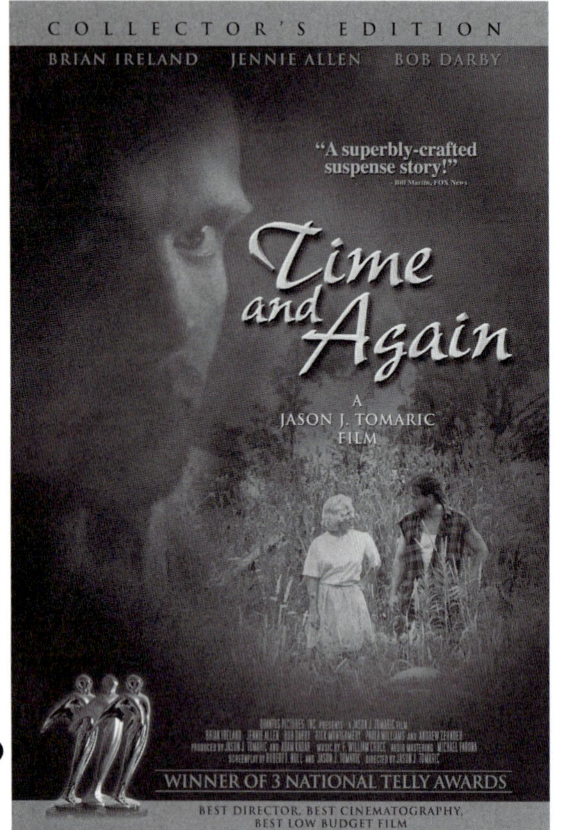

The official movie poster for "Time and Again"

- **Hire a sales representative.** With the complexity of the distribution process, hire a reputable sales rep who, for 10% of the gross revenue, will negotiate with distributors on your behalf, arrange festival screenings, assemble press kits, implement marketing efforts, set up private screenings with distributors, and try to secure the best distribution contract possible.
- **Submit your film.** Try sending the film, trailer, press kit, and a cover letter to a distributor and ask them to review the movie. Be sure to send a thank you note and follow up with any questions they may have.
- **Enter the film into festivals.** The easiest way to get your movie in front of distribution companies is to screen at major film festivals. Distributors often attend top-tier festivals looking for projects to acquire. Major film festivals receive thousands of entries each year for only a couple of dozen slots, so take the time to assemble the highest quality submission materials to help increase your chances.
- **Get positive reviews!** If audiences and critics like the movie, distributors are more likely to view the film. Positive word-of-mouth, critical reviews printed in newspapers and online, and news coverage of your project are all outstanding ways to attract distributors' attention.
- **Present the movie to distribution companies once it is finished.** Avoid circulating rough cuts, works in progress, and unproduced concepts. Unless you already have a proven track record, unfinished works may actually hurt you by wasting the one chance you had to impress a distributor. Always present your movie in its most polished form.
- **Arrange private screenings** in New York and Los Angeles, where most distributors are based. Renting a screening room can cost around \$500–\$1000 per showing, but you can help manage the screening by pitching the film before and after it runs, filling the screening with your friends and supporters of the movie to increase the excitement for distributors, and talking to distributors in person.
- **Hire a good entertainment attorney** who can read through and help negotiate the distribution contract. Distribution contracts can be long, complicated documents that, if unchecked, can provide loopholes for the distributor to write off profits so you may never see a dime, regardless of the number of copies they sell of your movie.
- **Begin assembling and organizing distribution materials during preproduction.** On-set pictures and copyright notices are easy to generate while

in production and are often required elements of a distribution agreement.

Before signing with a distributor, contact the producers of other films picked up by the distributor to see if the distributor has behaved ethically, paid the residuals, and kept honest bookkeeping records and how well their sales numbers met the projections.

PAYMENT

In addition to residual payments based on the number of sales, distributors may pay an advance, or up-front money to you, if they purchase your movie. The advance is intended to help you pay the costs of deliverables and the distributor will recoup the advance from the gross earnings of the film before paying you additional residuals.

There are a number of terms of a distribution deal, each of which can be negotiated in the contract. Distributors will usually take $25,000–$35,000 out of the gross sales to cover advertising and marketing costs, in addition to a budget for replication and distribution and recoupment of the advance before paying the filmmaker a percentage of the sales of the movie. In most instances, the only money filmmakers ever see is the advance, because low sales, creative bookkeeping, and exceedingly high marketing costs keep most of the gross revenues in the pockets of the distributors.

The amount of the advance, percentage of royalties, and payment schedules are often affected by a number of factors.

1. **Who is in the film?** Recognizable actors will not only help secure distribution for a film, but also increase its value. Audience members and customers at video stores are more inclined to purchase a movie if they recognize an actor on the box cover. When producing a film, spending $50,000–$100,000 on a recognizable actor may substantially increase the sales of the film, especially if that actor has international appeal.
2. **What genre is the film?** Typically, genres like action, horror, and animation are easier to sell in the international market than comedies and dramas because action works much better when the dialog is translated and dubbed in a foreign language.
3. **What is the technical quality?** High production values will increase the amount of money a distributor is willing to pay. Distributors will be hesitant to purchase a film with poor lighting, sound, special effects, and production design. Distributors usually buy only films shot on 35 mm film or HD formats.
4. **What types of films are popular at the time?** Current box office successes have a great impact on what types of films distributors buy. At the height of *Titanic's* popularity, dozens of movies about the doomed luxury liner, boats, and shipwrecks appeared on video store shelves.

5. **Is the film good?** If your film can hold an audience's attention and is entertaining, distributors will be willing to pay more money for the right to distribute the movie. Word-of-mouth advertising and reviews are just as important as purchased advertising.

DELIVERABLES

When a distributor agrees to distribute a film, they require the filmmaker to provide a number of materials in addition to the movie. Begin gathering these materials at the beginning of the production to simplify the distribution process and minimize your out-of-pocket costs.

1. **Delivery of the film on Digital Betacam, 35 mm film, or high definition:** The technical requirements of movies released on DVD, on television, and in theaters are very carefully regulated and must meet or exceed stringent guidelines. Most distributors require that you master the movie in the best possible format and that brightness and color values, audio levels, and picture resolution meet broadcast specifications. Producing a Digital Betacam master alone can cost upward of $1000 per tape and a conversion to PAL (for overseas sales) can cost an additional $1000–$1500 per tape. If your film was shot on HD or 35 mm film, you may need to provide a pan-and-scan full screen as well as a letterboxed version, which can cost thousands of dollars.
2. **Stereo mix on tracks 1 and 2—M&E on tracks 3 and 4:** When a film is distributed to non-English-speaking countries, the distributor will often dub the dialog in the audience's native language. To do this, the filmmaker must, when mixing the audio in postproduction, separate the dialog and provide a clean copy of the music and effects tracks. When the master copy of the movie is made, the complete English version stereo mix must be placed on tracks 1 and 2 of the master tape and the music and effects tracks, minus dialog, must be placed on tracks 3 and 4. This is an easy task if a majority of the film is ADR'd, but if the original on-set dialog is used, consider making a Foley and ambience track during audio post so when the dialog is stripped away, the M&E track still exists.
3. **Dialog script:** Distributors require a word-for-word transcription of every spoken word in the movie so that dubbing houses can rerecord the dialog in a foreign language and closed-captioning services can quickly type the dialog for DVD and television markets.
4. **Music cue sheet:** Distributors require a detailed list of every song used in the film, proof of the copyright holder's permission to use the track, label, and artist information.
5. **Song lyrics:** Distributors require a complete list of all song lyrics so they can be translated into a foreign language.
6. **Advertising materials:** Include photographs, behind-the-scenes photos, and any and all print materials for use in the advertising of the movie. It is extremely important to generate on-set photos of the making of the

film as well as "beauty shots" of the cast and crew during production so the distributor can create press kits and sales and marketing literature.

7. **Movie trailer:** If a trailer has been edited to promote the movie, the distributor will ask for a copy of it, either to use it to promote the film to potential buyers or to include it on the DVD. If the distributor deems the trailer to be unsatisfactory, they will produce a new trailer for around $10,000 to be deducted from the film's gross revenues.
8. **Chain-of-title:** The filmmaker must provide copyright notices and proof of ownership of the movie. Registration with the U.S. Copyright Office is required.
9. **Errors and omission insurance:** Required for almost all domestic distribution in the United States, E&O insurance protects the distributor from any third-party lawsuits stemming from the production of the film, such as theft of the idea or unauthorized use of copyrighted material in the film. E&O insurance can cost anywhere from $4500 to $15,000 and must be paid before a distributor will accept the movie.
10. **Additional materials:** A distributor may ask for behind-the-scenes clips, videos, news reels (copyright-cleared, of course), director commentary tracks, making-of specials, or any other additional materials to put on the DVD to increase sales.

The cost of deliverables can quickly add up, and wise producers include a line item for distribution in the budget. If the distributor doesn't offer an advance, the filmmaker must personally bear the costs of producing the deliverables himself. Ironically, these costs can be more than the cost of producing the movie.

FILM FESTIVALS

Producing a film is a tremendous amount of work, and most directors want to showcase their work. Whereas most filmmakers dream of receiving a million dollar check for their film, many are content just to have their work screened in front of an audience. Regardless of your intentions, film festivals are a terrific way to exhibit your movie and start down the path toward distribution.

- Most major cities both in the United States and internationally have film festivals. Check out www.filmfestivals.com or search for "film festivals" on the Internet to find dozens of guides to festivals, the dates they run, cost of application, and the genres they are soliciting.
- Film festivals are outstanding venues for meeting other filmmakers, agents, managers, attorneys, distributors, film executives, and financiers. Because the purpose of the event is film-based, most attendees are approachable and willing to talk about the business.
- There is a difference between the film festival and the film market. Film festivals are places to screen your work, gain recognition, vie for

Time and Again premiered to five sellout crowds. It was certainly an exciting, much anticipated day for the cast and crew . . . and for me too!

prizes and awards, and generate reviews and publicity for your film. Film markets, such as the Cannes Film Market in France, the American Film Market in Los Angeles, and MIFED in Italy, provide an opportunity for buyers to screen and purchase films that are already represented by distributors.

- When applying to a film festival, follow the application instructions closely and APPLY EARLY. Many filmmakers wait till the last minute to submit and the judges are often overwhelmed by the number of late submissions.
- Check the submission format. Does the festival require a DVD copy or a VHS copy of your movie? If it's a short film, can you upload it to their web site?
- Most film festivals require a nonrefundable application fee that averages between $25 and $150, payable by check or credit card.
- Although film festivals may accept rough cuts, or works-in-progress, send the most complete, if not finished, version of your film possible. Only you know what the final quality will be, not the judges. They will see only what you present them, and the better the presentation, the better the chances of your film being accepted.
- Send a detailed press kit that describes the history of the project, anything unusual about the production, or any other information that will help distinguish your film as being worthy of special attention. The film festivals are always looking for something new and exciting.
- Generate as much publicity and press during the production of the film as you can. The bigger the buzz, the more likely the film festivals will be to accept your film. Don't go to the festival . . . get them to come to you!
- Know the exhibition formats supported by the film festival. Although many festivals support digital projection, some festivals may require a film print. Film prints can be extremely costly, running into the tens of thousands of dollars for a feature film.
- If your movie is accepted, arrive at the festival armed with postcards and posters to advertise your movie and its show times. Much like a Hollywood release, potential moviegoers will be more inclined to see a film if they know about it and find it interesting.
- Bring lots of business cards. Film festivals provide the opportunity to network and build contacts in the filmmaking community.
- When planning to attend a festival, secure hotel reservations as early as possible, especially for larger festivals. Rooms fill up quickly and the hotels sometimes charge a higher price, so book early.
- Purchase festival tickets in advance, as popular films will sell out quickly.

TOP FILM FESTIVALS

Sundance Film Festival—Park City, Utah, in January, submission deadline is early October
(310) 394–4662; www.festival.sundance.org

Toronto International Film Festival—Toronto, Ontario, Canada, in September, submission deadline is April/May
(416) 967–7371; www.e.bell.ca/filmfest

Telluride Film Festival—Telluride, Colorado, in September, submission deadline May–July
(603) 643–1255; www.telluridefilmfestival.com

Cannes Film Festival—Cannes, France, in May, submission deadline in March
(33–1) 45–61–6600; www.festival-cannes.fr/default2.php

American Film Institute Fest—Los Angeles, in November, submission deadline in June/July
(323) 856–7707; www.afi.com/afifestm

Berlin Film Festival—Berlin, Germany, in February, submission deadline in October/November
+49 30–259–20–0; www.berlinale.de

Tribeca Film Festival—New York, in April, submission deadline November/December
(212) 941–2400; www.tribecafilmfestival.org

Los Angeles Film Festival—Los Angeles, in June, submission deadline February/March
(310) 432–1240; www.lafilmfest.com

New York Film Festival—New York City, in September–October, submission deadline June/July
(212) 875–5638; www.filmlinc.com

Consult www.filmfestivals.com for a complete list of film festivals around the world, submission deadlines, and festival dates.

SELF-DISTRIBUTION

Self-distribution involves replicating, marketing, and selling the movie without the aid of a distribution company. This gives the filmmaker complete control over all aspects of the film, for example, how much to charge, where to sell it, and how the monies are dispersed. The downfall is the filmmaker must also front all the money to produce, replicate, advertise, and ship the film, as well as the time required to promote and sell it.

Filmmakers can build a web site to promote their film and, using credit card processing companies like 2checkout (www.2checkout.com) or PayPal, accept, charge, and fill orders as they come in, managing the complete distribution

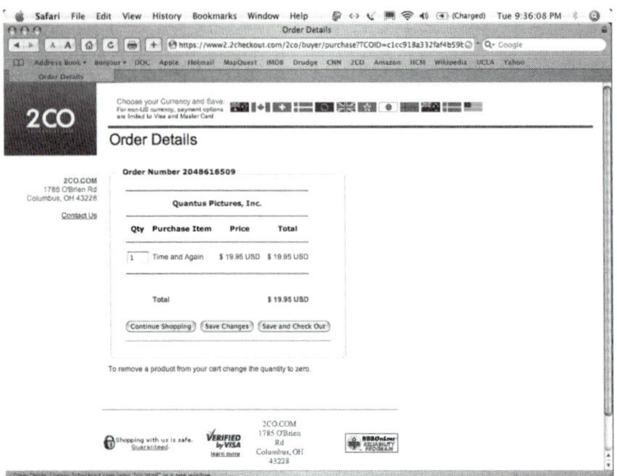

2checkout.com is a shopping cart site that I used to process orders for *Time and Again* (right).

The official web site for *Time and Again* (left).

process themselves. YouTube.com, MySpace.com, and a host of other video streaming sites are ideal for posting trailers to create a buzz, leading traffic to the sales-based web site.

Online sales outlets such as Amazon.com and Ebay.com can bring in additional sales. Although the number of sales probably won't be as high as if a distribution company were involved, profits per unit will be higher and the filmmaker can produce the product on an as-needed basis.

DVDs can be replicated either commercially in bulk, with on-disc printing, black Amaray case, and full color insert cover for around $1400/1000 copies, or using a DVD burner at home, producing single copies on an as-needed basis. Take note that discs burned in DVD burners are read on only about 92% of DVD players and are not reliable enough for commercial sales.

Another distribution option is to stream the movie online. Viewers can enter credit card information or transfer money with a PayPal account to view the film on a single, nondownloadable, stream. This eliminates the need to produce DVD discs and keep an inventory, although customers may be sluggish to pay for a film they won't own.

Premiering on your own

Filmmakers who choose to work outside the film festival system can organize their own screening in a local theater. Combining a smart advertising campaign with strong local support can attract a large public audience and even generate a profit.

- **Cost of renting the theater:** Local community theaters and one-screen theaters may be more willing to work with an independent filmmaker than large multiscreen chains dependent on revenue from studio movies. Small theaters are generally more flexible for scheduling, rental rates, and show times and can benefit from the added publicity generated by the movie. Discuss either a flat rate to rent the theater or a percentage of ticket sales.

- **Cost of equipment rental:** Unless the movie was shot on or transferred to film, it may be necessary to rent a digital video projector and/or appropriate sound equipment. These rentals range from $500 to $1000 a day; costs that can be recouped through ticket sales. When we premiered *Time and Again,* we rented the screen, projector, a complete sound system for the weekend, and labor to set up and strike the equipment for $1900. I played the movie off my Apple PowerBook directly through a FireWire drive to the projector and it looked AWESOME!
- **Cost of printing tickets:** Local printers can easily print tickets for the premiere. Print them on a colored cardstock to make it more difficult for people to copy the tickets. A different color per show or date can keep ticket inventories organized.
- **Schedule multiple screenings:** Even if the theater is available for only a weekend, schedule as many screenings as possible, both matinee and evening screenings, to maximize the possible number of attendants. We held the Friday night premiere for *Time and Again* at 7:30 PM and then screened it again on Saturday, at 4:30 PM, 7:00 PM, and 9:30 PM. Our rental arrangement with the theater and the equipment rental company was for one weekend, so the more screenings we packed in, the more revenue we generated.
- **Advertising:** Contact the local media and distribute press kits promoting the release of the film. Schedule interviews on the local television station or radio morning shows to talk about the movie and generate hype. Always include press photos, bios of the cast and crew, and some quotes the media can use in newspaper articles. Newspapers may ask for print-quality photos taken from the set or stills from the movie itself, so be prepared with these resources, as the newspaper writers are often under deadline.
- **Promotional materials:** Consider creating posters or DVD copies of the movie so the audience can purchase these souvenirs on their way out the door. It's a great way to make extra money and can help cover the costs of the premiere.

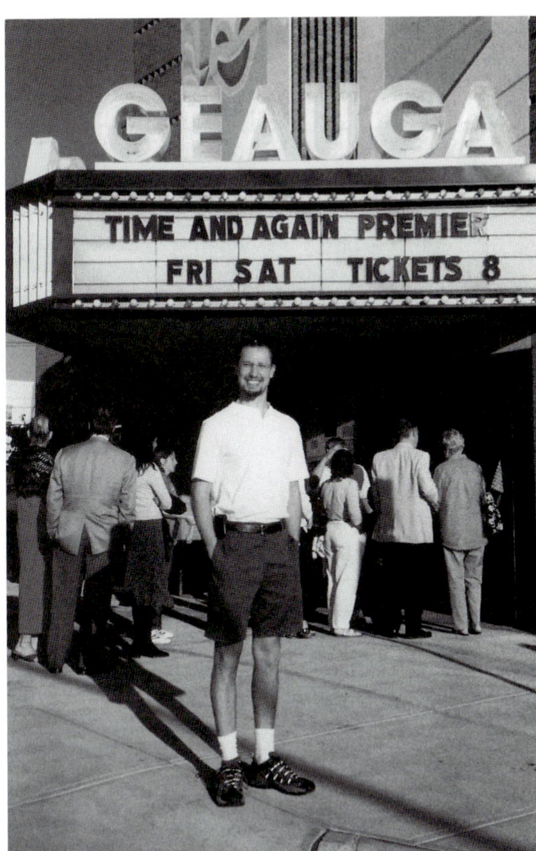

Here I am, before the premiere of *Time and Again.* It was incredible watching all the people who were interested in my film arrive at the theater. The feeling in the air was electric.

Quantus Pictures Inc.
Motion Picture Production Company

PRESS RELEASE-FOR IMMEDIATE RELEASE

Jason J. Tomaric premieres his latest film, "Time and Again" at Chardon's newly renovated, historic Geauga Theatre on June 20 and 21, 2003.

THE STORY

"Time and Again" is the story of Bobby Jones, a convicted murderer, who has been sentenced to thirty years in prison for a crime he didn't even remember committing. Bent on finding the real killer, he escapes from prison only to be thrown back in time to July 14, 1958... the day of the murder. With six hours to work, he must reconstruct a forgotten past to save himself... until he meets the sexy diner waitress, Awanda. It is only then that his true priorities are tested.

MAKING THE FILM

"Time and Again" was produced during the summer of 2002. Shot over fourteen days at dozens of locations, the filmmakers recreated the July of 1958 with nearly 75 period cars, hundreds of extras and the assistance of several local communities. Chardon and Chagrin Falls were the primary locations as the camera crew shut down several streets, including Chardon Square itself for the spectacular end of the film. But one of the most exciting scenes, the opening prison break, was shot at Grafton State Prison where filmmakers took control of the prison exterior for an entire night. Rigging spotlights, smoke effects and pyrotechnics, the director, Jason J. Tomaric, set the stage for Bobby Jones's journey back in time.

With the continued success of the digital medium, the filmmakers also produced a three-hour long documentary entitled "How-to-Make-A-Hollywood-Calibur-Movie-On-A-Budget-Of-Next-To-Nothing" which walks the viewers through every stage of the how "Time and Again" was made. Featuring dozens of interviews with cast, crew and local authorities, viewers learn everything from how to find actors and equipment to learning to read between the lines of a script to finding and using editing equipment. Cleveland weatherman Brad Sussman hosts the documentary which will be released with "Time and Again."

ABOUT THE FILMMAKER

Jason J. Tomaric, 27, has enjoyed national success as an award-winning director and renowned digital filmmaker. Winning six Telly Awards for his directing work last year alone, Mr. Tomaric owns and operates Quantus Pictures, Inc., a complete motion-picture production facility. In addition to directing films, Mr. Tomaric has produced and directed dozens of award-winning commercials and productions for clients such as McDonald's, Microsoft, Hitachi and RCA Records. His last feature project, "One," premiered to over 1,300 people at Cleveland's lavish Palace Theatre and attracted the attention of numerous studios including Sony Pictures who screened the film as part of the digital conference at the Sundance Film Festival. Mr. Tomaric currently resides in Chardon but will be relocating to Los Angeles at the end of the month.

ABOUT THE PREMIERE

"Time and Again" and another Tomaric short film, "The Overcoat" will premiere at the Geauga Theatre in Chardon on Friday, June 20th at 7:30pm and on Saturday, June 21 at 2:00pm, 4:30pm, 7:00pm and 9:30pm. Tickets are $8.00 and will be available at the door. The Geauga Theatre has special significance as it was used as a location in the film. The theatre is located at 101 Water Street, Chardon, Ohio 44024 right on Chardon square.

Press release.

Press releases

Catching the attention of the media by developing a strong press release is the first step in marketing a movie. Press releases are brief, one-page summaries of a news story that provide a reporter with all the information he needs to pursue and cover the event.

- **Story synopsis:** In a brief paragraph, describe the plot of the movie in the same way it would be written on the back of a DVD case. The newspaper will probably print the synopsis directly from the press release.
- **Cast and crew:** List the main actors and key crew members and include short bios of each person.
- **Quotes and funny stories:** Include a variety of quotes as well as interesting anecdotes from the set, especially those that may appeal to local audiences.
- **Premiere times:** Give concise directions of when, where, and how much tickets to the premiere will cost. Give landmarks as a reference if the theater is difficult to find.
- **Include photos:** Newspapers may ask for photos from the set or stills from the film. Have five or six pictures ready in a high-resolution, e-mailable format to send to the paper.
- **Clips from the movie:** If television stations express an interest in interviewing cast or crew members, prepare either a trailer or a series of short (10–15 seconds long) clips to be broadcast on the air during the interview. We had the greatest response not only from viewers, but also the news anchors, when we ran part of the trailer. Giving the audience a chance to see clips from the film is the best way to market it.

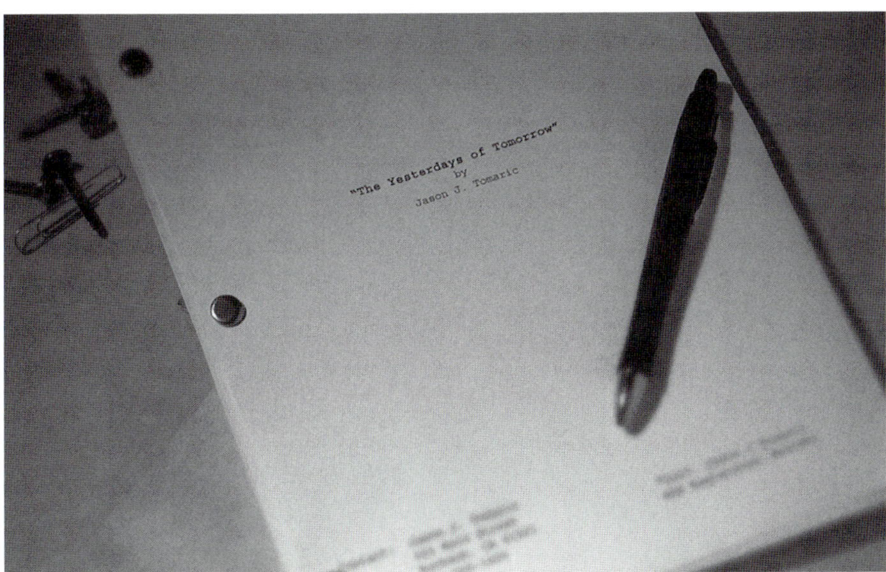

Remember that in order to get to this point, you need to have an excellent script.

Index

C

D

E

F

T

U

V